One Night

This book is dedicated to

Dr. Jack Winkler

Mary Catherine Mooney Winkler

Community Program Against Sexual Assault, Roxbury, Massachusetts
Director, Barbara Bullette

and

all the Heroic People who have survived rape and spoken and organized
against rapists

One Night
Realities of Rape

Cathy Winkler

ALTAMIRA
P R E S S

A Division of Rowman & Littlefield Publishers, Inc.
Walnut Creek • Lanham • New York • Oxford

PRESS

A Division of Rowman & Littlefield Publishers, Inc.
1630 North Main Street, #367
Walnut Creek, CA 94596
www.altamirapress.com

Rowman & Littlefield Publishers, Inc.
4720 Boston Way
Lanham, MD 20706

12 Hid's Copse Road
Cumnor Hill, Oxford OX2 9JJ, England

British Library Cataloguing in Publication Information Available

Library of Congress Cataloging-in-Publication Data

Winkler, Cathy, 1948–
  One night : realities of rape / Cathy Winkler.
    p. cm.
  Includes bibliographical references.
  ISBN 0-7591-0120-5 (alk. paper)—ISBN 0-7591-0121-3 (pbk.: alk. paper)
  1.Rape victims—United States—Case studies. 2. Rape—United States. I. Title

HV6561.W557 2002
364.15'82'092—dc21   2001045974

Printed in the United States of America

∞ ™ The paper used in this publication meets the minimum requirements of American National Standard for Information Sciences—Permanence of Paper for Printed Library Materials, ANSI/NISO Z39.48–1992.

CONTENTS

PREFACE

This book is nonfiction, fiction, fantasies, and memories. It is multiple voiced. It is a case study of me—both the person violated and the researcher. My argument starts with the rapist who attacked me one night. The details of the criminal cruelty and its impact are the crux of Part I, Raped Once. My education and ability to speak about the attack and pursue the rapist led to the second attack, the social assault by those who offered both a support and a challenge to me. This is Part II, Raped Twice. The ideas of the judge, lawyers, and scientists form the basis of what is defined as justice in this country—justice for the criminal. Their negation of me and my rights define Part III, Raped a Third Time.

In the last thirty years, the word used to describe a rape victim has come into question. We now use the words Victim-Survivor (V-S) for people raped to make it clear that a victim survived the attack and the aftermath. We need to define another area in which V-Ss take responsibility for their lives and decisions, even legally. Therefore, I use the term *VI*ctim as *S*urvivor and *A*ctivist (VISA). This term recognizes our voices. We had some control, albeit minute, during the physical rape, and our friends, coworkers, counselors, and people in the legal arena should likewise recognize our rights, outside of the attack, to exist. Action in living is our just respect. There are times in the book that I repeat the words of those speaking by using the word "victim." If the focus of their ideas is to denigrate, then I employ that word.

As people change ideas about concepts such as V-S to VISA, we need to also alter the structure of our language. In the argument on AIDS, we address victims, not as victims, but as People with AIDS, thus putting the adjective after the noun. Likewise, I do the same: person raped. We are persons first, and rape is something that we suffered but it does not define us. Moreover, when I refer to a rapist or VISA and need to use a singular pronominal adjective, I use "his/her." There are women who rape, and there are men who suffer at the hands of a rapist. While most rapists are men and most VISAs are women, we cannot disregard the significant number of other people in these categories. Further is the avoidance of the passive voice. Instead of "She was raped," a sentence that deletes the criminal, I use "The rapist attacked her/him."

As a case study, I use the work of researchers who impacted my ideas at the time. Therefore, most research stems from the 1980s, and unfortunately the significant research and writings in the 1990s were not available.

Since the focus of this book is on ideas, the identities of individuals representing these ideas are irrelevant. Many people duplicate the same ideas. For that reason, pseudonyms identify people, except me, the rapist, the media, and a few family members. I have also fictionalized descriptions of people as a further approach to anonymity.

The presentation of nonfiction in any form other than as it occurred is a fictionalized account. In books like other mediums of presentation, the author focuses on the ideas and is unable, due to the medium and space, to provide the exact presentation of the situation. I reduced one section from its original seventy-five pages to ten. Moreover, the use of any medium results in deletion of many points. In the legal case, I again stress ideas and not some details. For me, those details are tangential to the argument for justice; for lawyers and scientists, those details of the minutiae are more important than justice. This is a difference in perspective.

There are times that I represent people's conversations based upon my memory or notes. And there are other times that I duplicate people's words either because they submitted these to me in writing, the media recorded these, or the words are from legal transcripts.

Two experiences hallmark the difficulty in writing this book. Initially, one press showed great excitement to publish my manuscript. They gave me the red carpet treatment. A well-known researcher of rape read the first four chapters for the press and wrote that no reader would believe my account of the attack. Curious to improve my work, I met her at a conference and asked for her advice. She commented: "I've been raped. I know. You are too close to understand," and then walked away. Her perspective is that objective, not subjective, analysis is the only legitimate form of the study of rape. Another similar incident occurred; this time the professional stated that a poetic, not explicit, account is the only acceptable representation of rape. Their positional power stopped the publication of my book at two presses.

This book took years to write. I could not work and write at the same time because the horrors in the writing were as overwhelming as living through them. During periods of concentrated writing, I worked about four hours a day and relaxed every fourth day, and the buildup of these terror experiences emotionally exhausted me. After three or four months, I needed a significant period of relaxation to avoid an emotional breakdown. During periods of writing, self-therapy was hourly. The subjective experience in writing about terror is a ride on that terror. Feeling good came when I was not working on the manuscript. Both cases, my actions against injustice and my actions to write the insider's view of this injustice, are jobs of justice.

Part I
RAPED ONCE, PHYSICAL RAPE

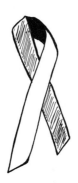

From the rural, and what some people would call "backward, primitive, uncivilized, and violent" region of Mexico, the site of my two-year anthropological research project, I returned to the United States, a country with educated people working for peace and safety and who enjoyed an age of computers and scientific advances. The advantages and disadvantages were apparent: materialism and money. Status superseded the quality of life. Hopefully, humanity was still a part of life.

CHAPTER ONE
ANOTHER RAPE SAGA

"**C**athy, this is Jack." My brother (see figure 1.1), my lifeline, the one who believed in me and my abilities to put my ideas into print as a professional, called. "I have AIDS." It was August 1987. Jack would die. He would die soon, and he would die before me. Life became meaningless and stagnant, but acceptance of his illness along with strategies for saving his life enabled me to focus on my teaching and research at the local university.

By the second week of school, those daily classes had endeared the students to me. They were alert and curious, had practical and insightful questions, and had come to class to learn—not to win me over or psych out my grading system. After class on Monday, I ate lunch in the park, a park awash in a sea of dark suits and white faces but with a backdrop of homeless, foodless, and faceless people. These people knew how to find decent, leftover fast-food lunches! That afternoon I spent finishing the grant proposal for a book on my Mexican research. Writing the proposal gave me great confidence and a pleasant high. The final edit on the research proposal to fund my book was due the next day. The day ended with my first tennis lesson of the year. The struggle to regain one's ability in a sport not recently played is both a frustration and a pleasurable challenge: a frustration at the realization of one's loss of some control, and a pleasure with those few good hits that remind one of their past skills. When your mind forgets, the muscles in your body—with their own memory—remember.

As I turned out the lights at 11:30 that Monday night, there were three men across the street, talking about life and drinking beer. The pleasant, easygoing sounds of conversation lulled me into a deep, deep sleep—a sleep that would let me escape into an oasis of peaceful dreams.

At first, I thought it was a nightmare. The top sheet flew off my body. This was not important enough to rouse me from my sleep. A kick landed on my foot. Although this awakened me, reality did not register. A man

Figure 1.1 Jack Winkler

stood over me. *This isn't true. This man is not in my room. This man is not invading my house. He is a nightmare.*

But he looked real. I quickly got to my feet, on top of the frameless mattress that rested on the floor, and leaned against the wall. Quick response was not yet a possibility. *Cathy, this isn't a scary nightmare. This is rape—a woman's daily fear.* A man was in my bedroom, a man standing with his arms open, and threatening me with his movements. In my sluggish, sleepy condition, action was impossible. He cornered me in a spot farthest from the exit. His body, just a yard away, blocked my escape. With his right arm slightly out in order to hinder my escape, he reached up with his left hand to close the front window that bordered the street. This would muffle any sound from the room, but the undraped window still admitted some diffused light from the lamp across the street. He quickly ran his hands through his hair.

Those voices that calmed me into slumber now meant something else. Now there were two voices. *This man in my room has the smell of beer on his breath. He had a beer with those guys, watching and waiting until I fell asleep. Those guys know his whereabouts. Nobody is stupid enough to break into a house with strangers standing across the street. This was a gang rape. Their plan is that he breaks in, closes the window to silence* my screams, and, at the same time, signals his friends for their turns. What good would immediately screaming out the window for help do, when I would only be yelling to his friends? They would laugh at my fruitless efforts. And my neighbors are no help because their bedrooms are not close enough to hear my screams. One or two shouts will not adequately awaken them from their deep and peaceful sleep. His trap was set.

In my terror, a ridiculous question came to mind. The rapist knew it was a stupid question. But I asked it anyway, desperately hoping that he desired only to rob me of my money and nothing more, or that I could talk him out of rape. "What are you doing here?" "You know. Don't talk." His simple phrase—"you know"—inferred that his presence in my room was obvious to me or any woman. Rape is so common that a rapist does not even have to explain his presence or intent. It's odd that "women do know this"; yet we deny the terror that we live daily. On the other hand, lawyers use this nonanswer approach to argue that the rapist had other intentions.

His first words sent another strong, unmistakable, beer smell in my direction. Were other drugs also part of his method to prepare himself? He was anxious and wide-eyed, nervous and agitated. Are these drug symptoms, or is this how a rapist displays his adrenaline-high? If he was on drugs, the pills of illusion would transform his good sense into criminal action. The safest solution was to prepare myself for the worst: I had to take the position that he was on drugs. I needed to find a way to rationalize with him beyond his curtain of imagined reality.

The literature on rape raced through my mind. Two problems confront people raped—guilt and denial. Guilt is a feeling imposed first by the rapist and later by others. I am NOT guilty for that rapist's presence in my room, for his actions, or for anything that I do to save my life. His guilt legitimized, at that time, my desire to kill him. Although he had not raped me yet, his presence was sufficient evidence of his intentions and a justification for actions of self-defense. His intention to terrorize me was clear. If I had had a gun, maybe I would pull the trigger—again and again and again. Thoughts about the repercussions of such an act surfaced. *What will I suffer for murdering a man who hadn't actually completed or even legally started the act of rape?* The answer mattered little then. To save myself was a form of justice even if lawyers unjustly judged my actions. Protection was legitimate. To stop a rape superseded the hell of prison. His terror was clear.

Denial is another part of the aftermath for people raped. People traumatized (I was already) have trouble admitting that a rapist attacked them. To say the word *rape* is to relive that terror. To deny the existence of rape is easier than to relive its horror. But burying the trauma delays and magnifies those land mines of horror. When I saw that attacker, I called him what he was—a *rapist*. What might happen soon is *rape*. What I am going to have to survive tonight, and the rest of my life, is a *rape attack*. With the knowledge that rapists attack as many as three out of four women in women's lifetime, I continued self-counseling: Now I was like most women. I was not special or unusual. No rapist had singled me out because of some peculiar trait. The only reason was my sex. He was in the room because I was a woman. His presence had nothing to do with my clothes, my behavior, or my looks. This rapist attacks women. Before me, he raped other women, and after me, he will rape more women.

It is sometimes amazing how much one can think about within a few seconds. These thoughts gave me guidance and, most of all, presence of mind. Although the rapist would dominate me physically and control me through terror for the rest of the night, I worked to control my mind, and I fought for that mind control throughout the ordeal. I clung to the hope that I could have a type of power through presence of mind and the persuasion of words. "Why are you here? What do you want?" "You know why I'm here." Then, he added, "I've got a knife in my pocket. Don't try anything." From that point on, we played a game of lying and telling the truth. This knife story, absurd as it was, began the game. Why would he tell me about a hidden knife unless it were nonexistent? If he had a knife, he would show it. He could have picked up a knife when he passed through my kitchen. He didn't. That is important. So his initial intentions are rape, not murder. This reinforced the point that most women who are raped are alive afterward. Survival was possible; I wanted to see daylight again. I had to keep in mind that saving my life was a possibility. Maybe the simple skills of walking and talking can happen for me tomorrow.

As he took off his clothes, his cutoffs fell casually to the floor without a thud from any object in the pocket. The shorts fell limp and weightless. Although I had already assessed him as weaponless, each bit of evidence helped. Alertness raced into my mind as my body felt the last remnants of sleep. *Be rational, be calm, keep cool. Assess the situation. Note his agitation. What does that mean? Perhaps he fears getting caught. Probably he's a little unsure about the security of the situation, and he doesn't have evidence whether or not I will succumb to his demands. I need to calm him down. I need to win his confidence in order to throw him off guard and escape. As a potential gang rape, I must find a means to get free of him before the others arrive. Think about potential danger and obstacles to safety. What other gigantic dangers are in front of me?*

Compliance was a strategy of power. He wanted his way immediately and grabbed my nightshirt in order to rip it off. I put up my hands, in a gentle manner, and said calmly: "OK, I'll do it, but you don't have to tear off my clothes. Let's make it easy on both of us." I would submit in order to make him believe that he was winning. I had to acquiesce and put him at ease. Only this way would a plan of escape work. As I took off my nightshirt, he quickly finished undressing. Within seconds, his underwear, shirt, and cap were off.

Preparedness defined his actions. Care was in the selection of his clothes for his night on the town. He wore cutoff jeans and a T-shirt: clothes that would not impede one's movements, clothes that were quick to take off, and clothes that were easy to run in. They were unidentifiable clothes. With empty pockets, nothing could slip out when he was running, jumping over fences, or getting in and out of windows. The trait of preparedness is true of most rapists—from stranger, to acquaintance, to date, to marital rapists. His only peculiarity was the cap. At this point, though, he lay it on the floor unnoticed for now. His tennis shoes were brand new—a shiny white, scuffless, and unmarked newness. As I glanced at his shoes, I wondered how he had walked up the wooden, noisy stairs without awakening the creaking echoes built into those planked steps. He must be a pro. Without his clothes, his body was slender, slightly muscular. He seemed the same weight as my father. The tone of his skin from his arms to his shoulders showed no sun marks of a day laborer. His skin tone, darkened by the shades of night, left the impression of a skin with much melanin. When the rapist entered the room, my dog, sitting in the bedroom corner closest to the door, made no noise or movement. The silence of my dog was a sign of familiarity: The rapist had made friends with her in the previous days.

"What do you want?" "Shut up." "Please, I'm afraid of getting VD or AIDS." "Shut up. You talk too much." "Look, you don't have to do this." "I'm here, and I'm going to get what I came for." Questions were a delay to the inevitable. I kept telling him over and over again of my fear of AIDS. The rapist smiled at me, pleased, as if to tell me he didn't care. Within another few seconds, he laid down on the bed and pulled me next to him, positioning himself between me and the door: "Suck ma dick."

Repulsion surfaced and held my body immobile and wrapped in fear. Disgust overpowered me. My eyes looked at his groin, yet nothing materialized in my view. My eyes were "blind." My body became paralyzed—

7

unable and unwilling to act. "Suck ma dick." I was immobile. How could I possibly follow his commands? I looked at his face. He smiled. His expression was one of pleasure and contentment. Nothing had happened except my demonstration of shock, disagreement, and extreme hesitancy. He took my wrist, pulled it toward him, and in a demanding voice ordered me: "Do it." "What do you want?" "You know what I want." "No, I don't." "Suck ma dick. You know how to do that."

Atrocious, dreadful, and horrendous repulsion swelled up and overwhelmed me. I could not touch or move nearer to this putrid and offensive person. My body was in shock. Fear froze me—I was looking down but seeing nothing. With his right hand, he reached behind my head and pulled my face down over his left groin area. He'd pushed my head right over the location of a scar. He had a scar! My eyes widened immediately. This scar—possible evidence—shook me into reality. The sight of it was like a bolt of lightning to my senses. Within a split second, I pulled my head slightly toward my body and to my right, to position it over his penis area, hoping to hide my discovery. He must not suspect that I saw evidence, evidence that could confirm his identity. The scar could put this maniac behind bars. Hope existed now.

A scar is distinct. His was round, about a dime in size and shape, with smooth, soft scar tissue in the center, surrounded by wavy, undulating tissue. I guessed it was a stab wound from an ice pick. For him, this scar was long forgotten. He had not brought a wallet or worn memorable clothes, but he did have a scar, a permanent identifier. Since the identification of a rapist's face does not usually convince jurors to convict, I could point to this man as the rapist by revealing the scar on his groin. This would convince everyone. The legal people's belief in my word was now possible. The rapist must not realize that I had noticed his scar. My rapid and sudden head movement back toward his penis, I was sure, indicated to him my willingness to comply. Eye control was critical: Never look at the groin area again. A slight glance could expose the ace in my hand. I began to collect data for the police.

With hope now, I made a plan for escape. I reached my right hand high up into the air and, with trepidation and fear, banged my fist on him, aiming for the base of his penis. I wanted to immobilize him with pain and run like hell for the front door. His reaction shocked me: He had no pain. Within a fraction of a second, he jumped to his feet and swung at my head. Darkness prevented a direct hit; he swung wide. Instead of a bull's-eye blow to me, his fist first struck the lamp, minimizing the force of his fist. Even indirect, this punch was sufficient to fling me against the wall. Unbeknownst to me then, I screamed as the battering began.

I fought back. I yanked on his penis. Yet again, instead of pain restricting him, it intensified his anger. He reacted with greater strength. With his left hand, he seized my upper right arm and, unimpeded, struck my head with his fist that carried the full force of his body. Anger and vengeance defined his actions; his vehemence was potent, determined. Screams shrilled from my mouth. Despite his hold on my right side, his force flung my body against the wall again and again as he continually punched the left side of my head.

My defensive strategies changed instantly. Survival, not escape, was the issue. To walk away from a rape without permanent damage was now my goal. The rapist's fists had printed his orders on my body. He would batter me until he got what he wanted. The pains that I tried to impose on him were his justification for his malicious beating of me. To succumb was to survive. Total submission was mandatory. To live became more important than his rape. I struggled not for a reprieve from that night of torture but for a reprieve from death. My initial actions had put him on alert and made another escape attempt doubtful. With both of his hands, he grabbed the hair on top of my head and held my two-inch strands tightly in his fists. From then on, he never forgot to ensure his threatening presence this way. His hands remained clenched to my hair most of the night except when he was on top of me.

"Suck ma dick, Suck ma dick." Feelings of nausea inundated me. "I don't understand." "You know how." "Please just tell me what you want. I'll do it. But you have to explain it to me." Anger emanated from his words along with insistence and a tone of retaliation. "Come on, you. This is *too much*. Just *suck ma dick. NOW.*" Despite my attempt to obey in the most minimal way, his foulness permeated my existence. Laboriously and with painstaking slowness, I licked the sides of his penis. Shaking defined my body. I tried to direct myself to follow his orders. I told my mind to convince my body to act. Feelings of fright and horror took precedence and controlled my body: Intense nausea, quivering sensations, and a dry mouth. My tongue was like sandpaper. With a desire to end the rape quickly, I moved my hand up and down his penis, rubbing it vigorously. I wanted to make him ejaculate, and now. I wanted him the hell out of my life, and NOW. Rub, Rub, Rub, Faster, Faster, Faster. Get him to ejaculate quickly and LEAVE. Rub, Rub, Rub.

"**NO**, I want it slowly. And don't use your hands. Suck ma dick. I told you what I wanted." I lightly licked his penis. "I said suck it." "I don't

9

know what you mean. Tell me and I'll do it. But I don't know." "Oh, you know all right. I know you know. Just suck it." "Really, I don't understand. Tell me." "Just shut up and do it. You talk so much." "Tell me." "Don't talk. Do it." I needed some sort of argument—whether he believed it or not was irrelevant because consistency might convince him. "Look, I was a nun and left the convent. Of course, I've read about sexual intercourse but I don't know how. You'll have to tell me what to do." "I don't believe this. Man, this is a trip. Just suck it." "Tell me what you want, and I'll do it. But I don't know what you mean. I'm doing what I think you want. What do you want?" "*Like a lollipop, suck on it like a lollipop.*" Delaying was not succeeding. In a gentle, conciliatory voice, "OK, I'll do it." And I did. I put my mouth around the top part of his penis and weakly acted on it—but not as if it was a lollipop. It was like a dead, decaying rat. "Is this OK?" "Yes, that's just fine." Browbeating me into complete submission was his enjoyment. He fancied acts of pleasure for himself, not me.

After a period of sucking his penis, he turned me over onto my back and placed his body on top of me. The closeness of his face to mine raised the level of his hate. My dog sensed this. She began to act confused. Agitated, she whined. She knew that I was in danger. Since the other person in the room had made friends with her, she cried in distress, bewildered. "Shut that dog up." With the rapist on top of me, I couldn't try to encourage the dog to attack. I wasn't even sure if she would. Instead, I told my dog to settle down: "It's OK, Logan." "That's a pussy white dog." These words showed his familiarity with my dog. He had mastered her friendship earlier. He was not a complete fool, at least not the type of fool who breaks into a house where a dog lives without ensuring that the dog won't attack. This was more evidence that the rapist had planned his night of terrorizing.

Fumes permeated the room: deplorable smells of harsh, pungent urine and of gaseous, putrid excrement. The strength of the smells directed my thoughts to its source. *Is it me?* I felt nothing. *Maybe it's the rapist.* Yet his actions and movements told me it was not him. The smells filled the air. *It must be Logan.* In the dismay of the situation, the dog evacuated herself, both urinating and defecating in the corner of the room. The odors were strong for a distance of twenty feet. Why doesn't the rapist say anything about these disgusting smells? Nasty comments are his style. Perhaps he is too attentive to his rape to care. The repugnant smells lingered, saturating my senses.

I could not write about this next point for years. The legal people never gave me that courage. Now I can state it. The churning disgust that I felt on my tortured body was the rapist thrusting and bludgeoning me and that horror left me with the strong and immediate desire to flee the terror. In a split second, my self—whether one calls it the self, the soul, the spirit, the essence—stepped outside my body on the right side and watched the rapist attack my body. Outside my self, I panicked. Incomprehension of my self outside my body further disoriented me. *One's self and body are one—always?!* I forced my self back into my body—back into the physical body that existed in a state of torture and terror. Dissociation is the name of that experience. Terror can panic us into dividing our body from our selves. My lack of understanding of that body/self-experience silenced me for years, and especially with the legal people who dwell on reproducible facts. Who could reproduce that? Other victims' experiences of dissociation educated me. Also as an anthropologist, I know that people in other cultures have learned how to leave their bodies for short periods of time. This happened to me.

In an effort to persuade him to leave me alone, I said, "My face and my head are in great pain." "You made me do it. It's your fault. I didn't want to hurt you." He transferred his guilt to me, but he was wrong. My goals were to refute his words, and find further evidence to identify him. I noticed some hair on his chest, a minor detail but clearly visible. As he continued to force himself on me, he repeatedly stabbed his penis in my vagina. At one point, he began to insert his penis in my anal area. "Please, don't do that." "Oh, you like that," he said with a wry smile. His comment implied that my pleasure was not his pleasure.

I said something to the effect that I use tampons. Why I mentioned this, I could not recall—even a year after the attack. My initial memory was that the tampon story was part of my nun cover-up story. But years later, when I no longer needed to protect myself, I recalled the reason. In order to avoid the lawyers' questioning my sexual history, I said I used tampons to explain the lack of a hymen. Rape shield laws prevent attorneys questioning a VISA on his/her sexual history, but if the history is part of the attack, then attorneys have the right to interrogate a VISA to the point of distortion and humiliation. That night, fear of the lawyers impacted me. After I mentioned the tampon, the rapist quickly pulled out and angrily demanded: "Get it out." "I only said that I use tampons, but I don't have any in now." "OK, then."

My lack of participation in the rape made his entry laborious. My vagina was dry, closed. He would have to treat me like those blow-up plastic dolls: The man works the doll that moves only upon command or when pushed. He started kissing me on the lips. I didn't move my face. "Open your lips." Ever so slightly, I did this. He continued slobbering his lips over mine and licking me with his tongue. I did nothing. "Move your tongue." I did nothing. "Move." "What does that mean? I don't understand. You'll have to explain it to me." "Man, this is a trip." At the same time, he pinched my breasts. "Please don't. That hurts." He didn't care and kept doing it. With his thumb and forefinger, he squeezed the nipples of my breasts; sometimes he grabbed, and other times he pulled on both at the same time. Hurting me was his pleasure.

I stole a few moments to try and study his face. The two features that stood out betrayed his possible age. First, the skin condition of his facial cheeks and his facial lines were evidence. His cheeks—clean and shaved, except for his mustache—left the impression that he had shaved for a decade or more. On one hand, he did not have that smooth baby-fine skin of a teen. On the other, his beard growth was not abnormally intense, which can speed up the signs of aging.

The second feature was his facial lines. I had noticed my own lines after the age of thirty. Ridges appeared on my forehead, the crow's feet highlighted my eyes, and laugh lines outlined my mouth. He had these too. The lines from the nose encircling the mouth were the most pronounced. He must be around thirty. I also had the chance to look at his teeth. They were medium-large, clean, white, without fillings or broken parts. Slowly I added up subtle but significant points to help identify this rapist. The police later informed me that the listing of features and traits pinpoints a culprit.

Without success, he continued jabbing his penis into my vagina. As his penis went limp—and this happened quickly each time, he turned me back on top of him. He yanked the hair on my head, held onto it tightly, and ordered me: "Suck ma dick." Laboriously and with painstaking slowness, I licked—lightly and minimally—again and again. My dry mouth was a constant reminder of my stress and disgust. Still horizontal, he swung his right leg to the other side of me, arched his back, which raised his pelvic area, and ordered: "Lick it." Again in my struggle not to obey him, I continued my strategy of filling time with questions: "What do you want? Do you want me to lick your ass?" "Yeah, do it." "Do you want me to do that because I'm white?" "Yeah." With a deep breath and thoughts about the distasteful and despicable chores in life such as cleaning up shit, I followed his mandates. "Is that what you want?" His face carried this immensely pleasurable look, and he was grinning. "Yeah, that's fine." Despite the briefness of the act, satisfaction was his. His pleasure came from strong-arming me to act in a repulsive way, not from the physical sensation.

With an unfathomably huge smirk, he switched his legs back: "Suck ma dick." After his penis was erect again, he maneuvered me onto my back with his body on top. The smell of beer still lingered. Although I tried watching him, finding unusual features in his face was difficult. More than that, to look at the rapist disgusted me. The struggle of penal entry into my vagina continued. My body—closed to him—made it difficult. For the rapist to be a part of me was vile. "This is a trip. You know how to do it." His frequent references to my past were attempts to humiliate me, to make me feel guilty, to imply that I was loose and well practiced: he implied that I was a whore.

I maintained my nun story: "I used to be a catholic nun. I don't understand." "What are they?" "Don't you know about nuns?" "I've heard about methodist nuns." His willingness to talk and my desire to combat his perception of me as a white racist instigated me to tell a story. I repeated an anecdote familiar to my anthropology students. "You know, when I was six years old, I learned my colors. I learned that brown and black were two distinct colors. The white people had told me to stay away from black people. For a long time, I had wanted to see a black person because the only people I had seen in the United States were white or brown. Since nobody said anything against brown people, I thought that they must be good people too." He laughed: "This is a trip." Even a person traumatized can still have enough control to tell a joke to the rapist. Joking was a means to safety: I hoped to calm him down and win him over.

Once more, his penis went limp. "Suck ma dick; do it." Without options, I followed his orders and surrendered to his demands—each time, every time. But I continued to let him know that my mouth was without saliva and only with great difficulty could I obey. Each of these times, he used his body to block the only exit from the room and held onto my hair with both of his hands. To remember how many times he made me go through those deplorable procedures was not a desirable memory. A number would further imprint that rape attack on my mind. At last though, during one of the reversals in which he again put himself on top of me, he finished. I assumed he climaxed, at least weakly. I say that the climax was small in that the size and strength of the ejaculation were minimal. Perhaps the drugs had an effect.

Finished, he put on his clothes and ran his hands through his hair. My heart leaped: *He'll leave at last.* "Where's your money?" "I don't have any." Unclear how to deal with him and fearful that I might make the wrong comment that would arouse more anger, I turned to my own thoughts: *I have to pay for this! I never studied such monetary transactions in microeconomics.* I wonder how much unaccounted money crossed hands in these types of crimes. "You've got to have money. Where's your money?" "I spent my money this weekend. I didn't have time to go to the bank today. I had planned to go there tomorrow." "Where's your teller card?" "I haven't got one. I just opened my bank account." He began searching the room. Half turned from me to block his face, he flicked on his lighter to peer into the closets. In the second one, he picked up my camera and placed the strap over his shoulder. At that time I didn't notice that he had also picked up the camera flash. He walked around the rest of the room; he touched everything and asked what it was. Most of the items on the floor were clothes. He tapped a bed stand and a hat rack and asked what they were. "You've got to have money."

"Look at my dirty clothes at the top of the stairs. To save money, I'm going to handwash them. I moved here and haven't received a paycheck yet." He didn't respond—it was as if he believed this statement. Only later did the puzzle pieces fit together. A four-foot-high metal fence surrounded the backyard. In the center, the landowners bordered off a section to keep their dog away from the new grass. The previous Thursday evening, I had hung my pairs of wet socks over this wobbly, three-foot-high, chicken-wire divider. When I went to collect them the following morning, I came upon the then-unrecognized sign of an event that would change my life: my socks were all over the yard. My first reaction when I looked at the indentation on the make-shift fence was that someone had stepped over it. This conclusion seemed preposterous. Why would anyone be in the backyard at night? I reviewed and eliminated other possible causes—broken branches, kids, my dog, the weight of the socks. As I reentered the house, nothing appeared out of place—neither the window locks, screens, nor the luminous night lights. Only later did I understand that the bent fence was his doing, and he already knew about my handwashing.

After checking the bedroom, he ordered me downstairs. He denied my request to put on clothes, but allowed me to carry my nightshirt in front of me. With his left hand grabbing my right shoulder to direct me, he walked us down the steps, synchronizing his movements with mine. It was impossible for me to run. *Be patient. He may drop his guard later, or maybe he'll leave.* At the bottom of the stairs, he pushed me into my office and told me to show him where my money was. On the sill in front of the bay window, I picked up my purse and retrieved $2 and a few cents.

He discarded the change but folded the bills and put them in his pocket. In the meantime, he was looking at the items on the window seat. He told me not to look at him and shoved my face away. Yet I was able to compare our heights. I guessed that he was 5′8″ or 5′10″. However, to note his height was difficult because his shoulders were hunched over as he looked through my things.

Escape was still unimaginable: He was between me and the front door. When he saw the phone, he yanked it out. "Where's the rest of your money?" He asked in disgust. He moved me over to the desk and pushed me into the chair. He forced my head down on the top of the desk and held his hand on my head to prevent me from escaping and from looking at him. "Where's your gun?" *What a ridiculous question! If I did have a gun, I would have used it on him long before this.* Emphatically, I said, "I don't have one, and I wouldn't have one in my house." This also left him unarmed. Access to a firearm would be his guarantee of freedom from conviction and the end to my time on earth.

He searched the top of the desk and opened the drawer. Finding a box with my checks, he asked me what was in it. I told him. He opened it and looked inside. Because I could not see exactly what he did, I thought he rolled the box of checks in his shirt. Pushed into the front part of the living room, I showed him some subway tokens. He left those. Also I pointed out a credit card with the name of Willie Nelson that I had found in my side yard within the last few weeks. "That's no good. I need money." *How did he know it was no good?* He then ordered me to go upstairs with him: At every moment, he was inches from me. His hands directed my body into the bedroom opposite mine. "What's in here?" "It's just an extra room." He checked out the few items and looked in that closet. Back in the hallway, he asked me what was in that closet. As I listed the details, he went through the contents, touching many of the items. He took me in the bedroom, put me on the bed, and sat down next to me. He sat back on his calves with his body blocking the door.

"Could you take the film out of the camera? Those pictures mean something to me." This was an unseemly request by me. Yet with his destruction of my life, those prints of reality seemed crucial. In a noncommittal manner, he removed the camera from around his shoulder and threw it onto the floor. He threw the other items in the same direction. Money was his object. He didn't want to believe he netted only $2: "I need money." "Is that why you are here?" "I have to have money." "Is that why you broke into my house?" "No, not really. I wanted some white pussy." After a few moments, "I've been watching you for three weeks. I know what I came for. But you gotta have some money." During this discussion, his face was reflective and thoughtful, deciding his next action. For me to be without funds was unbelievable to him. He seemed to ponder whether or not I would go to the police. Could he get caught for this? He had to discard the camera. It was traceable, incriminating evidence. If I could identify him, then he would end up in a most unwanted place. To get him out of my life, I said, "I do have a teller card." "Yeah, you'd lie about the code number." "No, I've got the bank's letter with the real number on it." Silence.

The dog began barking loudly. The rapist went to the front window to check, being sure that his body blocked any escape attempt. From the type of bark, I suspected that it was another dog outside, but said, "You'd better leave because the last time this happened the Hopes called the police." This comment drew him to the window that faced the Hopes's house. *How did he know in which direction was their home?* After a few moments, all noise subsided. My threat was empty. He went over to my bureau. "What's this?" as he picked up a plastic box. "It's a cosmetic case." "How do you open it?" "There's a catch that you push up." He examined the items inside and flung them everywhere. "Where's your jewelry?" "I only have costume jewelry." "What's that?" "It's fake or imitation jewelry." His anger surfaced. He threw all of my things from the top of the bureau onto the floor. My valueless bits of life flew through the air into the vacuous nothingness. I didn't move. Inside the small bureau drawer— surprisingly unnoticed and untouched by him—were pairs of diamond and gold earrings along with a pearl necklace. They were not his to pawn. He already took too much of me.

Still standing, he lit a cigarette and smoked it, thinking. He extinguished it on the wood floor, came over to the bed, knelt down, and rested back on his calves again. I was on his left—away from the door. The diffused light from the street lamp fell on the left side of his face. I had to get him onto a subject to distract him, to observe him, and to imprint the traits of his face into my memory. The contents of the conversation were unimportant. His control of the talking, pensiveness in selection of his words and topics, and his fixation on the subject would allow me to examine his facial details. This would be a good opportunity. To differentiate the minute details of his face was important because he did not have any outstanding facial marks, and, more to the point, I could not imprint his face as a whole into my memory.

At first, I had to fight with myself. Inside me, anger screamed out that tried to overtake my memorization task: *I hate this man. I don't want to remember the face I hate the most. I can't remember this hated face. I don't want to remember this disgusting person.* Another side of my mind said: *Control yourself, Cathy. Only you can identify and catch him. You can do it. Pull yourself together.* Frenzied and torn apart, I knew that whole facial memorization was not possible. To note each feature, though, was a more plausible goal. To interpose the image of this face—the most hated face—into my memory was unbearable. Instead, I memorized only the details.

His forehead was first. After marking the distance from the hairline to the eyebrows, I observed the shape of the hairline as it rectangularly framed his face. His eyes were next. They were small in comparison to the rest of his face. If I were an artist, I would have drawn his eyes a size larger. Moreover, if one placed a horizontal line across his eyes, one could note that there was a very slight slant downward on both sides. *How can I do this? I can't remember what I hate. Calm down, Cathy. You have no choice. You have to do it.*

Then I studied his eyebrows. They were uniform. What was noteworthy about these, like many of his features, was that they were not remarkable. His features fell within what one might call the normal range, almost as if a draftsperson had outlined his traits. His nose was medium in size, neither very large nor very small. *I can't go on. This is futile. I hate him. I hate him. Why should I have to remember his face? He's putrid. Cathy, don't lose control of yourself. Pull yourself together. There is no other recourse. Remember those features. You can do it. You have to do it.*

His mustache. The hairs grew straight down from the bottom of his nose to the top of his lip. It was not curly or awry like some mustaches. Also, the growth of the hair across the upper lip was uniform, unlike some mustaches that have slightly less hair in the middle section. It was trimmed on the sides with the mustache's outline matching his age lines from the nose to the far corners of his mouth. *Keep it up, Cathy. You are doing it. But I hate him. I cannot stand this man. Stop it, Cathy. You must identify him to prevent him from raping other women. There is no other choice. Make yourself do it.*

His lips. These were slightly larger than the normal range, but yet, they too, were not unusual in size, neither very small nor very large. His mouth and jaw minimally jettisoned from his face and, like so many of his features, were not exceptional. His was a nice-looking face. Some people would describe him as handsome. That is a rapist's look: Its pleasantness hides the violence inside.

He caught me staring at him. The intensity of my look alerted him. He put his hand over my face and forced it away. From then on, with each glimpse of him came his hand pushing my head away. "Don't look at me. You're a smart one. You'll go to the police." I probably asked him if he was worried about that. "The police know me. Well, you can't do anything about it." Unsure of the meaning of his last comment, "Do you have friends with the police?" "No, it's not that." He gave a mild laugh. "Have you got connections with the police?" "No, but they know me all right. I'm not going back in there again. I'm not going to get caught for this. I know what they'll do to me for raping a white woman." If he thought I was smart, he'd also think that I'd go to the police. Then, my task was to convince him of the uselessness of a police visit. "What could I do if I did go to the police? I'd have to absolutely identify you, and I can't see without my contacts or glasses. Besides," I pointed out, "how many men in the neighborhood have mustaches? You look like every other man around here." With an agreeable smirk, he said, "That's true." His last comment indicated two points: my argument had convinced him, and he knew the features of the people around here. This was another piece of evidence: He lives in the neighborhood.

He changed his position to hide his face from the light and leaned back on the bed. Time passed. Enjoyment of his monologue was my method of collecting evidence, my vehicle of defense. In the courtroom, I would throw his words into his face. Conversation was also my attempt to make him feel good about himself and about me. His looks, actions, and ease in his body indicated my success. If I wanted to walk out of this house, alive and unharmed, I had to make him like me. He had to feel that he needed me to feel good. That need was critical in order to persuade him not to cause me more injury. I was like a needle to his drug high: An addicted person, unless fearing capture, doesn't destroy the indispensable needle.

"Which subway station do you take?" My immediate response was the truth: "The one at Springfield." "I take that one too." Then I feared my honest response. He might try to attack me again in the future. "Sometimes I take Rellis Park." That was the answer that instantly—and also illogically—jumped to mind. Rellis Park station is too far away! "What time do you go to work?" "About 7 or 8." This question told me that he did not watch the house in the early hours, but at night. "How did you get into the house?" "I can break in any place." I had wrongfully suspected the side window in the basement, the one that stood in darkness and was easiest for forced entry. He said it was the window on the first floor he had broken into. "It doesn't matter because I can break in even on the second floor. No house can keep me out." This last statement was unclear: *Would he return? Could he break into any house? Was this a threat or a demonstration of his supposed control of all situations?*

"I'm hungry. What have you got?" "There is a casserole in the refrigerator that I could heat up." This topic ended abruptly: The lightbulb in the refrigerator put food off limits. Although it was burnt out, I wasn't going to tell him. His girlfriends were the next topic. "I've got five girlfriends that I can see any time I want." To build up his ego, I told him, "These women must like you a lot and enjoy having you in bed." He grinned. Saving my life made any strategy reasonable. "Are you going to leave soon? My face and head hurt." "It's your fault that I hit you. I didn't want to do it, but you made me beat you up." *NO, YOU are the guilty one. YOU are the one who chose to beat me up. YOU are the one who hurt me. I am NOT to blame.* He would not make me feel guilt for *his* acts.

Gently putting his hands on my face, he looked over the bruises. "These will show. People will know." "Don't worry. I can hide the bruises on my forehead with bangs and the rest I can easily cover up with makeup." I had no idea of the extent or amount of bruising. For him, the darkness of the room must have also hidden the whole truth. "I can call in sick if necessary. If I did go to work and someone noticed, I could say I ran into a door." He laughed. I wanted him to know that the bruises would not give him away. This time it was my turn to lie. I tried again to get him out of my home. "You should leave because I need to get some sleep, and my head hurts. If I'm going to work, I need some sleep." He ignored that comment. Surprisingly, with genuine kindness in his voice and a serious intent to follow through, he asked "Do you want me to take you to the hospital?" "Don't you think that's impossible?" Enjoyably, he laughed. His offer was ridiculous. His statement of consideration juxtaposed his act of force. "I might as well get all that I came for." He took off his clothes as rapidly and as easily as the first time. *Not again! When will this end?* The process of "suck ma dick" and his attempts to plunge his penis into my vagina began again—over and over and over.

At the beginning of this second episode, he let down his guard for a few moments. When he lay on the bed, he positioned himself in the opposite way from before. By placing his head away from the light from the window, he prevented the street lamp from highlighting his face. His body was no longer a barrier to the bedroom door. This was the first and only time that I had the "opportunity" to try to conceive of another escape plan. Strategically, I weighed my method of escape versus the chance of success: I could get to the top of the stairs, run down the steps, and put my hands around the two knobs on the front door to unlock and open it.

But, with his speed, I would never be able to open the door and get out before he was upon me. I could picture his body flinging down the steps in rage, launched to fall upon me, and physically poised to fully activate his insane anger aroused by my attempt to escape him again.

I went over this plan several times. With care, I timed each step of the escape. From the bed to the top of the stairs was half a second with at least another second to run down the stairs. I needed another half a second to grab the top lock on the door with my right hand, turning it clockwise while my left hand twisted the doorknob counterclockwise. My left hand would have to pull open the door the same time as my right hand turned and pushed on the screen door handle. This last step would take another second. If this succeeded, I would run out of the house naked, screaming like hell at the top of my lungs. Three seconds were absolutely necessary to get out of the house. *Do I have those seconds? Is there any way I could cut the time down to two seconds?* To succeed, I would have to respond like an Olympic gold medal winner, but without an Olympian's years of practice.

What will happen if I fail? The rapist, raging down the stairs, will hurl his body on top of me. This time the beating will not stop. He will bury his fury in my body. My life will end either at the door or just as I left the house. I envisaged him beating me up in the living room, and I then envisaged him beating me up in front of the house, naked, yet hidden by the shadows of the trees. The escape plan had to be fail-proof, or his wrath would leave permanent results. The idea was hopeless. He would either overtake me before I got to the door or as soon as I got it open. I did not want his body further imprinted on my life or death.

"Suck ma dick." After more times of forced oral sodomy, he got on top of me and again tried to get his penis inside my vagina. "How old are you?" I turned his questions back on him to avoid answering. "How old do you think I am?" "You must be eighteen." "Why do you think that?" "Because you are tight"; he was referring to his difficulty in entering my vagina. "I'm twenty-one." My age must remain a secret. The truth would jeopardize my life. A woman in her thirties might not hesitate to go to the police. Age meant experience and knowledge. It was an age that would make him feel doubly insecure about his safety. On the other hand, twenty-one pointed out a woman easily threatened and intimidated, and a woman whose fear for her life and security might make her hide the rape and the rapist. A woman of that age was one you still called a girl. Statistically a woman in her late teens or early twenties is the age at which rapists attack the majority of adult women. I hid behind that age—not for the sought-after youthfulness elicited in magazine advertisements—but for life.

"Did you ever have a black boyfriend?" "Why do you want to know?" "I know you haven't had a black boyfriend before. I'm your first." *How can he imagine that his treatment of me is like that of a boyfriend?* He grinned again and continued forcing his physical demands on me. Many times he touched my breasts. Although he initially started to pinch them with force as before, this time when I told him of the pain, he stopped that cruel treatment and touched them with a grab that was less intense, yet highly unpleasant. As his hands tightened around my upper arms, I told him of the discomfort. He reduced his hold.

This rape was different. Due to difficulty of entry, he licked my vagina. He spent several minutes during several periods orally sodomizing me. After each period, he would try to reenter my vagina. When his penis went limp, he repositioned himself, sucking and salivating on my vagina again and again. Each time, he would try to insert his penis, and when this did not succeed to his satisfaction, he would bend down and again spend horrible, drawn out, lengthy times with his mouth on my vagina. Feelings of disgust and abhorrence erupted over and over, and increased monumentally. Waves of putrefaction washed out my existence.

When at last he finished his second raping period, he did it with intense, rapid, and swift movements: backward and forward, pounding his body into and onto mine. Time and time again, he thrust his penis, striking like a fist, into my vagina. Repeatedly I felt the weight of his body banging down onto me. This time, the size of his penis seemed—in a slight way—larger than the first time. This time his efforts to rape me were with greater physical force and ponderous weight of pain. Perhaps the drugs had worn off. Two-thirds of the way through, he began to sweat, and those slimy drops fell over my face. I could not turn away from them. Finally after arching and stiffening his body, he alone climaxed. He pulled his body off of mine and lounged on the bed next to me. Like a statue, I waited and hoped that he perceived he had my full submission. *Will he at last—please God—leave?* My body turned into concrete: still and immobile, brittle if touched again. His hate beat me up.

"You liked it [his vaginal strikes of force]." "Why do you think that?" *This man is crazy. He raped me twice, beat me up, and robbed me.* With determination, I did not answer him or give him any hint of satisfaction. "You liked it because your nipples are hard." "They're like that because I'm cold." That was the truth. In reaction to the terror, my body closed down to prevent panic from consuming me. This lowered my blood pressure. Despite the warm weather on that late September night, fear chilled my body.

"Why did you break into my house? Why didn't you just come in as a friend through the front door?" "This is the only way I could have you." "Why didn't you try to talk to me?" Silence. This lack of response made me wonder: Had he approached me before? "Why didn't you at least try to come in through the front door?" In a slow, conversational style, almost matter-of-fact, "I'm a rapist. I know that I raped you. I know people don't like what I do. I am a rapist and a robber. That's what I do for a living. I watched you for three weeks. I was going to get you." "What about your five girlfriends?" "They're just five holes." Such a degrading term should not describe a woman, but that term probably best portrays his view of women. My students questioned me on this one word. They suggested that he really said *Ho*, referring to a whore, a common word used by black and white men of their age to describe a woman.

"I'm going to have to move out of the neighborhood now. Why did you do this? I'm going to have to leave." The rapist acted like my protector. "You don't have to leave. I'm not coming back. You can stay in the neighborhood. I'll take care of that." "How can I stay here after this?" "It's OK; I've had you." Then he put on his clothes while he kept up his parade of threats. "Don't go to the police. I'll come back and get you. I won't just hit you a few times." He moved to the end of the bed and put on his cap. The angle of his body in front of the diffused street light allowed me to watch him. He rested the cap about one-half to one inch back from his hairline. His meticulous arrangement of the cap into a specific and designated position was a common practice for him. In the right position, he felt comfortable. The cap, similar to a baseball cap, differed slightly. The front peak was oval, not squared off. This fell directly over the center of his face. The body of the cap, instead of sitting high off the head, fitted snugly to his head's shape. Although some people fold part of the back of their baseball cap under for it to lie flat, in this case there was no rise in the material in that area. His short and close-cropped hair revealed no fold. The close fit of the cap indicated a cap smaller than that of a baseball cap. The color, indiscernible due either to the lack of light or to many washes, left an impression of a camouflage look.

"Don't go to the police. I'm warning you. I have friends. We'll come back." In a low and submissive voice, these words came from my mouth: "Don't worry. I *know* better." A resigned and weak answer, spoken with fatigue. His despicable acts taught me not to cross him. Yet, in my heart I knew that I lied to him as I had so many times throughout the night.

"Where are your car keys?" "They're in the lock in the front door. Why don't you leave that way? It's faster. Just turn the lock to your right and the door will open. By the way, my car is hard to start. You'll have to wait a few minutes for it to warm up." This last statement was not an attempt to prevent him from stealing my car. It was the truth. If he had difficulty starting the car, his anger would bring him back. "Where are you going to leave the car?" Silence.

Halfway to the bedroom door, he stopped: "Stand up." "What for?" "I want to look." I stood up against the wall, slouching my shoulders and arms forward. Placing my right arm across my chest and my left arm across my groin. I tried to hide myself from his eyes. He stared at me, looking over my body. "You're fine. You have a fine white pussy." I would not look at his eyes or face. "Where's the phone up here?" *How did he know?* "The clock over there is a phone." On my last late-night phone call, I had heard a noise downstairs—*was it Thursday?* With the phone in hand and speaking loudly, I checked downstairs. Everything was in place. The supposed noises of the building dismissed the idea of an intruder.

He ran his hands through his hair, and then ripped the bedroom phone out. He checked around the room once more. When he came close to the foot of the bed, he unsuspectedly kicked something. "What's that?" "Probably my iron." "You know, you could have hit me with that." "Now you tell me." He enjoyed that comment. He moved toward the bedroom door, but before leaving, he touched the window at the top of the stairs. "These are the kinda locks you should use. You can't break into these. You'll be safe with these." Before he left, I told him: "Why don't you go out the front door? It's faster. Just turn the lock clockwise and the door opens." Repetition of this point was to speed his exodus. After he went down the stairs, I heard him rummaging around. Then the front door opened and closed. I stood there, wondering if he could really be gone and if I could finally hope that the horror of his existence in my life had ended. But the noise of the front door opening and closing was not sufficient to convince me of his departure. Maybe he lied again. "Are you there? Are you gone?"

The hollowness of the house answered my questions. I felt my nakedness and the reason for my nakedness. I ran to a hamper in my room that held dirty clothes and put on a pair of jeans and a top. Then I looked out the front window. The vacant peacefulness of the street stood in contrast to the torturous acts that had marked this bedroom, and the horror that still reverberated on the walls and floors. The car was there. He took my keys only to impede my search for help just as he had pulled the phones out. Somewhere in the mess of the broken lamp next to my bed, I found my glasses. Now with 20/20 sight, I saw that the lamp bulb, broken into pieces by his blow, was all over the bed sheet.

I ran downstairs, locked the front door, then rushed to the side windows in the office. As I started to check them, my foolishness dawned on me. Obviously a broken window was still open in the basement. And I wasn't going down there! I went upstairs, turned on the bedroom light, and, because he had pulled out only the telephone wires, was able to note the time on my phone-clock. It was almost 4:30 A.M. He had to leave then because the buses stopped for passengers directly in front of my house at that hour. As one of my neighbors, he knew this. I picked up the phone in my bedroom to call 911. Although I knew that he had yanked it out, I thought that if I could carefully hold those four torn phone wires and match them to the four colored wires on the wall, a temporary connection was possible. It didn't work. There was no reason to try the phone downstairs in my office. It would be dead also. With the knowledge that I couldn't go to the bathroom because the hospital had to collect evidence, I went downstairs to grab my hidden set of car keys. This information I kept from the rapist. My dog and I ran out of the house, got into the car, and locked the doors. I hoped that that last action had some meaning. I drove in the direction of the downtown area for my suburb. Since the courthouse was there, the police department must be nearby, I reasoned. If I rode around the square, I would either see a sign directing me to the station or a police car. Nothing. No person. No sign. Emptiness reached out to me.

Eventually a white pickup truck materialized. Traveling in the opposite direction, I drove my car next to his and stopped two yards away. Without an option, I spoke—at a safe distance—to this driver. "Where is the nearest Rape Crisis Center?" "Suburb Hospital is nearby." "Is there a Rape Crisis Center?" "No, but follow me." Realizing my hesitancy and state of shock, fear, and difficulty in comprehending, he pointed to a badge on his shirt and said something. Shock blocked my ability to hear. I assumed that he pointed to his badge as evidence that he worked there and I could trust him. I followed him with the thought that if I drove at a cautious distance behind him and on main streets, I was safe. When he did drive up to the hospital, I felt some confidence in him. After a few minutes in the emergency room, a nurse appeared.

"Does this hospital have a Rape Crisis Center?" "No, but we can collect the evidence." The evidence was a concern, but I needed counseling right now. Fear and trauma enveloped me: My sense of reality was about to slip away. I didn't trust a hospital without a Rape Crisis Center. "Where is the closest Rape Crisis Center?" "City Hospital, downtown. I can call you a cab." A cab would take time, but who would pay for it? I had no money. "Thanks, but I'll drive." As I drove past the subway station, I noticed a yellowish-orange car driving very slowly. On Heel Street, this same car suddenly showed up in my rearview mirror. This time the driver raced the car and passed me at 60 miles per hour. My speed was 40 or 45 mph. The car pulled around me, and then about two blocks ahead, suddenly stopped, leaving the motor running. Immediately I made a U-turn; one crisis that night was enough.

I applied my foot to the gas pedal and took Lion Street downtown. Speed was irrelevant. I drove as fast as I was able. I ran every stop sign and stop light, only slowing to glance for cars on cross streets. I passed the few moving cars in the opposite lane. I broke every traffic law in hopes that the police would stop me. Desperately, I wanted an officer to rescue me. No one was in sight. Once in the downtown district, I saw an emergency exit and assumed it must be the City Hospital. The locked door sent me back to my car until I found another sign. With emergency vehicles parked in front of the doors, this had to be the right place. I went in.

CHAPTER TWO
RAPE AS SOCIAL MURDER

Sense of Self

D o you remember your childhood wishes? My eighth year (1956) was the best of my life: old enough to comprehend but young enough to avoid responsibilities. At nine, my career goal was to be a fireman, but firemen are men. So I settled on arithmetic: It was a field of expertise that I could master, and I was too young to know that most math masters were misters. In math, I was always right. If $7 + 9 = 16$, then I checked the answer by reversing the process: $16 - 9 = 7$. What a great field: not confusing like english where one could always write the sentence better! High school years were great. In biology, we had parties and funerals for the frogs. In history, I ran for the President of the United States. Just like a real election, my opponent manipulated the outcome and won: Her campaign chair stuffed the ballot box! For our sixteenth birthdays, my friends and I gave each other a party. To get a party was not a surprise, but my surprise was that everybody came. They made me a scrapbook of our adventures and a seventeen-layer cake— disgusting in taste but heartwarming. It was time to move on to other adventures.

During high school and college, I worked to pay my living and education expenses. Luckily, my father's family's business offered an opportunity that, according to my father's standards, meant working all holidays, vacation days, and even Sundays. My parents also believed in education. As a matter of fact, my mother's first words to me at birth were: "Save for college." She taught me to be a strong person and gave me no guilt when my choices differed from hers. From my father, I learned by observing. He was a person of action. He aided people who needed a hand and never boasted. He'd help by giving a few dollars, changing a tire, or forgiving kids who stole. College life focused on my two jobs to pay expenses. I spent my time in classes, at work, or with friends. Over dinners with my roommates, we exaggerated on how our day was the most adventurous.

My major in mathematics was easy and boring. One could always find the answer: There was no challenge. During those years, my father's business suffered economically. A heart attack took him away from that business but gave him several more years of life.

After college, there were many types of jobs. An engineering company hired me, but that job was just the same as math: predictable, boring, and sexist. Then I taught math in junior and senior high schools. I enjoyed developing games to teach math principles, but the principals preferred math as work, not fun. So I traveled. On a teacher's salary, I could afford Mexico for the summer. That jaunt convinced me that I liked living with and learning from other people. Anthropology was my next challenge. While deciding whether to study anthropology, I lived with my brother Jack, who was a professor at Yale University. The university terminated his position because of his public support of the staff's right to strike. During that time, I got a temporary part-time file-clerk position that advanced me to assistant administrator of a clinical research project in neurology. I guess I was good. Still and all, anthropology was my interest.

Graduate school was next. At the beginning of my studies in 1976, professors were against research on women, but by 1980, when I received three research grants to study women's authority in Mexico, their attitudes had changed. My two years (1980–1982) of doctoral research were great. Culture shock was difficult, but the love of life by the people in the town of Olinalá won me over (Winkler 1987). They were artists, and I too drew (see figure 2.1).

In Olinalá, people knew how to deal with trauma (*el susto*): They supported people who cried and advised them not to store up tears because unreleased trauma explodes. They also appreciated life: They worked hard but found time for each other. Work, although not dismissed, was not more important than people. Rape occurred in Olinalá as well. At first, the people seriously, yet with a smile, said to me: "*Un hombre va a robarte* (A man is going to take you)." In the 1960s and earlier, mountain marriages—supposedly an agreement between a man and a woman—were common. The kidnapper—at a prearranged time and place—grabbed the woman off the street and carried her off to the mountains to be his bride. But by the 1980s, with changing social patterns, a woman took action and moved in with the man of her choice.

During the end of my second year in Olinalá, a man grabbed a woman off of the street, threw her over his horse, and rode off to the mountains. During the first hours, the townspeople—with an open mind—collected evidence on the case:

Figure 2.1 "Artist at Work" by Cathy Winkler

1) The kidnapper had bragged in the local bars that he would rape one of three women;

2) He had tried to grab another woman, but she had escaped;

3) Those who saw the kidnapping noted that the woman vehemently screamed and fought the kidnapper, but they did not intervene because only family members can stop a rape/marriage;

4) Other women spoke of how the kidnapper had inappropriately touched and grabbed them; and

5) The woman kidnapped had accepted a marriage proposal from another man.

Only with all the evidence did the community make a judgment against the kidnapper. One of the police units—known for its brutality—found and beat him up. They threw him in jail without food or medical attention. The reaction of the townspeople—including his family—was that, although this treatment was harsh, he was guilty, and it was a deserved punishment. Olinaltecans described the few cases of *robar* in the 1970s as *robar con fuerze* (to rob/rape with force). These cases were unlike most mountain marriages in the 1960s in which the kidnapper had sexual intercourse only with the permission of the woman.

More memories from cases in the 1970s surfaced. All rapists and men who aided the rapists received the same community sentence: death at the hands of the family of the victim or escape into permanent exile. In 1981, a rapist tried to sneak back during the night after years of exile to see his dying parents. The community alerted the victim's family, who shot him. He escaped with only a wound. The view of the community is that the crime of rape eliminated his right to live. The townspeople believe a woman's word, and the town's living history speaks of the injustices against women raped. Knowledge of a people who wholeheartedly believe and support women raped was important to my belief in my rights over the rapist and his criminal acts.

Another domain of women is men's sexual prowess. A local man and I were both out of town for the same two-week period. His story was that we were together. For weeks thereafter, the townspeople acutely observed me for information. Because I said nothing and acted no differently, there were two possible interpretations. Either the man lied that he had had sex with me or he was no good sexually. Being either a liar or a poor lover are both insults to a man's integrity.

Further evidence of the importance of a woman's word on men's sexual performance occurs after honeymoons when Olinaltecans ask the wife, not the husband, how the experience was. The bigger and more genuine her smile, the more status the husband receives. I also collected data at the market Sunday mornings. Women exchange information when they buy chilis—a vegetable used daily to flavor all meals. The word *chili* is also slang for penis. Women pick up a juicy looking chili and state how

flavorful the chilis were that they had that week. Others state that supposedly juicy-looking chilis can sometimes turn out to be duds. And some
women point to the old wrinkled, dried out chilis. Women laugh at each
comment. This experience of living in a community that values a woman's
word regarding sex and not a man's bragging gave me a belief in myself.

When I returned from Mexico, I finished my dissertation—what a
proud moment!—and then worked several years at a college as a visiting
professor. Thereafter, I got a promising permanent academic job. It was
initially a one-year position, but the administrator, Dr. Lina Sinta,
wanted me to apply for the tenure track job at the end of the year. For the
first time in years, I put down roots. I rented a darling house in a nice,
long-established middle-class neighborhood. My efforts at painting and
decorating my home led the landlady to take pictures of my work. I jogged
daily. That was my life on that Monday night in 1987.

Research on Rape

Most research on rape, unlike my subjective and insider's view, is objective
and emotionless. Statistical research is popular. In 1991, the FBI's Uniform Crime Report recorded 106,503 rapes, a rate of 292 rapes each day,
or 12 rapes per hour, or 1 rape every five minutes. From 1972 to 1991,
there was a 128 percent increase in the number of reported rapes. The
increase in the number of rapes from 1972 to 1991, although shocking,
does not explain the reason: Is it that there are more rapes, more rapists,
or more people reporting the rapes? National Crime Victimization Survey
(NCVS 1992), based on household interviews, noted a much higher figure: 171,420 rapes that year or 470 per day, or 20 rapes per hour, or 1 rape
every 3 minutes. National Women's Study (NWS) in 1992 noted that
people report only one out of every six rapes (Buchwald et al. 1993: 7–9).
Even more startling is to analyze NCVS's figures combined with the
results of NWS's study on unreported rapes. If we multiply NCVS's figures by 6, there were 1,028,520 rapes in 1991 with a daily rape rate of
2,818, or 117 rapes per hour, or 2 rapes per minute.

To understand these statistics on the personal level is to estimate the
probability of rape for each person. Studies reveal that

1) one in eight adult women endure rape in their lifetime
   (National Victims Center 1992),

2) one in three adult women suffers rape (Russell 1984: 49 and
   283),

3) one in four girls knows rape (Russell 1984: 194 and 285), and

4) one in seven boys experiences rape (Finkelhor 1979: 3; and Russell 1984: 194).

These are conservative figures because many people raped fear exposure, hide the truth, are not able to discuss it, describe their sexual assault as something other than rape, or have memory protection to block out the violence. These statistics are valuable, but they do not convey the experience of a rape attack.

Researchers' definitions of rape provide traits of the attack: crime of violence (Brownmiller 1975), depersonalization (Metzger 1976: 406), violence (Burgess and Holmstrom 1974a, b; Millett 1971; Sanders 1980), sex without consent (MacKinnon 1982: 532), terror (Sheffield 1987), total attack against identity (Weis and Borges 1973: 72), objectification as perversion (Barry 1979: 266), and sexualized violence (Chau et al. 1993: 8). While all of these definitions give insight into rape, only together do they begin to provide an in depth perspective of an experiential interpretation.

These definitions demonstrate two crucial points. First, one definition of rape can never suffice. There are many types of rapists and rapes. To describe all rapes as the same form of violence is in itself a form of violence against a VISA. Each VISA has the right to define the rape as she/he experienced it. Second, each rape has its own cultural context. We cannot deny the uniqueness of the experience of terror. Most rapists place their body on top of the VISA before they awaken her/him; yet the rapist who attacked me did not; only he knows the reason. The manifestation of the rape by the rapist and the cultural context are critical aspects in understanding the meanings of this violence.

To discuss subjective explanations of rape, one must accept that all of us "experience rape every day, whether literally through our own bodies, or experientially through those of our friends, through representations in the media, through fear" (Feldman 1993: 13). In some form or other, rape is a known act in our culture. The daily fear of it is a part of our definition.

Most accounts of a rape attack are brief and to the point:

In May 1974, a man held an ice pick to my throat and said: "Push over, shut up, or I'll kill you." I did what he said, but I couldn't stop crying. When he was finished, I jumped out of my car as he drove away. (Estrich 1987: 1)

In *Real Rape*, Estrich's purpose is to focus on a legal, not personal, analysis of rape. Her first chapter, though—an eight-page segment entitled "My Story"—focuses on her responses and police reactions with only a brief description of the attack against her. This is common. Katz's six-page account (1984: 1–5) also focuses only briefly on the actual attack:

> I was startled awake by a hand placed tightly over my mouth and by a voice saying, "Don't scream or I'll kill you" (p. 1). . . . [h]e removed his hand from my mouth. . . . [h]e . . . replied to my question (p. 2). . . . He slid down and performed cunnilingus (p. 3). . . . His penis attempted to enter my vagina but was unable to do so (p. 4). . . . His penis entered me, and he had an orgasm (p. 5).

Katz's description of an attack is typical. First, the rape attack was a brief twenty minutes like most attacks. Second, she spent a good portion of the book focusing on her reactions. This emphasis of self occurs for many reasons: the need to reassert her self into an event in which the rapist had tried to extinguish her; to justify herself to others; to help her understand the meaning(s) of the rape(s); and, to speak in order to break the silence experienced in the attack. A third reason for brevity in published descriptions of attacks is that spending time meticulously writing about each of the movements of the rapist is to relive the nightmare of the attack itself. Abbreviation is easier.

Rape differs from many other power relationships in that the rapist embodied us: one person imprints his/her body onto the body of another in order to control and dominate the other. My own experience conveys the intensity of this process of bodily torture:

> He amused himself with my body: in fact, *he masturbated inside me*. His intermittent actions of *bruising* me from *clenching my arms* to *pounding his body on my vaginal area* to *squeezing my nipples* implanted his body on my body externally and internally. *His sweat drenched down from his face and fell over my forehead and cheeks*, drops of which I could not turn away from. To leave his imprint in terms of body fluids on me, *he licked me with his tongue, salivating on my face, breasts, and genital area*. (Winkler 1991: 12)

Physical rape (see Winkler 1995 for another analysis) entails a rapist who imprints the definition of his/her body onto the VISA's body, domination of the VISA's bodily actions and space, and aggressive intrusion into the body of the VISA.

Both approaches—statistical and experiential—to understanding rape are valid. Sorrowfully, the qualitative and experiential approaches are few. Our research should focus more on in-depth, qualitative, descriptive approaches to violence to enunciate the details of torture. Researchers who have insight into the application of qualitative approaches—such as anthropologists—should help VISAs to verbalize the meanings of rape. To understand torture is to educate people against rapists. "To speak a true word is to transform the world" (Friere 1970: 60). Tomaselli and Porter note that a definition or an account of rape is insufficient. In their summary of rape definitions, they conclude that

> it is not just a definition that is wanting, it is a discipline, a language, a methodology or even simply a "classic" around which we could articulate our thoughts about the subject. (1986: 11)

In this book, I try to answer Tomaselli and Porter by using this case study to explain my perspective that rape is a process of victimization deeply embedded in our society.

Subjective Account

To survive a rape, self-counseling must occur *prior to*, *during*, and *after* the attack. Prior to the attack, acceptance of one's own vulnerability to such an attack and of a common bond with other people raped is critical. During the attack, a VISA has some mental control. The rapist tries to rule our minds, but we have the ability to control, or to try to control, our thoughts and preserve our sanity despite his/her attempts to terrorize us. After the attack, it is important to know that one was as heroic as in battle. A VISA survived a bombardment of hate and found safety. Just as the Vietnam Vets argue that they are forgotten heroes, people raped are likewise never mentioned in terms of heroic valor. Yet we suffered trauma symptoms like war veterans.

Prior to the attack, knowing statistics on women surviving rape aided me. Knowing that most women experience rape in their lifetime made me realize that I was like the majority of women, not special or unusual. The inner scar of people raped was now mine. Knowledge that most rapists do not kill their victims helped me to try to prevent hysteria from completely ruling me. I told myself that I would eventually be free of this rapist. Afterward, a record of the rape was my objective: Whether or not the police believed my story, documenting the rape for the record was the point. More than 90 percent of all rapes go unreported. If, on the other hand, the police rallied behind me but conviction was impossible, then the identification data might finger the rapist and help to convict him in another case. The least I could hope for would be police patrol of this neighborhood to protect other women. No person—even if I disliked him or her—should suffer what I had suffered or should know the trauma of rape. We should eliminate—absolutely and completely—this type of violence from our world. We must stop rapists from raping people. All rapists are repeat offenders. Rapists rape wo/men and rape for their own pleasure. Whatever is reasonable to stop them is necessary and justified.

Not only do we not understand rape, but also "sexual arousal is the most under theorized topic in human psychology" (Buchwald et al. 1993: 2). For almost ten years, I taught a course called "Cross-Cultural Sexuality," with a major section on U.S. sexuality. The students learned a lot about their bodies—structure, function, process, interaction, and other issues on arousal and bodily experiences. For the male students, the idea of male multiple orgasms with one ejaculation was a surprise and for female students, learning about internal changes to the vaginal walls prior to and during intercourse was new information. Many students commented, "even on the last day of the course, you learn something new." If we do not understand our bodies and good sex, how can we explain the difference between intercourse and rape?

Sexual intercourse is not the motivation of rape. Rape is hate. An analogy that explains the difference is our perception of a knife. On the one hand, we use daily a knife to cut vegetables in the kitchen. No one interprets that use as a threat. But when someone picks up that same knife and holds it in a certain way, that is a threat. We do not connect these two uses. Knifing someone is not an extension of tenderly cutting vegetables. In the same vein, sexual intercourse is not a link between love and rape. There is no connection.

That first year after the attack, something blocked my mind. A dark cloud enveloped me. Since writing is part of my job, the months lost were catastrophic. How do I explain this loss to my colleagues? Some said it was a lack of discipline. These people didn't understand that horror travels with people raped in our daily movements. VISAs know that rape is a loss of at least a year in a person's life. It is a year experienced, but not chosen. My analogy of that experience is that the rapist buried a knife inside of me. When you first move, the pain is excruciating. Over time, you learn to move in a way that it hurts least. Your organs grow around the knife, and you become part of it. Then the pain lessens. You learn to weave the pain into your understanding of life. Only the VISA remembers the embedded knife. Remembrance of that emotional pain is important to help us to speak out against rapists and to understand other VISAs.

Fearing that I would forget the facts of the attack, I wrote down my description in order to have a study sheet if I ever testified. I realized past-published accounts were silent about the hell of the experience. I wanted to explain to other people, inexperienced in attacks, what rape is. Only a detailed account of the intricacies of this horror might stop the rampant support of rapists. This writing took three weeks. With each sentence and paragraph came a torrent of trauma feelings, followed by a flood of tears. After a convulsive cry, I would take a break. Dishtowels were my handkerchiefs. No one who entered my home suspected how I'd used the towels. To calm myself, to remind myself of the better aspects of living, and to renew my energy to write, I read *All Creatures Great and Small* by James Herriot. His short vignettes about animals were humorous, distracting, well written, and sufficient in length for a break from my task.

In my writing, while I could feel the tears of emotional pain that streamed out of me, I felt that I was describing someone else. The event was too unreal. Many people call this denial, but for me it was part of the process of writing about torture. The emotional pain was the knowledge of the reality of the attack—I never denied that—and my mental self allowed me to accurately state the account. Writing about the attack allowed me to release trauma and made me recall some of the traumatic details. In contrast, editing and rewriting were calm activities. Following those weeks of unbearable pain, there was a feeling of euphoria, a catharsis. A catharsis, though, implies that one releases emotions, but those horror feelings never left. My feelings of elation were pride: I had faced the horror, published the terror. After the writing, the paper became my memory bank. Forgetting the details for testifying was not a worry now: I had my cheat sheet. In printing the details, honesty was my goal. I would not dismiss anything; it was my memory of that night, an honest writing of the horror. Yet truthfulness and honesty are never completely possible. There are still a select few points not disclosed because of my embarrassment or my fear of people's reactions. I privilege myself this secrecy. Please don't ask.

What is missing from my account, one person noted, is the feeling of terror as we people raped have had to feel it. That's right. It is not the details but the trauma of the torture that makes us friends in pain. By emphasizing my thoughts and mechanisms of preservation, the terror appeared minimal. Is it possible to put into words those feelings of complete loss of self caused by the rapist's attack? Hopefully, those writers after me will find some way to rectify this. Readers' emotional reaction to my account is only a small fraction of what VISAs actually live through. Readers, I advise you then to magnify your feelings of anger, hatred, horror, or other indignant emotions 10,000 times, and you will begin to know the impact of rape. Perhaps a poetic account is a means to understanding:

> A storm from behind, an impact. It sucks away the air around me in a great rush. I cannot breath. Rage is turning the air to pumice. I cannot hear. Something in my eyes. The pain is in my eyes. I am closing my eyelids but they do not meet. Something is in my eyes. Something is coiling around my neck, something alive. Something furious and terrible. Words, but I cannot hear them. I am thrashing in the air. There is a foul odor. My body is on fire from inside. My blood is rushing as if trying to escape. I hear only it. There is no air. It is all going out of me. Who is screaming? I do not know who is screaming. I cannot breathe. (Raine 1998: 9)

Why print the words of pain? First, the writing takes much of the pain away by giving meaning and understanding to the chaos of rape. Second, people, especially students, have thanked me over and over again for showing them how to stand up to their experiences of trauma. Third, this is my role as an activist. As a friend described it, "You are very lucky that you have the luxury to be able to stand up and state the truths of those horrors. You have the education and opportunity to aid others. You have support. Most people can never do anything about what happened." Fourth, to write on pain is a privilege to aid in stopping it. The medical and crises professionals, police and fire people, and others daily confront situations of trauma that they must deflect from themselves in order to continue their work. These are people who experience the worst to help others, and I wish to do the same.

Attack against Identity

Rapists attempt to murder the identity of their VISAs. Their weapons are words, actions, and spatial and temporal control. Their methods are as effective as bullets that maim and kill. Just like the experience of a gunshot that leaves one wounded or dead, rape is an attempt to murder our identity. During some rapes, the fear of physical death is ever present, and rapists do sometimes kill their victims. Although more subtle and difficult to discern than real bullets, the rapist shoots intellective bullets at our identity. Physical life has no meaning without identity: to live a life like an emotionless robot is not to live a life. Rapists are identity murderers who desire to crush and annihilate the existence of their victims. Only by realizing the depth of destruction of rapists can we encourage strong and severe action against all rapists.

Attack on identity is in our everyday interactions. Let's discuss the following exchanges:

1) *Man*: I'm hungry. What have you got?
   Woman: There's a casserole in the refrigerator that I could heat up.

2) *Woman*: I'm going to have to move.
   Man: You can stay in the neighborhood. I'll take care of that.

3) *Man*: I've got five girlfriends that I can see anytime I want.
   Woman: Those women must like you a lot and enjoy having you in bed. (Winkler 1995: 175)

These exchanges represent ordinary comments between heterosexual women and men. Because these exchanges occurred in the rape attack, they take on a more sinister meaning. But they are statements of everyday violence. Each comment demonstrates the man's attempt to have authority *over* the woman, to control her identity:

1) she should serve him,

2) she should accept him as her protector, and

3) she should accept his sexual "rights" to any woman.

Our everyday exchanges are the foundation for violence. Acceptance of male control in day-to-day conversations is equivalent to acceptance of the dominant attitude the rapist exhibits. Eradicating those everyday violent exchanges destroys the foundation of support that rapists enjoy.

The rapist's dictatorial injection of pain is in our culturing patterns. These patterns are threads of meaning and behavior. When multiple threads/patterns overlap, they form a set of meanings such as a rape. Therefore, expression of the patterns is the issue. Culture has meaning in an action; it is a verb; it is a movable, changeable, alterable, creative pattern. We culture, and in these culturing patterns, we share, learn, reject, duplicate, create, and recreate patterns of ideas and behaviors. For a rape to occur, I argue that at least five negative culturing patterns are present.

1) The rapist *isolates and silences* the victim: The man who raped me had watched me for three weeks to ensure that I was alone. He broke in at 1 A.M. on a weekday while the neighbors slept soundly. He threatened me several times during the attack not to go to the authorities. His pressure was to silence me about the attack. If the rapist ensures isolation, the VISA's hope is nonexistent. This isolation along with silence enhances the trauma and magnifies pain. To communicate is to defuse the pain.

2) The rapist *targets the self-esteem* of the victim. "You like this [the rape]"; "It's your fault; I didn't want to hurt you." The rapist is absolute judge of the meanings of his own and his victim's actions. His purpose is to destroy the victim's view of her/himself. The rapist denigrates the victim with words of vulgarity, words used to humiliate. In ordering me to stand naked and display my body to his staring eyes, the rapist desired not pornography but to subordinate me even in his last moments. Respect and belief in a VISA counteracts the denigration.

3) The rapist focuses on a *discourse of contradictions* with the victim. "I'm your boyfriend" and later "I'm a rapist. I know that I raped you." In another instance the rapist says, "I can break in anywhere," and then suggests, "Use these types of locks and you will be safe." Through contradictions, a victim enters a cavern of chaos in which logic is superficial and irrelevant. The rapist *intermixes violence toward* and *support for* the victim. "He beat me up until my lips and head were swollen," and later he asked me, "Do you want me to take you to the hospital?" Through violence, the rapist alienates the victim, and through support, the rapist barricades the victim with caring. The rapist is not logical, but the rapist's right to contradict is paramount. Consistency provides a stability against the abuse-care treatment.

4) The rapist *controls the movements and decisions* of the victim. Control, absolute control, characterizes the episode of terror. Besides the bodily controls through the rape attack, he held my two-inch strands of hair for hours. Any rejection of his control resulted in physical or verbal punishment. Rapists

thrive off authoring the victim's reality. Control transforms the person into a victim. My immobility at the end of the rape was a result of his absolute power. My lies about his "sexual prowess" and "his girlfriends' lust" refashioned me from an honest person to one who glorified the torturer. Decision making by a VISA counteracts the control previously established by the rapist.

5) *Cycling the Pain* into the life of his/her victim after the attack allows the rapist to continue controlling through hate the victim's perception of reality. Threats were one means. The scars on my body were another reminder, permanent in this form, of the attack. And the emotional knowledge of his hate was likewise unforgettable hate. Cycling the pain into a victim's existence after the attack reinforces the rapist's success in torturing. A VISA's ability to explain and alter the rapist's land mines of pain can minimize the damage.

These five negative traits betray the culturing patterns of rape. Separately, each is a negative cultural pattern that exists in our day-to-day exchanges. When combined, they demarcate rape. Identifying other cultural patterns may help us to further understand the process. To understand rape aids in dealing with its impact. Some of this information formed a basis of my education prior to the rape. Education gave me the knowledge and strategies to aid me in those traumatizing hours. It also gave me the strength to keep trying to stand up for my rights at the hospital and with the police.

TRAUMATIZED EVIDENCE: THE HOSPITAL AND POLICE

Of the 945,000 rapes reported to the police in 1989, only 24,912, or 2.6 percent, of the rapists received a conviction, and 11,663, or 1.2 percent, are in prison. Why do people not report rape, and why do jurors not convict rapists? When the rapist attacked me, the odds of finding him, getting legally plausible evidence, testifying in court, convincing a jury, and having a fair judge to sentence him were minimal. My initial goal was modest: to increase the recorded number of rapes by reporting it. My next goal was to attempt to find the rapist. Finding the rapist, people said, was like finding a needle in a haystack. To them it was impossible; but to me, if there really was a needle in the haystack, then patience would eventually uncover it. Remove one straw at a time from the haystack, and the needle will materialize. I committed to one year to find the rapist.

Hospital Concerns

"I've been raped." These were the words I spoke to the woman sitting in the information cage at the hospital's emergency room. What else can one say? At 6 A.M., I had finally found my way to the correct place. While waiting behind another client, I told myself I did not need immediate attention. Nevertheless, care was critical. *Wait, Cathy, obviously you are not bleeding to death.* My concern was the collection of the sperm in my vagina as evidence. The DA does not consider a person raped unless s/he carries such evidence buried inside her/him. Because the sperm would remain alive for twenty-four hours, I had time. The receptionist looked at me in a matter-of-fact way. Although I was one of the thousands of injured people she had seen, a subtle reaction of surprise seeped into her face. Fear of people's misjudgments began. "I've been raped." "Go to the Ob/Gyn.

Down the corridor, turn left and there it is." How many times a day does she give these directions to VISAs? I walked in and made the same statement to the person at the information desk: "I've been raped." Her face showed explicit signs of reaction. "Walk down the way and have a seat."

Within minutes the rape survivor advocate Cassandra was at my side. She was calm yet appropriately attentive. She had an effective style: While she sat next to me, she turned her body to face me. "I'm Cassandra, the rape survivor advocate. How are you?" Her gestures, expressions, and tone of voice demonstrated her all-out support. Her everyday questions and humane treatment of me demonstrated her concern. Within seconds, she changed the view I had of myself from one of victim to that of survivor. "I think I'm fine. I'll make it." "I was raped also. I understand what you are feeling." "What happened to you?" "A man I dated raped me in my home." "What happened to him?" "You know, I think he raped me because he knew I worked here. Immediately after he raped me, he asked for help. He went to counseling. I thought that was the best and only thing I could do." Her words held both doubt (the man is a criminal) and assurance (she protected other women). The hidden club of people raped now accepted my membership. The barriers for secrecy were down, and my hazing to become a club member was over. This response—"I've been raped"—became a common marker that lets each of us know that we can speak freely: We know what rape is.

"The doctor will be with you in just a few minutes. Do you want to call the police?" Subtlety defined her questions. She didn't tell me to call the police, and she didn't demand that the police be called. She placed the important issues up front and let me decide the action. She gave me control. "Yes, please call them. Could you ask the police to go to my house undercover? I don't want the neighbors to know. The rapist threatened to come back, and if the neighbors know, then the rapist might find out. Maybe I could drive the police to my house as if they were friends. The rapist threatened me. He'll come back."

Living in a tunnel of terror challenged my understanding. The rapist's threats defined my actions. I didn't understand that some rapists fear the authority of the police, or rather, the authority of imprisonment. Cassandra answered my doubts: "All rapists make these threats. Only 10 percent carry them through." The truth in these statistics was useless. As a member of the club, now I feared being a member in that 10 percent. No statistical argument could calm my fear of the rapist. If research showed that only .01 percent of the rapists returned, fear would still prevail. Rather the statistic magnified my mountain of fear. There was a 10 percent reason to worry! Gently she spoke: "The police can't go there undercover. Besides, rapists fear the police. That is your way of standing up to him." Her argument worked to overcome my hesitancy. I had to stand up to his threats. She left to call the police while I grabbed the phone to call friends: There was the need to change the locks on my house and for someone to be with me. It was 6 A.M. Social considerations were irrelevant in a crisis.

"Linda, this is Cathy. I'm sorry to call you but I knew you would be up." "What's up, hon?" She always addressed me and probably everyone else with this affectionate salutation. "I've been raped, but I'm OK. Can Don go over to my house later and change the locks on the doors? The rapist stole the keys and can get back in." Determination to stand up to the rapist and to stand up for myself was critical. "Sure, let me give you his number at work. It's 543-1234. Call him when you can be picked up. He'll take care of things." This call would lead to a list of people to be called in my address book. Next I tried Alecia. Although I knew her slightly, I needed someone with me. "Alecia, I've been raped. I'm OK, but I don't think that I should be alone. Can you come down to the hospital now?" "Yes, I'll be there right away." Her voice was supportive and convincing with a tone of urgency. "I'm leaving now." Meanwhile, a nurse took my blood pressure, a standard procedure.

Cassandra returned. "I've called the police. They'll be here shortly. We'll wait for them before the doctor sees you. I don't know how the police in your suburb are in their treatment of rape victims. I'm familiar with the detectives in the city, and most are good. There are a few you have to watch out for. Do you have any questions?" There was one pressing point. "I can beat this rape. The rapist doesn't have to win, does he? I don't have to become disabled by the rape, do I?" Doubt resided in her voice: "Well, no, but you should see a counselor in the rape center on the fifteenth floor." Her answer was both an unfavorable and a favorable response. Unfavorably, she questioned my ability. Favorably, she made me aware of the buried trauma. "Cassandra, I think he wanted to kill me!" "Most rapists threaten, but that's all it is. Few carry through with their threats." *Yes, he did want to kill me. It was not just a threat. . . . At least I don't think it was just a threat.*

To prepare me for the police, Cassandra asked questions about the rapist and the attack, and I described to her the details. Not trusting my memory, I asked for her help: "Remember these points, Cassandra: his scar, the details of his eyebrows and eyes. I'm afraid I'll forget. Please come to the police station with me. You can help me not to forget." "We'll see. You know, you have a lot of information about the rapist. I've never had a victim who collected these many details. This is impressive and will help the police." She described me as astute and clear headed—vacuous and meaningless words at the time. My jumbled insides took precedence over her compliments. "You are the kind of victim who I have always wanted to come in contact with. Sometimes, women can't reveal this information until a lot of time has passed. You have given more details in just five minutes than most women are able to pull together in the whole process." *What details?* The unremarkable looks of the rapist would make it difficult to find him. His features were average: neither ugly nor extremely handsome, neither distorted nor out of place. Nothing stood out, like a gold tooth or a mole. His most remarkable feature was hidden—the scar. My desire to have every man within five miles drop his pants, I knew, would not be well received by the police. But it seemed reasonable to me.

Her comments changed disbelief about myself into belief. Maybe the police would not view this rape as just a statistic on the crime books. Hope. Maybe the police could capture the rapist. Yet her complimentary words were difficult to believe. *How could I feel like a "good" victim when devastation defined my reality?* Externally my expressions were a false armor of defense because internally the terror of the rapist gnawed at me. "Well, I've taught and read about rape. I guess that helps. Cassandra, there's something I don't understand. I hit the guy in his balls, and I pulled hard on his penis, but he acted like nothing happened." "Some people say that rapists have such an adrenaline high and are so determined to complete the rape that nothing will stop them, not even pain." If that were true, are rapists impervious to pain?

Cassandra left to check on the police. Alecia found me. We gave each other a half-hug. "I didn't know that you had been beaten up." The bruises on my face were unfelt. Cassandra had responded to me without pointing them out. Alecia's next words should have been a shock to me, but how could a person be more in shock than I was at that point: "I was raped also." "What happened?" The process of counseling began. *Shouldn't Alecia be talking to me about the rape that I suffered? Or, maybe the attack against me made her reexperience the attack against her. Or, talking about her attack is her strategy against my terror.* "I knew this friend for about two years on an archeological dig. In the evening, the group sat around and drank a couple of beers, like always. I went to my room in the motel, two doors away. He came down to talk and made some jokes about sex. Before I knew it, he was on top of me, had all my limbs pinned down, and his hand over my mouth. It was over in minutes. I didn't tell anyone.

Who would believe that this had happened so close and in just a few minutes?" "Where is he now?" "He's still back there, working with my friends."

Since it was near 7 A.M. and I was to teach a class in two hours, I called the university. Gregory always came in early. "Gregory, this is Cathy. I've been raped. I'm at the hospital. I won't be able to teach today. Perhaps Vickie could cover for me." "Sure, but will you be in to teach tomorrow?" "Gregory, I can't make any decisions now. I haven't even been to the police station yet. I'll just have to notify you later. Please tell Dr. Sinta about what happened." "OK, but be sure and call her." "I will, I will. Good-bye Gregory." Minutes after the rape, Gregory expected me to be able to make decisions about work, and from his perspective, twenty-four hours was enough time for me to heal from a night of torture. Cassandra returned: "The police said that a detective came here but couldn't find us. Since it's seven o'clock, they'll send the female detective. This is better. Because she won't be here for another half-hour, the doctor can see you now. This is also better because you'll get a doctor who just came on duty and who will be fresh and not tired from the late hours."

In the enclosed room, the nurse left me half-naked with the hospital's flimsy paper gown. When the doctor came in, Cassandra went to wait for the detective. It was immediately clear that the doctor did not know how to use the rape kit for collecting criminal evidence. She left me alone to get help for herself from another internist. Returning, the two, whispering, hovered behind the sheet draped over my knees, the knees that they placed in those heinous stirrups. Luckily for them, my anger against the rapist superseded my anger against these doctors. If they don't know the procedure, why don't they read the directions *outside* of my presence? Usually, I would have told these people off: "You're both doctors, and you are a woman. You are supposed to know how to collect evidence from a rape. If not, at least be professional and read the directions somewhere else and then come back here and act as if you do know something." I had no energy to say a word. The whirl of trauma in my head silenced my anger.

The doctor's preparation matched her words of compassion: None. From the moment she walked into the room and almost until the moment she left I wondered if she was mute. Her only words were soft murmurings to her colleague to figure out the kit. After a rape, the feeling of aloneness arouses fear. The rape occurred—the rapist had reminded me of this—because I was alone. Companionship gives one the feeling of some protection and reminds one of one's own self. But the doctor did not speak and did not provide any assurance. Then Cassandra was back at my side. At last, the doctor found words to say to me, but her expertise was still in question: "Where are your bruises?" I had never looked at a mirror nor taken the time to examine any part of my body. Only when I had removed my clothes to put on the hospital gown did I see bruises. Cassandra pointed out marks: "There are some on this arm and over here and on her back." *Shouldn't the doctor be examining every part of my body? What type of an examination is this? People in trauma don't do medical examinations on themselves.* The doctor never looked at my breasts and chest area. These remained unchecked.

The doctor picked at my back: "I'll take out these glass pieces." *There's glass. There are glass bits embedded in my back.* She pulled out the broken lamp bulb bits, unfelt even then. The rapist's blow that swung wide and hit the lamp broke the bulb. The glass particles sprayed over the bed where the rapist had raped me for hours. The pieces embedded their way into my body. That night he had held me down on my back, pushing me into the splintered glass. I felt nothing.

"I think that these cuts on your back should be stitched up." *Forget it, just leave it.* As an anthropologist, I had learned from other societies that U.S. people have great concern for irrelevant medical points. "You could have a scar there." "I don't worry about such marks." I was too old and too sane to run for Miss America. *When would I have the time to get the stitches out? I would have to find another doctor and wait for hours in his office for something minor.* "Couldn't you just put some bandages over them?" With the investigation and the necessity of re-securing my home, time was of the essence. Besides, I felt no pain. "Let me get someone else to check this." She brought back a specialist who scrutinized my back. Their concern was proper medical attention, and my concern was to catch the rapist. Loss of time was the issue. "These should be stitched, but if you don't want the stitches, we could put butterfly bandages over them." Doctors always make a big deal about nothing. I didn't realize it then but trauma had left me numb. "Please, put the bandages on." After that, I never looked at my back. The butterfly bandages eventually fell off during a shower. The bandages in the bathtub drain were my only evidence of those scars.

"Because of the head wounds, we're going to take X-rays to see if your skull is cracked." It didn't feel cracked, but precautions were necessary. They wheeled me away on a gurney—on my back again, looking at the ceiling. Lying on one's back is a position of helplessness. While I waited, the detective charged up to me. "I'm Det. Carson," she spoke rapidly.

"Can-you-describe-the-attacker? I'm-going-to-put-out-an-APB-on-him." Her intensity and rushed actions upset me. I needed calm and peace. Perhaps her initial agitation was to impress upon me her intention of catching the rapist. She later validated this. "He's about 5'8" to 5'10", about 160 to 180 pounds, mustached, slender but slightly muscular, good teeth, and he wore a cap. He wore the cap one inch back from his hairline. The cap was camouflage-like. I'm not sure of the color, but the shape of the front part was duck-like or oval-shaped. He had a small dime-shaped scar on his groin, the left side." "I'll get this information on the police radio right away. Within the hour, they'll patrol for him." The speed with which she worked and her strong desire to capture this rapist were important types of support. Yet how can they find a rapist who did not have any distinguishing features except for a hidden scar? Hopelessness mixed with the intense desire to stop him.

"Who else was in the house, such as lovers?" "No one. I just moved here last month. I hardly know anyone. Also, I cleaned the sheets this past weekend, and there were no lovers, or anyone else. Except for my dog, and her hairs are straight, and of course, there are my own. Other than that, there are only the rapist's hairs." As the detective departed, the X-ray technicians wheeled me into place. They were people who did their job, were kind and efficient, and gently showed me where to place my body and head in the different angles for the X-rays. These people talked to me, but I didn't know if they knew about the rape or not. They treated me like a human being. Maybe they had no idea what happened.

The impersonal analysis of my body, some people might think, was a way of raping me again. That was not my feeling. On my body was the evidence of the crime. These people, even the mute gynecologist, did their jobs and gathered evidence against the rapist. The choice was unpleasant but necessary. I couldn't bathe until everyone had collected the evidence, but then again I didn't have an overwhelming desire to bathe and "get that rapist off of me." My body held the evidence *against* the rapist, and I wanted to preserve all of it.

After I returned to the Ob/Gyn clinic, the nurse told me to get dressed. "Could I wash the dried blood off my face?" No one took a photo as evidence. The crusty drops of blood over my lips pulled on the skin and that sensation gave me a feeling of disfigurement. At the basin, I saw myself in the mirror. Discoloration covered half of my face. My eyes—swollen and enlarged—were those of a war victim, ringed with colors. My hair, matted and tangled, stood awry. The dark red outline of blood around my lips added to the rainbow of beaten tones. How amazing that most people were calm when they looked at me! This face, grotesque from the beatings, is what the rapist enjoyed looking at! It pleased him to batter this disfigured entity with his hate! What type of person was he?

The staff had me wait for the pregnancy test, unimportant results to me. I had already decided that discarding an ill-conceived fetus was my choice. Three months were still available for me to deal with that. My one issue that morning was to stop the rapist. The nurse came over for another blood pressure check. "Why are you taking my blood pressure again?" "You had high blood pressure earlier. We can't release you until it's in the normal range." It was still on the high side. Cassandra let me know that if I needed anything I could call her. She gave me her phone number. I marked it in my address book but later forgot her last name.

The nurse explained the pills. After vaguely trying to remember these details, I asked, "Could I have this information written down?" "The pill containers have this information." She explained the different VD tests. None of that information reached my mental recorder. Details about the rapist were my only focus. But, I did not forget her advice for me to get an AIDS test in six months. Could my brother and I become companions with this disease? This was not a major worry now. My brother's diagnosis led to my education on AIDS. If the rapist had given me AIDS, the symptoms would not begin for five or six years. Maybe in that time some-one would discover the cure. When the pregnancy test came back nega-tive, enthusiasm mixed with relief were the nurse's reactions. I didn't care. While their focus was on pregnancy and VD treatment, mine centered on the rapist. Medical problems could wait.

Alecia drove my car home with my lonely dog. Cassandra followed so she could bring Alecia back to the hospital to retrieve her car. At my house, Alecia gave the detectives my keys to collect evidence. Five detec-tives, their whole group of detectives, worked on the case that day. On murder and rape cases, the detectives pool their efforts and work as a team the first days. This impressed me. The crime of rape against me was worth that much effort! While finding the rapist was improbable, to learn that the police department maximized their efforts in order to try to catch the "rat" was a great comfort.

The detective took me to the police station. During the ride, the rush of details about the rapist surged out, but she focused on her own thoughts: "Wait until we get to the station." I tried to get her to talk to me. Her response was the same: "You can put it down in your statement at the police station." Inexperienced about a statement, I didn't know what was necessary. More important, talking gave me a feeling of safety.

She didn't want to converse. The fear of loneliness plagued me as a harbinger to the threat of another rape. The rapist had said: "No one's in the house. You're alone. I know because I've been watching you for three weeks." *If someone else had lived with me, I would not know the rapist's terror. People are my armor against his attacks.* Rapists wait for the moment when a person is alone and then corner that person. Without witnesses, they know they are safe. Who believes the word of a person raped? Reality is a person's voice. Without the detective's voice, loneliness scared me.

"You know, this guy has a scar on his groin. It's on the left side." "We'll discuss it at the station." "His cap is kinda camouflage in style, but I think it was more like faded orange camouflage style. The peak of the cap was kinda duck-shaped not squarish like a baseball cap." "Let's get those details at the station." "I think I can identify him. I think I can pick him out. I'm almost 80 to 90 percent sure." "Good, we'll show you some pictures, but at the station, not here." Fear of losing the details and fear of loneliness prevailed. These issues raced through my mind, like a merry-go-round that goes faster and faster with a centrifugal force that pulls the riders off. The data kept whirling around and ate away at my sanity. "He left his fingerprints all over the house. Once you get these, you can match him?" "Well, it's not that easy. First, we have to have his prints on file." At least she spoke. "He told me that he's been in prison before. You should have the prints." "Well, there are other issues. He has to have touched a surface from which we can lift his fingerprints, like a hard smooth surface." "No problem. He touched everything. I know he touched surfaces like that. Well, then, you'll catch him soon. You'll just run the fingerprints through your police computer." "Most police departments do not have that sophisticated computer system, except the FBI, Los Angeles, and maybe Chicago. We have to hand check each fingerprint." If a detective needs to check each fingerprint by hand, this could take forever. But disillusionment did not exist yet. The rapist touched everything. Hope.

"Can we offer a reward for the guy? I'm sure my family and friends could raise some money." "We don't do that. People without money can't raise rewards. That would not be fair." "That's true. I'm trying to think of any means to catch him." "If we need information, we have a discretionary fund." Because I was new to the area, alone, and without lovers in the house, the police would try bloodhounds to locate the rapist. Hope. If he lived in the neighborhood, the dogs should pick up his scent and find him. The house, full of only my smells and those of the rapist, was a good place to use this method. The detectives had never had a case to employ the dogs.

Search for Evidence

When we arrived at my home, Det. Carson went over to talk to the Captain. Detectives Roth and Doil introduced themselves: "What identifying marks did this rapist have with which you could pick him out on the street?" "Nothing but a cap, and that cap he could have thrown away." "Do you know how long he was with you?" "I'm not sure. Maybe two or three hours." They gave me an odd look. "That long! Usually a rapist only stays 15 or 20 minutes." This surprised me. "Do you know what time he left?" "Yes, I looked at the clock then, and it was 4:30 in the morning. He had to leave by then because the buses stop in front of my house at that time. I don't know what time he came into my room because the clock was on the other side of the room, and I didn't have my glasses on." It's interesting that I wore my glasses at that time, and for the following week. Once the swelling diminished, I wore my contacts again. But no one questioned me on my ability to see that night without either glasses or contacts nor did they question the severity of my vision problem. To ensure myself as a creditable witness, I never brought this up.

"We interviewed your neighbor across the street. He was drinking beer with his friend. He heard screams at 1 A.M. but thought they came from the park behind you. He got off his porch and looked around but couldn't see anything." *I screamed!?* Those were unrealized screams. When the rapist slugged me, my voice automatically let out piercing peals of panic. My neighbor heard me: My voice took control of me without my realization and screamed for help. "The guy must have been with you for three-and-a-half-hours. That's a long time." *Are the police thinking that I wanted this guy to stay with me? No chance. Who would want a rapist in their presence for even a few seconds?* My crazy sense of humor, a basis of my sanity, surfaced: *Great, the guy who rapes me turns out to be one of the slowest rapists in town. Why couldn't I have gotten a "quickie"?* My thoughts rushed on: *Why didn't my neighbor call the police? If the rapist had seen a cruiser going down the street with a red light on, he would have left my house. Why didn't my neighbor at least call and report the screams? Wasn't it clear that those were screams of terror? He had to have heard the fear in my voice.* How complacent U.S. citizens are! A single anonymous phone call might have stopped the whole ordeal. Although my neighbor seemed like a good citizen because he told the police about the screams afterward, I had a different view.

"There were three guys on the porch drinking beer before I went to sleep. When the rapist broke in, there were only two. Those guys know who the rapist is. They drank with him last night. You should question them about that." "We did talk to them. One of their friends left earlier. We checked him out. That guy didn't react as if he knew who the rapist is. He seemed innocent to us, and this goes for his friends also. I don't think they're involved." Their view was hard to accept. I knew that my neighbor was a link to the crime, but my position didn't matter. The professionals had taken over, and I had to trust their judgment. They had experience in this area of gathering data and judging the validity of people's answers. I did not. I gave up that line of pursuit. "Did you see the guy as he left your house? Do you have any idea in what direction he went?" "No, at first I wasn't sure that, when the front door closed, he had really left. I called out. Only after the house echoed an emptiness did I run to put on my glasses and look out the window. By that time, the street was empty." "Did the guy have any distinguishing marks or smells? Was there anything particular that stood out, maybe his teeth?" "No, except for beer on his breath, he didn't smell; I think he must have taken a bath before he came in. His face did not have any unusual features."

"Do you think you could ID the guy?" "Well, I know you guys aren't the rapists. You are larger than he is, and you are shorter. But, yes. I feel 80 to 90 percent certain that I can ID him." To convince them and myself, I had compared these detectives' features with the rapist's. My insulting behavior was obvious, but the detectives were kind enough to ignore this. What these police detectives didn't know about was a past experience of mine when a rapist had terrorized my neighborhood for weeks. In that case, the rapist was a police officer. "Did he say anything to you?" "Yeah, there was a lot of conversation." "Oh, do you remember any particular statements he said that might stand out or be special to him?" "No. He did say 'This is a trip' a lot, but that's not special. Don't a lot of people say that?" "What topics did you discuss?" "He asked what bus station I took. I told him Springfield, and he said he used that one too. He told me that the police know him and that he is a robber and a rapist. That's what he does for a living. He seemed to know the Hopes. When my dog barked, he immediately looked out the window that faced the Hopes' house. That doesn't help, does it?" "Every little bit helps," the detectives said, but their faces showed disillusionment. "You said that he told you that he's a robber." "Yes, that's the term he used." "Are you sure?" "Yeah, why?" "Well, they usually use the term 'burglar,' and if the guy has been in prison before, he'd know the police term. Do you think he told the truth?" "Well, he wasn't always telling the truth. I know he lied a lot but on this point I think he was not telling me a lie. It's the way he told me. He used the term 'robber.' I don't know why, but I remember that term."

"Look, the guy told me he is known by the police, and that he is a robber and rapist. He left his fingerprints all over the house. He touched everything." "What did he touch?" "In the bedroom, he touched everything." "Can you name items, especially ones with hard, smooth surfaces?" "Yes, my camera case, my red cosmetic box, the window at the top of the hallway. Let me see, what else? In the downstairs office, the top of the desk, my box of checks and the checks inside, and the windowsill in that room. Oh yes, the red suitcase in the empty room upstairs on that side of the house. He touched that and opened it." "Why didn't you call the police from home? We could have gotten here right away. It's easier that way to catch the guy." "He tore the phones out. All my neighbors were asleep. I initially intended to go to the police station, but I couldn't find it." "We're down the street from the courthouse." "That's what I figured, but where?" "That same street, further down, just before the underpass." "Oh, that's why. I didn't drive down that far. There is no sign."

"I have a question for you guys. I punched the guy in the balls, and when that didn't work, I tried to pull off his penis." The words initiated an "Oh my!" and nervous leg movements from the detectives. "I don't understand why the guy wasn't hurt." "You said he had been drinking. Could he also have been high on coke?" "Well, isn't that hard to tell? He was wide-eyed and agitated, which did not seem to be symptoms from alcohol. Maybe he was on an adrenaline high?" "That could be, but if he was on crack, he'd have the same symptoms you described. He'd be feeling no pain. Police hate those cases. You could shoot that guy six times in the heart and head at ten feet, and that crack will keep him alive another ten minutes—long enough to kill you. You can't take chances with those coke heads." Through their questions came advice: "Did you mark him or scratch him with a fingernail?" "No, I don't have any right now." The knowledge that my brother had a fatal disease inaugurated my nail-biting habit. "You know, one of the easiest ways to catch a rapist is to leave a scratch on his facial cheeks. People are quick to turn in a guy with such a mark. Also it's hard for him to hide it."

The Hopes came out and stood on their front porch with a worried look directed at me. Det. Carson spoke with them. She then approached me and told me that I shouldn't talk to them: "It would just upset you. It isn't necessary." Without a word, I walked over. "I'm all right. The police have put all their men on the case." "Cathy, they asked us if we heard your screams, but we sleep on the other side of the house. We didn't hear a thing. Believe me, we would have called the police if we knew." "I knew you couldn't hear me. I'm not upset with you. I was just worried that you might be upset about me." "If there is anything we can do, just let us know." "I will, thanks. I better go now because the detective probably wants to go back to the station."

Instead, I went to see where the rapist had broken into the house. It was not the side window. The other detectives walked me around the house and showed me the back window, the one that was well lighted with two bulbs of 400 watts of power. The thick and durable screen, one of those old-fashioned steel screens meticulously attached to the building with big, heavy two-inch nails, stood open at the corner with a space large enough to admit the whole body of the rapist. Because there were no tools found on the premise, the forty or more nails that restrained the screen—a screen whose security I and the landowner had checked a little over a month ago—had been loosened days before the rape. The stretched holes on the screen indicated that it had been unfastened and then reattached to hide the rapist's plan: reattached well enough that casual perusal would elicit no suspicion of his preparatory work and no evidence to thwart his upcoming crime. The triangular piece of wood, hammered into the inside of the window frame to keep it locked, was gone. How much work did it take the rapist to loosen those forty or more huge nails and remove the jammed-in triangular lock?

On the way to the station, Det. Carson ran by the only fast food place in that area. I did not even realize I'd missed a meal. The transformation of my routine was so dramatic that the memory of day-to-day activities disappeared. With a vague sense of hunger, I ordered. We sat in her office to eat. I took one bite. Shock eroded my desire for sustenance. She asked me a few questions and then rushed off to do who knows what. I threw the food away.

Det. Carson brought back a handful of mug shots. They were pictures of men convicted or suspected of crimes. This bothered me because on the one hand blame falls on the same black men over and over again, and on the other hand, the rapist told me that the police knew him. He could possibly be in that set of pictures. "I selected pictures of men that looked similar to the characteristics you described. Now take your time and look carefully at each picture. In the meantime, I have to check on some other matters in the case. Study each photo. Don't rush. Examine each one. Any photo that you can confidently give an '8' or '9' to, we will bring that guy in for a lineup. I want to get this guy. Will you be all right?" "Yeah." What else could I say? *The rapist won't attack me in the middle of a police station. He probably doesn't care to know where I am. On the other hand, maybe the gossip from the neighbors has reached him, and he's angry that I had the gall to turn him in. If that is true, then he is either waiting for me or in hiding.* Even though Det. Carson's office was in the middle of the station, the safest spot, fear took the place of security.

Loneliness reinforced that fear. What I desperately needed was counseling, but that was not the job of the police investigator. I needed someone to calm me. The emotions of the previous night made me want to explode in uncontrollable hysterical crying! Those tears had to remain buried because self-control meant control over the details. *Am I to look at this guy again without anyone to counsel me? How can I look at the face I hate the most?!* Perusal of the pictures was quick, too quick. The investigator wanted a careful study, but for me to follow her directions while alone was impossible. I needed someone with whom I could discuss the points carefully and to validate my reality. Traumatic emotions dominated me; yet I had to do the task. I had to find that rapist. Some photos had features similar to the rapist, but none seemed to identically match my mental image. No face jumped out at me. I wanted to catch the guy, but I didn't want to see his face. No rapist is human, and, therefore, no rapist can have a human face. I needed support.

"Did any of the men look like an '8' or '9'?" "What exactly do you mean by an '8' or '9'?" "How closely the photo resembles the rapist." "Does that mean like grading a photo as a 'B' or a 'C'?" "Yeah, that's about it." Their coding system disturbed me: How do you rate a man as a possible rapist? If I pinpointed the wrong man, how horrible this would be for him! To be accused of rape and to be brought in for a police lineup when you are not the rapist must be a terrifying experience. How can I inflict that pain and terror on any man? For me, I had to feel 100 percent confident that I was picking the rapist. I didn't have the right to point out any other man in the pictures as having a similar face.

Det. Carson had information about the bloodhounds. The first try was a false start. Apparently, the dogs left the house, went right up to where I parked my car, and stopped. The police then returned the dogs to the house to pick up another scent. After the dogs exited the house for the second time, they headed in the left direction, turned down through a small forested area—where I had found the credit card—along a footpath frequented by the neighbors, and stopped at a trash can behind a duplex. The police interviewed the two people on either side of the duplex. The woman seemed innocent of knowing the rapist. No man was in her house that night. The police believed her story. In the other side of the duplex was a man with an Afro hairdo that stood about 4 inches high. Since my description included the detail of a man with short cropped hair, the police believed he was not the rapist. Moreover, he had had no male friends visiting that night. The police brought him down to the station to photograph him. When I saw the picture, I knew the police were right. But why did the bloodhounds stop at the trash can? I have my own unprovable theory: The rapist had hidden a pair of new shoes—shoes as yet without his scent—in that trash can and came back to retrieve them. He had been in prison before and would have learned such tricks.

Without a mug shot suspect, Det. Carson moved to the next stage: "What clothes was he wearing?" The captain listened as I noted the details of the cutoffs. "Wasn't it kind of cold last night for cutoffs?" "Well, maybe it was jeans that he was wearing. I'm not sure." His presence impacted my reality: "I think I'll be moving on." Jeopardizing my memory was easy. It was cutoffs that the rapist wore, but my insecurity challenged my certainty. Det. Carson said, "I'm going to be patrolling the streets these next couple of nights, looking for him. I want to get him. I want to nab that guy and pull down his pants to show the bruising. I want to find that guy, and his black-and-blue marks will expose him." "Look for the cap. It was camouflage in color, with washed out and faded shades, maybe orange. The light from the street lamp made it hard to discern the exact colors, but the front of the cap is unique. It's oval and not squarish like a baseball cap. I'm sure he's wearing it. He put it on like it was an old and familiar habit." Silence. I kept emphasizing the cap. No other feature stood out. Probably she realized that the cap was gone.

"I'm going to take you into Mary. Give her your statement." "What should I say?" "Just tell her everything." "Everything? But he was there so long!" "We understand. You just tell Mary everything that happened. We need information to catch him and on what crimes he committed." There was no way that I could tell everything. Selection was necessary: the details of appearance in order to capture him and the details of the crime in order to convict him. Would other details be helpful for the capture or conviction? I didn't know. No one advised me.

"This is the first time I've taken a statement like this," Mary said; she was nervous. The difficulty in speaking one's statement is to say the words at a slow rate for the typist, but my words rushed out like a runaway train.

I'd blurt out sentences and then try to repeat them. The situation was impossible. While Mary typed 80 words per minute, my rate of speaking was 240 words per minute. This disjunction in our methods resulted, I have no doubt, in a loss of data on the crime. Detailed accuracy was my goal. It would be clear to professionals on how to interpret the details, details that reflected my state of trauma. After almost five hours dictating the statement, not to mention the previous twelve hours, exhaustion reigned. I read, edited, and proofed it. She put my handwritten corrections in the computer. I never checked her corrections. I signed it.

I wanted a copy of the facts from that night. "Could I get a copy of my statement?" "Well, we don't like copies floating around. They could get into the wrong hands." The rapist did not trust me and neither did the detective. As I read the statement three months later, the disproportion of time spent on the most innocuous details of that night shocked me. One whole page—20 percent of the statement—described the least stressful and least endangering five minutes of the attack, for instance, when the rapist searched the other bedroom. I tended to spend time on "safe" details rather than pertinent and necessary points of the long and excruciating series of rapes. It resulted in not including crimes that the rapist could have been charged with.

"Let's go over the details some more in my office. We've picked up some items from your home for evidence. We will test the camera and sheets and give them back later. The suitcase had the wrong texture to lift prints from." "When will I get the stuff?" "As soon as the lab is finished. Did he touch any of the checks?" "Yes, he opened the box and touched the top one." "I'll pick that up when we return. Also, I'm going to need your underpants for evidence. You can change at home." "In a rush, I put on the minimal number of clothes in order to get out of the house as quickly as possible. I didn't take time to find any underpants in the mess. I don't have any on." "We'll need your jeans then, but after they get tested in the lab I don't think they'll be salvageable." "Whatever is necessary to catch this guy." "The other detectives checked your phone on the first floor. *It is working*." With a reprimand in her voice she asked, "Why didn't *you* use it to call the police?" "He yanked it out." "The detectives said it's in working order." "How could that be? Oh, I know what must have happened. When he yanked it, he must have busted the electric cord to the answering machine, but not the telephone wires. Since the phone upstairs didn't work, I just figured it was the same downstairs. I didn't try it!"

"I have to get pictures of you. Let's go into the women's bathroom for privacy. I can lock the door." I took off my clothes, and she photographed the bruises and contusions with a Polaroid and a 35mm camera. The true colors of those bruises didn't seem to show up on the Polaroids. Each shot was uncomfortable. Positioning of my arms and body for the best shots and best light in that shadowy windowless bathroom was like standing in those distorted fashion model positions. "I think these will come out all right, but sometimes it's better to take pictures a few days later when the bruises have surfaced more. The colors are persuasive to the jury. Do you have a friend who could take some pictures?" "Yes, I'll take care of that in the next day or two. I'll watch for the brightest colors for you." My poor attempt at humor did not arouse a response. The detective was all business. It was nearly five o'clock. The other detectives had finished photographing and fingerprinting the house. I called Don to meet me there. He firmly but gently told me that everyone on the "farm"—that was their nickname for their suburban home—wanted me to stay with them. I agreed. The detective and I left for my home. "Be sure and see a counselor." "Why?" "All rape victims need counseling." "I know I'm showing signs of trauma and shock, but isn't that natural after such a disaster?" "There will be more later. Everyone needs counseling."

The once-white door of my home brought shock. A black substance covered all the places the rapist had touched. Inside was the same: the office walls, the upstairs surfaces. The newly painted white walls were a dark, night-like shade. The oily, grimy smudges also obscured the walls of my bedroom, once my place of peace. "Don't worry. These marks come off easily with a cleaning substance." This did not avert my disgust. Det. Carson walked me through the rooms while I described where everything had happened. First, we walked upstairs to my bedroom. *There was no excrement or urine in the corner where the dog had laid!* "There's nothing here! The police cleaned it up?" "No." This wasn't a surprise to her. *How could something so real—the penetrating and pervasive smells of those odors—not exist?*

Smears of blood marked the linens on my bed. Another shock. I didn't remember bleeding, but the abundant evidence showed me otherwise. There was quite a bit of glass. The rapist had crushed me into those never-felt glass particles. *Did he feel them?* In the middle of the floor among the pile of objects thrown there by the rapist was the pair of earrings that my father gave my mother and that she had given to me. I grabbed these quickly and put them in my pocket: a memory I didn't want destroyed or lost. "My checkbook is missing." "Can you call the bank tomorrow and put a hold on those checks? Tell them that the police are interested in the case and to call us if any of the checks come through." "Could you catch the guy that way?" "It's possible." Hope.

On one side of my bed, I found the flash to the camera: "He must have had this rolled up in his T-shirt. I mistakenly thought it was the box of checks. They're the same size." On the other side of the bed were the ground-up cigarette butts. I never smoked, and these disgusted me. This was worse because he had ground those butts into the wood floor. His desire was to destroy. Retracing the steps of the rapist with the sun shining in through my windows did not reintroduce the rape terror. Instead, this was a method to catch him. The detective provided security. "Is it dangerous for me to live in this place again? Will the rapist come back?" "We can't advise you on that. You have to make the decision that's best for you." Her lack of a position was the professional one, but she never suggested ways to safely return. Then Don drove up. She quickly left. Thus began the long line of people talking behind my back.

Friends to the Rescue

With open arms, Don greeted me: "Well, how are you doing, young-'un?" "I'm fine." We hugged. This gesture became quite common with my friends and was a comfort. "I was just talking to the detective here about the break-in. You should have had bars on the windows." "Don, it wouldn't have stopped him. He would have jumped me getting out of the car." That was Don's only antagonistic statement. My speaking up instantaneously became a strategy against this and other discriminatory comments. Det. Carson spoke: "We haven't gotten your fingerprints yet. Maybe you could stop by in the next few days, and we could do that." "Let's go now if it's important. I don't want to hold up the case." "A day or two won't make any difference." "Can I go with you on patrol? I could help you find him sooner." "No, I don't think that would be a good idea." The best therapy for me was to be active on the case, but the detective discouraged it.

Don, a person of genuine kindness, held the car door open for me, and as he drove us home, he asked my wishes. "First, a Kahlua to drink and then a whirlpool bath. I want to relax in your tub for an hour while I sip on the Kahlua. You don't mind if I use your tub?" These were requests easily granted. "No problem, young'un. You know the specialties of the house." We laughed. After going thirty-six hours without sleep and enduring intense pressure, relaxation was my goal. A long hot bath was one of my favorite methods to reduce the adrenaline flow.

Don lived in a three-family, three-floor home. He and Linda lived on the second floor; Charlotte and Rick, Linda's parents, had the first floor; and Susan, Paul, and their two kids inhabited the third. Rick, who later wrote this excerpt, was one of the first people waiting to greet me:

> Our Cathy had terrible black eyes, and about all the flesh we could see was bruised, black and blue, or bloody. I put my hand on her shoulder, and she screamed in pain.

People carefully hugged and greeted me. Linda's brother Will and his soon-to-be spouse, Estar, stopped by with gifts. They were magnanimous: people who barely knew me! But I did not have the energy to be appreciative. The bruises shocked them. They weren't painful, only a symbol of the rape. Charlotte understood this and wrote her impressions:

> Cathy's vibrant and upbeat personality was crushed. It gave me a sickening feeling in the pit of my stomach, a roaring, as of a tornado, rushing through the head, a complete feeling of helplessness—where to find him—how to find him—would the police help enough—what would be the result of such an intrusion in one's life. All these feelings and thoughts piled one on top of another.

Linda's car could be heard pulling into the garage, and quickly Don left to greet her. At that time, I thought this was a routine response between husband and wife. Later, Linda told me that Don rushed out to prepare her for the sight of my head, which was bloated and distorted in the shape like an elephant's. This never bothered me, but it did disturb others. Susan's nursing instincts took over when she first saw me. Her journal held her memories of that night:

> In all my years of nursing, I have never seen anyone look as exhausted as Cathy did. Her face was swollen and discolored (I knew it would look worse in days to come), but at least she was walking under her own power, somewhat haltingly, like someone bruised in a car wreck. The exhaustion and pain were obvious. I was relieved when she spoke up because I have never felt so helpless in my life! Mostly, I could listen and be sensitive enough not to say or do anything stupid. Cathy was not a "rape victim," she was Cathy, and yes she had been brutally raped. Luckily, Cathy was in a very demanding mood. She was able to say "I want something to eat," or, "I want . . ." I knew she probably needed to regain some sense of control, and I was only too happy to oblige.

The Kahlua and bath made me ready for the sack. They gave me the study upstairs, prepared the couch, and then asked me if there were any other requests. "Yes, a night-light." Without hesitation, Linda grabbed the kids' night-light and remarked laughingly: "They're asleep. They won't notice it missing." Within seconds, I was fast asleep.

CHASING THE RAPIST

Fingerprinting

"Your identification is the basis for the investigation and conviction of the guy who attacked you. It is *you* who have to point out the guy, and *you* who have to be sure, absolutely positive, that the suspect is the rapist. It is *your* words in court that will convict him." That was Det. Carson's order, enunciated at the beginning of the investigation. She repeated it over and over again. Identifying the rapist was my obligation, and I had to point him out. The police doubted my ability even to identify a suspect: "Be sure, *absolutely positive*, that the suspect *is* the rapist." The police, like the rapist, attacked my confidence and abilities. Mount Everest seemed like a hill compared to this task—another challenge to survive beyond the rape. *I'll try.*

Stamina, self-control, and belief in myself aided me. I transformed my anger at the rapist into energy to use against him. That thunderous and destructive anger mixed with his hate, once his weapon, would become my impetus, my incentive to develop strategies against him and to find him. The rapist had succeeded in imprisoning me. Now I could imprison him.

Two days after the rape, Thursday, I went for the fingerprinting. "Det. Carson, how many fingerprints did you find?" "Well, Cathy, sit down first." The "sit down" phrase was ominous. "We have to take your fingerprints first, and then we'll see. But don't get your hopes up." "Surely, there is at least one fingerprint." "I'll let you know the results tomorrow." "I'll be by the phone all day." Thus began the first of many long periods of waiting.

As she rolled each of my fingers into the inkpad, I complied. But having the smears of black on my palm and fingers was one step too far. To see these smudged dots of grimy ink on my fingertips was not an issue, but the blackening of my whole hand, like the damage to my whole body, was another way the rapist had taunted me. I hurried to scrub those marks off.

The next day, Det. Carson called to say, "Cathy, there weren't any fingerprints, but we're going to try another method." "How could that be? He touched everything. Maybe there's some surface you forgot to check: the doors, door frames, windows, desk top, bureau, front area around the bay window?" "Cathy," she gently replied, "we tried everything. But there's still hope." "I don't understand it. How could that happen?" "If he had touched his hair and gotten oil on his fingertips, the oil and sweat could prevent fingerprints from adhering to any surface." "He did rub his hands over his hair several times, and I thought I smelled a faint odor of something on his hair when he was sweating. I was sure we had him." That defused my hopes. "If we can keep your keys for the weekend, we'll spray the walls with a chemical substance. Sometimes it works. It's toxic, and with this concentration of fumes, the house will have to be aired out for several days afterward." "Anything you want to do is OK with me. I'll do anything to catch that guy." The news tested my confidence. Disillusionment set in, and yet I had to resist hopelessness.

Saturday morning found me holding onto those last comforts of sleep, a time to mull over life and enjoy the respite from harsh realities. Two memories overlapped and nagged at me: one was of the rapist, as he had placed his cap on his head. The other memory was of an incident that occurred about one week after my arrival in town. I was at the bus stop. A man gently spoke up: "Excuse me. I don't want to bother you, but I'm new to town. Is this the right direction for downtown?" "Yes, you've got it right. I'm new to town also. These signs are unclear." The bus approached, we got on, and sat opposite each other. "I'm hoping to find work." "I know how hard it is to look, but I've heard it's not too hard to find work in this town. What do you do?" "I'm a house painter." "You won't have any problems. You could even go around the neighborhoods, and I'm sure you'd find work." "Well, thanks for the encouragement." "Why don't you stop at the university? They frequently have openings."

"Maybe another time. I can't miss my appointment. I'm in drug rehabilitation. I know I'm going to make it." The words "drug rehabilitation" left me reticent. Drugs make people crazy. I didn't want drugs taking over my life or the lives of those people around me. "It's hard, but you'll do it." My negative tone revealed my thoughts of discrimination. "Thanks, I could use the words of support. You don't need your house painted, do you? I'd like to do it." "No, thanks. I'm doing the inside now, but I like to do it." "Maybe I could help." "Thanks, but I'm practically finished, and besides, I'm a little short of money right now. I couldn't pay you." "I'd do it for nothing. I just want to see you again. I really like you." "Well, that's quite flattering, but you hardly know me. People in this town are all nice."

He stopped the conversation, and slowly, meticulously, with exacting precision, placed his cap on his head, straightening it again several times to fit it in the exact spot, that is, one inch back from his forehead. His cap had a duck-like flap that jutted out from the form-fitting body of the cap, and this flap fell over the front of his face. That was the same methodical way that the rapist had placed his cap on his head. "Really, I want to see you again." "I'm kinda dealing with some personal problems right now." "*Look-I'm-going-to-see-you-again*. When I want something, *I get it*. I will find you and I will see you. *I don't give up. I get what I want.*" The force behind his words brought glares from others. His threatening words came just as my stop arrived. I jumped out. I had forgotten about the incident until that Saturday. This memory confirmed my guess: The rapist was high on crack. The man on the bus went to a drug center, and the rapist was a druggie. Both men had the same formed cap and the same gestures. This was another clue to find the rapist. The drug center was on the west side of town at a public facility. Hope again. With this information, Monday morning found me on the phone to the police: "Det. Carson, I remembered something else."

"Cathy, first, we didn't get any fingerprints from the walls. The chemicals didn't lift any traces." Hope stemmed from my recent memory. Det. Carson said, "This drug center is a shot in the dark. Besides, we're not allowed into drug centers. The privacy act protects them." "That's OK. I believe in that. Can we do surveillance outside of these centers? I know that he had a morning appointment." "He might not be attending any more. He either finished the program he was in or got back on drugs." "We could at least try." "Well, we'll see." The famous "we'll see" response had multiple meanings. Sometimes it brought results; usually it was a means to put me off.

"Cathy, the artist for the composite drawing isn't available for two weeks. Can you make it on Friday afternoon?" "No problem. Finding the rapist has priority over everything else." "Be sure to remain calm the days before. You have to be at ease when you do this. Relax and don't let things bother you." "That won't be a problem. I'm numb." Friday arrived. Despite a fear of the bus, I walked down the first flight of steps to the platform. I saw a man's face that schematically resembled that of the rapist. Exact identification was difficult due to distance and my dark sunglasses. Without a crowd of people for protection, I didn't want to test my courage. I hurried to the far side of the bus stop, an area near another set of stairs. The bus came, but my eyes remained on that distant person. He got on in the front; I got on in back.

The downtown police department was easy to find: Look for a ratty, dilapidated warehouse. The unmarked entrance was identifiable only by the constant flow of people. Inside, a few overworked, bored, blue-suited people sat behind the information desk to confront questioning clients. Beyond were rows and rows of file drawers. No computer system existed. Once inside the station, I related how I had sighted a man who resembled the rapist to Det. Carson, punctuating my account with doubts and the impossibility of verification. "Pick up the phone, and you can talk to us. We can be there immediately." "There's another reason I am agitated." "What happened?" "My boss yelled at me." "Try to be calm now."

Det. Carson's badge was our passport inside the station. As we passed the sexual assault room, she pointed it out. Was the grunginess of the room meant to leave an impact on the practitioners of these crimes or as a demonstration of the investigators' revulsion in dealing with these criminals? More likely, the depressed room represented the level of funding for rape investigations.

In a closet-size room was the artist. Martha had more than a decade of experience. Her realistic renderings had caught many criminals. Her work, the detectives frequently told me, excelled beyond computer line-drawing that produced portraits without features, without emotions, and without the humanness of the criminal. "What have we got here today, Detective?" "This is Cathy Winkler. She's going to give you the details of the man who raped her."

"Oh my! You know, these are the hardest cases. Worse, though, are witnesses to murders. My goodness, are they upset." *Are these words of comfort? Is she labeling me a "difficult victim"? She is such a matter-of-fact person, though. Perhaps this is her way of calming me down by telling me she is accustomed to these situations.* I didn't feel calm. "Well, you just look through this pile of photos and see if you can find features on some of these men that resemble the guy. In the meantime, I'll start with the outer features. How is his head shaped, and what type of hair did he have?" "His head was kind of oval-like with close-cropped hair, black and curly. He wore a cap. Should you put that in the drawing?" "Well, if you want me to, I'll do it. What did the cap look like?" "It was like a baseball cap, but the front flap was oval in shape rather than squarish, and rested one inch back from the line of his forehead." She drew it in a cocked fashion over the left side of the face. "Well, he wore it right over the front of his forehead." "Oh, that doesn't make any difference. They can see the cap; besides, this looks better." It did make a difference. Shortly after the release of the drawing, the police wanted to bring in a man who wore his cap cocked in the same manner. I had to correct them.

While I studied the photos, the police officers socialized. "Do you know anything about an opening in section B?" "No, I hadn't heard about it. Do you want to change jobs?" "Yes, it's time to look for a new spot. I gotta get out of there." "Well, I'll check it out for you. It would be great having you work down here with us." Here was a detective who had my confidence talking about leaving her job right in front of me. I needed her right now. *Would she change jobs next week, leaving me with someone I didn't trust? Was she tired of us VISAs, or was I another bruise in her life?*

For each of the different features from the size and shape of the forehead to the eyebrows, eyes, nose, mouth, and chin, I selected a photo. Even ear placement was a descriptive point. Martha questioned most features. There were numerous erasures, but she was always compliant. Then came the issue of the skin tone. "Give him a dark complexion." "Did this happen at night?" "Yes." "Well, you know, honey, the darkness of the night always makes the skin tone appear darker than it is." "I know, but he did have a dark skin tone. I saw it up close. There was enough light from the street lamp for me to get a good view." "Well, let me shade it in, and we can erase it a little. We can try different tones." Despite her attempts to lighten it, I wanted the skin tone dark. She complied, yet repeated how night deepens our views of skin tones.

As she put on those last touches, she pulled herself back away from the drawing in order to judge its entirety. "Haven't I drawn this guy recently?" she remarked. "Does it look like him?" "I think it's an '8.' " "You can't do better than that." "The face is too long. Could you redraw it about one quarter inch shorter? It's too elongated for his face." "You mean redraw the whole picture! If it's a little bit too long, it's OK. Nobody expects it to be perfect." I wanted it perfect. The closer the drawing resembled his features, the easier it would be for the police to catch him. Without fingerprints, I felt desperate. "You're right. Redrawing it is too much work. But I've got an idea. Couldn't you just fold under this middle horizontal section between the eyes and nose? They have to photograph the drawing anyway. That would make it almost perfect." "Look, it's fine. Don't worry about it. If this can catch the guy, it will. We can't do any better." I relented. Det. Carson took the drawing to have it reduced for a wanted poster (see figure 4.1). The poster printed the words of pain. To speak about it was one reality, and to read it as a public document was

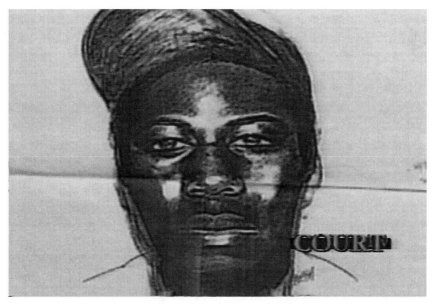

Figure 4.1   Artist Composite of Rapist

another. The words "raped her for about three hours" and "beat her severely about the face, head, and body" struck me. That sadistic act, a morbid act, was—against me.

Surveillance

The following Thursday, Det. Carson was to take me on surveillance, but Det. Roth greeted me instead. "Det. Carson is down with a cold. I'll take you." Roth, as he asked me to call him, was a personable fellow. His outgoing attitude, motivation, and energy expressed hope. He wanted to catch the rapist, he wanted to stop the criminal, and he wanted to help me. He treated me like a sidekick, despite my failings. We walked past the room where other artist composites were hanging. "See that one? That's the drawing of the rapist who attacked your neighbor two months ago. They look similar."

"Let's go. We're going to find him today. I can feel it." I laughed: *How could he know that in the next few moments I would see the rapist?* On the other hand, I appreciated his belief in my ability to identify the rapist. "First, we'll walk around the bus stop, and then peruse the neighborhood." "What will people think of me?" "Don't worry. They don't know who you are. They'll think you're a plainclothes detective like me." His confidence did not override my lack of confidence. How could anyone look at me and not know I was the victim of rape? I felt like one. My face showed it. I still wore sunglasses to hide the bruises. We walked around the bus station for half an hour. Det. Roth exchanged greetings with lots of people, and I eyed everyone as the possible culprit. Using my memory as I scrutinized each adult male face, I quickly absolved each one. He is too old. His skin is too light. Forehead too high. Jaw too square. Weighs too much. Too tall.

We moved on to neighborhood surveillance. Roth kept up the conversation. We talked about each other's past histories, although I think he did more of the talking. His first marriage ended in divorce. He had learned from that one. "Fidelity is one of *the* important values to maintain in your marriage." During the years between his first and second marriages, though, he had had numerous affairs to avoid despair. Despite his precautions, many of the women became pregnant. One woman admitted to lying about taking birth control pills; another confessed to having cornered him on one of the days when she was ovulating. Another put a pinprick in the condom. All wanted to marry him. While their methods were deceitful, I could understand the women. Roth was a great guy. He married a second time, to a super woman with several children. Together they had another child. In total, Roth had eleven children. For a thirty-year-old person, that was an inconceivably high number to me. Roth gave some money monthly to support each child. He worked two full-time jobs.

At a bus stop, I saw a man who seemed, at a distance at least, to have that face. Det. Roth said, "Let's stop and talk to him. You can come along with me." "What do I do or say?" "Don't worry. We're just going to ask a few questions." While reticence surfaced, I mustered my courage. Roth was my protection: He had the physique to chase the rapist and catch him. "I'm Det. Roth with the police department," as he showed his badge. "I'd like to ask you a few questions." Close to the man, I knew that his features freed him. Feeling that this man must be uncomfortable as a suspect, I piped up to reduce his anxieties: "That's not the guy." Det. Roth ignored me. "Let me just ask you a few questions. Could I see some identification?" He showed it. "Do you live around here?" "Yes, I've resided at 1412 Elm Street for the last ten years." "We won't bother you any more. Thanks for your cooperation." Det. Roth offered my only reprimand: "Don't say 'that's not the guy.'" "Why not? I didn't want him to feel guilty." "He doesn't know why we're talking to him. Besides, he could think that my questions were about a crime committed near his residence and not by him. Just let me ask the questions." "I see. I've never done this before."

"You know, I can usually tell if a guy is the rapist before we even talk to him." "How?" "Ninety percent of the time, they'll either run or give it away by the reactions on their face. Most of the time, the guy picks himself out as the guilty one before you have a chance to identify him." This was important. If the rapist saw me and ran, he would nail himself and not force me to be the first one to speak. He had to see me. That took some pressure off. At the end of the two-hour surveillance, Det. Roth offered to do it again the next day.

On Friday, Det. Doil greeted me: "Det. Roth forgot that he had to be in court today and asked me to take his place." Det. Doil was quiet and reserved and personified professionalism, contrasting Roth's chatty conversational (but professional) style. He walked with a slight limp. I was sure it was a battle injury from police work, but my error became clear when he described his fall from a tree. His inability to run after the rapist was a worry. "Roth told me that if the rapist saw me during street surveillance he would probably run." "Most of the time they give themselves away." "If the guy runs, will you run after him?" "I don't have to. I'll know who he is. I think it's important to be part of the neighborhood where you work. You should know the people. Work with them, and they'll work with you. I'll know the guy. I'll just pick him up later." *Won't the rapist leave the area?* "Let's ride around a bit. I want to show you some guys if we see them. I'll call them over to the car and talk to them for a bit." "I guess I shouldn't say anything." "It might be easier if I do the talking. After they leave, you can say something."

"There are not too many people out this morning. I'm going to park up at the 7-Eleven store that is down the street from your house." We sat there for awhile. Few people were around. Then, two guys came by and stopped near the side of the store to talk. "Hey, Kenny, come over here," Det. Doil said. Relaxed and without fear, he walked over. As I watched him approach the car, I placed my memory image over his face. The images were not the same. A vague, but insufficient, similarity existed. No click of recognition occurred.

When Kenny was six feet from the car, something happened inside me. The identical—I mean exactly the same—feelings of terror and shock from that night took over my body. Fear exploded from inside of me. But why? I wanted to reach out and grab onto the arm of Det. Doil for protection. *What will he think of me? Am I a frightened child, someone who fears everyone and all strangers? I want to get out of the car and run. But that fear is inside me; it will run away with me. What is going on?* "How are you doing these days, Kenny?" "Fine." "Are you working?" "I'm looking." His voice was unrecognizable to me. "You know of any trouble going on?" "Hey, I'm clean." "Take care of yourself. I don't want to have to visit your mother." Kenny's short statements also made no impact.

As he walked away, those feelings of terror dissipated. My emotional side spoke: *You're letting the rapist go.* Then my logical side argued: *But his face doesn't match that of the rapist.* That first mysterious inner voice, never before experienced, continued: *The rapist is going free. You've got to stop him from raping other women.* And my other self answered: *I don't have any visual evidence that's the man.* Why was this inner voice arguing with such intensity with me? I dismissed it. People say that the victim's intense desire to find the rapist causes them to manufacture those feelings to make someone out as the rapist. To pick the wrong man, to say that he was the rapist was not acceptable. It had to be the right man or no one. At a distance and too far from us to decipher his words, his body movements left me with the impression that he was telling his friend that he got away with something. It must be some other crime. He wasn't the rapist. There was no visual match. There was no vocal match. The very slight tautness in his muscles when he stood next to the car dissipated as he spoke with his friend, and a slight relaxation came over his body along with a smile on his face. Whatever he got away with was unknown to me. The fact is that his face did not identically match that of the rapist's. I said, "That's not the man." "I know." *How did he know—because Kenny didn't act guilty and didn't run when he saw me?* "But look at that man. Remember that body. That's the same size, shape, and head formation. Remember it. That looks like the outline of the rapist."

As we drove away, Det. Doil pointed to the house behind the 7-Eleven store, the one that Kenny stood in front of. "That's the house where a man raped a woman about two months before the rapist attacked you. The artist composites by both of you look like the same guy." "Martha thought that she had drawn this guy not too long ago." "Well, they look similar. Also, the MO is similar." "How so?" "He had beer breath, broke into her house, asked for money, and pinched her breasts." "How long was he with her?" "Well, her boyfriend left at 6:30 A.M. He watched the house, just like in your case, and then broke in when he was gone." "Did she scream?" "She has two kids and didn't want anything to happen to them." "How hard! Did she go on street surveillance?" "The attack set her off. We could hardly get any information from her." "But she did the right thing, didn't she? She went to the police and the hospital." "Yeah, that's true." "Maybe you could talk to her again. Perhaps by now, she is calm and remembers some more." Silence.

"I think I should tell you something before your neighbors tell you. The chief of police questioned why the guy was with you so long. He made the comment that you wanted him to stay. I know that's not true, but try not to let his words bother you. There wasn't anything you could do." My silence. That blame-the-victim information was public knowledge. "You know, Det. Carson doesn't seem as anxious to catch the guy as you and Roth. I know she wants to get him, but I don't know. There's something." "Well, I don't think Det. Carson is so much sick these days as she has a touch of burnout. You should know that." "Thanks, that does explain her attitude. I thought maybe she was angry with me." Though aloof, he educated me. "You know, if someone raped me, I would try every method to find that guy." "Like what?" "Private investigator, hypnosis, anything I could think of." "You think that I should push on with this investigation." "I'd try anything and everything to get that guy off the street." "Thanks, I'll do that." His words and my previous library readings on rape shaped my plan of action. I would apply and investigate each method. If one method failed, then I would move on to the next one. Ethically and morally, I must test every mechanism to find the rapist (see table 4.1). I might fail, but my tombstone would read "She tried."

Det. Doil educated me for a reason. Police investigations last three weeks: the first week includes intense investigation; the second week is the collection of secondary data; and the final week is the summation.

Table 4.1   Methods to Find the Rapist

Methods Tested	1. Bloodhounds—discovered direction the rapist left, but not his residence or identity.
	2. Neighbors—interviewed; noted time of screams at 1 A.M.
	3. Fingerprints—none.
	4. Signs in neighborhood—wanted posters out.
	5. Other rape victims—too frenzied to provide useful information.
Methods Being Tested	6. Street surveillance with police.
	7. Bank checks—ongoing surveillance.
Methods to be Tested	8. Drug centers—for surveillance.
	9. Downtown police photos—check out photos of sex offenders on file.
	10. Private investigator—hire one.
	11. Hypnotism—a last resort, not acceptable in court.

Then, they—not me—believe that the trail is cold and prospects for finding the criminal dim. They shelve the case. I had to become the investigator. I had to identify the rapist by myself. It was me, alone, who had to succeed when the professionals quit.

An experience in Mexico taught me that patience wins out. After the discovery of a man murdered in the fields, people had no idea who the criminal was. The locals advised me: In time, we'll find out. Two months later, in her fourth month of pregnancy and showing, the wife of the murdered man left town. Soon after, another man, her boyfriend, also left. Their departure revealed the truth to the husband's family. Fear of reprisal by the husband's family led to her confession.

Doubting the Professionals

The following Monday morning, I saw two men standing across the street from the entrance to my university building. Usually I wouldn't notice, but one of them stared at me. His look wasn't a glance or a look of curiosity or the interested-in-the-woman stare: It was a piercing look. His face resembled—at a distance—that of the rapist. Is he after me? I stood in the doorway to the building and studied his face. His shirt and pants were of an excellent quality, much better than the quality of the clothes the rapist wore. Anything was possible. No police officers were around. Noting my stare, he nudged his friend to move along. I had to find out if that was the rapist. If it was, maybe I could scream, and people would stop him. First, I had to be positive of the identification. As they moved up the street, I crossed. At the corner, they turned right. In order to get a close view without jeopardizing my safety, I ducked into the fast-food place. If I hurried, I could catch a closer glimpse. They saw me and rushed past the store. The angle of his body prevented me from seeing his face. As I left the other side of the store and stepped out into the sunlight, on a side street minimally traveled by pedestrians, there was no one! Quickly I ran by each store and checked inside. The men were not there. After three stores, there was an alley. They weren't there either! *These guys ran to escape me. Why?*

"Hello, Det. Carson. This might not mean anything, but I saw a guy across the street who resembled the rapist. I tried to check it out but the guy ran." "Why didn't you get a police officer? They're all over the place." "I did look for one, but of course, there wasn't one around at that moment. You're right, though. There's frequently a ton of police here." **"Look, don't keep calling me every time you *imagine* someone is the**

rapist." Her words shocked me. Despite seeing hundreds and hundreds of men, this was only the second time in three weeks that I had called, and both times I had qualified my statements. *Why has she stopped listening?* I changed the subject: "When can we do surveillance again?" "I don't think there's any need to do more surveillance." "Could we go down and check out the drug centers?" "No, I don't think that's possible." "What else can be done on the case?" "We'll call you if anything else shows up." "Is that it?" She said, "We don't forget a case, but we have others to work on."

"Chief Holmes, this is Cathy Winkler. A man raped me about three weeks ago, and Det. Carson is on the case." "Yes, I remember you. What can I do for you?" "Det. Carson's work is excellent. I have no complaints, but we are different types of people." "Hasn't she been doing her job?" "Oh, I have no qualms about her work. I want to try some additional avenues of investigation. I think I can identify the guy, but I need time to find him." "Would you want to work with Det. Roth or Det. Doil?" "You should make that decision. I don't care who. I want the best person to help me find the rapist." "I'll give your case to Det. Roth. He has the best record for finding rapists." "Thanks a lot. I really appreciate this."

When I went to see Det. Roth, Det. Carson saw me and abruptly veered away. Initially, I thought she would be thrilled to have me off her caseload. But my change of detectives infuriated her. She felt that I had judged her work as inferior. *Wasn't she burnt out?* Burnout is not a failure; it's a sign of intense caring and hard work. People without emotions do not have burnout. Whenever I saw her afterward, she snubbed me. No VISA ever requested to change detectives. I had made history in that department.

"You feel sure you can identify the guy?" "I'm almost 80 to 90 percent sure. There is a distinct image of his face in my mind." "You want to do some more street surveillance? Is 7 to 9 in the mornings and 4 to 6 in the evenings fine?" "Those are good times. What about drug centers?" "What do you mean? Det. Carson didn't mention that point." "The rapist, as he put on his cap that night, matched an image I have of a guy who had aggressively talked to me on the bus and who had told me that he was in a drug center. The location of the drug center is on the west side of town and is a public facility." "Well, let me check that out." He did check out the centers, and there were three in that area. Since most programs were only a month long, Det. Roth thought that it was a long shot.

"He said that the police knew him, and that he robbed and raped." "Do you think he was telling the truth?" "I feel confident that he told the truth." "It seems odd that he was honest," Det. Roth said. "If he has a long history of raping, he feels confident to get away with it again." "We did have another odd case. A guy raped a woman and told her that he was a high school star basketball player from the town of Logus. He gave specific, incriminating facts. You just never know." "Could the guy who raped me have bragged to his friends about his conquest? Maybe neighborhood gossip would reveal who he is." "I doubt that. Rapists never tell anyone that secret."

Roth and I went out on surveillance twice a week for the next few weeks. His energy level decreased but he was always enjoyable. One of the first mornings we checked the bus station at Rellis Park. As we drove to that station, I saw a guy get on a bus with a cap similar to the the type the rapist wore. We followed the bus to the station. While I always felt trepidation, standing up to my fears was important. What could happen? Roth was ten feet away, and there were tons of people. The cap-headed man was not the rapist. Relief. Roth spotted a pick-up with numerous men in the back. He thought one of the men looked like the rapist. "I can't tell. He's behind people." "Let's go up. I'll talk first to the driver, and then ask the man to step out. Don't say anything." "Don't worry. I learned my lesson." As the suspect stepped out, he greeted us with a smile. That smile revealed his innocence. He had a huge gold tooth.

We moved on to the stakeout at the bus station. Those words are more glorious than the experience, especially when one realizes the pain and horror that envelope a VISA. Since Roth was familiar with most people in the neighborhood, he stationed himself at an inconspicuous spot. If the rapist saw Roth before he saw me, he might disappear. Roth told me to stand at the top of the stairs and examine each person. He was ten feet behind me, but always watching. The signal was to place my hands akimbo on my hips. Earnestly I watched each person. I felt like a criminal viewing each man for his guilt. Fortunately I only saw innocent men. Each bus brought a large and different crowd of faces to check out. After a few hours, the repetition and boredom made me antsy. I changed positions. I rested my tired arms on my hips. Roth approached: "Cathy, remember what the signal is?" "Oops. I'll do better."

After several weeks of surveillance, Det. Roth said, "You know, a few years ago, a man mugged and assaulted this woman. We couldn't find the guy. We did a lot of legwork in her case. She had determination. She hired a private investigator, and sure enough, the PI found the guy. We got a conviction." "Det. Carson told me that PIs mess up cases, and police don't like to work with them. She told me to rely on the police and don't do anything else." "Well, each of us has our own approach, and some PIs interfere. There are some good ones. We cooperate in every way possible. We can't do everything with so many cases to handle." "Is it all right to look into it?" "I think it would be a good idea." "We talked earlier about my looking at the photos on file in the downtown police station. Could you set that up?" "I'll call Martha. You just go over there any time you want to. She'll show you the files."

Obligations kept me from that method of investigation during the next weeks. To Roth's surprise, I had put the case aside and focused on something else. I explained, "I didn't have much choice. Too much class work along with job applications for next year and a professional paper to deliver. That's life. But for the next two weeks, I have a few hours every day to check out the photos. I wanted to make sure that Martha was aware of what's happening." "I'll give her another call. You have her phone number. Call her whenever you want to be there. She needs to be there, and sometimes she works at other places."

For the next couple of weeks, I spent the first two hours of each day sitting in front of a huge file cabinet of mug shots. Quickly I learned to mentally detraumatize myself before and after each session. During these periods, I took breaks and gazed out into nothingness to clear my head and reestablish the rapist's image in my mind. These mug shots taught me a lot. There was a plethora of ways to present one's face in front of the camera to disguise features. People hold their heads down to enlarge a small forehead or blow up their cheeks to hide their slenderness. Pushing their chins into the air minimized a giant forehead and receding hairline. Inflation of their nostrils threatened victims. Mouths were an area of creativity from huge smiles to pursed lips. These guys were good. Not only did I have to envision each face as the rapist, reorienting the angled memory I had of the rapist to that of a frontal view, but I also had to recompose each mug shot into a undisguised facial expression and take into account changes due to aging, haircuts, or facial hair. I had to check features closely. Most mug shots were easy to discard. The hairline was oval in shape. The teeth were askew or in a different formation. The chin was too square or too pointed. Ears stuck out, or the eyebrows were too bushy. Even earlobes eliminated some men—too big, too wide, too long. Skin tones were another key to a guy's freedom.

Martha and the people who worked there were quite kind. In rare moments of free time, they talked to me. This made my time easier. Martha was the best with her great sense of humor, but most of all, she respected and admired what I did: "Girl, you've got guts. I don't know how you do it. But I know you're going to catch this guy." "We'll see. I'll have to admit that I don't like this task." "I want you to tell me when the trial is. Sometimes they have me testify." "What do they ask you?" "They ask me what the person was like when I did the drawing." "Can you remember?" "Are you kidding? By the time the case comes to trial, I've forgotten." *Martha, VISAs need every single bit of help when the trial occurs. Don't you realize that you could help get the guy convicted by describing the agitated state of the VISA?* But that was Martha's way. She was probably right in that the jury makes their decision based on the VISA's testimony and not the artist's.

The Private Investigator

With the semester over, I contacted a private investigator. My friend Will had told me that his lawyer friend Saul knew one. I had no idea what to do or if I could pay the cost. I called Marvin Dirkson, and we arranged to meet in his office that Sunday morning. Will went with me. Unfamiliar with PIs and still careful about my judgments, I knew that Will's law training could help me decide whether or not to hire the guy. One look at Marvin convinced me. He had disguisable features. His best qualifications were that he was African American, like Dets. Roth and Doil, and had lived in the neighborhood. These were important points. A white dude would stick out like a sore thumb, and someone unfamiliar with the neighborhood would lose time figuring out its layout. On his ability, he judged and then decided. A principled person; I liked that.

"Sit down, and let's start by having you tell me the details." I showed him the wanted poster, explained the case, and described the scar. "Marvin, I want to stop him from raping other women." "While my mother and sister just moved out of the neighborhood, I still have a lot of friends there. I want to do whatever is necessary to get rid of that guy." "Because you know the area is a major reason why I want to hire you. You have connections." "Why don't we drive over to the area right now and you can show me the house?" After we arrived on the street, Marvin passed a house about six doors down from the house where the rapist attacked me. "See that second to the last house from the corner? The white one. A guy who lives there received a conviction of rape. I don't know if he's out yet or not. I think it would be best if you work with my associate, Louis Ferguson. He's good, and I can help him on contacts. We always work together, but I have a lot of cases." "How much will it cost?" "I want to get this guy out of the neighborhood. This is a safe neighborhood, and I want it to stay that way. I care about the people. You can work out the fee with Louis. He'll be fair. We will get this guy, and money is a not an issue." Marvin's words revealed his qualities: He was a person of values who placed human caring above capital gain. Hope again.

Louis and I met in my office. He wore a smart looking suit; personally, I wanted to know the name of his tailor. "I'm Louis Ferguson, Dr. Winkler." "Please call me Cathy. Have a seat. Where should we start?" "Give me a rundown on the information about the case, and what the police have done so far." After the details, he asked for clarification on some points and gave an explanation of others. On the scar, "That's what a gunshot wound looks like and the size of the scar indicates he was shot with a 22 caliber. That supports the point that the guy probably does have a history of crime." He restored my confidence. "Louis, the rapist told me that he was a 'robber.' He used that word, I'm sure, but the police questioned me on that. They said that if the police knew him and had caught him several times, then the term of use is 'burglar.' " "You said the guy is around thirty years of age, right? Guys in that generation are more likely to say 'robber,' and the younger ones are more likely to use the word 'burglar.' It's just age difference." His explanations were reasonable.

"There's a number of ways we can start. First, I want to check out the neighborhood, who the people are, what they do, and where they live. This will help me to narrow it down to possible suspects. Also I want to hang out in the neighborhood, drinking with the guys. That will probably reveal the rapist." "Why would you do that? The police said that the rapist would never tell people what he did." "No, I agree with them. But, you know, when guys hang out among themselves," he embarrassingly laughed, "they're sitting around, then they lean back, drink their beer, and relax a lot by raising their shirt over their chest and opening their pants. The open pants would reveal the scar."

He asked me: "You've moved out of the neighborhood, haven't you?" "Yeah, why?" "Well, if we had gotten together sooner, I could have moved into your house. I think the guy would try again. Not right away, but later. Then I could catch him in the act." "I think it's too late to even get the place for a month." Now I knew: A strong possibility existed for the return of the rapist. And yet, the police could not inform me. "There's another way we can do it. We can set it up as if you are back in the neighborhood. What did you do in the neighborhood?" "I jogged every day." "That's great. We can set it up that you jog in those areas. But don't worry. I'll have several friends who would help me out, and you would always be under surveillance." "Great. Anything to catch the guy. I think my friends Will and Estar would help out too. They're willing to jog around the neighborhood and keep a watch." "That would provide you with more protection. It's kinda cold right now, but as soon as we have a warm spell . . ." Louis added an additional method to my list—decoy.

His most striking points were his professionalism and knowledge of the field of private investigation. What was critically impressive was his respect for and belief in my accuracy of data collection. "I do want to hire you, Louis, but I was wondering how much it would cost. I've heard private investigators are very expensive. I don't have a lot of money, but I want to be fair." "Just give me an amount you can afford. Marvin and I want to catch the guy. That's what is most important." He preferred not to give a number in dollars and maintained that position. "How about if we start with $350? I could pay you $200 now and $150 later. If the case involves more work, then we could renegotiate." I gave him a check and became his client. That money was not tax deductible. Louis began his investigation immediately.

A few days later, Louis called. "Cathy, I found the guy. I went down to the police station and checked with Roth." "Why do you think that's the guy?" "He's got a gunshot wound exactly where you saw the one on the rapist. He's the same height and weight. He lives two blocks from you, and his house is in the direction that the bloodhounds went that first day. He's got a record as a robber: He's been in and out of prison a lot. I checked the mug shot, and if you look at his hairline, you can see that he wears a cap one inch back from his forehead. His name is Kenny R_____." A name was meaningless. "That's incredible. What do we do now?" "I arranged with Roth to go down to the station and have you look at some mug shots."

"Was Roth helpful?" "He was quite willing to work as much as possible with me. I told him to look in Kenny's file and check for an abdominal scar. He said to me, 'How do you know that?' He had never checked the files for a suspect with a scar. He didn't know that Kenny had a scar." "You mean that no one ever went through the police files to match my data with that on record?" "They never looked." I said, "That's incredible. Of course, with their workload, they don't have time. They need a research assistant with a computer to do their office work, searching the files for comparisons. If I had studied their files, I could have found Kenny months ago." Years later, Louis told me more about how Roth reacted. Roth felt that the case couldn't be solved. He didn't think we'd be able to find the guy, and if we did, he didn't think I'd be able to identify him, but Roth didn't know how to get rid of me. There was more. Marvin knew Kenny's past history as a robber and rapist. He also knew about his gunshot wound in the left abdominal area. The details that I gave Marvin that Sunday morning were sufficient to find the rapist.

At the station, Det. Doil took Roth's place and put together a pile of mug shots. I went through them but couldn't select anyone as the rapist. While the one that Louis was interested in seemed a possibility, I could not identify the rapist from the mug shot. Was it the angle of my mental image—a frontal–left side view—to the angle in the mug shot—frontal and right sides? I asked for a police lineup. Roth's response to my request: Silence. When my review of the mug shots was over, Louis pointed out Kenny's photo. Even with Louis' information beforehand about the hairline indenture from the cap, I failed to pick up this point. Registering such information was an emotional challenge.

Before the holidays, I requested that Roth check Kenny's blood and hair in the lab. As shown in table 4.2, Louis' data on Kenny matched closely with the rapist's description: Either the data I had given the police were incorrect, or he was the rapist. The lab results would tell the police if he was guilty, and the police—knowing I couldn't identify the rapist— would know whom to go after when the next rape occurred. My description of the rapist was good—it matched Kenny's description!

Along with the similarities between the rapist and Kenny, the police knew that Kenny had a habit of hanging around the area close to my house, and they had observed him in that area in the weeks prior to the rape wearing the cap that I had described. They also knew that he was a heavy beer drinker, and my neighbors later informed me that they had

Table 4.2 Rapist v. Suspect

Trait	Rapist	Kenny (Suspect)
Height	5'8"–5'10"	5'9"
Weight	160–170 lbs.	170 lbs.
Age	25–35 years	32 years
Body Build	slender, but muscular	slender, but muscular
Police Record	robber and rapist	four-page rap sheet as robber, with an indictment but no conviction on a 1980 rape
Neighborhood	yes	house within two blocks and in the direction the rapist fled
Scar	abdominal	gunshot scar in left groin
Cap	yes	cap indentation one inch back from hairline on mug shot
Work	street person	street person
Mustache	yes	yes

met Kenny in a drug center. Of great relevance is that, to everyone except me, Kenny looked identical to the artist composite drawing.

After the December holidays, Roth took a few days off. This helps prevent burnout. In the meantime, Louis and I counseled. Louis said, "New Year's Eve is a great time to check out the neighbors. People are milling around, parties are open to everyone, and the weather is good." "You're not going alone?" "No, a couple of friends of mine will come along." The day after New Year's Eve, Louis called. "Cathy, this is Louis." He was upset. "What's wrong?" "On New Year's Eve, I got jumped in your old neighborhood. I went down to check the guys out." "Are you OK?" "Yes, just upset." To know that a professional could get as upset as a nonprofessional was a comfort. "What happened? Didn't your friends go with you?" "Oh, they bummed out at the last minute. I don't know where this guy came from. I didn't even hear him. He kicked me down on my stomach and held a gun to my head. He asked me for my money. I gave it to him." A professional like Louis who was well trained in many of the martial arts, physically fit, and alert to noises and movements was also a victim of crime. "How much money did they get?" "Two hundred dollars. I gave the whole wad to the guy. I didn't argue. It was my life at stake." "No, I agree, but why did you have so much money?" "I wanted to deposit it in the night teller at the bank before I returned home. I didn't want my checks to bounce. That's part of why I called you. Could you pay me that $150?" "Yes, that's fine." Due to cold weather, Louis and I had put off the decoy plan.

Hypnotism

In the first week of January, I called Det. Roth. "Roth, remember I told you about jogging as a decoy with Louis. Since it's warming up, we thought we'd try it this weekend." "I don't want you to do that." "It's my decision. The guy might attack me again, but this time we'll catch him." "He might get away." "You're right, but I have to try. There's not much else left." "Look, do me a favor and wait a bit." Roth had reasons for stalling, but I thought his reason was concern for my safety.

"I want to arrange for you to meet with the police hypnotist." I agreed, but I felt that it was too early in the case. That was my last option since hypnotism is not legally acceptable. Nevertheless, the police still employ a full-time hypnotist. Several months earlier, I had contacted some private hypnotists to learn more about the process. In a light sleep phase, one remembers everything that occurs during the hypnotism. Not only does the hypnotist help one to deal with one's fear of the rapist's face—in other words, to remember his facial features precisely—the hypnotist also helps to relieve one of the rape trauma. The last point sounded ideal. You're raped; you're hypnotized; you're relieved of the trauma. But to forget what rape is, is to dismiss the magnitude and severity of such a heinous crime.

Before hypnotizing me, the police hypnotist, Det. Lebbin, discussed the crime and answered questions. "First, let me tell you about the experience of hypnotism. If you are willing, I help you into a slumber-like state. I use a soothing scenery for you to view and music for you to listen to. Once in that state, I can question you. You will remember everything that happens while hypnotized, and I have no power to change your mind. Rather, I'll help you to remember details. I recently had a case where a woman saw the license plate of the criminal's car but couldn't recall the numbers. Under hypnotism, she remembered the first four numbers and that was enough for the police to locate the guy."

I asked, "How do I know that I will remember everything that happens during hypnotism?" "For court records, we film and tape everything. You can view it later for yourself." "I don't want to be alone when you hypnotize me. I want a friend with me. I would feel calmer." "That's quite reasonable. Let's discuss the crime." "My description of the rapist matches a suspect! I can't say for sure that the guy in the mug shot is him, but why don't the police at least do a lab check on blood and hair? We would know then if we were in the right ballpark." "I agree with you. If there are as many similarities as you have stated, I think that the police should do a comparison. I don't know why they don't do that." Here was an official of the police lab department telling me in front of another detective that the tests were necessary. When we reached the local police station, Roth was there, and I again asked him: "Why don't you write a search warrant to analyze Kenny's blood and hair?"

"I'm not so good at search warrants." Det. Moore chimed in: "I can help." "Det. Moore is always successful in writing search warrants. We'll need samples of your pubic and head hair for comparison. Can you stop by tomorrow?" "Sure, how long will it take for you to locate the suspect?" "We know where he hangs out. We won't have much trouble." The next day, someone had to supervise the collection of hair from my body. The only woman available was Det. Carson, who curtly accompanied me to the women's bathroom. "Roth told me that you have to take the hairs off my body." "You can pull out your own hairs from different parts of your head yourself. I'll just collect them and put them in this bag. Be sure you get hairs from the front, back, and side. They're all different. You can go into the stall and collect the pubic hairs yourself from different sections and then pass them to me." Those were her words: professional and distant.

A few days later, Det. Roth called. "I talked with the lab, and they're analyzing the evidence. I know you answered this question before, but they want me to ask you again. Was there another person in your bed prior to the rape, perhaps the week before?" Patiently I answered, "No, I had just moved into town and hadn't met anyone. Some friends stayed over at the house about two weeks before when I was gone, but they washed the sheets. The only other hairs besides my own were my dog's. Have the lab guys check some more. Det. Carson told me that there are many types of hair all over the head and that they're quite different. Those other hairs have to match another section of hair." "I had to check."

After another few days, Roth called. "Cathy, it's Roth. The lab insists that I ask you again if there was anyone else in your bed. Now they did look more carefully and found that some of those unmatched hairs did match. But they still have hairs unaccounted for." This was perturbing. "Roth, believe me. I'm telling you the truth. Look, I've always tried to be honest with the police. Since they found some more that matched, tell them to look harder. All the hairs in the bed were either mine, and those are the dark blond ones, or the rapist's, and those are the black, curly ones. They have to find a match. There was no one else but the rapist. Believe me, I wish I could give you a different answer." He laughed. "I'll tell them what you said."

New Line of Evidence

"Cathy, it's Roth." "Believe me, I know your voice by now. What's happening?" He was excited: "Good news. Not only did the hair and blood match, but there's a new method—DNA Fingerprinting—that just came out. The test matches the DNA cells of the suspect's blood with the DNA cells from the rapist's semen. If they match, the possibility of an error is only one in six billion. I have to get the official OK from the chief and the district attorney, but we will do it." "In other words, this would be scientific, absolutely provable evidence that the suspect is the rapist?" "Yes, this will convince any jury. They just convicted someone this way in Florida, and I'm sure your case is the same. The guy who did the lab work in your case is the same one who solved a child-murderer case several years ago with forensic evidence. He's confident from the blood and hair analysis that Kenny is the rapist. Since that analysis only placed Kenny's blood and hair in the correct groups, it isn't air-tight evidence. But the DNA evidence is."

"There's more. You might be the test case for this state." "This is good for you, isn't it, Roth?" "This case is a feather in my cap." "Do you still have the same opinion of my persistence in the case?" "Not now." "Thanks, Roth. I'm glad I changed detectives. You'd be the first to try out this new evidence." "Yes, but I always wanted to stop the guy. As soon as I get the official paperwork signed, I have to take a sample of your blood and send it along with a sample of Kenny's blood." "I can't understand why the guy doesn't skip town if he thinks you suspect him." "He is too confident. He doesn't know what we have. I'll be able to find him. The police have a watch on him." "Am I safe from him?" "Oh yes, he won't get away." *How could they afford to tail one person on the streets twenty-four hours a day, seven days a week—or are they just optimistic about their abilities to find Kenny again?*

Weekly, I called Roth for the blood-drawing appointment, but there were delays in signing the papers. One week the chief of police went to the hospital. Roth got sick the next week. Chief Assistant District Attorney Stan Rest was in a case and unavailable to sign off. Six weeks later, "Roth, what's the problem? I have a right to know after waiting all this time." "There is an argument between the DA and the chief of police who should foot the bill. The test is expensive, at least $1,000." "Oh my! That is not affordable for every case." "Once the State Supreme Court accepts it as evidence, the police lab will buy the equipment. The lab won't charge for each test after that." "What is their argument about payment?" "My chief says that we did the work in the case, and this is not part of our follow-up. We've put the evidence together up through the search warrant. After that, the DA is responsible for the costs of the case. The DA's position is that DNA Fingerprinting is part of the collection of evidence. We should pay." "What's going to happen?" "Someone will pay, and then we can do the test. They'll iron out this issue soon. Don't worry." At last, Roth took me to the hospital to have the nurse extract my blood officially, and he marked the tubes with great care. He was meticulous about details. That pleased me. "I'll send your blood along with Kenny's blood to the lab. I have to do everything perfectly. I'll pack the blood properly in dry ice and express mail it."

"Can you find the guy as easily as before?" Roth couldn't take my ignorance any longer: "Cathy, he is in the county jail." "How did he get there?" "We got him on a car theft and robbery at the end of December."

"Do you mean that he's been in jail for the last four months?" "Yes, that's why we always knew where he was." "Why didn't you tell me?" "I did tell you not to go on surveillance." "I've been safe from him for months. Do you know I would watch every nook and cranny when I went to the police station for fear that he would rape me again?" For four months, I lived the fear of rape and for no reason! But Roth couldn't tell me that Kenny was the suspect until he had evidence, and without the evidence, he couldn't tell me Kenny's location. The knowledge that the rapist was in jail ended my nail-biting.

"When will we get the results back?" "There's a backlog. It'll take nine to ten weeks." "Roth, you know when you will hear from me next." "I know I can rely on you, Dr. Winkler." Roth called the next day. "Cathy, this is Det. Roth." "Roth, Roth, I know your voice like the back of my hand." "Always professional, you know." "And I appreciate that professionalism. Did the lab speed up their testing procedures, and they already have the results?" "No, but I thought I should warn you. I called the lab to make sure that they had received the package. It's not there. The delivery company—with guaranteed overnight service—can't locate it. The package is lost, or maybe the dry ice won't hold up. We won't know until tomorrow. I know you want information and I wanted to prepare you." I was stunned. Anecdotes about mixups in legal cases are common in this country, and now it had happened to me. We were so close. We had found the guy, got the evidence on him, and now we had the best method in the world to convict him. Shock transplanted hope. In class that day, my mind had vacated me, and my responses were nebulous. After class, I called Roth. "Roth, it's Cathy. What happened?"

"It's OK. The package got held up an extra night, but you will be glad to know that I had put so much dry ice in the box that the samples were in perfect shape when they arrived at The Science Laboratory. Now we just wait." "Great." "There is still one more issue. If there isn't enough semen on the swab, then they can't perform the DNA test." "There was enough. I know it." The following day when I returned to my class, I discussed my mood during the previous day's lecture. "You might have observed me yesterday as distant." My students, never without words, said, "You better believe it. You were completely gone. We thought you were wacko." "Well, I hope I wasn't 'completely wacko,' but something bothered me." I explained the rape, the DNA method, and the "lost evidence." "That DNA test is something we do in biology class. It's easy. I can explain the method to you." One of my undergraduate students knew more about the method than the police! The ninth week arrived without news. The tenth, eleventh, twelfth, and thirteenth weeks brought the same response. By the fourteenth week, a conference took me out of town. "Roth, if you hear, call me, even if it's collect."

The evening before my return, Roth called. "When you get home, just disregard the message I left on your answering machine because I didn't understand the results at first. But, it's an absolute match. We've got him." "The wait was so long!" "On the results that the lab sent out, they state that the two samples are 'indisputably similar.' In my haste—I was a little anxious—I misinterpreted the phrase to mean that the samples were *not* the same. But I came in this weekend to quietly review the results, and I'd misunderstood. The results are a perfect match." "This is terrific. On my drive back tomorrow, I'll sing all the way." And I did. My joy was so expansive that I missed my exit, extending the original ten-hour trip by two hours. The two extra hours of jubilant, off-key singing was a pleasure! *He's guilty, and we've got the evidence on him. Yes!*

Part II

RAPED TWICE, SOCIAL RAPE

I took my walk as everyday, nothing unusual along the way.
Until at the creek that crosses the path, there was a bridge to make the
    way.
It appeared strong, made by loving hands.
But when I tried it, its wood with rot barely reached the lands.
I gave this bridge a chance and trusted that it would hold.
Devour me not the cold water rushing and swirling below.
Are you the bridge that is now my path to life?
Please take hold and be my strength.
If for me, this one thing you'll do,
I promise one day to be the strongest bridge for you.—a former student

Trust became an issue. Who would believe what I said about the attack?
Who would let me make my decisions, my choices? Friends whom I told
about the attack and the investigation questioned and judged me: "That's
a mistake, Cathy." "You're wrong." "You can't think clearly." Despite their
judgmental attitudes, I needed their support, even if it came with a distorted kindness: "We care about you, but you must do what we say."
Would I have treated my friends any better if a rapist had invaded their
lives? To survive together, my friends and I educated each other about the
issues. At times, we discretely disagreed with or avoided each other, and
then through time, we cemented over the cracks in our relationship. I
thank my friends for Part II and dedicate it to their greatness.

Part II focuses on how friends, counselors, coworkers, and administrators reacted to my openness. I didn't hide the rape or the investigation.
They didn't hide their views. These chapters reveal their perspective of
me through their written words and actions.

IT WAS JUST ONE NIGHT

M y friends were well-educated people. Their education varied from academic issues to liberal perspectives to activism. Due to their openness, I assumed that after the attack they would continue their insightfulness in their support. But their negative comments mirrored the negative culturing patterns of the rapist.

> While these second assault comments *do not INDIVIDUALLY* match the horror and trauma of the rape, the *accumulative effect* of prejudicial and antagonistic statements toward the survivor do have a compounding effect that is *MORE CRUEL than the rape attack itself.* (Williams and Holmes 1981: 2, emphases added)

The reason for these negative culturing patterns is due in part to the lack of understanding and in part to the fact that we VISAs, depending on people for support and comfort, experience a panorama of ignorant and intrusive treatment from these same people. I could have dealt with the negative comments if they'd been few in number. But they weren't. These commenting individuals were not rapists, but the cumulative effect of their comments and actions resulted in the same impact as a rape.

The Rape Club

For people growing up in the 1950s, the fear of rape surrounded us; a dread and horror of that crime permeated our existence. But how, as children, could we fear this? No one spoke about it; no one told us that a rapist had attacked him or her; and no one ever gave us the details of rape. News media minimally presented cases of rape. The weekly television show *Leave It to Beaver* never raised the issue. Then why did I and so many other girls fear that unspoken crime?

Now I know. Rape victims had crossed our paths. Their emotional pain seeped into our lives. We spoke with them, we sat next to them, we saw them. And those interactions were enough to spread the feelings of their emotional pain into us. Who were those people raped? I didn't know their names then, but the act of rape against me revealed the multitude of VISAs. All my life those VISAs had surrounded me. As a member of this rape club, I learned of the other members. "Cathy, I'm Cassandra. I know what happened to you is terrible, but I want you to know that I was raped too, date raped." Revelation of club members was continuous. At the emergency room, Alecia told me about her past terrors. Later, my friend Paula and my landowner Gerri called me with the same message: "Cathy, I told my friends what happened to you, and most have the same response: 'A rapist attacked me too.' I never knew that happened to them, Cathy!" My sister Mary Carol called me: "Cathy, I was date raped about fifteen years ago. A guy took me into a bedroom at a party. I wanted sex, not violence. But he jammed and battered his penis inside of me. I threw my clothes on and ran. At the bedroom door, I saw a line of guys expecting to have sex with me. I got in my car but not quick enough. The rapist jumped in. I made him believe I wanted more, and we should go to his place. When we got there, he got out; I locked the door and drove over to a friend's house where I cried all night. She helped but she didn't understand."

My cousin Maggie wrote:

The next day I was walking at 5:30 A.M. with my friends, I mentioned the rape. One of the women started crying and said she had been raped many years ago and had never told anyone but her husband and sister. She was touched by your openness.

The new manager of my home was Sandy. She had not heard about it. She walked into the house, looked around, and said that something horrible had happened here. She could feel it. "A man raped me." "A boyfriend tore my clothes off and raped me. The next day he came over; I beat him up. I couldn't stop hitting him. He didn't fight back. He knew he deserved it." Students in my class gave me responses that revealed that someone had printed the pain onto them: "I know what you went through"; "Thanks for noting that men and women get raped"; "Keep after the rapist, I couldn't do anything"; "I believe you"; "Could I be an informant in your research?" Stella called: "Nathaniel told me what happened to you. I'm dealing with the neighborhood boy who dragged me into his basement when I was twelve years old and raped me." Karla left this note: "There are many times when I think I'm not going to make it because of what I've been through. But you've shown me that with help and support I can." Sametta, another club member, read pain in my face and wrote this poem:

I see a tear form in your eye.
I long to reach and wipe it dry.
I know the pain you're feeling when you cry.

Past students called. "Cathy, I've got something to tell you." "Renata, a man broke into my house and raped me." "Cathy, this is going to be easier than I thought. I haven't called for awhile because a man date raped me, and I've had to deal with the fact that my father molested me for years after my mother died. He always said that I looked just like her. My father denied the rapes. I never know when I understand something." "Renata, is that why you would read the textbooks five, six, or seven times and then still not believe you understood the material?" "For six years, he told me that his sexual molestings did not happen. He made me question reality and my ability to comprehend." While not able to legally act against her rapists, Tasha's activism was through her poems:

It's a prison without walls, with rooms filled in the void of separation.
Walk through its rooms, and you feel its unwelcomeness.
Walk among its inhabitants, and you sense irritation.
You're a prisoner who cannot leave.

Rosemary, another past "A" student, called: "Cathy, my grades are fantastic at Harvard. The professors love my work. I've lost fifty pounds. Now that I feel great, I remember. I remember that my father had sex with me when I was a child. My mother wouldn't have sex with him anymore because of our poverty and the six children to feed. He used me instead. My therapist read my diaries and showed me how they reveal this truth. I wrote about it but did not know it. My diaries were always sacred to me, but I didn't understand why." "Rosemary, you would never rewrite any of your papers, not even your senior paper, which every student rewrote about five times or more. Is your writing part of your means of protecting your identity?" "That's it. Anyone tampering with my words tampered with my body. My words were my identity. I had control through my diaries." Four years later she wrote me:

I am doing well. I continue to work with my counselor. There are still memories coming up. I am not seeking ordination. In fact, I am no longer active in the church. Too many things I have to work out with the influence of patriarchy on the church structure before I commit myself to being part of the church again.

Kirk came to my office. "Dr. Winkler, may I close the door? I have something to tell you that might surprise you. Because you spoke up to the class, I decided to speak up to my high school friends. When I was twelve, a friend of my older brother raped me. When I told my four best friends, each one had also suffered a rape. We chose each other as friends because of our common history." One of my past teachers called: "Cathy, anything you need, let me know. I'll be there to help you." "That's great. But you seem to understand what's going on!" Years later, she told me: "My father sexually molested me as a child." "Is that why you played so many sports and other physical activities in high school?" "They helped." A past colleague had a small dinner party for me. Her significant other yelled at me from across the room: "Why are you always talking about rape?" Because I hadn't said anything that night about rape and because I noticed that everyone's shocked eyes focused on her, I knew that a past terrorizing experience defined her life. Later she wrote me. Her mother was a prostitute whose boyfriends raped her. The secretary at a past job called and offered to help me on my manuscript: "My uncle forced me to have oral sex with him. I can't forget it." My new neighbor stopped by because she had heard what happened: "As I was leaving a party, I went into the bedroom to get my coat. This guy followed me and then started to attack me. Luckily I screamed like hell. People ran in, pushed him out of the house, and stayed to comfort me. I cried the rest of that night. I still shake when I think about it." Attempted rape is traumatizing as well. Janet wrote her story:

When I was eight years old and my sister Carolyn was six years old, "Uncle" David moved next door. Within a few weeks, he began incesting us on a regular basis. We told our mother and father, who, after accepting Uncle David's denial, jokingly said Carolyn and I were having early crushes. As the years passed, Uncle David continually incested me, whether or not he continued to incest Carolyn I don't know as the subject was never again mentioned. When I was forty-two, my father died, and I returned home for the funeral. After the funeral when the guests lined up to shake the family's hands—a Quaker practice, Uncle David appeared. We looked at each other but did not speak as we shook hands. Several months later in a mental hospital, a psychiatrist diagnosed me as a manic depressive (a hereditary mental illness brought on by the traumas from Uncle David's rapes). When I shook Uncle David's hand, the stress triggered a manic episode. As a result of that handshake and the experiences connected with it, I now have a lifelong mental illness.

Louise wrote:

Dear Cathy, An old friend and I had a pleasant evening together and it turned into one of those petting situations where it then moved into his bedroom. That was OK. Then he assumed it would progress to intercourse. My surprise prevented me from stopping it. I didn't have much power. There was another man in the house, and I was in the country without a ride. The awkwardness of stopping overrode the potentially tense situation it would create. I went on. That was OK. I had made my decision. Bothering me is a comment he made during the evening. He was under the influence of something, either pot, beer, or a combination, and he never came. As he was lying there on top of me, still going, he said: "I'd like to go on raping you all night long. . . ." He felt the situation, the experience, the pleasure, and the control were all his and that I did not have a part in it. And I didn't challenge it. I haven't seen him again.

Trusted people, not strangers, raped my friends. These trusted people were fathers, brothers, uncles, neighbors, friends, dates, and coworkers. Many of my friends previously suffered the torture and carried its secret. Sometimes the torture reverberated in their work as with my students, and sometimes the torture remained silent. All of my life the pain had encircled me, and I, like most of us, never noticed it.

The incredibly large number of my friends who were in the Rape Club depressed me, but my students would remind me of my own words, demonstrated through the poetry of a former student.

I had a teacher once. I had a teacher once who said the same thing everyday.
She'd say: "You've got a brain woman, now use it!" She'd say: "If you don't one day, you'll soon be facin' the music!"
I used to want her to shut up and just get outta my face. But she keep on preachin' the same ol' stuff:
"Woman, I'm just tell' you straight. You gotta feed your mind and your body and your soul."
She didn't care if we didn't listen, she'd just keep singin' her song.
She'd never give up, she'd just go on and on.

I'd sit and smile and reply: "Aight." I'd say anything to get her outta my
sight.
And I'd watch my teacher sit and sigh. And I never noticed life pass me
by.
I had a teacher once who sang the same ol' song.
She'd say: "Life goes on. Are you a player or a pawn?" (Sametta)

Circle of Rapists

If so many of the people around me knew rape, then rapists must also
encircle me. While few rapists speak of their crimes, several accounts did
reach me. A tennis partner, Jerome, knew of my pain: "Cathy, I really
support you standing up against this guy. Rapists are nasty. I would never
hurt a woman. But I had a scare once. This woman and I dated for about
a year. I decided to break it off. She called me to come and talk it over. I
naively went. She wanted to have sex. You know. She wanted it rough
that time. Can you believe that after I left she went to the police and
charged me with rape? That Sunday afternoon, the police called me."
"What evidence was there?" "Well, there was bruising around her thighs
and the area around her vagina. But Cathy, she wanted it rough." "Did
she always want it rough?" "Well, no. But that day, she did." "What did
the police do?" "They told me to come in the next day. I was so scared. I
couldn't sleep all night. I don't trust the police; they'd take her word over
mine." "Jerome, you bruised her, and that was not usual sex." "Well, the
police let me go. That incident changed my life. Believe me, I am really
careful with a woman. If she doesn't want sex, that's fine. I'm never going
through that again." The police scare did work, and evidence from his
wife, Blossom, who he married later and who was raped by another
assaulter, was proof that rough sex was not one of his sexual methods. She
told me how respectful Jerome is with her sexually. Reporting the crime
to the police might not result in a conviction, but there is hope that a
VISA's action might stop a few rapists like Jerome.

One day the phone rang. "Dr. Winkler, I need advice and since you
are open, I was wondering if you could help my girlfriend. I know I lost
my temper several months ago. I know I raped her. I've apologized. I
won't do it again. I've offered her money for therapy, to pay for her education, to do anything that will help her. I've also talked to her mother."
"You've told both of them that you raped her?" "Yes." "Your honesty is a
help. Where is she now?" "We share an apartment. She's in her room.
She never leaves it. She's not eating. She's skipping all her classes. I'm

worried about her. I won't do it again." "If you did it once, why won't you do it again? Don't you need therapy?" I continued to have conversations with him and his roommate. This case demonstrates that some rapists do recognize their actions as criminal.

At the end of the semester of the attack, I visited John, who everyone described as passive and gentle. We met on the second floor balcony at a cafe, a peaceful place. A man came charging after our waiter screaming "I'LL GET YOU." The attacker tried to push the waiter over the balcony. Immediately, I jumped up and yelled: "Call the police," and turned my attention to the attacker. Standing at a distance, I said, "You don't want to do that. Think about what you are doing. He's not worth it. No matter what he did to you, don't hurt yourself." The words seemed to work because the attacker let up. What kind of tip do you leave after that? At the table, John was immobile.

John submitted this excerpt:

> My emotions hold sympathy, despair, and outrage for Cathy. Plus a measure of second-hand guilt. At a party at my apartment, a woman friend and I were both kind of stoned, kind of tipsy. We had been flirting all evening and finally went into my bedroom. We had some of our clothes off. I was aroused when she changed her mind—I have no idea why. I started using some of my strength. The struggle excited me. Then, I realized she was *serious*: she *meant* no. Now I was *mad*—totally aroused and feeling led-on, abused, toyed-with—all in my own home, no less. I started wrestling even more seriously, taking off her few remaining clothes. Why didn't she call out for help? Finally, I realized I was scaring a friend to death, and that I was about to commit an act—a crime. I stopped. We lay there inert. I apologized, almost in tears. She did the same. I put on my clothes. She did, too. We went back out to the party. Even today, I am shocked to have found this potential lurking in my psyche.

Lurking behind John's passivity was his fear that he was a rapist. Since a relationship is based on trust, I suggested that he share his words and my letter with his wife Louise:

> Dear John, For ten years, you have cared dearly for me as a friend. Your account was well thought out. We have all acted hurtfully in our lives. I know. One of my past students told me about the rape against her. I did not understand. She dropped out of my class. I was to blame. I want to kiss you for your bravery and KICK you in the ass for your stupidity.

But then, I would have to do that to myself also. At least now, we both have tried to change ourselves.

Around me were people raped and rapists. Some of my friends were criminals, and some were VISAs. I hadn't known. How did others treat me?

Friends' Reactions

Most friendships begin when life is calm and peaceful. Trust, respect, and caring are part of those times of enjoyment. Crises, though, expose the types of friends we have, and the type of friends we are. Kathy's crisis educated her, and she shared in writing her experience with me:

> What a weird society we live in. We grow up where everyone lives happily ever after. When "bad things" happen to us, we are not prepared to cope with them, and when "bad things" happen to people we know, we don't have any basis for dealing with them either. Somehow we muddle through. I can sympathize with your thoughts about having to deal with the reactions of other people to the rape attack. Most people don't mean to be cruel or insensitive, but they don't know what to say or do. In a crisis, you lose some friends and find out who the real friends were/are.

While I had chosen friends who were intelligent, honest, caring, and activists, all of us acted in ways that surprised even ourselves. Most of us did not understand the emotional turmoil we experienced and experienced in disastrously unique ways. Supposed acts of kindness to protect me became ways to prevent me from making decisions: Friends withheld information "for my own good." Words of consideration were judgmental, telling me how to act. Those who gave me time and space to feel better did so via avoidance. All of us had a range of actions: Sometimes we were great friends and sometimes we grated on each other's nerves.

During the first night of sleep after the attack, the luscious and titillating smells of gardenias, a flower that is a special favorite of mine, enveloped the room followed by other fragrances—roses, lilacs, and orange blossoms. They awakened my senses and hugged me with a peace and contentment that celebrated life. In contrast, my friends' night of sleep was horrible. "Nightmares haunted my dreams. You didn't sleep too well either," judged Susan. In a state of desperation, Linda hugged me: "Oh, Cathy. I had some horrible nightmares also. Several times I woke up throughout the night. It was rough getting to sleep and then staying asleep. I know it was terrible for you, hon." They assumed that their nightmares mirrored my sleep experience. Their judgments silenced me. The truth of my paradise dream would have stunned them. It stunned me.

My friends felt they needed to check on me. Yet I wanted only peace of mind. The people in the house received messages and passed them on to me. They believed that I acted in a distorted way. Other people needed verification that I was all right and would survive that ordeal. Hwei Chei's postcard demonstrated these feelings and needs:

> Piglet sidled up to Pooh from behind. "Pooh," he whispered.
> "Yes, Piglet?"
> "Nothing," said Piglet, taking Pooh's paw, "I just wanted to be sure of you."

Then there was my dear friend Paula. Emotional expression was her style, and yet impossible for me. I wanted peace! No tears, no drama, no exaggeration, no calls, please. She kept leaving messages. She needed to hear my voice to know that I was OK. I needed quiet. Paula's tears were for the fears that she had for herself.

> There is a steak knife between the mattresses of my bed. I put it there after I learned about the rape. If a rapist broke into my bedroom, I reasoned, I will try to kill him. I will be ready. You think you can be careful. You think you can beat the odds. You think that if you are physically strong and mentally alert, it won't happen to you. But it happened to Cathy. She was smart. She was strong. She was a jogger. She was invincible. If a rapist could attack her, it could happen to anyone. It could happen *to me*.

Later, I called my brother. "Jack, this is Cathy. Look, I'm all right, but a man broke into my place the other night and raped me. Don't worry. I'm OK." Silence. "Jack, I'm here. I'm OK. Can you say something? Don't worry. I'm OK." "Cathy, I'm in shock. Look, let me call you back in just a few minutes." Jack wrote how it felt then:

> It must have been the most stunning phone call I have ever received. I mean stun as in stun gun—no feeling, in a way, except an inchoate awareness that there was pain somewhere, in Cathy and in me, and a slightly clearer knowledge that I couldn't comprehend what had happened. She herself said that the events were too horrible, too explosively awful to relate—yet. But an atrocity of this order—and happening to

my own sister—well, I was stunned. Throughout, my feeling was: this experience is beyond my worst imagination.

"Cathy, I've contacted the airlines and have a ticket to come out and be with you tomorrow." "Jack, that's great, but isn't the ticket expensive?" "Yes, but it doesn't matter." "Jack, I'm feeling all right now. Besides, I'm not sure there's any room. Didn't you plan to come out and give a lecture here next month? Since the organization will pay your way, save your money. I'll be back in my place then. You can stay at my home." "I don't know, Cathy. I really think it would be better if I come now. Don't you think?" "Actually, I feel fine. Let's wait. By the way, don't tell mom yet. I want to be especially calm when I tell her. It's going to be rough on her. Her daughter raped!" "OK. You can call me anytime. I'll pay for your long distance phone calls this month. Call anyone you want." "Great. Could you pay for my long distance phone calls for the next two months?" Jack laughed. He was right, though: I did need a visit from someone who knew me well. As a person new to the area, my friends were recent and could not judge my prerape and postrape behavior.

The call to my mother was now at hand. "Mom, I'm feeling fine, but I thought you should know that a man raped me the other night. I've been to the hospital and police. It was several days ago. I'm doing OK." "You feel all right?" "Yeah, I'm surviving it." "Well, OK, Cathy." The call left her numb. My mother's friend, while discussing her problems at lunch, generated these words from my mother: "A rapist attacked my daughter, and my son has AIDS. Compared to my headaches, you have no problems."

Public Life

My first confrontation with unfamiliar people took place with an annual party at Linda and Don's the following Saturday. *How would people respond to my bashed-in face?* Apprehension seized me. After people had gathered in the backyard, I moseyed down to check out the scene with my sunglasses that blocked the front and sides of my eyes. Outside, there was a long table of food: That was a good way of blending in and a means to start a conversation. The first superficial conversations were fine: uneventful and brief. Bored, I decided to check out the house. This was a precarious decision because I would have to remove my sunglasses to see indoors. The discarded sunglasses brought stares. A woman surrounded me and backed me into a corner: "Oh, I am so sorry for what happened *to you.*

How could this happen *to you?*" Her emphasis demonstrated pity. Pity was her way of saying no one could rape her. This would never happen *to her.* I pulled away and fled for safety. Then there was Judy, known for her insulting comments. "Well, you must be the bruised lady that my daughter told me about. She told me there was a black and blue lady here. Ha, ha, ha!" "Did your daughter tell you the cause of the bruises?" "No, I didn't ask." "A man raped me." Honesty was my choice.

As time went on, some friends saw the pain. Katalin remembered:

> When I saw Cathy, I gave her a hug. She flinched. I didn't know I shouldn't touch her yet. I listened to Cathy. She was clearly a person in pain, a woman crying for help, needing to know how to heal or perhaps in the process of healing herself. But I didn't know what to say or what to do. So I just listened and said very little.

Knowledge of a rape attack intensifies people's fears. Some people feel the fear of a potential rape. Some people raped relive that trauma. And some people feel they need to define themselves as not victims. The rape left other friends in confusion. Ricky noted her dilemma:

> Mutual friends were little help to me. Their reactions varied from "oh my, how terrible" to "I told her she should carry a gun." The woman at the local rape crisis center was a calming influence. She realized *my own turmoil.* That talk with a disinterested but trained and sympathetic third party helped to put things into a better perspective. Rape is no longer distant or isolated. It is reality.

What my friends had in common was that they never asked me how I wanted to be treated. They forgot that I was still Cathy.

Friends observed me as if I lived in a fish bowl, a globe that gave off magnified and distorted features. People would accentuate their greeting: "How *arrrrre* you?" "*How* are you doing?" "How are you *now?*" "How are *you?*" "*Are—you—fine?*" "Hooooooow arrrrrrrre youuuuuuuu?" The casual salutation became overbearing. They constantly measured my feelings. I wondered if people had an emotional thermometer on me. For them, the attack, and only the attack, defined all of my emotions. Friends like Rose monitored our conversations:

> I listened more attentively to the things she was saying and the way she expressed herself. I kept score of how much of our conversation was

about the rape and how much about other things. At first everything she said was rape related. Then as time passed, other things crept in.

People's need to validate the rape as authentic surprised me: "*Your* rape is *real.*" The crime of rape is not mine: *His* rape is real. For some, the proof of the rape was the bruises, though I perceived them as minor and transitory. For many people, that was the only evidence of the rape: They couldn't see the trauma. Without bruises on my face, some people told me that they would not believe that the violent attack occurred: In other words, be sure to get beat up if someone rapes you. My details in words of the attack did not validate the crime.

Paul took me to the counselor at the hospital. Other patients gawked at my swollen and discolored face. "Paul, this is a hospital, but the patients, the sick ones, I think they're fixated on me. You saw them staring at me while we waited at the elevator. I thought patients would expect to see bruises in a hospital." Paul made me laugh: "Cathy, this is a hospital. You know, the patients are in competition to see who is the sickest. They want to see if they can beat you or not."

During my stay at the farm, Susan and I had become friends:

In the days to come, Cathy did talk. She could talk of nothing else. I was eager to listen. First, I was flattered that she felt that she could talk to us. Second, I needed to hear the details to try and understand the extent of the trauma. Later, I realized that no matter how much I heard about her experience, I could never comprehend, much less understand what she had been through. Feelings of my helplessness were setting in and becoming profound. I was also worrying more and more about Cathy. I had realized that talking about her experience was not bringing her peace. I wondered if peace would have to wait until the rapist was brought to justice.

People judged, scrutinized, observed, evaluated, and interpreted me, my life, my actions, my words, and my decisions. Paula and Susan had regular and close contact with me. From my viewpoint, I discussed the same issues in a similar manner with each, but they had contrasting inter-pretations of my reactions. Paula noted that she never saw anger from me and Susan noted that I was expressing more and more anger. A similar situation occurred at work. George and I were in the hallway discussing our committee duties. "George, when is the work due?" "Next week. Why don't I write it up, and you can look it over?" "Since we agree on the issues, and since I have no time these days, your offer is great. Thanks."

Georgianna overheard the conversation and pulled me to the side: "Cathy, don't let George dominate you. You are acting like a victim. He's controlling you." A few minutes later, Georgetta, who also overheard the conversation, pulled me into her office: "Cathy, you tried to control and dominate George by having him do your work. Don't act like the rapist." Rape defined both of these people's interpretations of my actions. Friends' responses had made me question who I was. My interpretation was that George's offer was to help during this crisis. These conflicting statements along with my migratory lifestyle made me wonder if there was any part of me that was constant. Rosaria noted: "Cathy lived like a political dissident, staying at different houses in different parts of the city because the attacker took the keys to her house and threatened to return."

Monitored, measured, and mismatched emotionally, I wanted to be free of everyone's scrutiny, as Tasha noted:

A declaration of freedom, being. I am strong, yet weak,
Striving for growth, but with no idea where to go, but with many avenues to turn.
The puzzles are (un)solved: what is the essence of life, love, truth, knowledge—no subject to control.
My pain, fear, is there, and subsides slowly. Friends, their love and strength, mismeasure me.
I may anger them—but they do not send me away.
My thoughts, beliefs, are my own. I am free to have them and to express them.
I may not be accountable to conformity. I am human, deserving of love.

Deana's words helped me restore faith in myself:

What I have learned is that you are still a good role model. You are still the same person as you were before the rape. You are still professional and competent. You are, perhaps, a much more patient person after waiting through people's denials. You still have a sense of humor. You still have your intellectual curiosity. You have not given up. You continue and you are strong. I feel privileged to call you my friend.

Moreover, Jan had advice:

I'm impressed with your ability to verbalize your feelings. Anyone who thinks you should appear completely OK is either: 1) insensitive, 2) nothing has ever happened to them, 3) an ostrich, or 4) they simply haven't lived long enough.

Rape-Defined Forever!?

Friends defined me now as rape-traumatized and tattooed emotionally, and those branded marks of pain, for them, would remain forever. The attack permeated all of my existence, or so they thought, and left everything about me damaged. Kate made me see the plight as a lifelong issue. Despite the passage of twenty years, friends who knew about the rape against her still defined her as a victim. And my friends like Gloria also demonstrated how right Kate was:

> There will never be any peace for Cathy. Even if the rapist were caught, convicted, and executed, it would not change her. The rape dominates her. Rape is something that we should forget and get on with our lives. It was just one night. Cathy, she has so much to offer to the world, her intellect, her sensitive cheerful spirit, her teaching ability, her openness, her understanding heart. How could she let this be taken away from her?

Tasha's poem duplicated people's perception of me as living in a rape-defined reality:

> I see a heart fading, slowly poisoned by anger and bitterness.
> Its fruits yield not hate, but indifference and self-absorption.
> A heart now questioning why, and how, it cannot feel compassion.
> The one who scored love's crumbs, now gives less.
> The one who fears chains of isolation locks herself in.
> Asking if the memories were only a shadow or an aberration.

And Karly had her insights:

> My friend has pine needles in her shoes, and it prickles her toes, a pain
> that beckons her forward, back . . .
> My friend has pine cones—in her sockets, growing behind her eyes
> She looks up at the overpowering pine trees, so clearly, strongly, they
> inhabit her dreams.
> My friend gathers love, doesn't know it, has fear, doesn't show it, has
> strength, my friend . . .

On my identity, Pamela understood:

> I do not call Cathy a "victim." Cathy did not want to be patronized. She
> did not want people to pity her. She did not see herself as a victim

because she was dealing with the situation. She was not helpless or weak. After the rape, she handled herself with grace and dignity. Yes, something horrible beyond belief had happened to her but she was in control of the aftermath. Immediately after the rape, Cathy had the presence of mind to drive herself to the hospital. She knew what types of medical evidence were necessary. She gave the police comprehensive data. As the consummate social scientist, she tried to piece together everything.

In helping me sort out negative comments, Susan was also sorting out her feelings of blame against me:

As Cathy related incidences, I wondered how people could be so insensitive. Why couldn't they see how they were imposing their own prejudices? One day we got onto the subject of vulnerability. She talked about how hard it was for her to feel safe, no matter how many times she locked the doors. I suggested that maybe she should take some lessons in karate, and she wouldn't feel so helpless. She argued that karate wouldn't have done her any good because she had been surprised out of a sound sleep in her own bed. The guy had obviously been on drugs anyhow and didn't feel anything; even the sharp blows that she delivered to his groin hadn't phased him. I made the comment that "When I had learned karate, it provided me with a lot of confidence. I would inflict some injury to my attacker before all was said and done." Cathy's response was, "Don't you think I did fight him? Why do you think he threw me against the wall? The guy was on drugs! Even if I had been able to stab him with a knife, I'm not sure it would have stopped him. It probably would have just made him madder. How do you think I got so beaten up!"

I was guilty, after all, of imposing my own prejudices on Cathy! I had been the one to take pictures of Cathy's wounds, and I had seen the damage this maniac had done and still presumed that she could have put up more of a resistance! I thank God that she didn't. She could have ended up dead demonstrating to the world (and me) her toughness! Instead of being supportive, here I was implying that she had been raped because she was weak or didn't fight hard enough.

During the third weekend after the attack, it was time to move my stuff out of the place I had called home. The move should pull people together. I notified those who offered to help. Vickie and Tod, my colleagues, had immediately said yes. Then I tried Paula, who I was sure would help too: "Oh Cathy. Uh. I have an asthma problem. Moving always aggravates it." She later wrote:

I felt guilty about the rape. I blamed the neighborhood where Cathy was living. It is true that I have asthma and get ill from dust. But the real reason was that I could not go to the house where it happened. I was angry at the neighbors—why didn't they hear Cathy's screams? I could not face the place.

People allow about three weeks for discussion of the attack and the police investigation, and then there is silence. Even though there was an ongoing police investigation, people gave me unacceptable negative comments. There were subtle hints to quit the case, but my thoughts protected me.

The Negators' Words	My Protective Thoughts
"Cathy, you tried hard. Let the next victim catch him."	*NEXT VICTIM! I don't want anyone to suffer or to know that hell that I have experienced.*
"Cathy, no one could do more than you. Believe me, you have tried harder than anyone else. Give up."	*Would you say it's OK to give up on finding an ax murderer? This rapist tried to murder me: He tried to take my identity away. He will physically kill next time. Is that OK?*
"Cathy, you can't do everything. You are obsessive."	*Stopping a rapist is not obsessive; it's sensible.*
"Cathy, we love you. Just relax and let the rapist go."	*If I stopped, a man does not go free. Rather, a rapist attacks again.*
"Cathy, if the police can't catch him, why do you think you can?"	*The overworked police is the issue, not their inability. If this one rapist is stopped, not only are a lot of women saved but also the police will have a hell of a lot fewer cases.*
"Cathy, there are other things more important in life than catching this rapist."	*What is more important than stopping a Hitler?*

There were also residual problems due to the move, bill errors, and reorganizational issues. For many people, any problems I experienced after three weeks were my fault. Susan observed this: "I began to notice people avoiding her. The intended support of people around her began to wane, and she experienced the cruelty imposed by insensitive, ignorant people."

I couldn't get a hold of some friends like Katalin. She never returned my phone calls:

> When I first heard of the rape of Cathy, I felt a number of emotions—shock, anger, pain, dismay, outrage, horror, nausea, fear, sadness—each competing for dominance. Anger won. I remember Cathy's excitement when she moved there. Her thrill at a new job, a new home, a new challenge. I was envious. Then this horror occurred. Her job tarnished, her home violated, her challenge compromised. And what was my response to Cathy and her rape? I did nothing. I didn't call her. I didn't write to her. I couldn't talk to her. I didn't want to hear her. I hugged my pain and my anger to my breast. I did nothing.

Cora also used avoidance, but in another way:

> I was having anxious fears, and I advised Cathy to put the attack behind her. She reacted in anger. I guess she wasn't ready to hear that, or she misunderstood my meaning. I wanted to see joy in her face. Later, I began avoidance behavior. I stopped reading and listening about rape. Even if she wouldn't, I put it behind me. I continued to talk with her about the discovery of the rapist's identity and the case, but I also encouraged other topics. Whenever possible, I changed the subject. I was doing a favor for both of us. Her pain had caused me distress. I didn't like it, and I wanted it to go away!

My students let me know that my efforts were important. A Japanese student, Akiko, wrote a letter to the chair of the department:

> Thanks to Professor Winkler, I had a chance to rethink the rape. Then I realized it isn't a mere private matter but it is one of the serious social problems that we have to tackle. Eventually I broke the silence, and being given the opportunity, I spoke about the rape experience in front of my classmates. That speaking experience made me feel good because I was convinced that all of my classmates, due to Professor Winkler's teaching, understood rape appropriately. Professor Winkler taught me that we need a brave effort to get rid of injustice in our society. I can say that Professor Winkler's class is absolutely the best I've ever had.

A letter from Tesias arrived in my mailbox:

> Dr. Winkler, not as a method of ass kissing, but as sincere appreciation from the bottom of my heart, I say thank you. You have given me a new

weapon to add to my collection of intellectual weapons: activism. The stories, jokes, personal information you have shared with us in teaching are both weapons and a personal encouragement. Thank you again. And to add to my respect for you, I thank you for realizing that not every black man is BAD. Gratefully.

A Roommate

Needing a place to live and not desiring to live alone again, I met Alecia's friend Lauren. She was young but fine as a roommate. I told her, "Lauren, I might be sensitive to sudden movements at night." "I work on the late shift and come home anywhere from one to three o'clock in the morning." "That's not a problem because regular noises do not disturb me. It's sudden loud noises or slamming of doors at that hour that would upset me." "No problem." We moved in together.

For a few days, my brother Jack stayed at the house. Because of my interest, we went to see some eight-week-old golden retriever puppies. "Jack, these are really cute." "You have to take one. You should both take one. And Cathy, take the one I'm holding." Instantly, Lauren agreed. For the first month, the puppies worked well. We had a front porch to train those fluffy and energetic animals. Lauren and I modified our schedules to watch and train the dogs. Then, one Monday night at 3 A.M. **JUMP, BOUNCE, SCRATCH, RUN.**

Over my sheets scrambled two highly active puppies. Leaping up from a deep sleep, I awoke with an adrenaline rush like the one that had occurred during the attack. "What's-going-on-here?" "I'm sorry, Cathy. The pups got loose." "Close the living room doors before you bring the pups in. I experienced the attack again." "Sorry, the nights before you were always so fast asleep. I didn't think anything would wake you." "Puppies jumping up and down on me in my bed in the middle of the night upsets me." "It won't happen again."

Two nights later: **JUMP, BOUNCE, SCRATCH, RUN, JUMP, SCRATCH.** Another more dramatic adrenaline rush exploded in my body. "What's happening? Lauren, didn't you close the doors?" "Alecia is here, and I wanted to play with the puppies. They ran so fast that I didn't get a chance to close the living room door." "Lauren, *take the time* to do that. I can't keep waking up with these adrenaline rushes. They are the ruin of me. Besides, I can't go to sleep the rest of the night because I am so charged up from the adrenaline. Lauren, don't let the puppies in the living room in the middle of the night *again*." "It won't happen again."

The next morning Alecia left me the sweetest note of apology, but there was no word from Lauren.

On Friday, just two days later, **JUMP, RUN, BOUNCE, JUMP, SCRATCH, BOUNCE, SCRATCH, BOUNCE.** Another bomb—even greater this time—of adrenaline, attack-like horror occurred, and the torture from the rape attack resounded in my mind and body after the puppies jumped on my bed again. I packed a weekend bag and went to the farm. Since I had not slept for the previous three out of five nights, I passed out for fifteen hours.

On Sunday, I called Lauren from a pay phone. "This is Cathy." "Where are you?" "I left you a note that I would be staying at the farm to get some sleep." "Yeah, I saw that." "Lauren, we have a serious problem." "It won't happen again." "Lauren, it should not have happened once. Maybe once, but not three times in five days." "It's not my fault." Lauren refused to accept responsibility. The argument escalated and finally, I screamed: "YOU ARE DRIVING ME CRAZY. DON'T YOU UNDERSTAND: YOU KEEP REPEATING THE RAPIST'S TERROR EVERY OTHER NIGHT OF MY LIFE. I CAN'T TRUST YOU." My anger surprised me. Lauren responded: "Well, I'm not moving out." "Fine. I'll find another place, and you can have that one. I'll stay with friends in the meantime." Lauren eventually decided to move back with her mother. She never apologized.

I was devastated by the cruelty of Lauren's actions, but other friends showed their belief in me. Mark wrote:

> What I hope you know about yourself is the depth of your strength, your incredible resilience and ability to cope. It will undoubtedly be very difficult, but you will cope, and you will go on, and you will find ways to make your life work and be happy. Write or call as you feel so inclined. You may be as expressive as you like—emote like hell, in fact. We will gladly listen and absorb.

Mark's words comforted me.

Rape of Alecia

Frequently in newspaper or media interviews with people extremely close to VISAs, those friends or family members comment that they likewise experienced a rape. Two of my friends, Alecia and Rob, said this.

Alecia was one of the most helpful people around me. She wanted me to receive strong support, not like the kind she had experienced herself. She identified with me in many ways, and for those reasons, the rape against me impacted her existence and her identity. At the hospital, when she looked at my battered face and traumatized body, she admitted: "I've been raped too. I never told anyone." She knew how rapists mark our bodies internally. She saw me at my most vulnerable moment when my sanity hung on the edge of reality. From me flowed trauma, terrifying and disfiguring trauma. Alecia could feel her past torture in my current pain. Later, she spoke to others about the rape against me, but could not speak about the rape against her. Her silence kept that trauma buried, like a time bomb. Alecia remarked, "Cathy seemed to be in a place where nothing really was going to feel good, safe, or secure—she had been terribly violated." But Alecia didn't imagine my pain; she felt it and stated it in a letter:

> I began to feel that she was trying to manipulate me and pressuring me to get caught up in HER RIGHT TO PAIN. I felt that Cathy was academizing her pain. I understood that as I did the same thing myself. Why didn't she cry? I felt like screaming at her "CRY GOD DAMN IT" "ADMIT THAT IT HURTS, REALLY FEEL THE PAIN," let it all out. She was so stoic. She wanted, she needed, to cry for herself, for me, with me.

Alecia knew the house where I lived. For one year, she had lived with Rob and Gerri. Like myself, she had jogged in the neighborhood. She drove my car and dog back there from the hospital. There was the house—her home once—surrounded by police detectives, dogs, and neighbors. Black stuff to lift fingerprints darkened the white walls. The rapist had violated her home, a home that held happy memories. She said, "I was able to cope with Cathy initially in, to borrow a medical term, an ACUTE state of pain. I could really imagine her pain."

Prior to the rape, Alecia stayed in my home for a week. Later, when she learned that the rapist had watched the house for three weeks, she knew that the rapist had watched her for one of those three weeks. Probably the visibility of her friend Lauren, who stayed there with her, protected her. But what would have happened to her if Lauren didn't stay one night? Did he watch for another rape victim? Seeing me made her realize that she had been moments, perhaps only yards, away from another rape, from another rapist.

Her support for me stood in contrast to the lack of help she received for the rape she suffered. Because she'd been with me in the ER, she arrived late to work. Her coworkers, upon hearing what had happened to me, treated Alecia royally, with great honor and esteem for aiding a VISA. Praise comes when one aids a VISA, but not when one is a VISA. Alecia knew that, at the time when the rapist attacked her, she received no comfort. Two years later, she did call the people with whom she had worked and told them that Mike, who still worked there, had raped her. She spoke up. Speaking, no matter how important and valuable, is not necessarily therapeutic; it is a reliving of the rapist's hate. To speak is to speak for justice; and yet to speak is to feel the injustice.

I confided to Alecia my negative feelings about my university colleagues. I thought Alecia, one of a group of past graduate students, had the same views as them.

> This is when I began to withdraw from her, the attack, and her life. She was putting words into my mouth. She prefaced statements like "don't you think that . . ." or "you can see that" and then proceeding to interpret things completely contrary to my view. She was twisting a lot of events in a self-fulfilling way, especially when it came to her accusations of "the entire department being extremely insensitive" to her attack. I simply did not believe her.

Alecia, like so many of us, idolized her mentors. She wanted to believe in their integrity and professionalism—at all times.

Alecia argued that I recycled my pain into abuse: "How and in what ways could CATHY very possibly have acted out her rape, her violation, her anger, her pain, her terror, on those of us who supported her? She became a VICTIMIZER, the attacker. A process occurs that is the contradiction of RAPE: she as the victim reclaimed her power by robbing others of their power." Her argument: I had become the abuser, and she had labeled me as an attacker, a rapist. While I disagree that I was an attacker, I do agree that what Alecia experienced was another rape. Her situation—paralleling mine—brought back her past torture and placed her life and career in jeopardy. Alecia knew the hate of a rape attack; she had experienced rape trauma again at the ER with me, she saw the rapist's acts in my/her home; support for her was in opposition to her right to be a VISA. The combination of all of these points of pain was another rape of Alecia.

Dee left me a note after hearing Alecia describe me as a rapist:

> You may have reason to wonder from time to time what you have done to deserve the hostility of occasional opponents. Take heart. The only

reason you become the target of their ire is that you disturb their consciences and expose their misdeeds. Some people who rest easy in their complacent toleration of evil resent you reminding them of their obligations to FIGHT it. They will disparage your motives and distort your true principles.

Rape of Rob

In August 1987, my landlords, Rob and Gerri, began new careers in a state over a thousand miles away. While Gerri's research job was an extension of her master's degree, Rob had returned to graduate school after ten years. Security in their investment in the house was crucial. My rent paid their mortgage, and Gerri's salary would pay the property taxes, house maintenance, Rob's tuition, and their living expenses. Their plan for success was secure as long as I was their tenant.

"How are you feeling? Rob and I are concerned." "I don't feel any pain; I just feel OK." "Is there anything we can do?" "No, but thanks. Look, about the house . . ." "Don't worry about that. We don't expect you to stay." "Actually, I want to stay. A VISA should stand up to the rapist and not give in." "You don't have to do that. Rob and I have talked about it, and it's our problem. We wouldn't want to stay if it happened to me," Gerri said. Rob wrote his ideas and sent them to me:

> I remember being shocked, very shocked. Even after talking to Cathy, it was hard to believe it was real and had happened, in part because she sounded so businesslike, untouched, and in control. Perhaps it was because she talked about it frankly rather than hiding it or merely alluding to a "problem."

Their distance isolated them from their home, a home tarnished by a rapist. Gerri, like myself, had jogged in the neighborhood. Had the rapist watched her also? Rob's thoughts were, *If we had stayed, it could have been Gerri. How could someone do this in MY HOUSE?* Rob had protectively reacted: The rapist could have attacked his wife and did attack his house. A rapist had placed his hate all over their home.

> After hearing about her rape, I felt conflicting emotions: I worried for her and felt anger that it happened at all—anger that it happened in my house and worry about what would happen (in terms of my rental). Hidden beneath all of it was anger at Gerri: "See, I told you this was a bad decision to rent the house. I told you we would have problems. I was

right, and you were wrong and now look at what *I have to go through.*"
In fairness to myself, I really felt rotten about Cathy getting raped. But
those "good" feelings soon got covered up, not anger against Gerri,
anger against Cathy. I was angry at Cathy just because she was the
victim.

Rob's initial contradictory emotions became transformed into one feeling:
hatred toward me.

Without the house payment, their economic situation was not viable:
They couldn't afford the rent on their current place, tuition, and a mortgage payment. Economic upheavals emotionally impact one's ability to
work or study. Besides economic jeopardy, the first semester in graduate
school can be one of professional uncertainty. During this semester, the
professors evaluate students' abilities or, as Rob worried, inabilities: "Her
rape forced me to have to deal with the house when I would have preferred to have life run smoothly," he said.

The following weekend I called Gerri and Rob and informed them I
had decided to move my stuff out on the fifteenth of October. I volunteered a month's rent and to pay the utilities until the new tenant moved
in. Sandy had offered to manage the house and to finish painting the second floor for $500. Joe had offered to have the locks rekeyed and put bars
on the basement windows. My friends had cleaned the police's black
fingerprinting substance off the walls. Rob and Gerri would not lose a
penny.

Sandy did find a renter finally, but she failed to collect a deposit. The
neighbors informed the tenant of the previous attack in the house. The
woman was furious that Sandy had endangered her and her child's lives—
knowingly. The tenant left after two weeks. Rob and Gerri were out
money, and the $200 utility bill was in my name. Gerri pointed out:
"According to Sandy, to clean and paint the house was a pretty major
undertaking. The police department had liberally smeared grease (for
fingerprinting) all over the place. She said that she had to evict the tenant." When these problems surfaced, she noted, "I didn't want to play the
bad guy to Cathy. So I let Rob do it. He became our economic spokes-
person throughout the torturous months. I was angry about Cathy leaving
us to pay the monthly house note and her final utility bills."

Without recourse from the tenant for the utilities, I sent the bill to
Gerri and Rob who sent me a note suggesting that we split the bills. I had
had enough: three months of bills for a place that I did not live in. I wrote
Rob and informed him that the other tenant's utility bills were not my
obligation. If anyone was culpable, then it was Sandy, the manager. I also

informed them that, while I would never sue them, my friends had suggested that idea. I didn't want nor could I pay any more. Thinking over the past, Gerri wrote me her interpretations:

> Cathy acted in her own best interest which is what she had to do. However, she should have been a little more understanding. She caused such confusion. We wrestled with horrible feelings, with each other, and with the rape. Unlike some of her interactions with other uncaring or inept legal investigators, employers, and coworkers, ours didn't warrant threats or manipulation.

Rob had his thoughts:

> When I dropped my concern for Cathy, I also managed to convince myself that she was a jerk, and thus I could legitimately dislike her. I always knew that no one deserves rape, but I had to continue to get along with Gerri. I needed someone to be angry at. She was convenient. I wanted to be angry at the rapist, but he was not available. I blamed Cathy for *her own rape*. The results of the rape triggered existing problems between Gerri and I. Having Cathy in the house was like putting a bandage on a festering wound. My main concern stemmed from needing to feel in control. I spent a lot of time envisioning catastrophes. I embraced only worry for and about myself. We lived between our pain and our financial burden.
>
> We decided to sell the house. Did I lose money when all was said and done? No. When we sold the house, we recouped all our losses and had enough left over to "justify" selling. Although Cathy and Gerri ended up keeping in touch and having a friendship, I managed to maintain my dislike for her until two years later when we spoke on the phone. I don't know if she realized how good I began to feel while talking to her. I was able to open up to myself and see all that happened with new understanding.

Gerri summarized the awakening:

> Untangling and acknowledging these layers of feelings has helped me realize the need to make others aware that there is more than one victim in rape. Our culturing patterns repress healthy sexuality and promote sexual violence and abuse. This creates ambiguity, anxiety, and fear about what to think or how to heal those involved in sexual assault, including those who, like us, are peripheral victims of sexual crimes. *We're all victims.* Thanks to Cathy who persevered throughout and had the courage and drive to offer an alternative to silence.

Rob added: "One ironic thing . . . as Cathy has gone through the healing process she has helped to heal others."

Myths or Discrimination

Rape myths are ideas invented or imagined about the attack and the VISA. Researchers selected the term "myth" in order to emphasize that myths about rape are false statements that express an insensitivity to the VISA. These comments are a fabrication. While I agree that the myths about rape are not the reality of VISAs, those myths do constitute the reality of those people around VISAs. More to the point, myths are statements and acts of discrimination. Just as we do not describe racism and sexism as racial myths or sexual myths, but actually existing forms of discrimination, we must also recognize rape myths as statements of discrimination.

Discrimination changes form over time. Burt (1980) exposes many myths that are insulting and debilitating to people raped such as "you should not have gone to that bar"; "It's your fault for wearing clothes like that"; or "You asked for it." None of those derogatory comments were part of my life. My friends knew not to make such statements. In my case, rape discrimination was in disguise. In avoiding the rape myths exposed by researchers like Burt, my friends revealed other forms of discrimination. I wrote in my journal,

> With fear in their minds, people treat VISAs as subjects of rape. In effect, they are subjecting us to rape again.
> If you discredit the "victim," the attacker walks free (Sezgin, personal communication).

Rape myths/discrimination discredits VISAs, not rapists. The examples in this chapter point out the experiences not of a physical rape but of a social assault—or second assault as identified by Williams and Holmes—that is the negative culturing patterns that impact VISAs.

Who are these people who hurt me? They're my friends. And what is a friend? A friend is a person like me with faults and kindnesses. We apologize to each other for our faults, and we give each other courage to speak up about these. I have some great friends. They wrote this chapter. Their honesty is immeasurable. I appreciate them for their desire to help by exposing *our* horrifying acts. As a nonvictim and as a VISA, I was/am no better. Like my great friends, we have to change ourselves, and then we can replace those violent patterns with patterns of support, kindness, understanding, and appreciation of people. These friends with faults, like VISAs, are heroic.

TREATING TRAUMA: RESEARCHERS AND COUNSELORS

Unknown Maze

*T*hat man standing over me wants to rape me. He hasn't raped me yet, so how could I already feel it? The following months, in a state of numbness, I wondered how such an emotional occurrence could leave me without emotions. A man's features did not match my memory, but his physical proximity reinstated the same rape-like fear as the night of the attack. Why? Six months later, still emotionless, reading an account of a murder-rape set off screams from my mouth. *What is going on?* What did these traumas mean? Why were there incongruities between my bodily feelings and my mental thoughts?

I went to the emergency room, worried about my future emotional state. Belief that I could stand up to the trauma embedded inside me by the rapist and that I could control my emotions was important to help me regain my self-esteem. Yet the rape survivor advocate, a professional experienced in the field of VISAs' reactions, had no words of encouragement: "You can't deny what's there. It has to come out, and you have to let it come out." I wanted words of optimism. "Yes, but can't I control it as it comes out? Can't I handle it if I understand it?" "No, everyone suffers the trauma as it comes out." The honesty in her response was a doomsday notice: My future would be a road of unpredictable cliffs and detours with bombardments of emotional reactions. The rapist had more than terrorized me for one night; he had planted a series of land mines to further destroy me. *When will I start down the road of terror? Will I wake up one morning screaming and terrorized into immobility?* At the hospital emergency room, I felt the trauma, and I felt as if I was on the verge of losing my grip on reality. The rape survivor advocate lifted me up from the cliff's edge and quickly helped me to reestablish my foundation. On the other hand, the advocate's words pointed to an unpredictable future of horrors.

How did I sleep the first night? After a half hour in a tub of hot water, while sipping on a Kahlua and cream, sleep quickly comforted me. My safe house was forty-five minutes from the rapist's neighborhood; I slept in a corner room on the top floor with three families around me. The next morning I awoke gently from one of the most pleasant dreams in my life. The day after the rape, my body rested in a pleasant state of numbness. Admitting to friends that I experienced these unemotional feelings was an embarrassment. The slight jitters one feels before teaching class were not there. The lack of emotions was specific: The emotions tied to the rapist, his attack, and his threats were feelings not felt or realized by me at that moment. Because my feelings about the attack were untouchable, discussion of the rape left me unscathed. I was in a state of nothingness.

Two days later I went to the house to get more clothes and remove valuable items. No one had stolen or destroyed anything. While there, the rape survivor advocate called. "How are you feeling?" "Actually, fine. I'm doing OK." "How does your body feel from the bruising?" "I don't feel anything." "You should feel like a truck ran you over!" "Well, I don't, and that's fine with me. I guess my body's morphine is in good supply." According to Burgess and Holmstrom (1974b: 51), victims experiencing this numbness are in a state of disbelief that the attack ever occurred; they describe numbing as reduced responsiveness and involvement with the environment. My emotional numbness silenced only my feelings from the rape; it did not induce behavioral restraints or denial, nor did my teaching suffer that semester.

Why didn't I feel that rage? In this society, professionals like me have no right to express it. People who express their rage are out of control and poor VISAs. While the tears and anger wanted to surface those first moments with the rape survivor advocate and with the police, I choked back the pain. Who would believe a person who screamed out that tortured hell? If you scream the pain, then people consider you unreliable and unbelievable. My numbness was a mechanism of control to deal with the oppression imposed by people around me. I waited for those rape traumas to pull my life apart, without guidance. When rape trauma symptoms grab us, our only possibility for survival, according to researchers, is to stay on the roller coaster and cling to the bar for safety until the ride is over. They said that trauma is an unstoppable and unpredictable avalanche of pain. I wondered: *Are researchers able to aid VISAs with rape trauma?*

Research on Rape

Researchers make several assumptions about rape VISAs. They assume that rape causes VISAs to be dysfunctional and that VISAs were not heroic during an attack. They put VISAs' reactions into categories as if rape attacks impact VISAs identically. Thus, they do not recognize the variability in the types of rapists, methods, and situations of attack. They treat VISAs as experiencing two separate and opposite states of existence: prerape and postrape. All traumas suffered by VISAs, or so researchers perceive, are a result of the attack, not people's negative comments or police and lawyers' inability to catch and convict the rapist. Researchers have low expectations of victim's abilities to recover from an attack.

Burgess and Holmstrom pointed out two stages in rape trauma syndrome:

> the immediate or acute phase, in which the victim's life style is completely disrupted by the rape crisis, and the longer-term process, in which the victim must recognize this disruptive life style. (1974b: 3)
>
> The main feeling of fear . . . explains why victims develop the range of symptoms we call the rape trauma syndrome. (1974b: 30)

Their research is foundational by demarcating the problem, legitimatizing the feelings of trauma, and exposing symptoms that range from physical to emotional upheavals. Symptoms mentioned by them and other researchers include: anger, withdrawal, guilt, suicidal traits, depression, eating disorders, addictive traits, psychosomatic disorders, flashbacks, moodiness, hysterical crying and screaming, phobias, irritability, overreacting, feelings of unreality, inability to concentrate, paralyzing anxiety, nausea, and psychosexual dysfunction.

The list left me bewildered and dismayed. *Which symptoms will take over my life? Will I find myself half-crazed and wandering the neighborhood nude at three o'clock one morning? How dysfunctional a VISA will I become?* Studies on rape trauma insist it is a foregone conclusion that trauma will disrupt the VISA's life. One is left with the impression that no VISA can have a functional life.

The New Our Bodies, Ourselves offers four stages of rape trauma: initial responses, the full impact of the physical rape pain that occurs in a safe environment, a temporary period of calm readjustment, and verbalization of deeper feelings by the person raped (Boston Women's Health Book Collective 1984: 103–4). However described, recovery is explicitly a victim-to-survivor process (Koss and Harvey 1991: 176–7):

1) Memory: The individual *controls* remembering.
2) Integration: Memory and affect are *joined*.
3) Affect Tolerance: *Affect* is not overwhelming.
4) Symptom Mastery: Symptoms are tolerable and *predictable*.
5) Attachment: Individual *reconnects* with others.
6) Meaning: Individual *assigns* interpretation to trauma.

The issue of "lack of control" is present throughout research studies, stressing that this lack of control is of paramount importance to VISAs. VISAs have a sense of loss of part of themselves and a battered self-esteem. Janoff-Bulman and Freize (1983) reveal that traumatic experiences impact (1) the belief in a person's invulnerability, (2) the perception of the world as meaningful, and (3) the positive view of ourselves. Colao and Hunt point out that "the victim needs to mourn the identity she feels she has lost in the assault" (1983: 208). More precisely, VISAs suffer issues of identity, loss of belief in their identity, and ability to express themselves. Further, three relevant needs are paramount: independence, resourcefulness, and survival skills. "The turning point in recovery often seemed to come when the victim began to internalize feelings of power" (Ellis 1983: 481).

Ellis noted that qualitative studies, such as those favored by anthropologists like myself, are "markedly impressionistic descriptions by victims and are thus not valid" (1983: 474). Instead, Ellis used a quantitative approach. The following is an outline of her methodology. Six data collection sessions occurred anywhere from a two-week to a one-year period. Length of time of any session was not stated. Victims had two major methods to follow: paper-and-pencil approach and interviews. In the writing, victims filled out these five lists: 1) Depression inventory, 2) Pleasant events checklist, 3) Mood scale, 4) Fear survey, and 5) Social adjustment inventory. In all of these, the researcher decided the criteria, and the victims responded either by agreement or disagreement: no explanations allowed. The interviews were of two types: structured interviews and depression scale.

The structured interview first consisted of an assault questionnaire that focused on the attack. Imagine repeating the words in chapter 1, but repeating them in terms of distinct questions, as lawyers force VISAs to do in a courtroom. Such an approach assumes that all rapes, rapists, rapists' methods of attack, and VISAs' responses are, by and large, the same. The researcher holds the right to frame the rape experience, not the VISAs. The second part was a prerape functioning history in nine areas.

The term functional implies that after the attack VISAs are not functional. Rapists' damage is extensive, but the researchers' perspective assumed that VISAs did not have the intelligence or strength to stand up to the rapist's internalized terror. The second interview centered on measuring depression. Notwithstanding that VISAs might suffer depression, aren't there other moods possible for the VISA to experience after an attack?

In Veronen and Kilpatrick's (1983) research project, informants participated in twenty hours of stress inoculation training. There is no mention of monetary compensation for VISAs' time. Whether or not their research aided VISAs of rape is unclear. Also, their research could not evaluate whether or not they speeded up recovery, prolonged it, or if recovery of VISAs would occur anyway as a result of time. Veronen and Kilpatrick do go a step further and state that they "expect most victims to recover from most symptoms in a relatively short period of time" (1983: 487). No evidence to support that supposition was available. Recovery for VISAs, according to Veronen and Kilpatrick, is the ability to mobilize resources and to have adequate coping mechanisms. Minimal functioning by VISAs is the researchers' goal. They work with VISAs without using VISAs' own words, without monetary compensation, without any offer of services, and without the willingness to change the research protocol if many VISAs drop out.

Ellis notes that the dropout rape in her and her colleagues' research projects, like other rape projects, is extraordinarily high. Almost 80 percent of the informants leave the project. Most VISAs drop out at the beginning of the project like I did. Well, I dropped out before I signed up; that's pretty close to the beginning. These investigators did not study why we VISAs refuse to work with them. Also, no one notes that VISAs who drop out take control: VISAs succeeded because we stood up for ourselves and rejected the scientists' approach.

In those quantitative studies, the researcher is the controller. She or he establishes the criteria, the criteria to which the VISA may respond. Constrained choices are a VISA's option, just like the rapist imposed upon him/her during the attack. If researchers agree that rape is a loss of control and rape trauma is a result of suffering without a sense of control, then shouldn't VISAs be in a position to regain that control? Methods in which the researcher controls times, locations, questions, answers, interviews, discussions, or questionnaires maintain the trauma for VISAs. Those were the reasons I refused to participate in research. Their structure emphasized my lack of control.

My Fantasies

Disregarding researchers, I sought out my own approach to therapy. For me, sleep is a highly valued commodity, and I like to do it for eight to nine hours every single night. No one should interfere with those sacred hours of my time, prerape or postrape. Yet, that night the rapist did, but he wouldn't succeed again. The first small tremors of discomfort in sleeping began. But I had a remedy.

Every night before I went to sleep, I would spend a few minutes fantasizing about killing the rapist. At first, he just got shot in the groin and the heart. Some nights, I'd shoot him a couple of extra times. There were those few singular nights in which shooting him was not sufficient. A more torturous measure, never to be practiced in real life, had to be developed. In my great fantasy, metal straps secured the rapist to a two-inch oak board. Leather would be too weak. Time in this fantasy lasted several weeks. The days began by my throwing knives at him; those initial knives severed only parts of his skin along his arms, body, and legs. The severed skin decayed and smelled, but I was numb to smells. The rapist had silenced that sense. As the days progressed, the knives cut off more critical parts like ears and fingers. Then I knifed off the testicles and penis. I never threw a knife at a vital organ because the rapist would die. His torture was to die while living in a state of decay. He would smell his decay as I had smelled it. The fantasies calmed me, and then I slept peacefully.

These fantasies continued for six months. They did not end because of the passage of a sufficient amount of time or because I had become strong enough to stand up to them. "Cathy," Det. Roth called, "We've got the evidence." "Great, but are you going to be able to find him?" "He has been in jail since December." That knowledge ended my fantasies. The imprisonment of the rapist deleted my need to fantasize about killing him. Other women were safe. Safety gave me peace of mind and vaporized the fantasies.

Whatever was to happen in regard to rape trauma, I wanted to educate myself about it. I began reading anything and everything about rape. I watched every news story. I saw every film on or about rape. In the film *Lipstick*, the rapist attacked one woman and then planned to attack her sister. The woman stopped the rapist and protected her sister by taking a shotgun and shooting the rapist. My reactions startled me. As she shot the rapist again and again, I yelled: "Don't stop shooting until there is nothing left of him." My body arched as if I had the gun in my hands, and I acted out that scene. In my mind, the rifle kept firing until there was nothing left of the rapist, not even the visible evidence that he was once a human being. Like the woman in *Lipstick*, I didn't want the rapist to ever touch another human being, and to shoot him once was no guarantee of his death, but to shoot his body into nothingness, like my feelings of nothingness, was fair play.

Body Trauma

During my period of numbness, I spent time on surveillance, and my emotions remained silent—except in one instance, an experience I discarded at first as a senseless response. The detective called a man over to the car. While my memory gave no spark of remembrance, for the first time in a month, I had feelings of trauma, and those traumatic feelings identically matched those during the rape attack. Nonchalantly, the man walked away. I proclaimed his innocence to the detective, but other words followed: "But remember that body. That is the same body as the rapist, and the shape of his head is identical."

Months later, I reflected on why I couldn't recognize his face. How could I point out the rapist by his back features, a never-before-seen side of him, and yet not discern his face? My logical collection of visual data, the basis for legal evidence that supported the man's innocence, stood in opposition to my body's supposed illogical trauma reaction. My memory of the rapist's face was proper legal evidence; my body trauma of him was not.

The body is able to circumvent the protective mechanisms of the mind. I learned later that, when the person raped is within a short distance of the attacker, a VISA's body provides information by duplicating the terrorized conditions. While the terror during that street surveillance episode matched the attack, the only meanings available to explain it were inadequate. Was I another dysfunctional VISA whose feelings of horror surface randomly and without reason? Did the intensity of the trauma leave me in an unstable condition and unable to distinguish my real feelings? Was I an unreliable witness, unable to make visual distinctions? Each of these explanations for my street feelings were wrong and were explanations that denigrated me and pointed out my supposed inadequacies. Bierwert (1990) provides a fourth explanation from her Native American research: The rapist altered his presentation of self in order to disguise himself from me. The closeness that occurred during the attack made me susceptible to these alterations in his body form. In other words, on the night of the attack, the man projected himself to me as a rapist; during street surveillance, the man projected his body as innocent.

By the third month, to prepare myself to handle the process of identifying the man who raped me—an experience frequently commented on by VISAs as another form of rape—I questioned my friend Kate Wininger. In a police lineup, she had identified the rapist who attacked her. I had intended to ask her the question: "What was it *like* to face the attacker?" but instead, I asked, "*How* did you identify the rapist?" The switch of questions from the experience to the mechanisms of identification revealed the database of information in my body.

> I had gotten a good look at the rapist in spite of the fact he had put clothing over my face. The presence of the gun, even though I didn't believe it was real, and being strangled until I became unconscious, along with the rapist's threats to come back and kill me and my husband, all made the trauma more real. Nevertheless, I still felt competent I could identify him. In the police lineup, the men singly walked into view. I was not afraid and had no reason to feel fear because these men were behind a one-way mirror. Yet one of them had an impact upon me. When he entered my vision, my body first identified him in the lineup. It was a *purely visceral response, a return of the fear and revulsion.* My body told me immediately that he was the rapist. After my body's split-second identification, I then visually recalled that man's face as that of the rapist [emphasis added].

Her experience of body trauma explained mine. Unlike Kate's experience, though, I did not have the protection of a one-way mirror or other witnesses willing to testify.

In continuing to seek help from other women, I talked with Jean, who told me of her experience identifying an assailant from a selection of photos. In that attack, the man had kidnapped her and beaten her with a crowbar. To save herself, she had jumped from a three-story building into bushes. Later, at the police station, she viewed a series of pictures and selected two. While she told the police that these men looked like the attacker, she told me, after the conviction, that she selected those photos because her body went into rape-attack shock as she viewed each photo. In the end, the selected photos were of the same man taken over a period of years.

Trauma reactions in rapist-identified contexts are those that parallel the repulsion and nausea experienced at the time of the attack, thus warning us of dangerous people. They are trauma markers of protection against the rapist(s). While attack-like contexts signify protection, rapist-identified trauma—more severe and more pronounced in intensity than the trauma in attack-like contexts—warns us of immediate, not just pending, danger. The *source* of my street-surveillance trauma was the context in which the rapist was present and was a danger to me; the *meaning* was his presence as a threat to my life. Interestingly, when I saw Kenny in police custody, knew he was guilty, and knew the result of DNA fingerprinting, I did not feel this body fear. Having Kenny in police custody and the absolute certainty of evidence against him, I believe, alleviated my body's need, in that context, to feel fear in order to protect itself.

While fear paralyzes our minds, our bodies aid our mental and analytical abilities by taking on, in a pronounced manner, the responsibility to identify the terrorists. In these cases, our bodies warn us: They scream at us by repeatedly duplicating, through feelings of terror, those same emotions experienced during the attack. Previously people had told me not to trust those body traumas because they were indeterminate and dysfunctional trauma responses to the rape; but now I know differently. My best protection is my body's built-in nonbattery-operated alarm system.

Screaming the Truth

At the emergency room, I experienced another trauma that remained buried. I told Cassandra that the rapist wanted to kill me. "All rapists threaten their victims, but few carry through their threats; besides, the rapist had no weapon." Acceptance of her position that the rapist's threats to my life were my fabrication left me with self-blame. I must have overreacted or distorted the rapist's words. This acceptance implanted a shock that had to explode later to help me support my original interpretation. On March 26, 1988—I remember this date more easily than the date of the attack—the newspaper ran an article on the well-publicized prep-student rapist-murderer. I read this—as I had read every other article on rape in the previous six months—to learn about and confront the trauma. I was alone. The rapist-murderer's Chambers' defense was that he had instinctually and accidentally defended himself against pain; he meant no harm. While the selection of words differed, their meaning matched the meaning of the rapist's words spoken to me during the attack: "It's your fault that I hit you. I didn't want to do it, but you made me beat you up.

I had to stop you." As I read the rapist-murderer Chambers' words, my body—spontaneously and without warning—
S C R E E E E E E E E E E E E A A A A A A A A A A M E D
in a death-defying manner. My body evacuated its contents. I sat on the toilet and at the same time bent my head into the bathtub to vomit the filth of the rapist who was inside of me.

The rapist had thought about killing me that night. I was near death. That feeling was not a fabrication. I had evaluated that hellish experience correctly and the rape survivor advocate, while trying to calm me down, denied my truth. The eruption of my body screamed out the truth to my mind, blocked by others' denial of the truth of the attack. My body knew that I was now safe to confront that fear of physical death. More than two years passed before I could read the rest of that news article. Both rapists had blamed their VISAs. Ms. Levin, the VISA, did not cease protecting herself from the rapist Chambers' battering until he had killed her. In my instance, if I, unlike Ms. Levin, had not quit fighting and not completely and absolutely given in, the rapist also would have ended my life. Rape was my escape from physical death.

While many people blame VISAs for the rape attack, and then also tell them that they are in denial, I wondered if these people around me were in denial. The bomb of emotions was my body's means of breaking the barricade of ignorance imposed by my "supporters." Somehow my body knew that this safe and secluded three-day weekend at home was a place to accept that reality and recuperate. An emotional land mine exploded and revealed the meaning of rape. Rape was an encounter with social and, now I know also, physical death.

Torturing the Mind

A conversation with Det. Roth opened up my understanding to past events. "Det. Roth, if he is in custody, we can do a lineup." "Cathy, I don't think that's necessary. We have the evidence." "But wouldn't a lineup just further strengthen the case?" "Not in this case." "Well, maybe I want a lineup, maybe I want to see him behind a one-way mirror, and maybe I want to be able to say that is him." "Cathy, it's not necessary." "Maybe it's not necessary for you, but can't I request one?" "Cathy, believe me, it wouldn't do any good." "Det. Roth, I want one." "Cathy, well, I guess I should tell you. You already saw him with Det. Doil on street surveillance and said that you could not identify him. That was when you were with him outside the 7-Eleven store." "Oh, I understand your position now. Thanks."

Topsy-turvy feelings dominated the next couple of days. Many negative events happened at the same time that impeded me from sorting out the source of the trauma. At the university Dr. Sinta yelled at me; police officers had stopped me several times for my expired license plate, a result of a title lost in a fire in another state; the IRS wrote that I owed them $1,000 and wanted to garnish my wages. A neighbor harassed me that my dog, not another neighbor's three dogs, smelled up the neighborhood. Too many problems at the same time.

It was spring break, and I went to my friend's farm to mend the seams of my body that burst with pain. For five days, I cried and cried and cried and cried. Rick found me in tears: "Cathy, what's wrong? You can tell us," he said. "Rick, I know I can tell you, but I can't tell myself. I don't know what's going on. I don't want to cry, but I just have to." A day later, Linda found me crouching under a bush. She sat down next to me and saw the buckets of tears like unending streams falling in so many different directions. Emotions gripped Linda: "Cathy," as she hugged me, "you can talk to us." "Linda, I just can't figure it out. I can't stop crying. What is going on? You better go to work. I have to finish my job of sobbing." We both laughed in sorrow. The tears finally exposed the truth. Throughout the rape attack and afterward, I thought that the rapist raped only my body, but not my mind. I had to face the truth. He had tortured both.

One of my best mental features that I had bragged to myself about for decades was my visual memory. I never forgot a face. I might forget people's names, but not them. In this case, the rapist was in my mind, that part of my mind held captive by the rapist himself. He controlled my ability to see and recognize him. He had terrorized my mind into setting up a strong barricade of protection against him. Accepting that truth ended the tears. The effectiveness of his methods of torturing me prevented me from using my own mind to identify him.

Reliving the Attack

About ten months after the attack, during a night of sound sleep, I awoke in an adrenaline rush like the one I'd experienced during the attack. With a frenzied reaction and a hypersensitized response, I jumped up to defend myself again. Inadvertently my dog had hit my ankle at the same spot where the rapist had kicked me awake. Deciphering the meaning of my emotional flare-up helped me quiet my nerves and return to sleep. My mind had remembered that spot on my foot. My body set off the alarm. With this knowledge, I squelched the attacks of trauma as they surfaced. As the octopus-like tentacles of terror surrounded me, I made the situation feel safe by turning on a light, checking the windows and doors, and calling a friend. Thus I prevented those tentacles from grabbing me and holding me down.

Why do similar contexts ignite the trauma? The answer that they are similar seemed insufficient, for it ignored the reasons for the surfacing. Why did my memory want to remind me of this horror? After the stranger's assault, the possibility that the rapist would return was real. This was an excruciating fear. Although initially numb from the attack, my self-preservation skills warned me that another rape could jeopardize my ability to survive. These fears of the rapist's return are real fears, they are valid fears, and they are protective fears. Contexts that correspond to the rape, rapist, and attack are *sources* of attack-like trauma. This trauma is the body's protective strategy to safeguard the VISA in order to provide space and time for her/him to heal in a situation of comfort and safety. This evidence gave me hope that by understanding the source and meaning of the types of trauma, one can put a check on its disruptiveness. There was hope.

Reclaiming My Body

Since the day of the attack, I'd monitored the contours of my facial muscles. Something outlined and marked my face, a diagram of pain. These lines fashioned my cheeks, highlighted my forehead, maneuvered my chin, and strained the areas around my eyes. My face was in an ever-present condition of darkened lines, inundated with wrinkles that weighed down the skin and muscles. After a year and a half of the facial distortions, a nervous tension began to invade my whole body. During the first two weeks, this agitation was tolerable, and as usual, unnoticed. By the third week, the tremors disrupted my ability to function, tearing me apart on the inside. Calling friend-counselors for help was futile; they repeated the dried-out list of advisory statements, and their ignorance only irritated and aggravated the shaking. They could not explain the meaning behind this sudden infirmity. Instead, they blamed and became annoyed at me, assuming I did not employ therapy in my daily life.

Then the pulsations suddenly stopped. Those nerve-racking feelings disappeared, as did the facial constraints, and the feelings of agitation ended. My face once again—after almost 540 days—relaxed. The facial tenseness, once unforgettable, evaporated. Pain did not spotlight my face and body anymore. Yet the dissipation remained unexplained.

A meaning did exist: My body had refused to suffer further the social attacks of rape. This occurred because I was in a context in which I felt safe—geographically safe from the second assaulters. My body erupted in a volcano-like explosion to say: "This is enough." There was a need to reconnect this disjunction between mind and body, imposed by negative comments. To reestablish those familiar mind-body connections resulted in squashing the terror that separated my body from my mind.

Experientially, my rape trauma, like that of all VISAs, is distinct. The lengthy numb period allowed me to differentiate the second assaulters from the original rapist. DNA fingerprinting that provided positive identification of the defendant as the rapist legitimated my reactions during street surveillance, not as manufactured terror, but viable trauma, inaugurated within the proximity of the rapist. Guilt feelings—common for some VISAs but absent in my case due to self-education prior to the rape, self-counseling during the attack, and self-defense against the blamers— were not part of my own trauma and did not then become intermixed with others types of trauma. Nevertheless, there were times when the meaning behind the disruptive feelings—whether brought on by the rapist, the second assaulters, or the legal experts—was barely decipherable. These periods of multiple overlapping traumas scrambled the meanings.

Historically, Burgess and Holmstrom's (1974a; 1974b) research is exemplary in establishing the concept of rape trauma. Now, three to four decades later, rape-trauma experts argue for an understanding of trauma as a process delineated by phases and symptoms. This typological approach, I argue, is but one approach in our understanding. For many VISAs, the intertwining of trauma contexts impedes their ability to translate the body's language. Even in a case such as mine—in which each trauma expressed itself distinctively—discovery of the meaning of that trauma was a challenge. Unscrambling the meaning behind the trauma can transform the rapist-defined position of *victims* into the position of *activists* who define the meanings of the rape attack, the trauma, and their identity themselves.

In attack-like contexts, the severity of the rape still hinders VISAs who need time to heal, and who, because of social and legal rapes, are not in a safe context. The body warns us of other contexts that do not have the prerequisite security "locks." Guilt trauma, which can wall VISAs from the world of people, reinforces the authority of the rapist and his/ her control; an understanding of its sources is a means of jolting VISAs into reasserting their rights. Rapist-identified trauma, a type not recognized as legal evidence, points out the rapist or other abusers to VISAs. Lastly, blame and denial trauma, which isolates VISAs, are incongruities between the blamers' reality and the reality of the VISAs.

VISAs' analyses of their traumas through a study of the contexts in which the traumas surface demonstrate their meanings. Knowledge of these meanings diffuses the rape trauma by bridging the gap between the mind and the body. Victims become activists when they interpret the meanings of rape trauma. If VISAs interpret these contexts and sets of meanings, they can better help themselves to deal with the rocky road to recovery. Four meanings affirm this activist approach:

1) PROTECTION. The rapist's physical insertion of his penis with bludgeoning force implants horror in a VISA's body's memory, and the memory later acts as an alarm system. As VISAs' bodies react traumatically, VISAs learn to guard themselves against the presence of the rapist or other abusers. The body brings to the attention of the VISA, in a dramatic visceral manner, the occurrence of danger. Although VISAs may not understand the meanings, the upsurges of emotions cause VISAs to find a safe haven, a place away from the presence of the rapists/abusers.

2) FOREWARNING. Because the impact of psychological, mental, and physical terror by the rapist and others can be extensive, and because the impact of the terror may not be cognitively perceived as a danger by VISAs, their bodies re-enact horror feelings to warn them of potentially unsafe contexts. Thus, trauma is important for self-preservation.

3) SAFETY. The nonrape context, while resurrecting past trauma, can also be a context of safety in which VISAs can deal with the trauma and its meanings without fear. The rape trauma is a pronouncement that the context does *not* contain other threats. In a safe context, s/he can let down her/his protective guard. Releasing her/his guard allows the trauma the reconnection of meanings viscerally and cognitively. It is this context of safety that enables VISAs to delineate and decipher contexts of nonsupport in order to translate those threatening contexts into peaceful ones. Such interpretive actions convert victims to activists.

4) INFORMATION. The momentous shock of the rape attack or other rape trauma may contain some devastating meanings for VISAs to confront. Denial of these meanings by those people around VISAs can further impede an understanding of our feelings. Acceptance of these meanings occurs when our bodies shout the validity of the meanings. Visceral reactions validate the minds' interpretations. This research is but one step in pursuing an anthropological understanding of violence.

Another VISA—Donna

My research on trauma began when Donna, one of my students, approached me. "Cathy, I want to be part of your research project." *What research project?* People who heard of my self-analysis wanted to try it. Instantaneously I realized that I had a research project and methodology. Each day and week thereafter, people materialized in my office or over the phone, all with the same request: "I want to be one of your informants." How unusual an approach to gathering informants! The informants demanded the research. Donna is an example of that.

She lived behind that wall of trauma David had built for a decade and a half. He began his amorous and chivalrous approaches with Donna when she was seventeen years old and just learning the meaning of sexual expression. His sexual approach alternated between pleasure and pain. During those good times, he affectionately and amorously made love with Donna; at other times, he raped her. His addiction for those love/hate sexual encounters became her blight. After David, Rob—on the first date—raped her. Yet Rob was easy to walk away from because there never was any tenderness. Donna thus had experienced multiple types of rape: first David's love/rape relationship, and second Rob's terrorizing and destructive rape. Despite therapists, counselors, and mental-hospital professionals, Donna experienced years of mind-body confusion. Her inner sensibility and strength persisted despite the trauma of the rapist-built walls of guilt that had silenced her.

During those times of self-blame, Donna lived with incongruous sensations between her mind and body. In the act of sexual intercourse, Donna felt her body react physically, but without those feelings of love. Waves of dread swept over her. David the rapist had attacked Donna's existence and separated pleasure from Donna's sexual self. While she could mend this split between emotional feelings of love and the physical sensations of sexual love, his attacks triggered episodes of manic depression. David did not cause the *condition* of manic depression, but Donna notes that David-the-rapist was the *initiator* of the episodes. The trauma from David's rapes set off the chemical imbalance for that psychiatric disorder.

In the presence of her parents, Donna's thought processes became interrupted with a loss of concentration and lack of desire. It consisted of nervousness, shortness of breath, deluge of dread, heaviness in her legs, and pain in her stomach. This guilt trauma centered on issues of premarital sexual intercourse, her failure to fulfill the role of a model daughter, and feelings that she had committed an awful wrong but without understanding the wrong, nor understanding that the wrong was David's and Rob's rapes. Moreover, Donna felt that she did not act like an adult and did not take responsibility for herself as an adult. She felt that, when she returned home after an evening in which David had attacked her, her parents would discover that she had had sexual relations.

Donna spent two weeks in a state of emotional chaos to decipher the meanings. She became the investigator. Although the examination of that horror almost broke up her relationship with her fiancé, Victor, a wonderfully sweet and gentle person, Donna had a determination to extinguish trauma from her life. Her ability to comprehend the traumas ended the guilt, and her analysis of the meaning of the contexts of the traumas stopped those feelings of self-blame during sexual intercourse and when she was with her parents. Thereafter, sexual intercourse became a pleasure for her. The guilt in the presence of her parents ended. Donna didn't have to protect herself anymore because *her* meanings returned her identity—an identity with a foundation stronger than the rapists' terror.

Her body generated feelings of guilt, fear, and lack of mental concentration. The guilt, an assault on her self-concept, was to keep her quiet; yet her body, separated from her self, screamed for affirmation. Her connection between her silence and the trauma-shouts of her body in those contexts revealed to her the meaning of David's acts as rape and the meaning of her parents' presence as authority figures. Her deciphering of those meanings allowed Donna to feel, for the first time, a unified connection between love and sexual intercourse. She wrote me:

> I have carefully read the paper. The first thing I said to myself when I finished was "Wow!" You totally captured my thoughts, feelings, and experiences. As I read it, I could relive the feelings I had at the time; so it must be a good article. I can tell that you really put your heart into it. I appreciate its accuracy. I consider our talks to have been a very healing

and liberating experience. Now when I make love, I feel *no guilt*, and I have *total trust* (personal communication, emphases added).

VISA as Researcher

To aid victims in reestablishing their identity and self-esteem, I argue they must become activists who direct the research and who enunciate the meanings of the trauma. Crucial to diminishing rape trauma is for VISAs to interpret the details of the attack themselves. A person's interpretation and set of meanings reinvoke control and recenter a person as an active participant and a cultural negotiator of social interactions. My experience as a VISA and a researcher opened up research opportunities to reveal this silence:

1) to generate an insider's view analytically;

2) to bridge the gap for informants to become Investigator-VISAs; and

3) to transform the VISA into an activist.

Unlike most anthropologists, whose decision to study a research area is by choice, for a crime victim, there is no choice. Yet it is in that lack of choice that a crime victim–researcher fully comprehends the subject matter. A life-threatening situation can heighten one's power of observation and accentuate one's ability to decipher the meanings behind a criminal's words and heinous acts.

The Investigator-VISA has that distinctive blend of double-consciousness, conceptualized by Dubois (1967), that allows one to understand the issues of a VISA and the issues of an investigator. As one subjected to rape, I did not become ruled by the rapist. Unlike many VISAs, I had a background in cross-cultural experiences that enabled me to analyze the meanings, contexts, interactive process, culture shock, and trauma reactions. More importantly, the experience of rape aided me as an investigator to frame research more appropriately, to develop an analytical approach for this type of data, and to search out issues previously unnoticed by nonvictim-investigators.

Second, investigator-VISAs are more than describers of data; they are the interpreters of the rapist's acts and meanings. While the investigator can provide them with a framework for analysis, the distinctiveness of each rape and the rapists makes it necessary for VISAs to research the meanings of the rape trauma experiences. Investigator-VISAs are the ones to interpret and analyze the rape trauma because, 1) trauma occurred in a secluded, inaccessible area known only to them; 2) the inflictors of the torturous emotions are rapists whose identities remain unknown to investigators; and 3) breaking the silencing of the VISA—part of the rape trauma—reestablishes their voice and identity.

Third, structured interviews are not a method for this research; they don't work. Rapists have already tried to take away our decision-making choices; interviewers must not duplicate this type of behavior. In my study, investigator-VISAs select the time, the place, and the duration of our exchanges, and they decide on the extent of my participation. In the research, most exchanges averaged three to five hours. If something arose to alter the time of the interview, the investigator-VISA chose the next time that would accommodate both of us. The sites chosen for exchanges of information have varied from my office to restaurants to parks, and have also included telephone conversations and letter writing.

Finally, investigator-VISAs have had the right to edit the work and delete portions of their interview. Word choice and phrasing was an interactive process between us. This editing not only clarified points important to the investigator-VISAs, but also gave them decision-making rights. The ethnography thus holds the ingredients of their thoughts, feelings, and experiences as only known by them, the VISAs.

Each rape attack has a set of meanings, and each VISA must sort out those meanings. For me, rape was an attempted social murder; the rapist failed. The discovery of the meanings of that rape helps VISAs sort out the torturous experiences. Rape is a loss of control. To decrease trauma then, a VISA must have control. To aid a victim in reestablishing his or her identity and self-esteem, the victim must become an activist by directing the interviews and discovering his or her own meanings of the trauma. Crucial to diminishing rape trauma is for the VISA to interpret the details of the attack. A VISA's interpretation and set of meanings reinvoke control and recenter a person as an active participant and a cultural negotiator of social interactions. Inversion of control-based methods aids VISAs into becoming investigators, and this approach thus becomes an asset in diminishing rape trauma.

To unscramble the trauma, victims must gain control and self-esteem, and I argue that this can only happen when VISAs become the investigators. Researchers such as myself can play the role of advocates. The illogic of trauma is logical. By guiding VISAs through the labyrinth of authority in research and recognizing VISAs' abilities to interpret meaning and create valid research, researchers like myself use a qualitative, structureless methodology that enables VISAs to establish meaning. Their ability and right to establish the parameters of interaction, interpretation, negotiation, and decision making reconstitute VISAs' control and self-esteem. Our methodology and research are successful when we give up our rights to control VISAs' recovery. Relinquishing our status recreates the status of people traumatized and feeling without control in life. By losing our status, we researchers regain our status again. When VISAs breathe life into our research, our research will have a life for VISAs.

CONFRONTING INSTITUTIONAL BARRIERS

Honesty did not aid me in problems with institutions. These problems, a result of moving, reorganizing, and readjusting my life to new circumstances along with working with the police, became major dilemmas in my life. Institutions generally do not have policies to aid people in crises. Instead, the VISA becomes the target. And when we seek counseling, we find that it has set up its own barriers.

Counseling

Alecia's ideas about counseling stressed counselors as the only problem solvers.

> Over the weeks, I became angry with Cathy. I started realizing that in several months she had only been to a counselor one or two times. She told me that the counselors did not deal with her rape "in the way" she wanted them to. I became angry at her because in her own pain and anger and hurt, she distorted her personal relationships. I saw her as not coping.

On the second day after the attack, I called the counselor, Jan: "The people around me think that I should feel horrible. I feel OK. Should I feel worse?" "No. You are just experiencing a numb period. In time, those feelings surface. This is not unusual. Many people react this way." "Then, it is OK for me to feel good." "Yeah. Enjoy the pleasantness. There's nothing wrong with it. Come in and see me tomorrow." To feel neutral after a horrifying experience was not unusual, not bizarre, and not wrong. My mind protected me.

The next day, Jan sat across from me, but at a distance of almost ten feet. Did I have a contagious disease? Her eyes, instead of looking directly at me, watched the walls and floor. Her seated body leaned back in the chair, away from me. I explained to her my reactions and my friends' reactions. Silence. I described briefly the rape and used the word "rape." "What do you think of the sexual assault?" "Jan, why do you call the rape a 'sexual assault'?" "Well, most people can't handle that word at this point." "I've used the word several times with you; can't I handle it?" She did not listen. Then, I let tears flow: Tears to get her attention. Silence. I asked for advice about the future: "If I don't feel the trauma now, when and how will I? Can I control the trauma so that it doesn't get unleashed in front of, say, a class of students?" "You'll just have to wait and see. Do what feels good: Eat food if you want to. Gaining some pounds won't hurt you." This was Jan's advice. For a person whose weight has been the same for almost twenty years, a ten-pound gain does feel different, from fitting into one's clothes to effects upon the monthly cycle. But she, like other counselors, regurgitated what I considered poor advice: Eat without restrictions. Other survivors informed me: You either gain or lose 50 pounds. To exchange one problem for another was not my goal. During our session, Jan was blasé, uninterested. Probably she had heard this story over and over again: Raped, numbed, hidden trauma, surface trauma, survival. Counseling left me depressed: unhelpful advice and minimal explanations.

As Cassandra later informed me, Jan suffered the trauma of a divorce. This did explain her lack of empathy, but it did not justify it. Objective professionals like Jan are not allowed to explain their behavior to patients. Professionals must never reveal themselves, but VISAs must expose their intimate details! Feeling unwanted as a person, first by the rapist, and now by the counselor, I was upset: Is this counseling?

I did speak to many counselors. I used the grocery store approach: I visited each counselor for half an hour to find out who was the best one for me. Insurance does not pay for most counseling, and to pay fifty dollars or more per hour per week was an expensive proposition. I was in no rush. The majority of counselors gave me the same advice: "If you are raped, you need weekly counseling." "What if I am doing fine?" "All rape victims need weekly counseling." "Could you tell me what symptoms or issues that I'm having difficulty with?" "If you are raped, you need weekly counseling." "That may be true, but how am I not handling the situation?" "Well, I don't know, but I'm sure there is some way that you are not acting correctly. If you are raped, you need weekly counseling." Their economic interests superceded their therapeutic knowledge.

Cassandra was originally a terrific help to me. She was the exception. Throughout the first year, I had called sporadically. Each time her advice included the words of help I needed, and she treated me like a person who could succeed. I owed her a great deal of thanks. In an article, I cited her tremendous efforts: "I thank the rape-survivor advocate whose approach helped me regain my sense of reality" (Winkler 1994a: 286). Moreover, I cited her advice to rape trauma: "You can't deny what's there. It has to come out, and you have to let it out. Everyone suffers it, and everyone suffers the trauma as it comes out." I sent her a prepublication copy for her suggestions on changes for the article. She was furious. Her boss Lorraine wrote me of Cassandra's anger and then moved on to other points:

> For me, it seems grossly unfair to write of a volunteer's perceptions paralleling our lack of understanding of the rape victim's [survivor] trauma. For my part, you never gave me a chance; you can't speak fairly about what we know. We have much understanding, and skills, and *success* in supporting women in directing paths to their own true power.

Lorraine had other suggestions. She wanted to coauthor my book. She said that we would work on our book the weeks before I was to testify against the rapist, a time of acute distress when a VISA lives with the memories of the rapist and his attack. I wrote to her that pretrial trauma made her suggestion impossible. She never answered. In the DA's file was a letter from Lorraine: "Did we talk about this patient? She can't take 'NO' for an answer from our volunteer who accompanied her to court previously and is misquoting her in a 'book' about her difficult experience—even though she declined therapy [from me]." Lorraine assumed that, if I did not go to counseling with her, then I had no counseling at all. She also assumed that I intentionally misquoted Cassandra. Why did I ask for Cassandra's suggestions? Lorraine objected to my article published by Cambridge University Press.

Ellen was a budding feminist on campus and the Director of Women's Studies. I needed feminist advice to deal with the impact of the attack on colleagues at work. She initially wanted my help to rewrite the sexual discrimination policies. But, when I requested that she accompany me, as a listener, to meet with administrators in regard to the sexual discrimination by my boss she responded in writing:

> After hanging up the phone last week, I had second thoughts about sending our procedures draft to you. It is still going through changes weekly. Instead, I am sending a copy of the old procedures. I wish I could be more help to you. As you said, this time will be very difficult for you. If you need extra or new support now, I'd like to suggest these

women, all licensed psychologists who were suggested by my husband. If you have any questions, call my husband.

She denied me a simple request of her presence and transformed my request into a need for counseling.

JoEllen was a specialist in rape survivors. After I explained what happened, the case, and my research, she likewise and initially reacted professionally with me. "I'm writing a grant to do research on the paralysis that victims suffer during an attack." "Could I read it? Maybe I could help you with the writing. I've gotten several research grants funded." "That would be great. I'll make a copy for you." "Other counselors told me that I need weekly counseling. To tell you the truth, I don't understand. Wouldn't I know if there were odd feelings going on?" "Most victims do not go to a counselor and do well. I also think you are right about how you are handling the situation. At this point, you are doing everything possible to deal with the situation that a counselor could suggest. You are at the place where I hope to get most victims."

JoEllen described me, as so many other counselors did, as an ideal rape survivor: "You are a great victim-survivor and should feel proud of your actions." JoEllen suggested a different type of counseling for me. "Cathy, it's true that I have never counseled anyone like yourself. I think it's marvelous what you have done. I'm willing to work with you through the investigation and your friends' and colleagues' problems." "At this point in time then, you have no advice on what I may experience?" "Few people have taken the actions that you have taken. We can work it out together." While this seemed like a healthy perspective, the working-it-out process would cost me fifty dollars an hour. In other words, if I paid her $200 a month, I could teach this counselor what to expect with other VISAs who take action.

JoEllen's attitude changed quickly when the bank mistakenly bounced my check. On my answering machine was a harsh message: "Cathy, *your check bounced. You owe me $25.* Please bring the money in cash over to my office *today or tomorrow.* I can't afford to do counseling *for free.*" "JoEllen, the bank accidentally stopped payment on all my checks instead of just the ones the rapist stole." JoEllen was known as an open-minded counselor with victim-survivors, and yet her first reaction to the bounced check was that I wanted to hurt her financially. Instead of asking for an explanation, she assumed that I was guilty.

She had more to say, "By the way, I've decided that it's probably not a good idea to give you a copy of my research proposal." "Uh, why?"

"Well, um, you probably have too much to do." "Everyone has that excuse. I'd like to read it, and I know most of the research on rape." "Cathy, it's just not professional. You can call me for counseling. That's our only relationship." Even this liberal counselor wanted her patients to be victims, not professionals. "I suspect that you might want a counseling visit in the future, and you can call me. I can arrange a time for you within twenty-four hours or so. But, there is one point I do want to add: Do not feel guilty if you give up the investigation." She and other counselors suggested that I quit looking for the rapist. Why didn't she offer me support to endure the investigation? I never returned to JoEllen.

Marley was a therapist friend of Estar's, who worked with women battered. We met in a local bar where the darkness would hide my face if I took off the sunglasses.

> When I met Cathy, I was not prepared for the bruises on her face. She talked openly about the experience of being raped, an act of courage itself. Dealing with my own feelings of anger and nausea was no small matter. I had to experience the discomfort and then let it take a back seat to Cathy's tortured experience. The torture only began with the rape and continued throughout her dealings with her friends and colleagues. It is a shame that rape victims have to survive societal abuse after the rape. It's like a repeated rape.

Marley's approach was unique: "Would you like me to be a friend or a therapist, or we can just stop with this meeting? Whatever you want." In my experience, counselors do not allow themselves to be a friend of a VISA. But that was what I needed. Ignoring my professional status was a denial of my identity. "A friend, please, I need understanding friends." She kept that promise of friendship with counseling—for years. She included my letter in her newspaper column. She advised me that if stopping a rapist is an obsession then we should all be obsessed. During that time, she told me how she helped a high profile woman who was battered but, when the woman abused wanted to coauthor a book with Marley, Marley felt the other woman wanted to control her. She dropped her as a patient. Marley confided to me that many counselors respect her work, but note that she has trouble dealing with people battered when they gain equal status. This happened to me too. After the local media interviewed me, she stopped answering my phone calls or letters.

Lily acted humanely. She listened to my mountain of reasons causing depression and my strategies to combat it. As I told her about the legal case, the civil case, my brother with AIDS, and relocation annually for work, the level of shock in her eyes and face kept increasing. I asked for her advice. She said that my depression was legitimate, and if there was no depression, she would worry. She said that I had more suggestions for combating depression than any counselor could suggest. When I asked her for the cost of the session, she told me to put my checkbook away and to donate the money to aid me.

Alecia was right that I did not pursue the formal avenues of counseling. The weekly aid in understanding my VISA's issues were through my friends who ranged from VISAs themselves to professional counselors to minorities who comprehended the never-ending blight of discrimination and the need not to give up or give in. My phone bills increased to $150 monthly for those informal sanity sessions. Those friends counseled me and always worked to understand my perspective. Those friends were activists. Those friends were humanitarians.

Rape Crisis Centers

In place of counselors, I approached in the next city of my residence the rape crisis center and spoke with the director, Magdeline, to volunteer my services. She asked me to work instead with a low-income rape crisis center directed by Barbara, and I did. Barbara received me like a human being: with respect and understanding. Magdeline's rejection of me as a volunteer was unexplainable then. Later I met a woman whose crisis training was with Magdeline. Her view: Magdeline wanted to control everybody, and from the beginning, she knew that I was not a victim and not controllable. Instead of support, Magdeline preferred volunteers who acted like victims.

The next state I landed in, I approached Magda, the director at that Rape Crisis Center. They had a forty-hour preparation program for volunteers. Most of the training centered on issues that I had either experienced, read, taught, wrote about, or lived through. They asked me to give some of the lectures. Since attendance at training sessions involved a two-hour round trip at night in winter weather, I asked if I could just attend the sessions in which I needed training or where I would meet the local specialists. The director rebuked me as not being a team player. Several months later, one of my students, Kara, called a volunteer at this rape crisis center to ask advice on telling her father about the date rape. The volunteer was terrific: She encouraged her to stand up for herself in a protective way. Several days later, Magda independently called and ordered

Kara not to tell her father because Magda's own father had disowned her in a similar circumstance. Kara asked me, "Dr. Winkler, why does she think that my father is like her father?" "Kara, what do you think is the best decision?" "I want to tell my dad." "Well, I think you know better. Do you think that he will react negatively?" "Yes, he might, but speaking up is more important." Kara told her father, and while the experience was emotional and difficult, Kara succeeded in being herself, in deciding about who she was, and in convincing her father to accept her and to understand that rape was a part of her past life. Her father did not disown her. Instead, they became closer. Both Kara and I chose control over our lives.

My own unfavorable experiences with Rape Crisis Centers should not diminish their great importance. These centers have only a few underpaid and overworked people. The centers are run on shoestring budgets with constant political harassment and economic stress. Many of the staff have suffered one or more assaults personally, and in helping others, they must relive the negative emotions of the assaults suffered by other VISAs. These centers need decent support. Instead of *increasing* our defense budget by $5 billion, why not give the money to these centers for women's defense?

Corporate Discrimination

My checks began bouncing. The bank had put a stop order on the wrong check numbers and refused payments on my bills. Moreover, the bank had not changed my address as I had requested, and they sent the notices of bounced checks to the old address. I hadn't received them. The bank also did not review my account to see if the rapist cashed stolen checks. I sent creditors a copy of the letter from the bank explaining the error, and each one responded favorably except one credit card company: "If the bank makes an error in your account, it is not the credit company's fault. Pay the penalty." The next month, the bank repeated the same error. Again, they put a stop on the wrong check numbers. Once more I sent creditors a copy of another letter from the bank. That one credit company's policy persisted: "You are culpable for all bank errors: Pay the penalty." I canceled that credit card, but the company continued to charge interest on the interest.

After four months of bill problems, another credit card company contacted me by phone about an unpaid bill. I had prepared that bill on time but due to the move the bill became lost—and thus forgotten. I explained the situation to that company person who responded: "I am so sorry. Our company understands. You will have no problem with us. There is no harm to your credit. We will not charge you interest or late fees, and we will help you any way possible. When would it be reasonable for you to send in a payment?" "I really appreciate your kindness. I'll make sure I find the bill today. Thanks so much." That company won my business and my heart. The company's kindness energized me to resolve the bill promptly. I kept that credit card.

Granting Agencies

Back at work after the attack, I mailed in a grant proposal on my Mexican women's research to the Pediker Foundation. Although five days late, I figured my letter of explanation would clear up the matter. The grant was to study problems of women. Rape is a woman's issue because the majority of VISAs are women, so the granting organization will understand. Instead, the Foundation refused to read my proposal: "We do not review grants postmarked after October the first." "Elizabeth, did you read my explanation that a rapist attacked me several days before the due date, and that's why the grant was late?" "Yes, and I'm sorry."

"Elizabeth, if this grant is set up to study problems that women suffer, don't you think that many of the grant writers who are women would also suffer those same problems? Isn't rape a gender-specific crime?" "Would you hold on just one minute?" And several minutes later, "Dr. Winkler, what you said upset me, and I think you are right. I went to check with our supervisor, and we will review your grant." "Thanks but haven't the reviewers disbursed the grant money?" "Yes, but we will reconsider it. Please send it in." Her offer was superficial. They were not going to get the reviewers together again to review my grant. While Elizabeth was genuine, she did not have the ability to change the organization's policy.

During the following years I submitted grants on rape research in the United States to several prominent agencies. The insiders had the same response: "It's a great grant. It needs to be funded. But these white male reviewers will only grant money for research on women raped if it is not in the United States. You can try but expect nothing." And that was the result.

The University

While the incidents described below did occur, they are an amalgamation of examples from different universities and from different years after the attack. I altered the original case. Paula initially advised me about Dr. Lina Sinta, the administrator: "She was my teacher as an undergraduate. We had remained in touch through the years. I knew her bad side—her manipulative side. Cathy could handle Dr. Sinta and do well in the department as long as she was realistic about Dr. Sinta's motivations."

Dr. Sinta called and asked, "Cathy, when are you coming back?" "Dr. Sinta, how are you doing?" "Oh, uh, yeah, I'm doing fine. I took your class last night." "How was the teaching?" "OK. When are you coming back?" "Dr. Sinta, the man raped me yesterday. Could I decide in a few days?" "OK. Call me every day." "Dr. Sinta, would you tell my students what happened?" "What should I tell them?" "Whatever you feel comfortable telling them. The crime is against all of us, not just me."

The next day, Dr. Sinta called again. "Cathy, I took your class last night and explained the rape." "How did the students react?" "OK, I guess. You are coming back on Monday? We can't keep substituting for you, and doing *your* work." "Dr. Sinta, could I make the decision on Monday?" "*NO*. We would have to pay a substitute. There's *NO* money for that. The students have missed two classes. We have to do something." "Well, the students didn't miss two classes, Dr. Sinta. You and Vickie taught them. Both of you are professionals. Didn't you tell me that you know so much you can walk into a room and just talk about what's on your mind, and that's new information to the students?" "Well, that's true, but someone has to take over the classes permanently. Either you come in on Monday, or we make other arrangements." "Then, the answer is yes. I'll be there." "Call me every day."

I was calm when I returned to work. People would understand the horror of rape. They were social science professors. Dr. Sinta was in the hall and I went to shake her hand. She pulled back. "*I didn't know that you got beaten up.*" In a low voice, I asked: "Can I get an appointment with Dean Dulle this afternoon, and could we get the locks on the door of the department's office changed since the rapist has the keys?" "I'll take care of the appointment with the dean. And on the key change, I'll see about that." I walked downstairs to talk with George, the maintenance person. "Is there any problem in changing the locks to the office door? A rapist attacked me last week, stole my keys, and knows where I work." "No problem. I need an order from your boss. I can do it any time today." By three o'clock, George had no order form. "Dr. Sinta, I checked with George, and he has not received an order form yet." "Cathy, you are paranoid. There's no reason to change the locks." Losing my keys to a rapist is ample reason to change the locks!

Dr. Sinta insisted that she attend the meeting with the dean and myself. For three quarters of an hour, they bantered back and forth. Finally, I inaugurated the reason for the meeting: "Dean Dulle, I asked to see you regarding the rape attack against me. I want to be active in the investigation to find this rapist, and I want to know that I will not suffer any repercussions academically. I will cover my class obligations; that's my first priority. Also, I would like the locks on my department office door changed. I teach at night, and the rapist stole my keys. He knows where I work. Can this be done?" "Yes. Dr. Sinta, take care of that. Is there anything else?" "Yes, I would like your assurance that my involvement in the investigation will not jeopardize my application for the tenure track position opening up in the spring. I'm going to have to spend time with the police. This will take away from the full dedication that I would like to put into the present job this fall." "Of course, there's no problem. Are you able to work?" "What other options do I have?" Silence. The dean stood up and extended his hand. After we left his office, Dr. Sinta said, "Cathy, you are paranoid about that lock. What's the matter with you?" "Dr. Sinta, this man rapes women. If I'm not there, he'll rape you." Reality sunk in. She had the locks changed within the hour.

Colleagues' Greetings

"Hey Gregory, how are you and your wife?" "Cathy, I'm sorry for what happened to you. A stranger raped my wife before I met her. You'll get over it." Gregory was up front, and yet reserved. "Vickie, I want to thank you for taking my classes. You did a good job of preparing the students for my return." "HOW ARRRRRRRRRE YOU, CATHY?" "Fine. The police want to find the rapist, but despite the rapist's police record, there were no fingerprints found in the house to pinpoint him. It's probably a guy in the neighborhood." Silence. "I've decided to move, but I'm going to take my time and find a comfortable place to live." Silence. "Uh, your class went fine this morning?" "Yes." Silence.

The next day, I asked: "Vickie, what's wrong? Yesterday you didn't say anything. We've always had good conversations." "I guess I'm afraid to say the wrong thing and make matters worse." I punched my left upper arm with my right fist: "I fought the rapist, and I'm still fighting. I'd feel more comfortable if you'd disagree with me like you did before. I'm still Cathy Winkler." "I'm sorry. I was too cautious. I'll continue disagreeing with you from now on." That shared laughter restored the friendship.

Vickie informed me of the histories of the members of the department: "Cathy, you know that my brother raped me but did you know that for years the alcoholic father of Joan the secretary raped her. You should also know that Dr. Sinta told people that her father beat her after her mother died when she was twelve. A lot of people also think that her father raped her between the ages of twelve and eighteen. At eighteen she left home for college and never returned. Also, about Gregory . . ." "Yeah, he told me about his wife. This information is unbelievable. Every woman who works in this office and at least one of our two male colleagues' wives have suffered rape!" Later that day, I saw Gregory. Since Vickie altered her behavior after I spoke with her, probably Gregory would also. "Hey Gregory, how's your work?" Speaking rapidly, "I've-got-a-lot-to-do-right-now." "Any interesting projects you are working on?" "*All-my-proj-ects-are-interesting-and-I-don't-have-time-for-chit-chat.*" I left. Then I knew that Vickie would be an anomaly in the department.

On the third day, Dr. Sinta said to me, "You have to pick up the new key, and here's the form." "Dr. Sinta, could you send one of the work study people, we have three here, to pick up the key? I don't want to walk around campus with this bruised face." "No, you have to sign for the key." "In August, I did not sign for the key; a work study student did. When these bruises are gone in three weeks, I'll go over there and sign myself." "No, you have to go NOW." If Dr. Sinta was immovable, I had to use the authority over her: "The dean told me that he would help me any way necessary. I think this is a reasonable request. Do you want me to contact him?" "No, I'll send a student. But remember that I am the administrator. I make all of the decisions."

The atmosphere in the office became unbearable. People were uptight, haltingly communicative, and avoiding me. They talked with an edge in their voices. I represented their tortured past. After my morning class on Wednesday, I decided to confront the problem in order to resolve the issue: "Gregory, what's going on in the office?" "What-do-you-mean?" was his brusque response. "What are people saying about the rape?" "Nothing, everything-is-fine. Everything-is-absolutely-normal." Gregory desperately wanted life to be like the prerape time. He wanted me to be all right; he did not want to know that his wife suffered. To see my bruised face forced him to confront the past pain of his wife. Ignoring her past pain was easier. The office atmosphere was too unpleasant to work in so I took the afternoon off and drove out to a national park where I sat in my locked car and cried. The tears streamed down my cheeks. These were not tears because of the abuse of the rapist; these were tears because of the abusive treatment by my colleagues. They had shut me out like we shut out people with leprosy.

That same afternoon, Paula ran into Dr. Sinta:

> Dr. Sinta saw me at the university's post office and exploded. She ranted and raved. She was hysterical. She blamed Cathy. She said Cathy was causing havoc in the department. I calmly asked a few questions. What was the problem? It hit too close to home. Dr. Sinta could not handle the rape. It brought back memories from her own past. She wanted to patronize Cathy—"Oh, the poor victim." She could handle it on that level. I told Dr. Sinta to wait a few weeks. After all, the event was still fresh.

Late that afternoon on the phone, Dr. Sinta informed me, "Cathy, I had to do something about this. You understand that I'm the administrator, and I have to take responsibility." "What's wrong, Dr. Sinta?" "The people in your department are upset with you. YOU ARE CAUSING HAVOC IN THE DEPARTMENT. YOUR RAPE IS DESTROYING THIS DEPARTMENT. I have to stop this. I'm going to have everyone meet with a psychologist next week as a group. You will be part of that group. It's for *your own good*." "If that will help, sure. I'm going to stay away from the office except for my classes for the next two days." "Yes, *that would be best*." Her harsh words were followed by a cordial request: "Shall we go to dinner tonight to celebrate our birthdays?" "I don't think so. Good-bye." (See figure 7.1.) As I hung up the phone, tears and screams wretched from me. The hateful words from the rapist were easier to accept; he was not a friend or a colleague. He was not someone I had to deal with daily.

On Monday morning, I returned to work early in order to be on top of all issues and preserve some form of peace in my life. As I approached the building, my legs began shaking: I walked on ground that seemed to be in a constant earthquake state. The muscles in my face tightened and outlined my features; my face felt distorted. These were pains caused, not by the rapist, but by the social abusers around me. Confronting me as I opened my office door was a dozen dead and faded yellow roses (figure 7.2). To cheer me up, a friend had sent me these flowers on Thursday, the day that I had absented myself. That was the first time in my life to receive roses. No one called me about the delivery. And there was no water in that 12-inch deep vase. Why had someone done that to me?

The first chore was to smooth things over with Dr. Sinta. "Dr. Sinta,

Figure 7.1   Cathy Winker on her 39th birthday, ten days after the attack

I know that this past week has been hard on people. No one knew about the beating and seeing my face in its multitude of colors must have surprised people." "Cathy, you didn't tell anyone about the beating, only about *your* rape!" "I know, but the beating was not the part that pained me. I can't feel the physical pain. The bruises are like a bad makeup job. The horror that is like a dark cloud over me is the rape." "I guess I understand. Perhaps I had a little anger last week, but I had to take control." "Dr. Sinta, you probably didn't realize it, but you used the phrase 'your rape.' It is not 'my' rape: it is 'his' rape against me. I don't claim any part of that rape. I didn't want to be there." "That does seem like a reasonable point." "Dr. Sinta, I know this rape is hard on everyone. I want to do my job, be able to work with the police when it doesn't interfere with my classes, and get along with people. Perhaps the first shocking week is over, and everyone can calm down." "Yes. That's a good idea." "Well, I hope this calms any doubts you have." "Yes. This is fine."

Her behavior belied this declaration of truce. Delay tactics and withholding information were her methods. I had one day to complete the

Figure 7.2   "Vase of Dead Roses" by Cathy Winkler

department's project for the library—a two-week project. A year later, I found the following memo from the library in my department file:

> According to Dr. Cathy Winkler, she never received those library lists, which were hand carried over [to the department] and put in her [mail] box. While I cannot understand it, I apologize for the extremely short notice.

What happened to the missing lists?

Redirected anger was another of her techniques. Dr. Sinta set up a meeting with Joan the secretary and me. "Cathy, you cannot use all of Joan's services. Joan is my secretary and for the rest of the department." "Dr. Sinta, I type 150 words per minute on the computer. It's faster and easier for me to do my own typing. Joan takes my phone messages, and that's it." Dr. Sinta placed Joan in a difficult, if not impossible, position. "Well, it's just your attitude." I said, "Joan, give us an example." With hesitancy and doubt about what was happening, "Dr. Winkler, you are always trying to put me in my place like right now. See that, Dr. Sinta." "Joan, I'm asking for details." Dr. Sinta wanted Joan to discredit me. Since Dr. Sinta could not get me to lose my temper, she had tried to augment a dispute between Joan and me. I interjected: "Joan, why don't we all accept that each one of us, including me, made mistakes in the past. I apologize for treating you, or anyone, unfairly, and I will try to be more fair. I will make sure that I do all my work. Do you agree, Dr. Sinta?" Once I humbled myself, Dr. Sinta ended the meeting.

Backstabbing occurred, as I learned from students. "Dr. Sinta is verbally attacking you in public meetings and in her courses. She talks about your inability to work and your paranoia." Student workers overheard Dr. Sinta's comments: "Cathy is disrupting the department." Unbeknownst to me, the students called a meeting with Dr. Sinta regarding her verbal mistreatment. What was Dr. Sinta's response to the students' protests? She called me into her office and told me that I had launched a counterattack to take control of the department from her. Her evidence was students' reporting my negative comments about her. I asked: "Please give me one example. Could you name one instance, one phrase, one time, one class, one situation in which I mentioned you?" Silence. Without evidence, Dr. Sinta had to let the issue drop. I had never mentioned or made reference to her; my focus was on stopping the rapist.

Dr. Sinta gossiped that I had changed my anthropology course to a course on rape. Discussion of the attack was one twenty-minute period the day I returned. I connected my facial bruising with a point made in another class session: "In our last class, we discussed perceptions on how people from other cultures actually 'see' differently than ourselves. Today, we have an example of that. You notice that I am wearing sunglasses at night and inside a building. I will have to take these off in order to see my notes. But at first, the bruises will surprise you because they are bright red and purple. As the class hour passes, you will notice that you become accustomed to looking at me with these multiple colors, kind of like a punk look. Each class period thereafter, I will have different shades of colors, and each one will have a look of what we might call 'natural.' Here go the glasses." Several weeks later, students asked me to explain my calmness: "Why are you not hysterical, crying, or upset?" A ten-minute explanation of numbness satisfied my students' interest. That was the sum of our discussions on rape during that fifteen-week semester.

In the department, insignificant issues became magnified. One day Gregory broke his silence: "Cathy, your material for the bulletin board is due today, and it's late." This was a bulletin board hidden away in an untraveled hallway. "Sorry, Gregory. With the move, the police investigation, and my research paper for presentation at the national anthropology meetings next week, I'm busy. The material was due today? I'll turn it in tomorrow." "You can't do that. It's too late. I already put the bulletin board together yesterday. What about the newspaper account? I did the bulletin board." "That was the job you volunteered for, Gregory. We are to work on the news article together." "WHAT'S THE MATTER WITH YOU? WHY DON'T YOU GET YOUR WORK DONE? I CAN'T DO YOUR WORK. WHAT DO YOU WANT?" Suddenly, he stopped with shock in his wide-opened eyes. He had screamed. He had never seen me, as the "victim," screaming or losing control of my temper. Embarrassment covered his face. "Just forget it."

I fulfilled my obligations, taught my classes, attended department meetings, and my research and writing were activities at home—away from the office. Each week I checked in with Dr. Sinta to list my accomplishments. During the prerape period, Dr. Sinta frequently had discussions with me such as: "About your work in the department next year . . ." After the rape, she made no comments about next year.

Fear of colleagues' comments became a daily anxiety in my life. Little things occurred that showed that the people around me viewed me differently. Conversations became formal. Distorted interpretations were routine. Everyone avoided me, and I reciprocated. Paula noted that "Cathy bravely went on with the routine tasks of work. She behaved in a very professional manner. She continued teaching. She was direct and straightforward. She told her students what had happened. I never saw any anger from Cathy during that entire time."

Would the new year begin a fresh slate? The month's respite in December left me with the expectation that time would diffuse the burden and pain of the attack, with renewal in the air, and calm, soothing, and go-along atmosphere desired by all. Instead, silence, avoidance, and disapproval continued, highlighted by Dr. Sinta. Those first days back left me with feelings of paralysis. While in the previous months I jogged two to three miles without much effort, now my body gave out within a quarter of a mile. Exhaustion captured my body.

The emotional pain from my colleagues' attitudes had punctured my energy and sapped my strength. My jogging disintegrated into a walk that quickly deteriorated into immobility. I sat emotionally paralyzed in the gutter, hoping for energy. My mind began to wonder: *Can I walk back home? What would a person in a house nearby say if I requested a ride home!* This is a supposedly able-bodied person, healthy, and without physical impediment, who couldn't walk! Could I explain that emotional depression disabled me? Would anyone understand how the emotional terrorism of Dr. Sinta made me physically inert? My will told me to move my legs. As I stood up, I leaned against the tree and measured the distance to the next post. I leaned on front-yard fences. I willed my emotionally impaired legs to move. Pain throbbed in my muscles. Each step meant that I was closer to the next tree, lamp post, or fence. This emotional fatigue crippled me.

With the new year upon us, I prepared my urban research proposal for the department. Securing a tenure track position in the department depended on generating research ideas embedded within city living. The fall semester was a time of pulling together that urban project, and yet my time had focused on saving my life and the lives of other VISAs by finding the rapist. During December, I mulled over my predicament, and one logical conclusion arose: My project would be the "culturing of rape." The investigation gave me the connections with relevant people in the city: police, therapists, crises center personnel, district attorneys, private investigators, hospital personnel, and others. The project focused on the reconstruction of the lives of the families and friends of VISAs of stranger rapists. In particular, the project dealt with the ramifications of this violence on those not directly violated in the attack and analyzed how the ramification of the violence upon their lives hindered them and altered the interactions between VISAs and supporters. What was Dr. Sinta's view? In a memo in my file, she wrote: "We discussed her proposed research on rape. I said that it is not an urban project. She agreed." I never agreed.

Before the rape in September, Dr. Sinta had asked me to lead the next summer field school to a Latin American country. This was an opportunity for students to experience anthropology firsthand, to learn the culturing patterns of people from another society, and to apply their classroom ideas to life. For me, it was an additional three months' salary. After the rape, Dr. Sinta could not disqualify me from leading the field school because she had already sent letters about my excellent qualifications to the Director of International Studies and to the government officials and university professionals in that country. She found another method. Although many students intended to apply for the program, there were *no* applications when the March deadline came. I contacted the Director of International Studies: He was furious. Since he handles about forty programs annually and had worked in this particular job for over ten years, he had an idea of the number of applications to expect. Insufficient applications had *never* happened for this particular program, and the complete *lack* of applications locally and nationally was highly suspicious. He contacted Dr. Sinta and accused her of sabotaging the program. Students likewise confirmed our suspicions. Locally, Dr. Sinta informed students not to apply insisting the program would not occur. Nationally, Dr. Sinta strongly discouraged students who called. The director suspected that Dr. Sinta actually threw away applications that were submitted to her.

Dr. Sinta's method of evaluating my work for the fall semester of the attack reconstructed reality. She wrote that my work was barely passable, and I needed help in all areas. She failed to mention the students' excellent teaching evaluations of my work. A full 20 percent of my Introductory Anthropology students signed up as anthropology majors. Forty students did individual research projects on people homeless, bus lifestyles, gay people's response to AIDS, and urban Latin American patterns, among others. I wrote five committee reports and sat on three other committees. I submitted a grant proposal and had a paper accepted. Students wrote comments:

1) Cathy Winkler's anthropology class is the one class at this University that has an atmosphere that is very comfortable for the student. You didn't mind answering questions or responding to a topic. It was the one class that I made sure I came to;
2) Dr. Cathy Winkler has gained the respect of all of us in the class with her strength in carrying out her classroom duties after her harrowing ordeal.

Most important, Dr. Sinta did not mention *it*. She did not mention that I had lived through a severe personal crisis during the semester. There is no university policy on crises. To formalize the category of crisis means that administrations would have to admit to the existence of sexism, racism, homophobia, and other areas of discrimination that impede people's ability to succeed.

As ordered by Dr. Sinta, Vickie informed me that I was not a candidate for either of the two tenure track positions in the department. I asked Dr. Sinta to put in writing the process of selection:

The position you applied for had 23 applicants. Each faculty [4] ranked them and turned into me their top five candidates. From these names, the Executive Committee [3] ranked the top three candidates. Your name was *not* among the initial five candidates ranked by the faculty. This basis for the decisions of each faculty member was *not placed in writing*. Therefore, I cannot speak for them. As with any hiring decision, the candidates are ranked according to their qualifications and needs of the department [emphases not added].

When my contract was over at the end of the year and I had moved to another state, Dr. Sinta continued her harassment long distance. First, she sent a registered letter informing me that I owed $378 to the department for phone calls and photocopying. When I did not respond to that letter, she sent a second registered letter that stated that I owed $623 for phone calls and photocopying. The third letter increased the amount to $789. I sent a letter—with a lawyer's approval—explaining my teaching and research expenses. Copies arrived also at the offices of the president, provost, dean, and teachers' union president. Dr. Sinta's letters stopped, but she sent out one more memo to the faculty members: She personally had to approve all letters of recommendation for me from that department.

When classes ended, Vickie asked to have lunch with me. "Cathy, did you know that Rob did not work this spring?" "What are you talking about?" "He was sick in the fall. Remember?" "Of course, he had a horrible case of the flu." "Well, he asked for paid release time, and he got it." "He got paid for not teaching?" "That's right." "Why didn't he tell me?" "Because he knew your situation. But I thought you should know." "He never comes to the department more than one hour per week, and instead uses his lab as his office. That's why I didn't know. Dr. Sinta did not announce Rob's release time at a department meeting. Isn't that a major issue?" "Yes, Dr. Sinta didn't want you to know." "Why didn't Dr. Sinta offer me time off after the attack?" "She didn't?" "No, she demanded that I return to the job or lose it. She stated that there was no money for a replacement." "Cathy, she did discuss with me about letting you off. I said that it was your choice, that you might want to work, and that work might be a better solution for you." "Vickie, that's all she heard: Cathy should work." "Maybe so. Dr. Sinta does do that."

"Vickie, as long as you're telling me this, tell me what happened about the tenure track position. Did every person vote me down?" "I didn't. You were one of my top candidates. I pointed out in the meeting that we should consider you because of your contributions to the department this year, because of your excellent teaching, and because of what you went through. Dr. Sinta was against that." "What do you mean, exactly, that Dr. Sinta was against it?" "At the beginning of the meeting, she made the announcement that you were not a candidate." "You mean that she explicitly told everyone to exclude me?" "That's it. But I didn't do that." "When did everyone make up their lists?" "Well, we had looked at the vitae previously. Rob and Greg told me that they had planned to put you on their list. But we made up our lists for Dr. Sinta at that meeting." "In other words, everyone gave Dr. Sinta their final list of candidates after Dr. Sinta told the faculty members to exclude me?" "Yes, that's how it happened." My conversation with Vickie was my impetus for filing a sexual discrimination case against the university.

CHAPTER EIGHT
JUDGING CIVIL JUSTICE

N
ausea overwhelmed me as I sat down to write this chapter. My work as an anthropologist is my self, my pride, my focus, my identity. To take away my job because a person raped me is destructive. Dr. Sinta succeeded in inducing nausea that still impedes me from working whenever I reflect on that horrifying period. University administrators stamped their approval on Dr. Sinta's actions, and my colleagues cowered under her tongue.

Institutional discrimination occurs when the policies along with the administrators' patterns of behavior belittle an individual or group of individuals, or create an environment of antagonism. University administrators culture patterns of discrimination into our schools of learning. People who duplicate the hierarchical authority in order to maintain their positions reinforce these negative patterns. When people are inhumane, our logic to explain life becomes uncertain. Humanity is logical; inhumanity is illogical. The combination of humanity and inhumanity in one person is not rational, but it exists.

The rapist demonstrated his hate, and further support for that belligerent behavior comes not only in institutional practices as noted in the previous chapter, but also in our institutions of justice from the affirmative action department in the university to state-level affirmative action to civil courts. Injustice defines our institutions and, I learned, defines the lack of justice.

Affirmative Action

Vickie had given me evidence of Dr. Sinta's discrimination:

1) No time off from work offered while a male colleague received release time for a severe case of flu;

2) Discrediting my application for tenure track job;

3) Verbal debasement at department meetings;

4) Verbal denigration of me to students and colleagues;

5) Lack of department support; and

6) A negative atmosphere.

There were witnesses: Rob, Paula, Steve, and students. To educate myself on the process for filing a case against the university was the next step. People told me that the *process* is the legal issue. A victim of sexual discrimination or harassment who legally follows the steps of the process receives, as so many argued, justice. More importantly, if the case has explicit evidence with strong witnesses, then when the case arrives in civil court, the judge knows that the discriminators had every opportunity to rectify their crime. In this particular state, the process consists of three steps:

1) University Affirmative Action Committee;

2) Either *S*tate *E*mployment *C*ommittee for *A*ffirmative *A*ction *M*anagement (SECAAM), or EEOC. The latter federal organization in this state, like most other states, does not investigate cases. It files them.

3) Civil suit against the university.

Another legal case began in my life to coincide with the criminal case.

On June 6, 1988, nine months after the rape and at the end of that school year, I met with Ms. Castora Spithey. She was the affirmative action director at the university. "Ms. Spithey, I'm Dr. Cathy Winkler. Please call me Cathy." I stretched out my hand to shake hers. She had a warm smile: "How does your office process complaints of sexual discrimination?" "Well, when a person comes in, we discuss the issues." "What happens then?" "Usually, a discussion is sufficient." "Do you file a report?" "Only if requested by the complainant." "How many complainants filed last year?" "Since I've been here for a year, all have been satisfied with the issue after discussion." Her answers revealed her effectiveness: to talk people out of justice. "How many faculty members have had complaints of sexual discrimination or harassment?" "Actually, none have come to this office. I have mostly students." "None?" "Yes, that's right." Job security is a method to keep faculty and staff silent.

"Ms. Spithey, I want to file a sexual discrimination complaint against Dr. Sinta. What is the process?" "Well, you tell me what happened, and then we proceed from there. Isn't she a woman?" "Yes." "How can that be sexual discrimination?" "Well, legally the name of the law is inaccurate. The issue is gender discrimination." "What does the word gender mean?" The director of affirmative action was unfamiliar with the word gender! "Let me explain what happened," and I did. "I have witnesses to verify these points." "Why don't I check on these issues? I'll talk to our lawyer and then get back to you." Two weeks passed and I returned to her office. "I thought I would start off by asking you what you want." "Since Dr. Sinta discriminated against me, I feel the university owes me a year of employment." "You know there are no positions open." "Then they can open a position for me." "That's if you win your appeal." "I want to appeal. What do we do?" "Well, I need a statement from you on what happened. Then I interview you and those involved." "Here's the statement and list of people in the department."

"I'd like to know your method of interviewing." "I'll invite each person in and question him or her on the issues." "What method of questioning do you use?" The method influences the answers. Frustrated, she answered "I'll ask questions over the issues." "Yes, but there are different approaches and formats for questioning. Which one do you use?" Silence. She had no idea that there were different interview methods. Would she use open-ended questions like "Explain what happened" or direct questions like "Did Dr. Sinta make the statement . . . ?" She abruptly stood up: "*I'll* handle this case." My case was dependent upon someone not educated. "Ms. Spithey, can I explain different interviewing approaches to you?" "*I'm THE Director. I'll* take care of it. Good Day." In her file memo, she wrote:

> Dr. Winkler asked me what a person needed to do *to get information out of* the Affirmative Action Office. *She also attempted to tell me how I should conduct the investigation. She proceeded to tell me how to do my investigation.* I explained that I would be in touch with her as soon as I had finished the investigation [emphases not added].

In her memos, Ms. Spithey demonstrated her lack of education: "He did *not* observe *no* interaction between Dr. Winkler and Dr. Sinta." Her memos repeated the same points two, three, four, or more times: "He never saw Dr. Sinta and Dr. Winkler interact with each other." "He never experienced any interaction between Dr. Winkler and Dr. Sinta." "He did not observe interaction between Dr. Winkler and Dr. Sinta." Contradictory points were present: "Dr. Sinta became *more impatient* with Dr. Winkler." And, "In all of his experiences with Dr. Sinta, he thought Dr. Sinta treated Dr. Winkler *fairly in all ways.*"

After some phone calls, I learned about a woman administrator at the university who was also a feminist. She was pleasant but, as I quickly realized during the discussion, a task-oriented person. "Dr. Detolur, let me get to the point. I am pursuing a case of sexual discrimination against Dr. Sinta. The reason I came to you is that I don't understand Ms. Spithey, the director of affirmative action. She doesn't know about interviewing methods and doesn't want to know. She's never heard the word gender. What's going on?" "Ms. Spithey's position is an appointment. Her job depends on the administrators. Because the administrators like her, and not because she has the education, she has that job. She isn't free to act on cases of sexual discrimination because that might make the university look bad. Instead, her job is to stop complainants." "Well, she does a good job. No student has ever filed a case of sexual or racial harassment or discrimination at this university."

"Then, according to the administrators, she does her job. Also, she is one year from retirement. She does not want to thwart her retirement." "She will turn a blind eye to discrimination of any type for that reason?" "Yes, she protects herself and does not care to protect other women or ethnicities. Ms. Spithey is a patriarchal feminist: a person who succeeds by protecting the foundation of patriarchal abuse. These people believe in feminist issues but will not act upon them until, as they say, they are secure. Alas, what is security? When Ms. Spithey gets retirement, she will have economic security, but not positional power. When they are in positions of power, they take no action to build a foundation of support to protect their or others' actions." A fearful feminist controlled my recourse to fairness.

Ms. Spithey's first step was to send me the university guidelines for sexual harassment:

Harassment on the basis of sex is a violation of Sec. 703 of Title VII. Unwelcome sexual advances, requests for sexual favors, and *other verbal or physical conduct of a sexual nature constitute sexual harassment when*
    1) submission to such conduct is made either explicitly or implicitly as a term or condition of an individual's employment,
    2) submission to or rejection of such conduct by an individual is used as the basis for employment decisions affecting such individual, or

3) *such conduct has the purpose or effect of unreasonably interfering with an individual's work performance or creating an intimidating environment* [emphases added].

Ms. Spithey then interviewed each person. The witnesses discussed their results with me. Paula gave Ms. Spithey specific evidence on the multiple times she had heard words of harassment by Dr. Sinta. Mrs. Spithey wrote: "Ms. Doran believes that the problem between the two was a personality clash. Ms. Doran knows that Dr. Winkler will get upset if you don't see things her way." Vickie's interview centered mostly not on the crime but on how horrible rape is. Ms. Spithey had her interpretation: "Dr. Convex believes that sometimes Cathy goes to the extreme. Dr. Convex thinks that the problem with Dr. Winkler was happening before, but the problem just escalated after the rape." Rob stated that Dr. Sinta had told the faculty members to exclude me as a candidate for the tenure track position and had threatened the faculty. Rob admitted that Dr. Sinta's threats worked with him. Ms. Spithey wrote: "In all of his experience with Dr. Sinta, Dr. Bennett thought Dr. Sinta treated Dr. Winkler fairly."

Worried about Ms. Spithey's credibility as the affirmative action director, I contacted Ms. Insiteful, a legal specialist in the area of discrimination. She advised me to ask all informants to write down their version of the interviews. The fact that their versions differed from those recorded by Ms. Spithey was significant in a legal case. One witness responded: "Cathy, I'm sure I'll remember. Don't worry." But if we did not go to trial for five years, which is the usual delay time, would their memories be accurate? I did understand their reason for not wanting to write down the incidents: It is hard to write about hate.

I contacted Ms. Spithey to let her know that Dr. Sinta harassed people involved in the investigation. "Without evidence, I cannot act" was her response. In her memos, she wrote:

> Dr. Convex telephoned after leaving to say that Dr. Sinta did ask her to stop listening to Dr. Winkler. Dr. Sinta told her that she thought talking to Dr. Winkler would probably get her in trouble. It made Vickie feel as though it was a *threat* [emphasis not added].
>
> Dr. Barnett was concerned about the confidentiality of this interview. He said that Dr. Sinta has a history of not treating people fairly and is concerned with her own career only. She has shown insensitivity to other people.

Steve Favor said that Dr. Sinta has a record of harassing, lying, breaking rules. She is vindictive. She harassed him and tried to fire him.

In regard to my phone call, Ms. Spithey wrote: "I told her [Cathy] I could not do anything about the harassment unless the names were revealed." She already had the names and the evidence.

In August, Ms. Spithey rejected the case. What was the evidence? Dr. Convex had pointed out that she "had noticed coldness, hostility, and silence in the office. Hostility seemed to escalate." In regard to time off, Dr. Sinta submitted her own words: "*I decided* that it may be best if [Dr. Winkler] continue to teach" [emphasis added]. On a history of hostility of Dr. Sinta, Steve Favor stressed that "Dr. Sinta had problems with others. She got rid of Dr. Nilan, and she treated Sally Harrison terribly" [past faculty members]. On August 10, 1988, Ms. Spithey's letter concluded:

> In examining the documentation presented and through personal interviews, we have found no evidence to support your allegation of "Gender Harassment" nor any evidence of sexual harassment or discrimination on the basis of sex. Therefore, the charge is hereby dismissed.

The State Appeal

The next step in the process was the state office. Before going through that process with SECAAM, I wanted assurance of fairness. "I've heard that the EEOC in this state rejects all complainants who file discrimination and before I put myself through this ordeal with SECAAM, I would like to know the success rate of cases that appeal to you. Let me explain my situation of discrimination." And I did. Ms. Stephenson responded: "Well, you have a good case, and we do a great job for the victim. I think it will definitely be worth your while to apply. The investigation only takes ninety days from the submission of your application." Three weeks after the university affirmative action case, I filled out an "Intake Questionnaire." This form provides only four lines for answers to very complex questions. "1) What action has been taken against you? 2) What reason(s) was (were) given for the action which was taken against you? 3) In what ways were you treated differently than others?"

The questions focused on information pertaining to the person, not group, discriminated against. Specifically, question #3 states "differently than others." On September 19, 1988, three weeks later, SECAAM wrote: "In order for the investigation to proceed, you must contact us within *five days* of your receipt of this letter to discuss your charge with the assigned compliance office." SECAAM demanded a quick response despite the fact that I had to simultaneously deal with the upcoming criminal trial of the rapist, a trial that was to start any day.

One week later I met with Harriet Borrows. It was a great pleasure and enhanced my spirits. She showed dedication, caring, and understanding, and focused on the issues of justice. I began by explaining in detail the discrimination. She listened intently and asked astute questions. She showed concern. Then came the question: "Who else in the department has suffered this situation?" "Ms. Borrows, why do you ask that question? I'm here for myself." "Cathy, the federal laws state that discrimination is against a group of people; otherwise, it is not discrimination. Action against an individual is not against the law." "What are you saying? You expect the other women in the department to go out and get raped to prove that same type of sexual discrimination? I think that's unfair." "That's the law." And I rushed out of the room, shocked and on the verge of tears. How could my case be a group case? She followed me.

"Ms. Borrows, you asked for other women to get raped for me to get justice." "I guess I was insensitive, but the law specifies group." "Ms. Stephenson said nothing about this when I called, and it is not on the form. The questions focused on me, the individual, and nothing about group discrimination." Ms. Borrows did interview the witnesses. Vickie and Ms. Borrows spent the interview redesigning a world without discrimination, and not discussing pertinent issues. Vickie offered no evidence. Paula made sure that Ms. Borrows had the evidence against Dr. Sinta.

At the end of November, the due date for the decision on the case arrived and I called. "No, it will take longer to determine." I moved to another state for a job. "No, it will take longer." It was now six months. "No, it will take longer." I gave up calling. The waiting period increased my anger, anger about the misinformation, anger for the false expectations, anger for the ridiculous, dysfunctional interviews, anger for wasting my time, anger for waiting. Finally at the end of May, almost nine months later, "Cathy, we find no cause or evidence of discrimination." My built-up anger exploded: "Ms. Borrows, you are a woman. A Black woman. You suffer a double discrimination every single day of your life. You live with the threat of rape like all women. How could you conduct those interviews in such an unprofessional manner? Of course, your conclusion is against me. You didn't even do an investigation. You didn't even ask people questions. You fantasized about the world instead of confronting the world. You put me through hell." When I ended my ranting, she said quietly: "Do you have any other questions?" I regretted screaming and terrorizing that woman. She was wrong, but I was wrong to deliver my comments in such a forceful, nonstop torrent of pain: That was unjust. Soon after, she quit her job.

Harriet Borrows' official record of the conversation was in a memo:

> The compliance officer [Harriet Borrows] informed the Charging Party [Cathy Winkler] that a predetermination of no cause was being recommended in the case. The compliance officer indicated that testimony and evidence did not support her allegations of sex discrimination. The Charging Party stated that she was not surprised about the outcome because the compliance officer was biased from the onset of the investigation, and she had been told how the compliance officer questioned the witnesses. The compliance officer did not attempt to defend herself. Instead, the compliance officer was silent while the Charging Party further explained how she felt about SECAAM.

This is the only writing by Harriet Borrows in the two-inch file. There was no information on the interviews. SECAAM sent their own letter:

> Careful examination of the evidence indicates that there is no reasonable cause to believe that a violation of Fair Employment Practices Act of 1978, so amended, has occurred. Consequently, in accordance with that act, the charge is hereby dismissed. Timeliness and all jurisdictional requirements have been met. The Charging Party may apply to the administrator for reconsideration of this order of dismissal.

At the same time I received this letter, my mother called to say that my brother was near death. Instead of appealing, I flew across the country.

When I called to request my file from SECAAM, Mr. Bullach told me that I had to sign a form not to use this material publicly. All material was confidential. I made another call to Ms. Insiteful, my free-advice lawyer, who called SECAAM. "Cathy, besides signing your name, also add that you do not agree with the above statement." Mr. Bullach was cordial and indirectly inquisitive: "Were you satisfied with the outcome?" "No!" "You could put that in writing. It would have an impact." How much more could people ask of me: Reform the department and reform all the institutions that support Dr. Sinta's discriminatory behavior along with stopping the rapist and caring for my dying brother?

The Civil Suit

For this case, I contacted Ms. Insiteful again. She told me, "Cathy, I've checked and I want to tell you up-front the case doesn't look good. While this doesn't mean we won't consider the case, I want you to know initially the barriers." Finally! Someone who is honest! "I did some checking on Dr. Sinta around the university. She is a person who discriminates against every single person with whom she comes in contact. Everyone hates her." "That's good for our case, isn't it?" "No, not really. She treats everyone equally the same—rotten. Discrimination means differential treatment. Dr. Sinta isn't nice to anyone. Next, sexual discrimination cases are usually a man against a woman. This case is unique in that regard." "But the law would still allow it?" "Yes, I believe so, but it is a rare case and would have to change people's thinking about discrimination." "What else? By your voice, I know there is more." "Rape is a difficult subject. The rape was off-campus, people were traumatized, and this would muddle the case." "The muddling was the discrimination." "I know. The other point is that the U.S. Supreme Court has not been favorable to cases anyway similar to this. Therefore, I have my doubts."

Nevertheless, I knew that I had to pursue the civil case.

SETTING: U.S. CIVIL COURT, CASE #619543

Plaintiff: Dr. Cathy Winkler (Dr. W) with attorney Ms. Insiteful (MI)

Defendants: Dr. Sinta (Dr. S), the university with attorney Mr. Badger (MB)

Charge: Sexual Discrimination and Harassment

MI: Dr. Sinta, did you offer Dr. Winkler a paid leave of absence after a rapist attacked her?

Dr. S: Yes, on the second day after the attack, I offered her the rest of the semester off with pay.

MI: Did you use those exact words?

Dr. S: Perhaps not exactly, but I did ask her what was her decision about work. She was quite clear that she wanted to work, and that work would be therapeutic for her.

MI: Did she state that she thought work would be therapeutic?

Dr. S: No, but she said she wanted to return to work. She spoke competently.

MI: Dr. Sinta, isn't it unusual for any person, whether or not they are traumatized, to refuse a three-month paid leave of absence? Wouldn't you take such an offer?

Dr. S: Yes, I would, but Dr. Winkler wanted to work.

MI: Isn't it true, Dr. Sinta, that, when Dr. Winkler returned to work, the bruises on her face shocked you?

Dr. S: Yes, what a surprise! She had not told me!

MI: How healthy is a person who forgets to mention to her boss that bruises cover most of her face and body? Isn't it unfair to ask a person with an extensively bruised face to stand up in front of a group of students and speak?

Dr. S: For some people, this is therapeutic, and Dr. Winkler wanted to talk about the rape. She was obsessed with telling everyone that she was raped.

MI: Dr. Sinta, you use the word "obsessed." I take this word to mean a behavior not normal. But didn't you just say that Dr. Winkler was competent to make the decision about returning to work? Now you state that she acted in an obsessive way.

Dr. S: It was Dr. Winkler's decision to return. How was I to know that she had emotional problems?

MI: Dr. Sinta, are you aware of the feminist literature that states that rape victim-survivors have emotional problems after the rape?

Dr. S: Many do.

MI: Why should you think that Dr. Winkler was different?

Dr. S: She's a specialist in feminist issues. She should know how to handle herself.

MI: Are you stating, Dr. Sinta, that a researcher of trauma is free of its traumatic effects?

Dr. S: No, but she should have told me if she didn't want to come back to work.

MI: Let me get this clear, Dr. Sinta. You expected Dr. Winkler, even though she had just suffered a severe trauma of multiple rapes, an extensive beating, forced sodomy, and robbery—a three and a half hour ordeal followed by thirteen hours at the hospital and with the police—to be able to make a decision the second day after this vicious attack in regard to her return to work?

Dr. S: Everybody has different ways of dealing with rape.

MI: If you thought that Dr. Winkler acted inappropriately, did you suggest again that she take a paid leave of absence?

Dr. S: If she wanted it, she knew that she could take it.

MI: Dr. Sinta, the day you offered her a paid leave of absence and she rejected it, you also informed her that if she changed her mind later, she could take the paid leave of absence?

Dr. S: No, but once it's offered, she knew that the option was available.

MI: In Dr. Winkler's statement, you said: "Your rape is destroying the department, and your rape is causing havoc in the department." Did you make these statements?

Dr. S: Absolutely not.

MI: Isn't it odd, Dr. Sinta, that Dr. Winkler's memory of your statements matches the memories of the rest of the members of the department!

MB: Objection.

MI: Moving on to the next point, your Honor. All the members of the department have stated in depositions that you disqualified Dr. Winkler as a candidate for the tenure track position. Do you agree with that?

Dr. S: No. Faculty members are jealous of me and are in league against me. Who are you to believe, unpublished teachers, or myself, an administrator and well published?

MI: Dr. Sinta, do you control the budget and make decisions over the faculty?

Dr. S: Of course, an administrator decides fairly the allocation of the budget.

MI: Isn't this allocation of funds, which faculty members desperately need to advance their careers, a control you hold over each member of the department? Couldn't this influence faculty members' vote?

Dr. S: No, everyone votes independently. I have no control over the faculty.

MI: Thank you, Dr. Sinta.

MB: Dr. Sinta, didn't you offer Dr. Winkler every opportunity to take time off and deal with her emotional trauma?

Dr. S: Yes, I immediately offered her a leave of absence.

MB: Isn't it then Dr. Winkler's responsibility to let you know that she is not capable of making decisions at that time?

Dr. S: Yes, absolutely.

Summation:

MB: Jury members, rape is a horrible crime. None of us disagree with this nor do any of us doubt that a rapist brutally and horribly raped her the night of September 29, 1987. No person should have to suffer rape. Dr. Sinta tried to help Dr. Winkler. She offered her a leave of absence; she offered her counseling; she told her that she would do anything that would help her out. Dr. Winkler, unable to find the rapist, unleashed her anger against my client. Dr. Winkler was full of frustration and anger. She had every right to have anger against the rapist, but, unfortunately for my client, she redirected her anger toward her. Her evidence against my client is weak at best. Since Dr. Winkler didn't get the tenure track job, she blames Dr. Sinta. She wasn't qualified. We know that raped women act in a traumatic and unpredictable way after the rape. My client wishes she could have done more.

MI: Dr. Sinta selected an excellent defense attorney: One who, like her client, blames the person raped. Dr. Sinta called my client obsessive, and Mr. Badger describes my client as unpredictable. Let's review Dr. Winkler's credentials for that semester, a record that speaks for itself: Excellent teaching, presentation and publication of professional papers, and extensive praise from her students and colleagues. This high performance demonstrates her credibility as a witness, an excellent witness under stress, but we must remember, despite what the defense attorney has said, that Dr. Sinta and the university's administration are the ones on trial.

The issue at hand is Dr. Sinta's reactions. Dr. Sinta, as she has stated, is a professional. Wouldn't a professional put in writing any alteration of a contractual agreement? Dr. Sinta admits that she did not tell Dr. Winkler that she had several weeks to make up her mind regarding a leave of absence. As Dr. Sinta stated, Dr. Winkler knew this without words. If that point is true, maybe Dr. Sinta's offer of a paid leave of absence was also one made without words. Further, Dr. Sinta had absolute control over the budget. Did Dr. Sinta make sexually harassing statements to Dr. Winkler after the rape? Dr. Sinta says she did not. Yet, six people testified about Dr. Sinta's harsh words against Dr. Winkler: "Your rape is causing havoc in this department."

Jury members, the defense lawyer believes that a person raped cannot control herself and cannot act appropriately. I argue that Dr. Winkler did suffer trauma and shock not only from the rape attack but also from Dr. Sinta's sexual discrimination and harassment. Performance of her job appropriately does not mean that she did not suffer. Her suffering was private. The central point is Dr. Sinta's conduct and inability to act professionally and honestly with Dr. Winkler. Let Dr. Winkler end her suffering. Decide in her favor so she knows that people can believe the words of a person raped.

Decision:
After twelve hours, the jury returned and read the verdict: Guilty. They made an award of $2 million against the university to make institutions aware of injustices against others victimized. While Dr. Sinta received the humiliation of a guilty verdict, the university's insurance company—not Dr. Sinta or the university—paid the $2 million and my lawyer's fees. After deducting a two-week vacation, I disbursed the money among the

rape crises centers in the state. Each of the ten centers received almost $200,000, which paid low salaries for only a few employees and some overhead costs for one year. This amount was little to help the extensive number of VISAs.

Truth:

There was no legal case filed against Dr. Sinta or the university. Since the journey for justice in a legal case against institutions is long, expensive, and unlikely to succeed, this fantasy script will have to suffice in making justice a reality. I decided against pursuing the civil action against the university, not out of lack of desire but because I had to deal with the legal case against the rapist, annual job moves, and my brother's dying. I had reached my limit of pain.

Part III

RAPED A THIRD TIME, LEGAL RAPE

Law is a status game, a game that deletes justice. DAs, defense attorneys, judges, and scientists work to maintain their privileged positions. What do these men have to worry about! Rapists rape women, not male DAs, not male scientists, and not male judges. (Winkler, journal)

Legal justice is our formal recognition of fairness in evaluation of crimes, in treatment of torturers, and in respect for VISAs. Criminals, with a right to a lawyer and legal protection, receive a justice denied to VISAs, who are only the witnesses and sufferers of torture. Because judges, DAs, and defense attorneys mute and distort the voices of VISAs, where is a VISA's legal protection and legal rights? Isn't justice for all people?

After the physical rape, a VISA looks to the DA for protection and justice. Instead, protection and justice are for the defendant. The legal process then in the DA's words "We might go to trial" become for the VISA "relive the rape." The DA's words "prepare for trial" mean "be in that state of rape." Announcement of a trial date means "Live with the rapist's terror." Our justice for VISAs is a trialing of horror that is ever present. If there is any justice, it is slow to torturous. This is what I learned.

CHAPTER NINE
LOOKING FOR JUSTICE

A Fairy Tale

Once upon a time, there was a girl named Little Red Riding Hood. While she was walking through the forested hood with a basket of food for her grandmother, the Big Bad Wolf raped her. She didn't live happily ever after.

"Are you Kate Clark, the activist detective?" "Yes, how can we work together?" Kate, who was pleasant and respectful, listened attentively with a relaxed posture and comfortable pose. Kate believed Red and treated her as a professional. "A big bad wolf raped me. The forest—a haven of beauty—hides and protects all types of wolves, but I want to find that wolf." "We'll find him." Kate outlined her plan of investigation. She would 1) Provide Personal Protection: Kate would move into Red's life and carefully watch over her. If the wolf attacked again, Kate would catch him. 2) Scrutinize the Neighborhood: Red would continue her daily routine with security on watch. 3) Use a Tape Recorder: A voice-activated, soundless tape recorder on Red would document the evidence. Meeting a rapist the first time after the attack is his vulnerable moment. Unsuspectingly, he might—thinking no one is around—admit his crimes. 4) Duplicate the MO: Because the rapist targets new people in the neighborhood, Kate would set herself up like a young, look-alive "Red" but with karate expertise. She too would walk with a basket through the forested hood and present a demure persona. 5) Use Video Cameras: Video cameras, disguised as flowers and squirrels, would decorate the woods. The rapist's next deadly deed would not go unwitnessed. Trying to attack Red again, the rapist got caught in one of Kate's traps.

From the moment Red arrived at the police tree house, investigative questions protected the rapist-wolf: Why did she talk to the wolf? Why did she stay so long behind the bush with the wolf? Why, despite the fact that he beat her up, did she not even try, beyond the point of mutilation and perhaps death, to get away? Why did she stop trying: did she place her life above that of freeing herself from the rape by the wolf? She must have wanted it. Why didn't she see the path in the woods on which the wolf ran away? Why did she walk in that part of the woods? Why couldn't she run after the wolf? Why couldn't she run as fast as the wolf? Why did she let the wolf enjoy himself with her?

"Follow the system," friends advised Red. Other professionals emphasized: "Just give the system a chance, and it will work for you." "It will be just. It's a slow and tedious process," reiterated the tree house police detective, "but it will work." "Our legal rules," stated the forest DA, "are to protect everyone, but our goal is to get the criminal." "Justice will win out" was their common refrain. "Let me be optimistic," spoke up Kate. "Let us believe that the lawyers work for justice, no 'errors' occur, and a jury of *his* peers convicts the rapist-wolf. Have you really won? The case will take one year to go to trial, and the judge sentences him to one year in jail, time already served. The convicted wolf walks out of the courtroom with you, Red. OK, let's try to be even more optimistic and the judge sentences the wolf to twenty years. In some regions in the forest with overcrowded jail trees, a twenty-year sentence equals twenty months in jail. In others parts of the woods, the wolf can get off early for good behavior. His good behavior in jail outweighs his bad behavior with you."

"Red, these are the procedures of justice. You will lose at least a year in your life working for those values, a year that will test your friends, your job status, your ability to endure as a whole person not wrecked by the antagonism of THAT group of legal people. But, remember that your work for justice is a lost cause. I want to be completely honest with you, Red. Using probability figures—a common practice for life insurance companies, the wolf—even with conviction—will know freedom soon. While the legal rights of the wolf are meticulously respected, no one tells you about your rights to justice, or that you even have rights to justice, or that you have the legal right to protection. During the whole process of catching and convicting the rapist, errors—or what are called 'errors'—make everyone act as if they are walking on eggshells, and not one eggshell can be cracked. If so, the rapist wins—AGAIN. Justice doesn't work, Red."

"Should we play fair?" asked Red. "Why should I believe in lawyers and judges who take away VISAs' rights and don't protect people raped? Why should I put faith into a group of people who subjugate me? Why should I work for values that in the end lawyers and judges fail to support? The disease—legal idiotology—that causes our pain, we must obliterate in order to stop wolves. What is an alternative? The wolf is in jail now awaiting trial. He is safe, barricaded from me. What can I do?" "Red, you could hire a killer, but would a killer really object to a wolf? Or would he murder him and then turn you in for murder while he goes free? We call this type of justice—plea bargaining." "Kate, if I am to live in this society, we have to have justice. I know women raped who have left the forest forever to live in a woods on another continent where peace does exist. If the legal people in these woods will not exact justice, then I must find a way to have the justice enacted against the wolf myself. We must stop the wolf before he hurts another person."

The trial occurred. Red testified. After the jury left to deliberate, Red went into the bathroom stall. There in her purse was what appeared to be a curling iron, but was a cleverly designed gun. She put it together and loaded it. She returned to the courtroom. The judge asked for the jury's verdict. When the foreperson stood up, so did Red: "There is but one justice for a wolf." She cocked the curling iron gun and pulled the trigger until she had emptied the bullets into his body. The wolf died on the spot. "Justice for all!" Due to Red's temporary insanity, her lawyer got her case dismissed.

"Red, that was a great fantasy," said Cinderella. "How clever! I had a fantasy too. I poisoned Prince Charming. While he gave a speech at one of the top universities in the forest, he died on his words." Each person in the VISA group laughed hysterically for hours at their creative means of justice. With smiles on their faces and tears in their eyes, they hugged each other, promising to continue to work for justice in all forms: fiction, nonfiction, and fantasy.

The Red Riding Hood fantasy was another strategy to prepare myself against the legal labyrinth that had to be navigated to imprison the rapist. Like the physical rape and the second assault, this "third rape" tested my spirit to the limit. Nothing in the fairy tale was nearly as fantastic to believe as the real events in trying to get the rapist convicted. The writing for the next two chapters occurred at two different time periods. The updates on personal and legal issues to my friends were a means to maintain and educate my support community. I sent out 125 to 150 letters every 3 to 4 months. I wrote the rest of each chapter shortly after the events occurred.

Meeting the Prosecuting Team

In May 1988, Det. Roth called and announced first, the positive results of the DNA Fingerprinting evidence; second, the trial as the state's test case; and third, future media coverage. On Friday, June 3, 1988, across from Assistant District Attorney Stan Rest and District Attorney (DA) Bill Will Sr., I sat alone. The rape survivor advocate had a baby and did not want to return to her job. They had not replaced her. "Hello, Miss Winkler. Bill Sr. can only stay a moment." Stan was then, and as always, a gentleman. He had a relaxed manner and an approach that centered—in a nonintrusive way—on the person with whom he was talking: "Did you have any trouble finding this office?" "No, your directions were clear. There is a problem if people couldn't easily find this office." Stan laughed. "Well," he added carefully and meticulously the next sentences: "We are going to work *with* and *for you*. I want you to know that we have *your* best interest at heart." The way he punctuated and accented those words, while giving me cautious but sincere eye contact, made me suspicious. Someone's description of me was negative.

Bill Sr., who could never remain silent and unnoticed for long, piped up: "Cathy, I'm going to have to go soon. But I want you to know that we place high priority on *your* case." They loved to use the word "your" case, when it was really Kenneth Redding's case; it was *his* case. He was the rapist. "Both Stan and myself will handle this case. You've got the two best lawyers in this office. I'll take you through a practice run before I question you on the stand, but Stan will handle most of the rest of the issues." Bill Sr. wanted the status position: interviewing the poor victim. "If you have any questions, please feel free to call us. Stan, how does the case look?" "Judge Ekele approved the search warrant." "There should be no problems there."

"We need to figure out what crimes he committed. Cathy, you have a degree, don't you?" "My doctorate is in anthropology." "This police statement has a few errors. It doesn't seem to reflect the way you speak. Oh well, those errors don't make any difference. What crimes did Redding commit against you?" "I'm not a lawyer, but isn't it against the law that he broke *in*, beat me up, raped me a number of times? He just kept raping me. And he kidnapped me." "First, for kidnapping, he has to transport you from one place to another." "He held me against my will, and I couldn't leave." "Well, we've got him on breaking-and-entering. That's clear. Physical assault, that's two. Rape, that's three. With the evidence, no one will question if a rape occurred. Everyone knows someone raped you. What else did he do to you?" "Is it against the law that he forced me to lick his penis and he almost put his penis in my anus?" "The first is sodomy. Did he insert his penis all the way into your anus? I'm sorry about these questions." "No." "Then we can't put that down."

"You have only one rape! He raped me more than once. If rape is the forced entry of the penis into the vagina, then he raped me hundreds of times. There were definitely two periods of raping. Between them, he put on his clothes." "Did he rape you in different rooms?" "No, but the rapes were not the same. Not only was he in different positions on the bed, his behavior was different. In the first period, he kept pinching my breasts, and in the second rape, he salivated on my genital area." "We can add two counts of rape and sodomy." "Did he threaten you with a gun?" "Yes, he threatened me, but not with a gun, with his fists." "Didn't he rob you?" "Well, yes, but he only took $2 and some subway tokens. That's all the money I had." "If you had had $500, would he have taken it?" "Oh, yes, and he might not have raped me a second time. With money, he'd be too eager to spend it on drugs." "Well, we've got him on robbery. Let's see. We've got nine counts. That would put him away for a long time."

"By the way, Cathy, I can't believe you can't identify him. Your artist composite is an identical match. It's incredibly accurate." "I don't see the similarity between the composite and Redding." "This is really surprising. It's one of the best artist composites I've ever seen." Bill Sr. chimed in: "Since everything seems together, when should we go to the grand jury for an indictment, then the arraignment, and trial?" "We need time to visit the lab to learn about DNA. So we want to put the grand jury off as long as possible. If we go to the grand jury on June 30, and you don't need to be there Miss Winkler [not "Dr."], then we can arrange for the arraignment in August, and the trial in October." "Good. We've got everything together. I've got another meeting. Nice meeting you, Miss Winkler. I'm sure after the trial we can meet on better grounds." He shook my hand, grabbed a toothbrush out of his top drawer, and left.

"There's just one point I need to let you know. As Roth told you, this trial will get news coverage. But I don't think there will be anything on it for awhile. Your name won't be mentioned." "You can use my name." "It's better not to. Do you have any questions?" "I was wondering who is Redding's lawyer. He doesn't have any money. It isn't that I care who his lawyer is, but he should at least have reasonable defense." "Yes, I understand what you mean. Marble is a private lawyer who has his case." "How could Redding hire a lawyer?" "This guy wants the case for the publicity. Redding's mother put her house up for collateral, but it is not worth that much to Marble." "What's he like?" "Well, I've tried several cases against him and won. He does prepare, but juries don't like him. That's where I succeed."

"Stan, I don't want to plea bargain in this case. I'll go the distance to stop Redding. I don't want him to get off with a short jail sentence. He's raped too many women." "OK." "Stan, when can Redding be tested for AIDS? If he has AIDS and refused to use a condom, he attempted to murder me." "He can't be tested unless he is convicted." "When he's convicted, will you have him tested?" "We'll cross that road when we come to it." He didn't answer the question. "Can I watch you in a rape trial?" "Sure, there's one I'm trying next month. It's a tough case. She knew him; they were coworkers. There are some other problems like drugs and her interest in him. This is a good case because Judge Foible, the same judge assigned to Redding's case, will preside." "Great. Call and let me know the date."

When I got home, "Hey, Roth, this is Cathy Winkler." "Great to hear from you." "Did you describe me to Stan?" "Well, yes, he asked." "Could you tell me what you said?" "Oh, only good things." "Would you, please, repeat those good words to me?" Roth felt cornered but answered: "Intelligent, humorous, a good person, pushy. . ." "Roth, women are the only ones who are described as 'pushy,' not men. Could you do me a favor and the next time, use the word 'persistent'?"

The next day I said to Stan, "I saw the article in the newspaper. Everyone got a kick out of your comment about the impossibility of explaining how a man's semen got into the victim." He laughed. "Yeah, yeah. But that is the issue. You know, Cathy, I didn't realize they would run it so soon." "Didn't you have any idea?" "Well, I gave them the information but they usually run it when they have extra space or need a filler." "I was wondering why you hadn't notified me. Could you do me a favor? I don't mind the news coverage, and I know that it's important for the case and to educate other VISAs, but could you notify me next time? It did upset me a little when my friends started calling me about it." And I had another question: "Stan, can I go to the arraignment? Since I'm not identifying Redding, I want to see him and find out how I react." "You don't have to go, but it's all right. I'll let you know the date."

June 6, 1988: The news coverage has begun. Reading the article is like walking through a fog: in one respect the case centers around what happened to me, but on the other hand, there is no mention of my name— thank goodness—prior to the trial. Because the grand jury had not yet indicted the rapist, the newspaper did not publish his name or information of his present jail sentence. As far as I'm concerned, no rapist should have a human name.

Get out your eraser because as usual I'm moving again. I'll be sharing a house for the summer and fall with a third-year med student in a nice quiet neighborhood. Since my roommate works at the hospital most of the time, I'll have the house to myself in order to work and write. Most importantly, I can keep both of my dogs—laid-back Logan and snuggly Sneakers. Also, I have a replacement job from January through June of 1989—ANOTHER address change! For that time period, please send my mail to the university. Remember: write all addresses down in pencil. I'm on the move. That's migrant work. Moving minimizes materialism. My academic books are the real problem: I need to design book shelves/ moving boxes. The decorative and look-alike wood bookcase shelves that can transform into packing boxes. The difficulty is that wood is too heavy, and plastic is not environmentally friendly. If I have trouble next year getting a job, maybe I should try to market my "bookcase/moving box" idea. Keep in touch. All support is helpful.

On June 30, 1988, Stan informed me that there might be another news article the following day and that the grand jury indicted Redding. Here is what the jury found:

Kenneth Charles Redding
1) Did have carnal knowledge of Cathy Winkler, a female, forcibly and against her will
2) Did perform a sexual act by placing his mouth on the sex organ of Cathy Winkler, with force and against the will of the said Cathy Winkler
3) Did perform a sexual act by inserting his sex organ into the mouth of Cathy Winkler, with force and against the will of the said Cathy Winkler
4) With intent to commit theft, did take from the person and immediate presence of Cathy Winkler, by intimidation, by the use of coercion, the following property, two dollars in money
5) Did make an assault upon the person of Cathy Winkler, by attempting to commit a violent injury to said person, and did beat said person, with his fist, which, when used offensively against said person, was likely to and actually did result in serious bodily injury
6) Without authority and with intent to commit a felony, to-wit
7) Rape, therein, did enter the dwelling house of Cathy Winkler, located at 666 West Willow Drive.

Another Rape Trial

Two other people, besides the judge, jury, lawyers, defendant, and myself, were at the rape trial that Stan prosecuted: a female legal intern and a friend of the defendant. When the woman raped was on the stand, her horror was clear to me. She held her hands tightly, and her facial muscles were taut. Her whole body was rigid like an emotional bomb ready to explode. I understood the need to hold back and prevent the explosion: the gut-wrenching screams and the waterfalls of tears would scare the calmest observer. That was one of the reasons I hid my emotions, and I suspected that she had a similar reason. Nevertheless, she was articulate and clear with only a slight nervousness in her voice. The defendant called her at the end of her shift and came by to see her. She got in his car to sit and talk. He took his belt and tied her hands behind her: bruises from the belt marked her wrists. In the struggle, he broke her light blue hair band. Of interest is that most of the hair band, except several small pieces lost under the passenger seat, were not in the car.

The woman lawyer intern commented: "She's lying." "Why do you think that?" "If he raped her, she would cry." "What about the other evidence?" "She didn't cry. She wanted sex and lied about all the rest." This woman, a future lawyer, refused to believe the evidence. "You should know the suffering of a rape. Then you would know the truth." "That's a horrible thing to say." "You're right. That is horrible what I said, but what you said is just as horrible. You believe neither the word of that woman nor the massive amount of evidence. Perhaps your words are more horrifying because as a lawyer you will put into practice this disbelief of people raped. Is this how you will conduct your business?" She left.

The friend of the defendant testified. His testimony was secondary information revealing that the woman had called the defendant and had sexual interest in him. After testifying, the friend of the defendant asked me: "Do you know the woman?" "I don't know any of the witnesses. I wanted to observe a rape case." "I can't believe that woman has railroaded my friend. He's spent ten months in jail because of this. I'm his only friend. I've tried to visit him every month. I even brought him clothes for the trial. I want to know what you think. You don't know anyone in this case." "If it was sexual, why were her wrists marked up? Why did she have bruises on her face? Why did he try to get rid of the headband if he innocently broke it during sexual play? Why did the police detective, who has seen hundreds of victims, and her friend point out how she was in a state of shock and trauma after having 'good' sex? He's guilty. I'm glad he has a friend like you, but your friend is a rapist." A shocked look of realization came over his face, "I see what you mean." He headed for the bathroom. Every ten minutes he rushed out. He left pale and returned wiping his mouth. How hard it must be to accept that your best friend tortured a woman, and then your best friend lied and used you to try to cover up his rape. The jury returned with a guilty verdict.

"Stan, congratulations. How was your visit to the lab?" "Great, it's incredible what they can do!" "This case is an education." "You bet." "If a jury convicts a rapist on DNA, and after he serves his term, moves to another state to rape, the other state could catch him by his DNA, right?" "I never thought of that, but not necessarily. Every lab has its own method of analyzing DNA. They are not comparable." "That's terrible. The FBI should regulate that." Silence. Six months later, I read an article on that. The FBI plans to regulate all DNA testing for uniformity from state to state.

The Arraignment

The day for the arraignment arrived. Face-to-face confrontation can bring out trauma, and preparedness was my goal. With Cassandra and my friend Estar on either side, we waited in the hallway in front of the elevator outside the courtroom. The three of us had comparable features: short blonde hair, light complexion, and similar height and weight. There were about thirty other people. Would I recognize Kenny and would he react to me? At most arraignments, VISAs are not present because they are the ones identifying the defendant as the rapist. Defense attorneys would argue that prior contact prejudices the VISA's testimony. But, in this case, I could not identify the rapist. I was not even sure I could recognize him after seeing his picture many times. Redding expected my absence. Surprise was on my side.

August 27, 1988: On August 12, Kenneth Charles Redding came up handcuffed with twelve others in identical blue cotton garb. All had the same letters on the back of their shirts, like a football team. The elevator doors opened, and the fifth man caught my attention for two reasons: first, he vaguely resembled the traits of Redding, and second, he looked directly at me with a sense of surprise. He did not look at either woman on my left or right side. He kept his eyes focused only on me. I turned to Cassandra and said I think it's the fifth man. "Yes, that's what I thought. He looks just like the artist composite." She could visualize the match while my mind still protected me. Why? Before the "rapist" (and this is his appropriate title: he's earned it) left the courtroom, I again positioned myself at the elevator to see his face. This time it was worth it. He was angry, and that was a look that gave me satisfaction.

I was alone watching him. Right before the elevators closed on Redding, with the security guards standing behind him, he whispered the words of the rapist: "I told you I would get you for this." These were words that only I and the rapist knew. These were words that I had not put in print. These were words that I had not repeated to the DA. Only two people knew the exact words, and one of those two people just spoke the words to me from the still-open elevator. At that moment, anonymity disappeared from the rapist's voice. While Redding had admitted to me during the attack that he was a rapist, rapists and incestors admit their guilt only once to the VISA, and that is when no one is around. That was Redding's one and only time. He, like others, goes into a terminal silence about his crimes. Redding's voice now validated that he was the rapist. I knew the voice now, and yet the trauma continued to protect my visual memory.

Then began the waiting. I became dysfunctional. Menial tasks were manageable, but writing articles on my research from Mexico was impossible. Originality and creativity did not exist. Remembering the details of the rape was necessary in order to be prepared for the grilling by the defense attorney, but each moment of horror made me feel insane. What if the insanity of those horrors mixes up the details and chronology of the acts of torture? I couldn't write professionally nor could I run away from the fear of not remembering. My remedy was to write down the details of the attack. The result was chapter 1 of this book.

Cassandra read it. I was proud. "What do you think, Cassandra?" "Well, you know this does *not* sound like rape." "I put down the details. The next writer will have to figure out how to go beyond this." "You are too much in control. It doesn't demonstrate the trauma and shock. You lead the reader to believe that you knew everything that was going on." "I did. I did have some control. But you're right: I don't know how to demonstrate the terror and shock. How does a writer who controls words present rape without control? Besides, I wasn't a dysfunctional nincompoop. I knew that he raped me; I understood his intentions throughout the night. Maybe the words I put down demonstrate too much control, but VISAs do have control; they can control their minds." Cassandra turned her back on me and walked away. Recognizing a VISA's control in an uncontrollable situation is a significant step toward survival and activism.

The DAs called me in for a meeting. I sat alone on the couch. Bill Sr. and Stan leaned toward me and paid close attention to each word. "Cathy, we are a little concerned with the search warrant." "What's wrong?" "Let's review a few points. You know that you saw Redding on the street in front of the 7-Eleven store. What did you say to Det. Doil?" "As Redding walked away, I said 'That's not the man.' " Bill Sr. and Stan sat back with a mild but disgruntled reaction. "When he was maybe twenty feet away, I said to Det. Doil: 'Remember that body, that head size. That's exactly the body shape, height, and head that we are looking for.' " "Did you say anything else?" "No." "Are you sure those are your exact words?" "Yes. What's the problem?" "Det. Roth wrote in his notes that you could not identity Redding when you were with Det. Doil, but he didn't add those last lines." "I know I said them." "That might help us. In the search warrant, Det. Roth did not even mention them." "Could I see the search warrant?" He passed it to me. "This isn't it. This doesn't match how I described him."

"Let's discuss another point. Tell us about the scar." I described it. "We need to know exactly where it was." He then stood up in front of me. "You can show on my body the location of the scar." Next, Bill Sr. quickly stood up in front of me: "Why don't you show its location on my body?" Both of these men wanted me to put my hand on their groin area. At the same time that I had a case of sexual harassment and discrimination under review with SECAAM, this pattern of negative treatment continued in another context. There were no witnesses. Here were two men that I desperately needed on my side to stop the rapist. While the location of the scar was critical information, their method—not a picture or drawing to point to—was unacceptable. They knew—by memory—the laws against sexual harassment. *I have to placate these men. I do not want to touch their groins, I do not want to duplicate actions that would remind me of the rape attack or the rapist, and I do not want to pick which man would receive an unwanted touch from me. There had to be a strategy, a solution for this situation.* Like so many people, I used my naivete as a power source, "Would the judge allow this in the courtroom?" "Uh" and "Um" noises occurred before they sat down and responded in low voices: "No." The harassers backed out of their power trips. My anger calmed because I had a strategy to expose them later: the printed word.

"Maybe I should show you the location of the scar on *my* body. That's how I would probably do it in the courtroom. Right?" "Yes"—a unanimous answer. I stood up and put my left hand over the left side of my groin. "Cathy, you stated precisely that the scar was located two inches below the hip. Is that correct?" Bill Sr. pointed to his hip bone. "What I meant was two inches below the hipline on the left groin, not below the hip bone. I don't know if I stated this point incorrectly because of exhaustion and trauma, or maybe the secretary typed it incorrectly. We don't have the originals." "It is better to be vague." "Why? I thought you guys wanted people to be exact." "When it's too exact, the defense attorney can then argue that he is not the defendant. If it's general, then there is leeway: Perhaps the scar is three inches instead of two." "No one legally gave me advice until today." Terrific! The first time in my life at a police station and in a state of trauma and the lawyers feel the need to analyze my statement under a legal microscope.

"Did you see another scar?" "I never looked. After he pushed my head on top of the bullet-wound scar, I never glanced at any other part of his groin or the rest of his torso. If he saw me glancing at the scar to get further verification of it, he would kill me. I couldn't look again. When he was standing in front of me without his clothes on, about three to five feet away, I couldn't see any scar because I didn't have my glasses or contacts on. I took actions to save my life. Isn't that important?"

Excitedly, Bill Sr. spoke up: "Cathy, I've had this job for fifteen years and I have never seen the legal issues in this search warrant before. This is a unique case. I can argue this in front of the state supreme court." Always concerned about the VISA, Stan pointed out: "This might delay the case but we are going to argue for the acceptance of the search warrant. We have doubts. Judge Foible will accept it if he possibly can. He's against defendants getting off because of technicalities. That's why he became a judge. If the judge does not accept the search warrant, we'll take it to the court of appeals." "If necessary, we'll argue this in front of the Supreme Court for you." *What did I care about the state supreme court?* A trial as soon as possible was a necessity to stop Redding. Is a speedy trial a consideration only for the defendant but not for the VISA? "If that doesn't work, we feel sure we can get another search warrant." "Do you have another case to be the test case for DNA?" "Yes, we have two other cases. None as good as this one, but something will work out." We shook hands, knowing that in three weeks were pretrial motions.

The waiting period became horrendous. "Marley, the pretrial and trial are in about a month." My friend and professional counselor responded: "I'll be there. Don't worry." "I don't need help then. Everyone says they'll be there for the trial. It's this period that's hard." "What do you want me to do?" "I'm not sure, Marley. But I can't work, and it's hard to get through the day." "Maybe you can volunteer at the center?" True to form, Marley called me every day and discussed my activities. She suggested ideas to keep me active. While volunteering at the center did not work out, those five-minute phone calls were a tremendous help. My brother noted my anxiety: "You don't sound good, Cathy." "You're right. I finished writing the description of the attack and that made me feel good, but on most days I can't do anything." "Bob and I are going up to the lake for two weeks. Why don't you fly to mom's and meet us for the long weekend?" "Getting away will help me through these days. I'll go."

The upcoming trial unleashed information within my family. They needed to read the first chapter. If the trial was on television, the details might traumatize them. After my sister Mary Carol read it, we sat and discussed it. My mother sat silently behind my sister watching television. Mary Carol began: "You know, Cathy, even though readers should not deny what happened, I still didn't want to believe it." I asked: "What else can I do to get people to believe that they're vulnerable?" "I agree. The details are great; they make it believable." "The unbelievable can become believable." "Well, it helped me. One feels the panic and the inability to escape. I wanted to rush out of there like you wanted to do."

"I didn't mean to say it isn't good," said Mary Carol. "Even though a man raped me, I still have that urge to deny it could happen again." My sister had not told our mother about the rape. Inadvertently, she blurted out the secret. My mother's eyes opened widely, and she gave me that questioning, stunned look. My sister soon left. "Mom, after the rapist attacked me, she told me about the rape. It was twenty years ago. That rapist never even realized he raped her. She said she's dealt with it in therapy. She's right that we would not have supported her then nor understood her. That's probably why she moved across the country and lived in a commune for years." "I just can't believe it. My daughter! What can we do now?" "She doesn't need or want anything. Just treat Mary Carol like Mary Carol, as always." "I feel like I should do something. Maybe buy her something." "No, I don't think that's a good idea. I don't think Mary Carol wants a gift for the rape. Really, she's OK. It's sad that we did not support her or help her." She had more queries: "Cathy, what is rape?"

I began my mother's education process. "Rape is when a person doesn't want sex, and someone forces him/her to do it against his/her will. There was a case I heard about in New Zealand where a woman invited the man to her bed and agreed to sex, but during the sex, the angle of his penis in her vagina hurt her. She told him to stop. He wouldn't. The jury convicted him of rape because she said no. There are all types of rape: date rape against Mary Carol, stranger rape against me, incest against women like those in the anthropology department, acquaintance rape, and even marital rape. There ought to be another type called 'drug rape' when guys secretly drug women in order to assault their bodies. Their minds might not remember, but their bodies do."

Pretrial

"Cassandra, the pretrial will be this Monday. Can you be there with me? I don't have anyone else. Besides, you understand the procedures." "Uh, when did you say?" "Monday." "Oh, uh, at what time?" "9 A.M. Do you want me to pick you up?" "No. We can meet there." "It is the same place as last time." "Yes." "I'll see you there?" Silence. "I can count on you?" Silence. "Is something wrong, Cassandra? You're not upset with me because of that chapter I wrote." "I'll be there. Bye." The hesitancy in her voice and her failures to answer worried me. I wanted an experienced person there.

Her abruptness caused me to continue to call my friends for therapy. "Hey, Susan, the pretrial is next week." "Well, that's just another part of the process." "Well, that may be *the* process. The DA thinks that the judge will throw out the search warrant." "Then what?" "Then, they go to the court of appeals and then to the state supreme court and then another search warrant. I just want it over. Now." "Who's going to the pretrial with you?" "I think the rape survivor advocate, but she sounded hesitant about supporting me." "Why's that?" "A month ago, I gave her the description of the attack to read." "Jack told me about it. He said it's fantastic, and you should publish it." "Well, ever since she read it, she avoids me. I'm not even sure she's going to show up for the pretrial." "Do you want me to come out? I don't mind." "Susan, that would be great, but this is the last minute and tickets are expensive." "Cathy, I'm glad to do it." "I'd love for you to come, but are you sure you want to go through it?" "I've attended to trials before. Look, I'll get the ticket and call you about the times."

At the pretrial, the first day involved the hearing on the search warrant. I sat in the hall because I was a witness. I was alone. Susan was in the courtroom monitoring the hearing for me. Every so often, she came out to report the proceedings and check on the whereabouts of Cassandra. At ten o'clock, I left a message on her machine, assuming that there was a mixup. At noon, I called again. Finally at two o'clock, I reached her. "Cassandra, this is Cathy. Where are you? I'm still at the courthouse." "You are? I thought it would only last for the morning. Another victim needed my help, and that person *really* needed me." Because I did not display dramatic expression of trauma, even a trained rape survivor advocate assumed my trauma as insignificant. "Cassandra, will you come over to the courthouse?" "Are the proceedings still going on?" "Yes, and they will continue tomorrow." "Did you go by yourself?" "A friend flew in to be with me, but she is in the courtroom. I'm alone in the hall." "Well, you are not alone. You're OK." She hung up.

At the end of the proceedings that day, Stan walked out of the courtroom: "Cathy, it doesn't look good." "What does that mean?" "Det. Roth couldn't remember many points. He wasn't a great witness. The police are frequently our weakest link in a case." "Have you tried working with them?" "Yes. We've set up meetings, and we've told them that they should just call us when they have a questionable search warrant. Now we wait for Judge Foible's decision." "When will that be?" "He always decides quickly. If he doesn't make a decision today, he will decide tomorrow." "At least we'll know where we stand." The job of police officers with a high school education is to write search warrants that can withstand the legal scrutiny of the Supreme Court. How can DAs fault police officers and detectives? Why aren't all search warrants written by legally trained DAs if they want to ensure legal accuracy? Doesn't a four-year college education plus a three-year legal education make a significant difference in one's ability to perform his or her job? Police risk their lives physically, not legally.

Bill Sr. excitedly left the courtroom: "This might go in front of the Supreme Court. Think about that." My fury at his priorities exploded inside of me. I raced down the stairs and out of the building. On the drive back to the house, I told Susan: "Nothing should allow a rapist to go free for his crimes." "This is really an interesting and important legal point. They can't exclude exculpatory evidence." "I don't care. We have the evidence. Everyone agrees that he is the rapist. Where's the justice?" "But, Cathy, that is a relevant issue. We have to protect the defendant's rights." "And my rights?" "The detectives did not do their job." "How could the detectives do their job? DNA testing did not exist when they wrote the search warrant. They wrote it based on standards that went out of date with the new methods of evidence. Yet the laws governing search warrants focus only on VISA's identification and are still the legal standard. That standard is irrelevant now. Yet the judge, the lawyers, and you feel that old standards for search warrants are necessary. That's ridiculous. Look, Susan, everyone says the rapist is guilty. That is the only relevant issue. There is no legal mistreatment of the rapist. This is a technicality. Rape is hell, and incarceration is the only remedy."

While my emphatic response abruptly ended our conversation, my mind screamed: *Could I find a gun and kill Redding?* Marley had one in her car. If Redding was in front of the courthouse and the television cameras were on, nothing would stop me. I'd kill Redding in front of an audience, in front of a television camera, in front of the world. Then, everyone will know that they are safe. Never before had this fantasy come so close to a reality.

At home, I went for a run. My shoes quickly took me on the customary route. Two miles into the run, my feelings broke through. In the middle of a beautiful suburban neighborhood, I sat down on the curb and cried uncontrollably, hiding my face in my arms. For almost half an hour, my body shook with the outpouring of tears. No cars stopped, nor did any neighbor check on me. Bitterly, I drowned myself in those salt-filled drops, the tears of living in a society in which the people in justice protected the rapist from responsibility for his crimes. The tears broke my desire to murder. I had an experience of temporary insanity: The people in the legal system set up the conditions for this temporary insanity. Yet they are not guilty! I vowed then to always have a strategy to stop the rapist if faced again with the ineptness of the legal people. Susan and I went out for dinner. My appetite was large: one humongous steak, a huge pasta dish, salad, several glasses of wine, and plenty of ice cream. The run, the new strategy for future crises, and a super, great big dinner worked. I felt calm and resolved.

November 4, 1988: As always, I wish this was my last note to you, but the saga continues. On Monday, September 26, the first of the two pre-trial motions began. The issue was a question on the validity of the search warrant. While the facts are that the police erred, the specifics include misrepresenting evidence, that is, failing to present both exculpatory (the guy is innocent) and inculpatory (the guy is guilty) evidence. The exculpatory material is in regard to an incomplete statement. Det. Roth wrote that at a photo lineup I said that Redding (the rapist) looked like the attacker. What he did not add were three other points. First, I saw Redding on the street, and after he was called over to the car, I said to Det. Doil that "he was not the rapist." This point was not in the search warrant. What Det. Doil had forgotten to relay to Det. Roth for the search warrant was the second point that as Redding walked away from the car, I said to Det. Doil that the rapist had the same body shape. Third, he said in his police report that I had also stated "but that is not the man." This was not mentioned in the search warrant. The truth is that I had said "but I can't say that this is the man": a slight but significant difference.

Inculpatory evidence left out was that the artist's composite looked just like Redding. In addition, Det. Doil saw Redding regularly hanging around my block during that time period, wearing the same-shaped cap. Other misrepresented information in the search warrant was the issue of the scar. My description was of a 1/2" circular scar, located about 2" below the left hip line. Instead, Det. Roth described an 8" vertical scar in the stomach and chest areas, of about 1/4" to 1/2" in width. Needless to say, this was an error: Two different scars in two different areas. The attorneys argued my data as literally factual and failed to note that written into the statement was trauma. The defense attorney noted that the scar I saw must be located exactly on the left side of the body where the hip is and not in the left groin area. The lawyers got into a dispute about the boundaries of the hip, abdominal, groin, and stomach areas. No one asked me for my interpretation.

The judge who makes up his mind immediately ended that first day in silence. The next day, we returned to the courtroom to hear the pretrial motion on the DNA Fingerprinting. The researchers—Sefaborb and Gemal—from The Science Laboratory were great. They avoided those silly big academic words. The family members of Redding the rapist showed that they believed this evidence: Their faces became long and drawn, and their mouths hung open in disbelief. The laboratory people were so good that none of those windy, long-talking attorneys made a summation. That pleased the judge. The scientists stated: This is the picture of the DNA from the sperm collected on the vaginal swab taken from the victim; this is the picture of the DNA from the blood of Redding; they are an exact match; and only 1/49,000,000 could have this same pattern. They showed that there was no contamination in the sample or error in the procedure. Just beautiful! The judge said that he would consider the issues further and give an answer by Friday, whether or not to begin the trial on the following Monday, October 3.

Judge Foible postponed the trial. At the end of the pretrial, he made this comment:

This evidence as to the DNA testing would be admissible. My problems [on the search warrant] are, one, the victim's statement when she saw the photographs and she said, it's similar, but he's not the one or something like that. To me, when you split that in half and just put "he's similar" or "it's similar," whatever the exact words were, and that's all, that leads you to believe that he's probably the one who did it, or least there's some possibility. But, when you put in the other half, that he's not the one, it leads you to the opposite conclusion. So that really does disturb me. I will reserve any final ruling on either motion.

My students' comments boosted my spirits:

Now I know why the voices of women are so full of anger and hate. There is so much injustice in our society. Yes, Cathy, we are not yet all free.

You've given at least one person a whole new perspective on rape. New perspectives give birth to new ideas. New ideas give birth to geniuses.

You are one of the most impressive teachers. Your experiences broke the "socialization mold." You really make me think and make me want to take more action.

I have found it much easier to stand up for what I want/believe now because I'm not afraid of someone's status.

Hwei Syin Lu, my Taiwanese friend, explained how her people would react to me: "In my country, Cathy, people would give you a parade." At the same time as the pretrial motions, my brother Jack was a week-long guest lecturer at Bershar College. Despite his second year living with AIDS, he still enjoyed life. He knew that on Monday and Tuesday I was in court. On Wednesday night, he called. "You sound chipper, Jack. What's happening?" "This is incredible. The first talk was highly successful. Everyone loved it. They all said it was the best talk that they had ever heard." "Jack, the *best* talk that they had ever heard? How many people said that?" He laughed because I was his sounding board who ferreted out the truth behind grandiose statements of his out-of-this-world success. "I'm sure at least one person, but a really, really intelligent one." "Was this one person an undergraduate who had never taken a class in Classics before?" He laughed again. "I do have evidence that they loved the talk. The students put together a play based on the talk and presented it to me after the dinner tonight." "That is incredible! They only had forty-eight hours to do that!" "That's the way this school is. Professors dedicate themselves to teaching, and students' lives focus on these types of projects." "That's a great honor, Jack." "Cathy, what's happening?"

"I'm going to kill Redding." "Cathy, don't tell anyone." "Jack, I can't do it because Redding's in prison. Damn it." I called again the next night: "Susan just called me, Jack. I'm sorry you are depressed. I'm not going to kill Redding. As a matter of fact, it's a good sign that I'm talking about wanting to kill him. The dangerous period was when I didn't mention it." "Are you sure?" "Jack, Uncle Eddy gave me another strategy. I'll find out who are the lifers in prison and send them a copy of the attack. At the end of that article, I'll write that this guy should never leave prison. Eddy thinks they'll kill him. I'll let someone else do it." "I do feel better. I don't want to see you go to jail for that." "Jack, wanting to kill Redding and killing him are two different issues. It's healthy to want to kill him. He tried to destroy my life. If I get quiet again on this subject, then worry."

Waiting

Life became a waiting period, a time not to make decisions. A research trip to Mexico was on hold because I had to be in the United States to keep the case alive. My emotions became muted: I drifted between anger and numbness. The rape trauma subsided, festering like an internal sore. When would the judge make his decision? My task each day was to wait. I was at home between 8 A.M. and 5 P.M. The first week went by. The second week. On the third week, Monday passed without a telephone ringing. On Tuesday, the phone was silent. Wednesday. Thursday. Friday arrived. It was the day. "Cathy, this is Stan." "Your voice sounds like it's bad news." "Well, not exactly. The judge did accept the search warrant and wrote an incredibly strong decision. That guy is brilliant. But Marble told me that he will appeal it immediately." "What does that mean?" "The court of appeals will decide if it needs to hear the appeal or if it could just rubber stamp the decision. In 80 percent of the cases, the court of appeals rubber stamps the judge's decision." "And their decision?" "It's hard to say." "Don't you have any idea?" "This is a touchy situation. We'll have to wait. It could go both ways. Don't worry. We can always submit a second search warrant." "When will we have the court of appeals' decision?" "Probably in a month."

The wait resumed. I was calm the first week. Probably no call that week. Week two included minor aggravations. Week three was a bit more unpleasant. Week four arrived: My glances at the phone increased. "Hello, Cathy, how are you doing?" "Fine, Stan. You are always cordial, but your voice could sound happier." "As we feared, the court of appeals wants to review the judge's decision on the search warrant." "This is unusual." "It doesn't happen often. We'll keep our fingers crossed." "When will the court of appeals make its decision?" "That's hard to say, Cathy. A few months, six months, or even more." Due to the trial, my job postponement until January meant a monetary sacrifice and no benefits. To travel back and forth between the cities during the trial would task me too much. Now, the case was on the back burner. Nothing would happen for months. Other issues would occupy my daily life instead: The first priority was the move.

My dreams reflected my life. The rapist was in my apartment about to attack me with the police and DA standing outside the door. I could see them through the blinds, but the rapist didn't notice. My mind, in the dream, kept projecting my thoughts to the DA and police: Open the door. *Just knock. Break in.* DO SOMETHING! Any action will stop the rape. DO SOMETHING! Then I woke up. I had this identical dream—without feeling fear—three times. In the dream, the police and DA had cornered, but not captured, the rapist. Since the DNA evidence fingered the rapist, my dream symbolized my life: living with the pain of rape and with the security of conviction but a few steps away.

November 4, 1988: After three weeks, specifically on Friday, October 21, we received the official favorable decision from the judge. He stated in his decision that on the scar the police had made a blatant error and described the wrong one. Clearly, Redding the rapist had a scar similar to the one I described and in a comparable area. He said that, while there is a question about ID, that is the reason the DNA evidence exists to take the place of questionable IDs. The defense attorney submitted only one brief on the search warrant issue and did not challenge the issue of the DNA evidence. Even he knows that his client is guilty. The court of appeals will hear the case. The roller coaster is still on the move, going up and down. What a thrill! Whoever loses at the court of appeals level wants to go to the state supreme court. Oh goody! Of course, the DA's thrill is that this becomes a landmark decision. In his power terms, this gives him "a lot of political exposure." A police officer's "error" is legal precedent. Wow!

When the DA told me about the judge's decision and he read me statements that the judge had made in castigating the police, I—slightly, just slightly—raised my voice and asked if there was going to be some ass kicking. If so, I would approve. Don't worry. I do appreciate the fact that this same detective went after the DNA Fingerprinting evidence. He deserves a kick in the pants right before you congratulate him. As a result of my raised voice, the same police detectives in a recent sexual assault/murder case took extra precautions and called in the lab people and the DA to make sure that they collected the data accurately and that the search warrant was precise.

I saw "Redding the rapist" (I think this should be his official name) at the arraignment and at the pretrial motions. While it was clear that he had gained weight and shaved off all facial hair, I could not make an association between the two faces. I could recognize Marble in a crowd after only seeing him once. But for Redding, I "saw" two different but similar people. Every image of Redding from that night, the mug shots, the car surveillance, the arraignment, and the pretrial experience stand out as distinctive, separate persons. As a result of this lack of memory association, or this block in my memory like a form of amnesia, I have PTDS or post-traumatic depression syndrome, sometimes referred to as psychogenic reaction. The amnesia or memory block problem is a result of a trauma usually associated with a threat of death to oneself or friend/ family. This makes sense in my case because I studied his face at the same time that he discussed the need not to go back to prison for this.

Redding is on trial this Monday for robbery. I'm thinking about stopping by the courthouse and giving him a couple of wicked and threatening stares. I asked a lawyer friend what he thought of this, and his retort was that he would go with me. As time goes on, I become more convinced that there must be something to witchcraft. Perhaps it is the only type of power I can have. No, we can't have that. My life goes on in some form or other. I wrote one paper for the anthropology meetings at the end of November with one more to complete. I'll move over the Thanksgiving holidays. And the waiting game continues. The truth dies, and people begin creating their own facts and their own history.

Even with the postponement of the trial, I wanted to let Redding know that I would not give up. In November, Judge Foible oversaw the robbery case against Redding. None of Redding's family came for that trial. As a fast-food chicken restaurant closed, Redding grabbed the back door and entered with a gun. Five people saw the gun clearly. The fifth person immediately exited through the front door and ran across the street to the police car. As the police entered, Redding exited through the back door. The police chased him through one mile of forest. When they caught him, he was without a gun. The jury convicted him, but the judge ruled that he was nonviolent because the police did not find the gun. Later, Redding appealed the burglary charge. He argued the bias of the judge: "During the trial, I was being investigated on other charges. This judge knew. I think this prejudiced his decision. I was really convicted because I was being investigated for other charges."

In March, I picked Jack up at the airport and noted his weakened condition. He slowly took the three flights of stairs and remained upstairs for days. I drove him to the first lecture and made him comfortable in the back seat where he could recline among the pillows. For his talk, he stood for an hour and a half, a practice that would end. On the way to the second university, he reclined again comfortably in the back seat with the sun beating in to warm him. At the next university, I took on a more active role of protecting my brother. I drove him as close as possible to the auditorium to save him a few steps. I ordered a stool for his talk. After the talk, a friend put him on the plane back home, and I returned to my home to await news of a job. Poplar College in a nearby state offered me a job for the 1989–1990 school year.

In June, my mother called in distress with her telegraphic message: "Jack's dying. Get out here right now." I found my brother bedridden but thrilled to have his three sisters pampering him. "Well, that's the way it should be," he laughed. He needed specially enriched drinks every day: I bought cases. He wanted his favorite foods from when he grew up. I made them. He needed a cushioned toilet seat: I installed it. With weight loss, new clothes were a necessity: I bought those.

When Jack stabilized, I called Stan: "You sound great." "It must be a cover-up. I'm with my brother Jack who has AIDS." "Oh, I'm sorry." "Have you heard anything from the court of appeals?" "Yes, they turned it down. Judge Foible makes the decision what to do. You know, we have a second chance with another search warrant."

In July, I called Bill Sr.: "Excuse me for bothering you, but do you know the status of the case?" "Well, Barbara, who handles the cases that go to the Supreme Court, has it." I called Barbara: "My name is Cathy Winkler, and I'm involved in the Redding case. Do you know if the DA will pursue the case to the Supreme Court?" "I'm deciding now whether or not the DA should pursue this case to the Supreme Court. This case involves a lot of work." "If the case did go in front of the Supreme Court, would it have an impact on future cases or police procedures?" "No, this is a rare incident. The result wouldn't impact any other case. I'll suggest to Bill Sr. to drop it. The case isn't worth the work." "Bill Sr. said he follows your decision. Is there anything else I should know about this decision?" "Now I understand why Bill Sr. said you are a difficult witness." "What does that mean?" "Oh um, nothing. I've got to go." "One more point: When will you officially make the decision?" "In the next month." She later wrote a letter to Judge Foible that "the bulk of the argument contained herein is probably academic [irrelevant]."

Another Crisis

In August, I packed up my stuff. The phone rang: "Cathy, I'm going to die," my brother told me. Emotions stifled my words. "Jack, how do you know?" "I have a blood disease. They gave me an experimental drug, but they don't think it will work. They have never given the drug to anyone with as high a reading as mine." "What was the reading?" "It was 16,000. The drug worked for those whose reading was less than 12,000." "I'll get a ticket and be there right away." I left the boxes stacked up. When I arrived, the disaster was worse than I had thought. Jack was dying in one room, and my mother was ill in the next. I spent my days moving from caring for one patient to the other. Every hour, I went to the other side of the house and cried for five minutes. That's all the time I had between their needs. Each had different problems and issues. I made every food imaginable to satisfy them. Since the morning is the most likely time for the heart to give out, I woke early and peeked into Jack's room, looking for signs of life. In dying, body movement is minimal, breathing shallow, and leg and arm movements few. Each morning after I confirmed he was alive, I then proceeded to my mother's room. What illness did she have? She had so many symptoms. By the fifth day, my energy level was low. "Please, someone, get better." My mom began to get up, eat a little, and move around the house. One of my patients was on the road to recovery. After a week, Jack asked to go to the clinic.

The doctor loved Jack, and the staff called him the "little soldier." He would always sit quietly, without complaining, until they called him. When Jack first got AIDS, he asked a friend who was in the hospital for a year with a kidney problem how he got people to take care of him. His friend said that he was the kindest, friendliest, and happiest patient in the world, and then people did everything for him without asking. For Jack, that was an easy role. I wheeled him into the doctor's office and sat next to him. "How are you doing, Jack?" as the doctor touched him affectionately. She always showed intense interest and care with every word and gesture. "I'm fine." "Are there any symptoms or problems?" "No, I'm feeling fine." "What about that afternoon nausea?" "Oh, yes. I forgot that." As a great patient, Jack forgot his symptoms. "Jack, I have the results from the blood test. Your rate is 10." "What scale did you use to measure this new result?" "Same scale. It decreased that much. The experimental medicine worked!" After we picked up more medicine, we left the hospital that day in celebration. He wanted new clothes to match his good feeling.

September 14, 1989: Keeping with my migratory pattern, I have another abode. Of course, this time I hope that I may actually be in the same place for one whole year. Then again, such a peaceful life is a shock to my system. While this area is desolate, its beauty is magnificent. There are over 25 lakes and ponds in the county alone. Every road passes a lake with views that distract the driver. Probably after a period of time, I'll not notice these stupendous countryside panoramas. With my concern for Jack and my worries about the trial preoccupying my daily existence, I fantasize about life on a deserted island.

Crises are a regularity in my life. When the tenants refused to leave the rental house, this was an almost expected result. Not knowing where to send my boxes was part of my day-to-day uncertainty. Actually, certainty or dilemma-less situations were suspect. If it's not a crisis, then something is wrong. To end on good news, my classes are full; my sense of humor—most of the time—is a success with my colleagues; and the rent for my abode includes heat: at least inside the apartment this year, I won't freeze. The legal saga for conviction continues. We will win the case. Don't worry; I informed the DA of my prognosis. Take care, and a zillion thanks.

Another Search Warrant

Poplar College offered to pay for the trip to get my books. While there, I made my monthly DA check-in. Stan reported: "We will submit a second search warrant. That's why I wanted to talk to you. First, I want to let you know that I went to the police station and found another victim. Redding also raped one of your neighbors, Haily Betten." "Oh, the police detectives told me that a year ago." "They never mentioned it to us. I'll get her blood and send it for DNA analysis if we get the search warrant." "Do you need my blood again?" "No, that's fine." "Doesn't the first search warrant throw out his blood and won't that cause a problem?" "Yes, it does rule out his blood, but your blood and the semen are intact. There is no problem." "Don't you need all the tests done at the same time?" "No, that's not important. Lab controls show that all the tests are the same or comparable."

"For the search warrant, how did you describe Redding?" I gave him that information. "Cathy, if you think of anything else, call. We'll put the search warrant together in the next two days." "Stan, I'm leaving for my next job, but I'll call you on the road in case you have any other questions." The next day, I checked in and clarified several points for Stan. The following day, we spoke for the third time: "Stan, did you include the information about the bloodhounds?" "What's that?" "The bloodhounds, that the detectives brought to the house after the attack, left and followed a route in the direction of Redding's house. Stan, I also have another concern. The private investigator told me that Kenny has a brother. I'm afraid his lawyer will try to raise reasonable doubt by inferring his brother, who must have similar DNA, raped me." "I'll look into those points." "There's one more question that I want to ask you. Why can't you identify Redding? The composite looks just like him." "I can't, Stan. That's the trauma. I don't even see a similarity between the composite and Redding."

"By the way, some of the other lawyers in the office rated the search warrant between a 'D' and an 'F.' There is reason to worry about the judge approving it." "With all of my information matching Redding, you don't have enough for a search warrant?" "We need an identification. You can't identify him." "What a joke! We can't get the DNA result that absolutely identifies Redding until we get a search warrant! And we can't get a search warrant without already having an absolute identification. Is this the law?" "Well, Cathy, that's about it." "When will the legal people stand up for the truth?" Stan laughed.

September 14, 1989: The gist of these letters—Conviction of the rapist. Can you believe how long this process takes! We're at the two-year mark, and hopefully, only six more months in the legal system. The DA thought there was a 50–50 chance that the magistrate would accept the new search warrant. Problems included contradictory information such as my statement "That is not the man" to the artist composite that looks like the rapist. To enhance the case, they also threw in the case of the rape of my neighbor that occurred two months prior to his raping me. A further DA precaution was to tape their conversation with the magistrate on their oral arguments for the search warrant.

Another problem was timing. The search warrant is valid for ten working days, but the rapist—now residing in a county penitentiary—needs transportation to that county to extract his blood. With paperwork, that process can take a month. This time the magistrate—knowing the whole truth—accepted the warrant and within a day the detective sent off the rapist's blood to the laboratory. Of course, the DA is now very good about letting me know about every possible up-and-coming problem. They can't find the woman in the other case to send her blood in for the DNA Fingerprinting test, and the defense attorney plans to attack the new search warrant. It's as usual a wait-and-see situation. Surprisingly, this case is still the test. These days, who knows!

"The real problem," noted Stan, "is Redding. The last time we got his blood, six large men had to hold him down, and even then it took half an hour of his struggling before he gave in. Our detectives and the guards at the jail don't like this job." "Well, they won't have to do it again. When do you think we'll have the results?" "The DNA testing takes eight to nine weeks." "Yeah, but last time, the lab took fifteen weeks." "With results in December, no one wants a trial like that. The jury members are in the holiday spirit. We try pickpockets and shoplifters then. Let's aim for January." If everyone agrees that one's blood equals one's blood, or one's own DNA matches one's own DNA, then why draw Reddings' blood again for testing? Shouldn't the second search warrant validate the previous blood test? The six officers who sat on Redding can verify that part of the chain of custody.

The DA let me review the papers on my case. I found a copy of a letter sent on October 23, 1987 to the police by the Advocate Investigation Agency on behalf of Haily Betten: "I am requesting a computer run to identify previous rapes in that area from January 1, 1982 through August 5, 1987." This evidence demonstrated two points: Haily was a gutsy, not-easy-to-give-up-or-in type of person, and the police had reports on other rapes.

I passed the next big wait cheering up my brother and mother long distance. Daily, I either called or sent them a card or some trinket. In the meantime, I got involved in an AIDS group. The closest one was one hour away. While the weekly trips gave me time to cry, there I was somber and unemotional. One time, when a snowstorm prolonged the trip to two hours, my tears fell due to fright from the weather and fright on the double trials in my life. What will happen this month: my brother's death or the court case? In November came the call. "Jack's in the hospital. He's dying." "Are you sure?" "This is it, Cathy." "How long does he have, mom?" "Cathy, he'll die any day. I don't know if he has another day. They think it's pneumonia." "Mom, is Jack talking?" "No. He's not responsive." Each day he got a little better, and four days later he was back at home. AIDS was as unpredictable as the court case.

November 30, 1989: We're still hoping for a trial in January. This would be a good time for me since I'm between semesters. The written report from the DNA laboratory is positive. We need the results in print by December 7 for a January trial. The DA interviewed Haily the other day and said that we are two extremes in types of rape victims. I think that's good. The attacker rapes women. Our sex is the issue.

"Cathy, the DNA evidence for Haily is a match, but it's band shifting." "What does that mean?" "With deterioration over time, the DNA begins to break down, but the lab corrected for that, and it's a match. Trial date is January 4, 1990, if the judge accepts the pretrial motions." "You know that I'll be there." "By the way, we got Kenny's brother's blood, and we've sent it off to the lab." "He volunteered?" "Well, not exactly." "Does he do drugs like Kenny?" "I think so." "Did you corner him and plea bargain: give blood or receive a charge of rape?" Stan laughed. On September 24, 1990, Roth wrote in his notes:

> Scott Redding was arrested on another charge. I interviewed him in reference to the rape of Cathy Winkler and Haily Betten. Scott stated he didn't do anything like that. I asked him for his consent to draw his blood. He said that he consents any time. I asked Scott, did Kenneth ever talk to him about any rape, and he said no. Scott signed a consent form to waive need for search warrant.

In December, Jack called. "Cathy, I'm dying." "You know I've heard this before. Are you sure?" "The AIDS is in my heart. There's nothing they can do. I might live until the next year, but not longer than February, or I could go any day." "Can you last a few days, please? It's Thursday. I need to finish my schoolwork and write my exams. I'll arrive on Monday." "Oh, I'm sure that's fine." "Promise?" "Yeah, I think so." My mother asked my friend Nicole to pick me up: quite a pleasure, but unusual. I assumed my mom didn't want to leave Jack alone. When we drove up, she ran out: "Cathy, I did it. I held Jack's hand this morning. He's OK. He told me that he was about to die, and he asked me to hold his hand. He didn't think he would live to see you this afternoon." My mother had feared her powerlessness: She could not deal with Jack's death or surviving her son—her firstborn and only boy. Today, she learned she had strength. "Hey, Jack, how's it going?" "Oh, Cathy, I felt my heart not moving this morning. Mom held my hand. This lasted hours, and then I got a little better." Teary eyed, I asked, "Does this mean you won't live until January?" "I don't think so, Cathy. Why?" "Well, I have a last wish. I want you to be there for me, at least via the phone, during the trial. It's scheduled for January 4." "I don't know, Cathy. I'll try. I would also like to see my book out." We hugged.

Luckily, both my brother and I had a sense of humor: "Jack, does this mean you want your holiday gifts early?" "Yes." That was one of four holiday celebrations he enjoyed. "Cathy, I'm not going to make it through the week." "Oh, I think you'll be alive next week. You don't look that bad." "No, this week is it." "I'll bet you that you'll be alive next week. If you live until next week, you owe me a hot fudge sundae. You know, though, if you die this week, it's going to be hard for me to collect the bet." Like children, we wrapped our baby fingers around each other, bet, and then pulled them apart. Each day followed, and each day Jack made it through the morning. At 10 P.M. on Saturday I said to him, "Jack, do you think I'll win my bet?" He laughed embarrassed: "I'm going to make sure you don't win your bet." As the days passed by, he became constipated. I bought him some over-the-counter medication. The next day, he reported, "I couldn't stand it any more, and I took several doses. Will you help me to the bathroom?" He stood up, I stood in front of him, he put his hands on my shoulders for balance, and we choo-chooed to the bathroom. This parade occurred many times during the morning with either my mother or me helping him to the bathroom. After four hours of bathroom trips almost every fifteen to twenty minutes, Jack yelled really loud: "Help, I need help, right now. MOM. CATHY." We ran as fast as we could.

"Hey, guys, I feel much better." Another practical joke in the face of death. That next week, his jokes continued. He always wanted to die in a dramatic way. He put a clean white sheet over himself and held a lily between his crossed hands. His pale skin blended into the sheets. My brother asked me to somberly call mom. "Mom, you better come here right away." She gasped. Jack opened his eyes: "Hi. Just wanted you to know one of the ways I would like to go." Jack and I bellied over in laughter. My mother quickly left to recover.

Each day brought new, unrelated surprises. Early one morning, our caucasian neighbor called: "I've called the police." On our garage door in red, someone had painted: NIGGER LOVER LIVES HERE. She had also called several friends to scrub off the words. I suggested another solution: "Let's call the newspaper. We can make a slight change with just a few letters: SNICKER LOVER LIVES HERE. We'll say that we can't understand how people knew about our love of candy." The police questioned us, asking if we were members of the NAACP: "Of course." We suspected it was a random act of hate: our garage was in a dark area. We installed a light sensor.

"Hey, Cathy, how's your holiday season?" "Stan, we're surviving everything." "The court of appeals has to review the pretrial decisions." "Judge Foible did decide in our favor, didn't he?" "Yes, but the court still has to review the search warrant." "Again?" "I didn't suspect any problem." "Thanks for keeping me in touch. Do you have any idea when the trial will be?" "Maybe March." In our family, we had agreed not to hide news—good or bad. "Jack, be there for the trial." "Maybe I can live a little longer. When is the date?" "March. We are part of each other's struggle for three years. I guess that, if they both have to end, they could end together. I need your support." "I'll try, Cathy."

In the following week, Jack, quite unexpectedly, wanted to see the doctor. "Well, how's our little soldier?" she asked. "Actually, I'm feeling better." "That's great. Let me check you." She started listening with her stethoscope in all the different sections, feeling, thumbing, and whatever: "Jack, this doesn't change the general diagnosis, but you don't have AIDS in your heart. Last time you had five symptoms that indicated that diagnosis. They are gone. I have never seen a case like this. No one survives AIDS in their heart. But yours is gone. Your final diagnosis is still the same." In July, he beat the odds; in August, he survived; in November, he lived through the imminent threat of death; and now in December, he was here. "How long do you think he'll live?" "Jack beat the odds several times, but, Jack, you won't always do that. Maybe a few more months." As we drove home Jack said, "Well, Cathy, maybe I will be there for the trial." Good news magnified: An advance copy of Jack's book arrived and a book reviewer, knowing Jack's situation, sent him a copy of her review. He was ecstatic.

Back at home, I checked in with Stan. "Cathy, I don't think this should be a problem. . . ." He said those dreaded words: "I don't think" and "problem." "But I wanted to let you know that the lab tech who drew your blood died in a car accident." "He was so young. That's terrible." "I think the chain of evidence is fine, though." "With Det. Roth's carefulness, you can believe it. He watched the blood drawn and watched everything like a hawk. He did not want anything to happen to that blood." "That's good for our case. Well, I wanted to keep you informed."

To share my personal research results, I offered my students a method to minimize their own past buried traumas. In my Social Problems class, they wrote a paper that analyzed a past personal trauma. Those with past sexual traumas who wanted the opportunity to speak were guest lecturers in my Victimization and Violence (V & V) class. The grade that day for the students in V & V class depended on how the speaker felt after the experience of exposure. My students provided an environment of belief and trust. The speaker received a purple heart for bravery. It was the only symbol of justice that s/he would receive for the sufferings from that crime. Would I ever leave the maze of injustice?

The deterioration of Jack's body continued. At the beginning of February, I went to the AIDS support group meeting. Each person explained their current troubles and state of existence. For the first time, calmness disappeared. This group knew about my brother's condition and the trial entanglements. "How's it going, Cathy?" Tears flew down my face as my hands flew up to cover my embarrassment: "Horrible." A few minutes later, my tears slowed, and the words flowed. I apologized to the group. "Oh no, Cathy. Gosh, I'm so glad you cried. Your crying made your pain real." Tears are evidence.

Tension grew inside me. Running four or five times a week in freezing winter weather was not sufficient exercise to control the stress. Like my brother, the night sweats began. From Jack's experience, I knew what to do: I kept towels next to the bed to cover the wet bottom and top sheets and always had several changes of clothing nearby. Sweats occurred three or four times a night. Feeling my nerves avalanching out of control and worried about the wet sleeps, I called a medical friend. She refused to allow me a crutch of addictive drugs: "Figure out the problems. Stand up to them. Do not substitute one problem with another." She was right, but how was I to survive?

My life had many obligations: fulfilling my present contract, visiting Jack, finding a job, presenting professional papers at conferences, and awaiting the trial. With the arrangement to fly back for Presidents' Day weekend to visit my brother, I made a deal with a school that offered me a job interview to combine that trip with the interview. Jack's disappointment was obvious when I flew in and out within hours. Every day was precious. Rationally, I explained to him the reasons for a short visit: I had to get a job. But he needed me too. Returning home, I saw the light blinking on my answering machine. Those first words left me dizzy and confused: "Cathy, I'm sorry to tell you, but he had a massive heart attack." I had to listen to the message several times to register its meaning. It was Jack's voice—weak and devoid of energy. Jack's lover's brother—a healthy person, watchful of his diet and exercise, and recently examined thoroughly by a doctor—had suddenly died. The shocks of life continued.

In my dreams then, there was a voice in my brain screaming louder and louder, continuously, one word:

R R R R R R A A A A A A A A A A A A A A P P P P P P P P P E

A scream of just one word, a scream of that word, a scream that kept hanging on to that word and bellowing unceasingly. Oddly enough, the other side of my brain calmly counseled me: *Hold on. Stay calm. It will pass. It seems worse than it is.* Unlike those people whose dreams mystify them, I understood the meanings. The constant threats of the trial and the perpetual pretrial existence were too much. I wanted it to end; it should end. These ongoing legal delays were not acceptable. For some damn reason, the people in the legal process expected a Herculean strength from me. They did not care about my turmoil. It was not easy to act peacefully while emotional bombs endlessly kept ticking and exploding.

During spring break in March I was able to make my next visit with Jack. We spoke the day before I left. "Cathy, I want to die. I don't want to live." "What's happened, Jack?" "The pain is too much. Sleep is the only way I can live. If I'm awake, it hurts too much." "Hold on. I'll be there in two days." Hold on; that's what we want a dying person to do who is living with excruciating pain. When I arrived, Jack wanted to leave copies of his new book for his colleagues to show them his appreciation. When we reached his department office, his body shook with death. The secretary and I grabbed clothes from the lost-and-found and wrapped him up. The secretary, the only person around then, was on the verge of tears. She had never seen death up close. With trembling hands, Jack wrote a personal message in each of the six books and sent them through campus mail. His colleagues did not reciprocate with a thank-you note. When I left for my home, his last hug was feeble. We did not doubt this time that death was at the door.

Upon my return, "How are you doing, Cathy?" "Stan, my brother is dying. How are you and what's up?" "I'm sorry about your brother. That's really hard. I called because I've decided to go into private practice. I'm leaving the DA's office." "What happened? Aren't you and Bill Sr. life-long friends?" "It's a hard decision. I've waited to make the decision because of Bill Sr." "What about the trial?" "That's why I called. I want to try the case before I leave, and I'm leaving May 1st. Could we have the trial in April?" "No, Stan." For the first and only time, I said no. "Jack is going to die any day now. I can't deal with both in one month. It's too much. What will happen then with the trial?" "Joel Prey, the new Assistant DA, will take over, and he'll try it." "Stan, let him know that I can testify in May."

April 1, 1990: The date of April 1st—fool's day—is perfect for this letter. Almost three years have passed and still no trial date. Stamina and patience are gone, and anger at the ridiculous and overbearing legal people has taken over. The latest: Another legal case will present the DNA-as-evidence argument to the state supreme court whose decision should occur anytime between now and the middle of June. Thereafter, they will assign a trial date in Redding's case and without the complications of proving the DNA as valid evidence. Tentative trial date is between June and August. Is it possible that they can think up any more excuses or delay tactics? I finish teaching at the end of April and will present a conference paper on the meanings behind rape trauma. Then I travel across the country. Hopefully I'll have three to four months to work on my book. The Chinese say that after disaster comes great things. My belief in this Chinese philosophy is strong.

The charging and uncontrollable roller coaster rides of pain had to stop: My nerves were unraveling. Was this a breakdown? Working, job hunting, brother dying, and the rape trial absorbed my time, my energy, and my emotions. Besides all of these, I had a conference at the end of April. There was only one solution. Finish classes early and leave. Student attendance at out-of-class movies terminated the semester two weeks early. My male colleague, who had skipped seven weeks of classes that same semester, was furious that I had completed all the hours and assigned material two weeks early. He ran to the chair and protested my neglect. The chair questioned me, but he had little to argue: He had approved the movies to substitute class time. The chair's main worry was students' complaints. No one complained. Many of them were fond of me and knew of the stresses in my life. It also reduced their own end-of-the-semester stress. On the drive to the city for the conference and trial, a feeling of bliss came over me when I heard Jack speak: "I'm not in pain anymore, Cathy." When I arrived, I called my mom and told her: "Jack died this morning." "How did you know?" How could I tell her that Jack had told me himself!

Another Trial Date

July 24, 1990: Re: Bets on Latest Trial Date. As you may have noted on the letterhead, my migratory pattern continues with another one-year job. From what I've heard, the department consists of a good group of people. The best part of the summer was jogging. I'm up to four miles and hope to reach five miles someday. There is one fact: jogging is not a favorite sport. I know that it is good for you, and I know that I feel better after it is over, but it is not an enticing activity. At least now I've reached the point where I easily jog along the first one mile, then note the mile-and-half marker, then the two-mile marker, followed by the two-and-one-quarter sign. Desperation sets in: two and one-third, two and a half, two and five-eighths, two and six-elevenths. By the time I reach the last mile, I speed up in order to escape those horrible fractions.

While I lost a year of work by helping Jack fight AIDS, I am now back in the dungeon of the library, struggling with words and phrases. People comment on this as therapeutic and give me a sense of control. Wrong. A therapeutic act is to walk away from this case and this book project. The only reason I'm doing it is to stop rapists. Writing is a chore with hours of recuperation necessary. Pastries and ice cream are helpful. The writing is unpleasant because the picture of oneself in the writing is not favorable. Wouldn't we all like descriptions of ourselves as perfect human beings, and that everyone around us was also that way?

News on the mysterious trial date: Stan, who was handling the case, has left this job for the private sector. I think I wore him out. He did say that he will use Redding's case on his resume to demonstrate that as a defense attorney he can stall cases. Now that is a new approach! Judge Foible has set the pretrial date on September 20th to hear the presentation on statistics by the experts. If there is no catch-22, and in this case there have been a few—from two court of appeals' rulings, two search warrants, supreme court ruling, witness's death in car accident, to Stan leaving the case, not to mention the current glitch—then the trial dates tentatively set—the DA always says to me, "the trial dates that we're working on"—are September 24th through October 5th. Are these dates a reminder of the three-year anniversary of the attack and that I'm a year older?

Let me know what odds you want on that trial date occurring or not occurring. Each time, I keep saying that I cannot think of a reason that they could postpone it again, but they always come up with something. This time the pretrial motions are complete, and the supreme court has ruled: What else is there? I have my fingers crossed that the trial occurs, and I can get on with other stuff. No one thinks the defendant will plead guilty; he has thirteen counts against him. A guilty plea is like asking for life in prison. His only hope is that the jury does not understand DNA Fingerprinting. We don't want that to happen. Maybe this is the second-to-last letter that I'll send you. The last is the letter of victory. I hope, I hope, I hope.

The department faculty had strongly voted for me for the position: There was no hesitancy in their minds about their support. My importance as a candidate of choice was of interest: Each faculty member had some reference to rape—family, friends, personal, or self-fear. Because of their acceptance of my research and VISA position, the energy I received in that department along with the successful summer of writing and the current success in teaching bolstered my desire to work even harder. Work is an elixir when there is an environment of support.

September 25, 1990: I realize that the DA thinks these subpoenas are real, but to date each one was a phony. I love their calls: "Cathy, are you sitting down?" I immediately do sit down and grab the laughing gas. Last week was a minor catastrophe because the geneticists for the DA argued that the lab tests of DNA on the semen and on the suspect's blood occurred at different time periods. To be absolutely scientific, simultaneous performance is a necessity. A scientific test means that it is valid whenever performed or at another time period if conditions are under control. Also, the laboratory said that they couldn't run another test on the semen sample because it is all gone. The result is that the DNA tests on the semen and on suspect's blood are valid despite the difference in calendar times.

With that problem supposedly cleared up, the DA had to still change the trial date because the scientists scheduled that time to appear in another trial. Of course, other problems could occur. The doctor who examined me in the hospital is now in the army and may be sent to the Middle East. Another reason to postpone the case and again. Why not? There have been so many changes, and I can't say "ups and downs," so many downs, that I have now developed a factory line of emotions. Within five minutes, my body passes from anger, nausea, fury, rage, to relief—relief that I can get out of the trial mode mentality and think about my life. In other words, I can again resume the freedom to be. Oh well, back to the running track. Good news: My apartment overlooks a lake and is terrific.

The week before the trial was the date to present a paper on my research to the university. My life was in order: I had finished the paper on trauma over the summer, I had arranged the two weeks of lecturers and films to cover my absence, I had completed my conference paper for December, and I had asked all of my family and friends to attend the trial. Then five minutes before I was to present the paper on campus and three days before the trial, Joel called. "Cathy, we postponed the trial." "Why?" "The scientists want more tests." "What other tests are necessary?" "They want a DNA test run with your blood and Redding's blood at the same time." "Why is that necessary? There are lab controls to prove that all tests have the same results." "They won't testify for us without another test." "When did they tell you this?" "I got them the results a few days ago." "You mean that you gave me a date for the trial without the scientists' review of the evidence." "I didn't think there would be a problem." "Shouldn't the scientists review the evidence before you establish a trial date?" "Cathy, there is no reason for a problem." But there was. After I was sure that Joel was to blame for the delay, I yelled at him. He should know my hell.

Never have I delivered a paper with such anger in my voice. Usually, my calm side presides while the details scream the meaning of the pain. At the end of the paper, I explained my angry voice. Anger that emanated not from the rapist but from the continued mistreatment by the DA: The legal people kept me in a state of rape. When would my trial trauma end? Exhaustion from the emotional roller coaster ride immediately took over. My friendly colleagues agreed to do their lectures, even with the postponement of the trial. My body was limp from the endless chain of emotional downfalls.

October 25, 1990: The DA called me on October 15th to reschedule the trial for October 29th. My chair gave me permission to take off those weeks. My sister bought her plane ticket, my uncle altered his work calendar, and friends rearranged their schedules. The DA informed me that another case involving murder and incest was the first test trial case of DNA in that state. Not disturbing news. I have only one goal: stop the rapist. On October 22nd, the DA called to inform me of the postponement of the other trial because of complications, and that this trial in which I have to testify is, after a two-year wait, the test case again. Fine, let's just do it. While I feared the trial, I felt good this last week. Now, the end of the ordeal. Whatever the trial was like, I would survive it. After that, my life could center around new plans.

Unfortunately, the DA said that there was a miscommunication. The "experts" assumed that the lab had run a third test to further verify the original results. The DA assumed also that the "experts" had checked the lab's work. These assumptions led to an unfortunate miscommunication. A third test as a check is now necessary before the trial. Believe me, I explained to the DA the difference between miscommunication and assumption. You do not assume that people do their work; rather, you ask for the results in writing and then check them. Can you believe that Joel told me that he really knows the case—now! Three days before the trial, he cancels it because he has learned what he doesn't know and what data he doesn't have!

The DA's latest strategies: First, the DA in the city where I live will get a blood sample from me, and Joel will get another search warrant and get a blood sample from the suspect who is still in jail. They will send these to the lab. They will run another DNA Fingerprinting test. Why not spend some more money on this trial! This rapist will have the pleasure of knowing that he has cost the state a ton of money. These results will match the previous results and act as further controls and confirmation of the original tests. By the way, the statistics now demonstrate that the probability that this is the wrong man is 1 out of 3,000,000. I had one request for Joel. I want *in writing* verification that the rapist would not be released before the trial. He said we could "assume" that, and I told him again that I do not work on assumptions. Because of overcrowding in jails, states frequently give nonviolent criminals early paroles. Judge Foible considered this rapist—at this point—as nonviolent. I know that he will kill the next woman. This legal process has also educated him.

January 7, 1991: At the end of November, I went to the Anthropology meetings and gave a great paper. But that's not the point here. On my return trip, I changed planes in the trial city where the police escorted me off the plane—just another routine step in this case. The DA and medical staff took me to a secret room where they extracted my blood—those vampires. Well, maybe the room wasn't secret, but they needed a key to get into it, and maybe those people weren't vampires, but I didn't get a lollipop. My blood along with the suspect's blood— suspect, ha! we know that he's guilty—is on its way to the laboratory for a third DNA Fingerprinting test.

I ended the semester exhausted. A friend had invited me to recuperate at her place. Shock was on her face when she saw me. At times, I cried; at times, I was seriously depressed; and at times, I vegetated. During those days, another VISA also awaiting trial called me. A gang of male college students had raped her. She had to testify against the six rapists with their six expensively suited lawyers. The trial was high profile and in the news regularly. How could I help someone when exhaustion defined my existence? Few people experienced these pretrial tremors. So, despite my limited energy, we shared feelings. Yes, you are going to explode. Yes, it is almost impossible to work. Yes, just living through the day is an accomplishment. And, yes, you will survive.

January 7, 1991: I'm back from the holidays where I visited several different friends. Each place I visited became a winter wonderland. I arrived and within minutes there was six inches of snow falling. This happened thrice, and of course there was no surprise when I returned to my current home and six inches of snow fell upon my arrival. I wanted to let you know that the snow is on the ground, and it is time to make your reservations for cross-country skiing. There are beautiful trails through miles of forest. If you've never cross-country skied, the process is easy. You put on all the clothes that you own. Then, you start off on the trail and as you progress, you take off scarves, coats, sweaters, and the rest and hang these on the trees. On your return trip, you pick up your belongings. It is strongly suggested that you take the same trail home. For reservations, you can call either of the two numbers above. But remember, there are few reservations left. This is a popular, still an unknown secret, cold spot. By the way, if you plan to come the weeks of February 11th or 18th, please be aware of my possible absence.

According to the jocular Joel, there is a possibility for the trial on those dates. We are sure that this is just another one of those New Year's Eve jokes, isn't it? For those interested in participating in the betting, you can call 1-800-tri-gess, and place your bet on the probability of the trial. Although Joel is also betting that the trial will occur, what does he know! I informed several people of these dates, and responses were similar: "Again." "Yeah, sure!" "Can you believe that?" I continue in my optimism. This time as always, I questioned Joel on every aspect of the case. Why I question Joel, I don't know! I never discover the loophole for the delay. Frankly, I wanted March for the trial because that is the loveliest month there. All the pink and white dogwoods along with the zillion types of azaleas and a trillion other flowers are in bloom. I hope I don't arrive with six inches of snow. That would close the city. People don't believe in shoveling snow. NO-O-O-O. Let the snow melt naturally! Just in case, I'm taking my skis for fun and frolic. Don't tell my boss. This letter, like the last twelve, is the second-to-last letter I plan to send to you. If this ever ends, you'll miss my notes. Who else writes to you this often?

January 31, 1991: You guessed it. Trial postponed until March 11th. All parties moved up one month. Joel informed me that the lab work is late. I then called Bill Sr.—his boss—and in a gentle way demonstrated my wrath. He informed me that he is more persistent than myself and will guarantee—unless God intervenes—that the trial will occur on March 11th. I do hope both of these guys meant the year of nineteen hundred and ninety-one A.D. If someone blew up the courthouse, would he consider that an act of God? He said yes. I said that I could find another building to hold the trial. He agreed. I suppose their situation of overwork makes it hard for them to think. That's my nice diplomatic side speaking. My other side is unspeakable except in a closed room with six foot cement walls and no other human being around. My patience is gone, and they are now in trouble because they are tampering with my humor. Oh well, off to the slopes to woosh and swoosh.

The ultimate reliable fact in this case was that this evidence was perfect; it was textbook case evidence. The lab's brochure had promised this:

If the two patterns match, investigators can conclude with an average of 99.9% certainty that the biological specimens are from the same individual. If the patterns do not match, investigators can be assured from the biological evidence that the suspect is not the perpetrator. Forensic scientists get no false positive results.

On August 24, 1989, the lab had sent out this notice:

As the pioneer of DNA identification technology in this country, our lab is still the most experienced DNA testing laboratory in the world. We have performed testing in nearly 1,500 criminal cases and testified in 75 trials in 20 states.

Spring break was the beginning of March and the trial was the week after. Joel called the day before the break was to begin: "Cathy, there's a lab error." "What happened?" "Your blood does not match your blood. Your DNA from the 1988 test does not match the present [1990] DNA test."

CHAPTER TEN
CONFRONTING STATUS, NOT JUSTICE

ow could I not be myself? I laughed. "There's a lab error." "Can't they find the error? It's my blood, not the semen or evidence. There is no error in the evidence." "Cathy, Bill Sr. dropped the case. With an error, it's not salvageable." "But, Joel, the error is in the lab. I was with the detective. He didn't mix up the blood samples, and he didn't handle any other samples. He was excruciatingly careful. There is no problem with the chain of custody. If the error is in the lab, can't they find it?" "Cathy, we don't pursue cases with errors." "Joel, can I make an appointment to see you Monday in your office?"

During the next twenty-four hours, I made up a 100 diagrams of the case (see table 10.1):

Table 10.1   DNA Comparisons

Year	VISAs	Rapist		Defendant	Lab Controls
1988	1) blood of CW	2) semen of KR	=	3) blood of KR	XYZ
		=		=	=
1989	4) blood of HB	5) semen of KR	=	6) blood of KR	XYZ
				=	=
1990	7) blood of CW		=	8) blood of KR	XYZ

The discarded first search warrant excluded sample #3. But, #2 = #5 = #6 = #8: all match. Absolutely identical matches over three years. The controls in the lab demonstrated that the tests worked. Because scientists accept these results and because this area of biological science depends on excellence, is the legal evaluation of evidence more stringent than science? When there is a lab error such as the mixup in my blood,

205

the test worked because it showed that there was no match. Errors are all right, if they can be explained and have not hampered the evidence. This error did not hamper the evidence. The semen evidence—#2 = #5— matches, and Redding's blood—#6 = #8—matches. Sense of humor was critical. The party scheduled for that Friday went on as planned with a new theme: "I am not who I am" or "Whose DNA are you anyway?" I had a backup plan. If the DA threw out the case with me, they could try the case with Haily. During the drive to the DA's office, my fantasy was that I was the expert witness in the case with Haily because I had published on rape trauma. Such a great strategy would never play out, though. For some reason, the defense attorney would argue my bias.

March 15, 1991—Re: Spring Break or Persuasive Influence: Disagreement with the DA. Dear Supporters: Sit down. With the official notice of the dismissal of both rape cases, several members of the Anthropology Department expressed their support: Go get them. To be part of a group of people who believe in me, show me confidence, and have the same set of values was marvelous. You don't get the bad guys alone: you get them when you have terrific supporters. Counselors fail to prepare us for this stage of the game: activism. Here I am the victim, and now I have to take over and organize people. While the rape trauma by the legal people speaks eloquently from my mouth, the experience leaves me in shock. During the car trip, I wondered what could I do? First, Joel must explain his position. And if necessary, I must be willing to accept this horrible defeat. What a pleasure if this ordeal ends! While my book would also and unfortunately end with the disparaging position, that is reality. To end it with the conviction is false for the majority of cases. I want to believe that there is a light at the end of the tunnel. For most people, there is only darkness.

That Monday, I went and saw the Hopes, my past neighbors. They wanted to organize the neighborhood in protest. Also, they told me an interesting point: The guy who lived across the street at the time of the attack and who heard my screams is now in jail—just like his incestuous father—as a rapist.

On Monday afternoon, my friend Saul and I showed up at Joel's office. "Joel, this is Saul. He's here as a friend but he is a lawyer by profession." "Yes, I know Saul. Didn't we try a case together?" "Yes, it was that defendant Jones." "You convinced the judge to lower the sentence. That was my position." In siding with Saul on that past case, Joel tried to make an alliance against me. It didn't work. Joel said, "I don't know what I can do for you, Cathy." "Joel, would you explain to me again your position?" He did. His final word: "Cases with errors are over." I explained my position and took my stand: "Joel, how can you drop a case without finding the error? If the error is in the 1988 sample, then the 1988 evidence is in jeopardy. But if the error is in the 1990 sample, then the 1988 evidence is legally admissible. Let's do another DNA test to find out who I am before you drop the case. Isn't that legally reasonable?"

"Look, Cathy, I know this is frustrating, but the case has an error. Anyway, I've reviewed your description of the attack and the defense attorney would have a heyday with what you wrote. Throughout your account, you express your thoughts. Those thoughts are indefensible." Vehemently, I raised my voice: *"JOEL, this is a rapist. My thoughts aren't the issue. The issue is that we need to look for the lab error before we discard the case. This man will rape again. Don't you get it? We have to keep trying."* It was 5 P.M. Monday afternoon with lawyers still working in the outer offices. All of them heard my screaming voice. Catching a glimpse of Saul's face in my peripheral vision, I noted his look of shock, but continued: *"This guy is crazy enough to blame you for his legal problems and go after your wife."* "I don't *live* in a neighborhood like *that*." "Joel, rapists have transportation." He illustrated the denial of his and his wife's vulnerability by shaking his head. "Joel, I want to discuss this decision with Bill Sr. Will you at least ask Joel to meet with me?" "Yes."

Turning Activist

On Tuesday morning tears flowed nonstop. Janie yelled good-bye several times as she went to work but not even a whimper left my throat, it was so choked with misery. Later, the electricity went off, and the cellular phone went dead. Since Saul's office was several blocks away, I drove there and explained the lights-out situation. "Is the case salvageable?" "Yes, I think it's still worth fighting for. There's an extra phone in the next office. Start making phone calls." And I did. The whole day I called everyone: NOW, politicians, action groups, the scientists in the case, the lab, legal experts, scientific experts on DNA, experts on rape trauma, newspapers, and any phone number I could find. I spent nearly eight hours nonstop on the phone. My requests were concise and to the point: Do you have a moment of your time? I'm a rape victim trying to stop a rapist. Could you explain _____ ?

My issues were:

1) Scientifically, check the validity of the evidence for both cases.

2) Legally, check the validity of the scientific evidence for both cases.

3) Check out rape trauma as evidence.

4) Organize a protest and press release. Call for support: NOW, women's groups, action-oriented groups, politicians, Men Stopping Violence, other antiviolence groups plus neighbors, people who influence the DA, and the media.

I began with the scientists in the legal case. "Dr. Musher, this is Cathy Winkler, one of the victims in the DNA Fingerprinting case. I want to understand the evidence better." "OK. That seems reasonable. Does Joel Prey know you are talking to me? Didn't they throw that case out?" "Yes, therefore our discussion is not legally relevant. Two points: First, if the controls in the lab are valid, then if they throw out my 1988 blood test because it was not me, do you scientifically believe that the 1988 semen sample is still valid?" "As long as the lab controls are valid, so is the evidence." "My second question is in regard to the DNA in the case with Haily. I know that it involves band shifting. Do you think it is scientifically acceptable evidence?" "Yeeeees." "Would you be willing to testify on the validity of that evidence?" "Of course. I told Joel that." "I just wanted to check."

Several minutes passed before I could reach Dr. Pompousie, Dr. Musher's boss. "Dr. Pompousie, this is Cathy Winkler, one of the victims in the rape case that Joel Prey is handling." "I can't talk to you." "Dr. Pompousie, I want to learn about your expertise. How could I influence your testimony? I'm not a scientist. The case will probably never go to court." "You don't need to know anything. I'm the expert and make the decisions." "That's right. You are the expert, and that's why I'm talking to you. Is the evidence of DNA band shifting for the case with Haily Betten valid?" "I already gave that answer to Joel, and he knows my position." He hung up. His lack of a response was his answer. We answer "yes" by not giving an answer, and for answers of "no," we state that word up front and quickly. The evidence was valid.

The next expert was the FBI scientist who testifies in DNA cases. The telephone operator in DC gave me the FBI phone number, and that operator passed me to the DNA Fingerprinting expert. "Dr. Priestley, do you have just a moment to answer a few questions on DNA testing?"

"Sure. This evidence is great. I've testified in over 300 cases and won all of them." I explained briefly the issues. "Is the DNA Fingerprinting evidence valid in both cases?" "In the case that involves you, lab controls validate the evidence. In regard to the band shifting, I know the work of that lab, and it's rock solid. They have a 3 percent margin of error that covers the band shifting. We're not as strict: We have a 5 percent margin of error for the FBI." "Can you testify in this case?" "I'd love to. Have the DA call me. I love this evidence because I'm always right."

Next I needed to check with the lab that made the error. I reached the CEO. "Dr. Sefaborb, I'm Cathy Winkler, the rape victim. I wanted to know if you have been able to find the lab error in the Redding case?" "The police goofed up. You have no right to talk with me." "Dr. Sefaborb, I was with the police the whole time. The detective had only the blood of two people, which he carefully, immediately, and with painstaking accuracy labeled with our names. There is no error by the police. I know the error is in the lab. You only have 1,500 samples. The error is recoverable and explainable." "You have no right to call me." He hung up. His nonresponse meant a yes-he-was-guilty-of-an-error answer, and either he couldn't find the foul-up or didn't care. They don't get paid for looking for their mistakes. Because the CEO would not talk to me, I tried others who worked at the lab. "This is The Science Laboratory. How may I direct your call?" "I'd like to speak with Dr. Gemal." "What is this in regard to?" "She did the lab work on a case." "Is this in regard to the Redding case?" "Yes." "I'm sorry, but you are not allowed to talk with anyone here." She hung up. I called several other DNA labs and experts. All validated the evidence.

I then tried the rape trauma angle. Since I had read the research, I knew names and universities of the researchers. First was Dr. Kowler. "The artist sketch looks just like the defendant. Eighty percent of my evidence matches the defendant. But every time I see him, I have a different memory. While everyone thinks the sketch is an identical match to the defendant, I don't see the resemblance. We have DNA Fingerprinting evidence to validate the defendant as the rapist, but the DA wants to throw out the evidence. What I want to know is whether or not I'm suffering from Post-Traumatic Stress Disorder (PTSD)?" "From what you have told me, yes. This is common." "Have you ever testified in cases like this?" "Yes. This seems like a great case because of the 80 percent match and your inability to even see a resemblance between the defendant and the sketch. I'd be willing to testify after I review the evidence and interview you." "Great. I'll give your name and telephone number to the DA."

The same response came from several other rape trauma experts. I now had a list of experts for Joel.

With legal and scientific support, I was ready to meet with Bill Sr., but I needed a backup strategy and a threat. The threat was a press release that announced a rally in front of the courthouse on Friday at noon. Since this case initially had media coverage as the first DNA case, we had a headline: Rapist Freed Despite DNA Evidence. Friends helped: "Cathy, how can I pressure the DA?" "Christine, what organization do you belong to?" "I just started a group called Women Against Violence and for Equality (WAVE), and nominated and elected myself as President." "Could you get the president of WAVE to call the DA?" "No problem." We laughed and continued our campaign.

> March 15, 1991: Activism is exhilarating. Here I was an unknown, both as a person and in regards to the process of persuasion, and yet the telephone calls demonstrated my legal rights. My action-oriented friends gave me names of people to contact and made calls themselves. Many networks of communication went unrealized. I had so much fun that afternoon. It was a thrill to call up unknown people, explain the issues, and then hear their words of support. Most calls were like this. These super people had the same set of values: to stop rapists. After twenty years of hundreds, probably thousands of people's efforts to change others' misperceptions of rape, their words and efforts paid off in this case. Thank you, thank you, thank you.

Confronting the DA

"Bill Sr., would you have time to see me tomorrow regarding the case?" He answered immediately, "I can squeeze you in at 11 A.M. but only for a few minutes. By the way, you don't have to fill up our telephone lines with calls. No one pressures me into a decision. Also, you have no right to do the legal investigation in this case. We are *not your* lawyers." "Thanks for seeing me tomorrow." The fact that he offered to meet and to meet immediately with me was evidence of my power.

Saul agreed to go with me as a supporter, not a lawyer, to the meeting. I outlined my argument. At the top of the sheet were the two central points—Trial Continuance and Redo My DNA. Saul dressed in a shirt—without a tie or suit coat, formal but not aggressive. Warning Saul about Bill Sr.'s habit was accurate: As we entered, he put away his toothbrush. Saul and I stifled our laughter. To begin the meeting, the ole boys placed themselves in a circle, leaving me on the outside. Saul stepped back and made a place for me. Next, the ole boys focused on legal control verbally with Saul. After all, Saul was a lawyer like them. He was ready. "Bill Sr. and Joel, I'm here to support Cathy. She'll speak for herself."

Standing over us, Bill Sr. began in a gentle voice: "Cathy, I care a lot about you, and I'm only saying this for your own good. You need therapy. You have an obsession; you can't let go; you can't understand others' perspectives. You need therapy now." The rapist, after beating me up, spoke gently about taking me to the hospital. Bill Sr. belittled me like the rapist, and without evidence, made an instantaneous evaluation of me: His was not a solid legal position! Only one month ago, he was on my side and supportive! Too many feminists and too many past personal experiences expressed the meaning of Bill Sr.'s words: Words of denigration meant the discriminator felt cornered. My comment inverted his interpretation and smothered his position. "Thanks for the compliments." His look of surprise was a precious moment. Knowledge is great.

"Bill Sr., isn't it true that we do not know which DNA I am?" "Yes." I started with a lawyer's approach: Present questions of the facts and through the questions expose their legal illogic. "The error is either in the 1988 or 1990 sample. Correct?" "Yes, but . . ." "Let me finish, please. If the error is in the 1990 sample, then isn't it true that the 1988 semen evidence sample is legally viable evidence for a trial?" "Yes." "Then, would you test my blood and find out who I am? I could have my blood drawn tomorrow." "Yes, that's fine." "If the error is in the 1990 sample, then I ask you to proceed with the case. If the error is in the 1988 sample, then I realize we are in a different position." "Cathy, lab errors are always a problem in a legal case." "Bill Sr., isn't it true that if the lab error is in 1990 sample, then that blood is not part of the case?" "Yes, but the defense attorney knows about it." "The defense attorney also knows that the 1988 DNA sample of Redding thrown out matched—exactly—the semen sample." "Cathy, the policy is not to proceed with any case if there is an error." "Isn't that policy too absolute and too obsolete? Shouldn't the policy depend on whether or not the error is explainable? We are human beings. We make mistakes. If an error is explainable, then we can proceed with the case."

"We don't know where the error is: the detective or the lab?" "Yes, Bill Sr., I know where the error is. I was with the detective. He was excruciatingly particular. He immediately labeled the tubes of blood and sealed them in envelopes. The detective did not make a mistake. Second, we know that there was no mixup of those blood samples because we have

Redding's blood and semen samples from 1988, 1989, and 1990: they all match. The detective could not have made the error. The error is in the lab." "Yes, that seems logical. But whether you find the error or not, it still existed." Since this approach was not successful, I used a Mexican technique: Change the subject and give time for the other issue to germinate in their minds: "Bill Sr., what about the issue of trauma? I know experts in that area who are willing to testify." Emphatically and definitively, Bill Sr. said, "This state does not accept rape trauma as evidence. That will not change." Bill Sr. is the one making the decisions. He is the state. Instead of taking responsibility, he blames an abstract entity. Time to change subjects again. "Bill Sr., you know Joel and I have different perspectives on this case [using diplomacy], could I work with a different lawyer in your office?" "*No*, Joel has the case and wants it." "Maybe Joel doesn't want to stay on the case. Maybe some other lawyer has more interest in the case. Maybe another lawyer and I would get along better." "Joel is on the case and that is the issue."

Joel spoke for the first time: "Cathy, I'm sorry about Monday." *Was his apology part of Bill Sr.'s scheme to quiet me?* "Joel, I appreciate your apology. On Monday, you attacked my thoughts during the rape. My thoughts are not evidence, but ideas. Trials center on criminal's actions. Please don't ever attack a VISA's thoughts again. Your words horrified me." Humbly, Joel accepted my berating. Meanwhile, Bill Sr. stood up and walked around his desk to end the meeting. For me, it ends when he employs his own legal logic and agrees to a continuance.

"Bill Sr., can one of your detectives get my blood drawn tomorrow while I'm in town?" "Yes, we'll assign one." "Bill Sr., are you going to ask the judge for a continuance on the case? At least let's keep the case open until we discover the results of tomorrow's DNA test." "I can't promise that." "Bill Sr., I can't leave until I know that you have agreed to that." "Cathy, I don't know what the judge will decide." "Bill Sr., didn't you tell me that the judge usually abides by your decision?" "Yes, that's usually true." "Then, Bill Sr., why can't you ask for a continuance?" "Cathy, I just can't promise it." "Doesn't Judge Foible want this guy convicted? Wouldn't he be reasonable and at least give us time to find the error?" "Cathy . . ." "Bill Sr., you haven't given any legal reason why you should not ask for a continuance." "OK, I'll do it. Will you be there Friday?" "Yes, as always. I want Redding to know that it is not over yet." Joel looked down and away. Suspicious behavior. The failure of Bill Sr. and Joel to legally explain their position angered me, and I turned my anger into a source of strength to find new strategies.

March 15, 1991: Methods of lawyers are important to learn. First, at the Wednesday meeting I asked that Joel not be present because of his verbal abuse on Monday. I would not tolerate that abuse. Bill Sr. approached Saul, presenting the point that Joel was not abusive. Saul was a gem: "I'm here to support Cathy. She knows what is abusive." In other words, Bill Sr. wanted to get Saul on his side and change the odds from two people versus two people to three men versus one victim. Saul ensured the odds remained two versus two. I did lose on that point of exclusion of Joel from the meeting who sat on the far side of the room. Bill Sr. began by letting me know that no one pushes him around, no one tells him what to do, and he makes his own decisions. I figured that every time he said "no one pushes him around" meant that he had received a phone call. I did not tabulate how many times he said that, but he got a ton of phone calls. Then, he let me know that I have always been a problem in this case. Luckily, Saul spoke at the right times: "You know, Cathy is the one who hired a private investigator who found the rapist. I know this because I found the private investigator for her." That quieted them for a moment.

And then Bill Sr. argued that there were two boulders (problems) in this case. Of course, his perspective differed from mine. "Only two boulders! I have already jumped over 50 boulders, a mountain of boulders. What's two more?!" At least he did give the appearance of listening to my argument and agreed to a continuance. Before the meeting was over, Bill Sr. made it clear again that I needed counseling and therapy due to my serious psychological problems. Also, he stated that he knew that the legal system had raped me. Isn't he the legal system who is raping me? Here this man is raping me, verbally abusing me, aware of the four years of waiting, admitting like the rapist that he, alias the legal system, raped me and thinks that it is bizarre that I'm not 100 percent calm. How many times does one have to stand up for one's values! Am I the only one who has this weird view that we should stop rapists? Bill Sr. grabbed his toothbrush and left for other meetings; his words left tire marks all over my body.

Immediately after the meeting, I walked over to see Stan. I didn't tell him about my meeting with Bill Sr. "Hey, Cathy, how are you doing? Let me show you my new offices." When I saw that the only framed picture on his walls was the news article of the Redding case, surprise widened my eyes. That was his status symbol! "Oh, I always regretted not trying that case." "Stan, I want to know your position on the case. Let me explain the current situation." And I did. "Do you think that another DNA test is necessary to find out where the lab error is?" "Cathy, Redding is a horrible character. He's the type that, if he were out, he might attack my wife. Yes, I think they should find the error. They should do everything necessary to stop Redding." Stan recognized his own vulnerability. The next day, Stan, who never initiated a phone call without a purpose, called. "Cathy, just wanted to check in with you." *How did he get the phone number?* "You know that it is hard to defend cases with errors in court. This is one case." His call explained the network of power. Stan was part of Bill Sr.'s plan to silence me.

The meeting with Bill Sr. pounded my body into a state of emotional turmoil. The day after the meeting was one of the most physically traumatic in my life. After the detective drained my blood for another DNA test, I went to the farm to recuperate. Lots of walks, baths, and times of nothingness were a necessity. When my friend Don and I went on a walk, some detectives from the county approached us. *Why were these detectives half an hour from their district? Bill Sr. was out to get me!* But there was a sighting of a stolen vehicle from that district in this county. False alarm.

On Thursday afternoon, Joel informed me that the judge agreed to a continuance. I canceled the press conference. The court hearing was at 9 A.M. on Friday. It usually started late, and I was late. When I got to the courtroom, the case on the continuance was over. I saw Redding. Then I went to the DA's office to get copies of some papers from the case. Joel was attentive but always looking down and away. Suspicious.

Feeling complacent because of my ability to stand up to the DAs and win, I went to peruse the legal papers. Finally I recognized the similarity between Redding-the-defendant and the artist composite drawing. He looked *identical* to the composite. The composite was more than an identical; it was Redding. Release of a piece of my trauma occurred.

Now I knew the truth. During the physical attack, Redding was not the only person in that room. The DAs, defense attorneys, and judges were there also. The thought of another attack from the lawyers on identification of the rapist was a trauma. Standing up to the legal people—which involved my experiencing an emotional upheaval equivalent to a heart attack—enabled me to break through part of that trauma and see what was always in my mind. I couldn't yet identify Redding with the attacker's face. There was more trauma. But I knew I could rid myself of it.

March 15, 1991: The hearing on Friday morning was the official filing, but not an issue in contention. That same day in the DA's office, the link between the face of Redding the defendant and the artist composite congealed. Now I can see the incredible photographic similarity. This is only one link in my memory that has come back. I thought the remembering experience would be different: a lightning bolt would sap my memory back into existence. Guess not! But since then, I noticed a number of changes in my own body. Friday and Saturday were days in which I felt pleasant to be myself again, and my desire to eat all the time and to eat lots and lots of carbohydrates vanished: Vegetables satisfied me. This is all kinda funny. By the time my memory comes back in order for me to identify the rapist, the evidence is illegal! In other words, my word is not legally valid because my traumatized memory does not fit the legal system's time schedule. As an anthropologist, I know that people in other societies would laugh at the absurdity of our legal practices. Everyone thinks that the defendant is the rapist, and yet these believers are also the ones who legally argue for his freedom. Lawyers strategize for power and status. My strategizing is to escape the rapist's intentions: rape and murder next time.

After experiencing and writing this newsletter, I felt depressed. But a friend, Sally—a very wise woman—made an astute comment: "You are lucky to have the chance to stand up to this. Imagine how many people have to live with the horror of rape and the rapists, and cannot even try to do something about it." Friends like this are the best therapists. And, that was how I spent my spring break. How was yours?

P.S. To make life more interesting, the DA lied to me. He dismissed both cases of rape against Redding. Don't worry: my gyrating mind is at work. Next installment soon.

Broadening the Network

At the end of the week, Saul called me: "Cathy, you won't believe what happened today." "Wasn't last week enough?" "I ran into Judge Foible. I told him that I had helped you with the case. Then he said: 'That's an incredible case. Bill Sr. asked for a dismissal.'" "A dismissal? He didn't ask for a continuance?" Bill Sr. lied. "What can I do now? Is it over?" "Actually, I do have good news. Bill Sr. wants this supercop job. The governor asked the legislature to create a new position to oversee all police and legal forces in the state. That's why Bill Sr. wanted to get rid of the case. He didn't want any bad publicity." "How could winning the Redding case be bad publicity?" "It took Bob four years to get a case to trial!"

215

"He would avoid convicting a rapist because of that?" "I'm afraid so." "What can I do?" "Start using the phone again." And I did.

The feminist politician Cheryl Standup needed to know me better to support me further. The following weekend, I drove to the DA's city again. I met with her and her friend. "Cathy, this is Quincy." "Glad to meet you, Quincy. What do you do?" "I'm in public relations." "Honey, why do you think I brought him along! He could be useful to us. By the way, I know someone in television who wants to interview you. Let me know if you want to go that route." I stored that information away for later. Quincy explained his personal reasons for supporting me: "About a year ago, a man raped my grandmother in a city south of here. She has Alzheimer's and couldn't remember the details. But we combed that area, and with DNA Fingerprinting, got the guy. My brother and I had a lot of problems convincing the DA that this man was the rapist and then convincing him to use DNA Fingerprinting. The rapist is now rotting in jail." "Wow, that just happened last year!" "Yes, so I understand your problems with the DA." "I'm so sorry for your grandmother. Does she remember the attack?" "Not really." "Her mind might not remember, but her body does."

During the meeting, Cheryl got a chance to size me up. I gave her several of my articles on rape and trauma, and we decided the first strategy: another meeting with Bill Sr. A letter to the news media connected this rape case with the supercop issue: How could a person head all legal and police institutions if he could not convict a rapist with DNA Fingerprinting evidence? My question would raise eyebrows, especially those eyebrows that were against Bill Sr.'s appointment. Also attached was my article describing rape as social murder. While no media coverage came as a result of my letter, people in the media did make phone calls to Bill Sr.

Bill Sr. willingly scheduled me in for a meeting the following Monday. This time I went in with more support: Marley, a therapist of people abused, Dale, a therapist for abusers, several politicians, a minister from the neighborhood, the wife of the mayor, and neighborhood representatives. Eight of us surrounded Bill Sr. The issue was how to stop the rapist legally. Although Bill Sr. had his plan of action, so did we. He began the meeting and tried to direct it, but Marley came prepared. She used a feminist strategy: Soak'em in honey until they choke on their hate. "Bill Sr., Cathy asked me to attend this meeting, and I am certainly willing to sit in and offer advice," she said, hinting that she was not a friend of mine. "Bill Sr., while we've worked together on trials [she has testified as an expert witness], I've never had the chance to tell you how impressive your work is. It is clear that you work to help victims. Your intelligence and diligence always impressed me." I glanced at his face. *He believed her!* I played my part, acting double crossed with a look of astonishment on my face.

Feeling on a better footing with Marley in his corner, Bill Sr. directed again the conversation: "Cathy, this is a very serious issue. It is extremely important that we stop rapists. I do everything possible legally to do it. I've even started a home for children incested in order to protect them from those rapists. The difficulty in this case is that *you* cannot identify Redding." "Bill Sr., you told me years ago that the evidence did not rest on my ability to identify the rapist, but DNA Fingerprinting. Have you called the lab to find the error?" "Yes, but they have had no luck. They didn't make a mistake." "Bill Sr., you and I both know that the error is in the lab, and it's their responsibility to find it." "Cathy, if you could identify the rapist, we wouldn't need the lab. You are the one who is the jinx in this case. You can't identify him and . . ." Marley broke in and changed her position from his friend to his therapist: "Bill Sr., stop blaming Cathy. We are not here to blame the victim. We are here to discuss viable legal issues. If you proceed with this argument, we will have to leave." Stunned was his reaction—caught in a terrible error: He had condemned the victim! And Marley, his supposed friend, had reprimanded him—in front of politicians.

Dale asked *the* question: "What would have to happen for you to say that it is impossible to go to trial?" "We are working on all leads. We will find a way to get him to trial." Dale had rephrased the question—"What is necessary for you to stop your abuse?"—to fit the legal context. Dale exposed Bill Sr. as a legal abuser who, like all abusers, avoids answering the question. As the meeting closed, Rev. Hope asked all of us to join hands and pray: "We ask you to help our DA make the right decision. Amen."

Expecting no resolution from the meeting, I put my next plan into action. I sent out a press release. The first response was from a reporter who refused to support a person raped until the trial was over! Several days later, a rather conservative columnist, forceful on issues of crime, called. He must be a good journalist; he had tracked me down at a job interview. His message was supportive and to the point: He loved my article and would call Bill Sr. to stop this rapist. After a word with Bill Sr., his support dissipated. When I returned home, Jane Hanson—a columnist who was well known for her work to support VISAs' rights—called. Thus began my first step into the media limelight. The result of the attention was that the lab reexamined the case and found the error: It was a result of mislabeling. Surprise, surprise! The DA got a third indictment. Surprise, surprise! The trial was scheduled to begin August 3, 1991.

July 5, 1991: Re: Good news—1. Job = Permanent, and 2. Yes = Reindictment of Rapist. Let's start with the first piece of surprising good news. I have a job for next year. That piece of news is probably not a surprise. The unexpected news though is that I have a contract until 1998. In other words, I have a tenured track position. I'm in recuperation in a hideaway from the most recent struggles and making plans for my next home with a used piano, a dog named Sneakers, herbs growing around my kitchen window, and a guest bedroom.

Let me begin with the "P.S." from my last letter: "Just to make life more interesting, I found out that Bill Sr. lied to me. He dismissed both cases of rape [the case with me and the one with Haily] against Redding. Don't worry: my gyrating mind is at work." Unfortunately, most people completely misinterpreted these sentences, emphasizing the power of Bill Sr. and dismissing my mental gyrations. Never doubt an anthropologist's mental gyrations: we have cross-cultural possibilities! To begin, there are two types of dismissal. For those of you who are interested in my legal education: 1) the first is a "null process" dismissal in which the DA still has the life of the crime (7 years) to reindict, and 2) the second type is a "dead docket" dismissal in which the possibility of reindictment is only six months, or in this case, the deadline is September 8, 1991. Of course, Bill Sr. asked for the second type of dismissal (the worst possible scenario).

I flew for another official meeting with the DA. This struggle cost me more than $1,000 [only one person ever helped me with money]. Despite yet another loss with Bill Sr., I felt emotionally healthier: the therapists protected me from verbal accusations, and I had legally and fairly presented the issues. The following points I stressed to the press: 1) The lab report verifies the DNA Fingerprinting results for the other VISA, and these results specifically name Redding as the rapist, and in addition to Joel's letter to the Board of Paroles, written in January 1991, states that the DNA for the case with the other VISA is valid, and 2) in that same letter—may I please have the pleasure to quote him: "Mr. Redding is as dangerous and assaultive a criminal as I have seen in my fourteen years as a prosecutor." While stressing that Redding is one of the really bad guys, he dismissed the cases!

On the error in the lab results, both the lab and Bill Sr. gave up. I hadn't. As stated in the last letter, I had Bill Sr. take another blood sample from me and send it to the lab. This test demonstrated that my DNA was the 1990 sample and not the 1938 sample. With this point clarified, the lab then discovered what happened in 1988. Apparently, the lab mislabeled someone else's blood as mine and never tested my blood in 1988. You know—the usual number switching—a familiar practice of all human beings. Without testing it, the lab had sent the box of my 1988 blood samples back to the police evidence room and there they misplaced it. For two months (May and June), the police and Bill Sr. looked for it. Lo and behold (there's a lot of "lo and beholds" in this case), it surfaced. This box is important to demonstrate that the lab never tested my 1988 blood sample, and the chain of custody was intact. On June 27, 1991, the DA reindicted Kenneth Redding the rapist for the third time, and the trial date is in August. The hardest part of this process was not the confrontation with Bill Sr. While I admit that was difficult and quite emotional, I did recover quickly. People's verbal attacks against me with their explicit negative comments are an experience of horror. These uneducated statements by a terrific number of people who felt that Bill Sr. was right, I was wrong, and therefore I had an obsession, paralyzed me at times. But I always remember my set of values:

Rapists are wrong, rape is *always* wrong, and *all reasonable avenues are necessary to stop rapists.* All rapists are serial, and this rapist considers rape his occupation. If freed, he will continue raping women, and I suspect that *murder is on his agenda next time.* Conviction of a rapist *frees* all past victims of most trauma—and for this guy, I have no doubt the number is in the hundreds—and conviction *protects* hundreds of women from experiencing in the future the terrorizing hell from this rapist's hands.

For those people who think that I have an obsession and whoever else is interested, I am selling T-shirts with the following logo: I AM OBSESSED, WHY AREN'T YOU? These T-shirts are available in all colors and sizes. Of course, they are 100 percent cotton and shrink proof. T-shirts sell for $25.00 plus $3.00 postage. Please send your money, size, and color preference to one of the above addresses. Profits are for the case [One person ordered a T-shirt]. All the crazy routes in this case actually excite my book editor who keeps letting me know that even the author Kafka could not have dreamed up such a plot. Much love and a ton of appreciation,

P.S. At this point, I would like to have a theme party: "I am not who
I was, but I have been found."

The Friday before the trial, Joel called. "Cathy, the trial is postponed."
"What happened?" "This is Redding's third indictment. In 1988, the
state supreme court stated that the court of appeals prior to trial must
review all third indictments." "Did you know this a month ago when you
called me about the trial date?" "Yes." Sometimes even the discriminators
tell the truth. "What about the case with Haily Betten? Isn't that just two
indictments?" "Yes, but we don't want to go to trial without both cases."
"Thanks, Joel." I got off the phone before the fit of crying erupted, and
then with a gut-wrenching force I exploded into tears. The shaking and
sobbing went on for hours.

Going Public, Rape Trial

A television interview was now a necessity. I had no desire to go public,
but I had to stop the lying by the DAs. They knew that I had been waiting
in the city for the trial; they knew that I was in a state of pretrial jitters;
and they didn't tell me the truth. "Laurie," as I muffled the sobs, "This is
Cathy Winkler, Cheryl Standup's friend. She stated that you want to
interview me." "I'm glad you called. I ran it past my manager, and he
OK'd it. I'll also interview Bill Sr." For the next forty-eight hours, I
engaged in intense self-therapy to prepare myself for the interview. Every
four hours, I jogged three miles and then took a long hot bath. I ate well
and relaxed those other hours. When the time came for the interview,
trauma and anger did not dictate my life. The interview was fine.

Bill Sr. was smart. His only available time for the interview was after
mine. As he knew, the reporter questioned him based on her interview
with me, and he discredited my position. He argued that the legal difficulty was with Cathy Winkler, a victim who could not identify the rapist:
Victim's identification convinces juries. Unfortunately for me, Laurie
sided with Bill Sr. In the end though, the media pressure worked: Joel
tried Redding for the rape of Haily.

This was Joel's first DNA case. As Joel questioned the scientist Sefaborb, the jury members leaned their bodies forward to listen carefully to
the evidence. Since the first pretrial on this evidence, Sefaborb was not
the same. Like Joel, he spoke rapidly: he raced through his explanations.
The speed and multi-syllabic words left the jury with the impression that
Joel and Sefaborb did not want to explain the evidence. Both men were

arrogant and self-centered. The jury became angry at the speed of and unnecessarily complicated explanations. Dr. Mismanaging testified for the defense. He did not deny the validity of the DNA but raised issues that it was not the best evidence. Joel wrote the following note on him: "Mostly does paternity testing and does some DNA. Always testifies for defendants; has testified against the Big 3 labs. Financial interest in knocking off other labs because he wants a contract with state government." During Mismanaging's testimony, Sefaborb sat in the audience-less pews and smugly laughed. He chided at his comments. His attitude disturbed the jury.

After several days out, the jurors returned and explained to the judge that they did not agree. The vote was six to six. The judge excused them for the day, but informed them to return Monday and resume deliberation. They left. As I walked out, Redding turned to his sisters and gave them a victory sign along with a huge smile that stated "I showed them." His attitude set off my trauma and ignited my speech: "YOU WILL BE STOPPED," I yelled as I pointed my finger at him. My peripheral vision revealed the astonished looks on the faces of the judge and Joel. Previously, the sisters had offered to share their lunches with me. Now the family of Redding knew who I was! With such extensive knowledge of the courthouse, I went to hide and cry. In the meantime, Joel had sent people around the building to look for me. No one could find me.

"Cathy, there's still hope." "Yes, if the court of appeals approves the third indictment." "No, this is in regard to a detective from Mumford Highway. He stopped by and has several unsolved cases. He thinks that Redding is the rapist. The MO is similar. I'd bet my job that Redding raped all three women." "Mumford Highway is quite far away, and there's no public transportation there. Do you think Redding really raped those women?" "Yes, it's a strong possibility. I've spoken with Bill Sr. We'll get DNA tests run on the three cases." "I hope it works." As I left the courtroom that last day, I misplaced my textbook with my new address inside it. Did I leave it in the courtroom where Redding or his sisters could find it? In a panic, I ran to the courtroom. Redding's sister was at the door, observing me. Did she have my book and address? I retraced my steps throughout the building. At the exit, the security guard handed me the book. The person who found it knew me and which exit I used. It wasn't a member of Redding's family. I was safe.

As I arrived at the university for my first day of classes and parked my car, several faculty members told me to go home: Our building was on fire. Is this some type of indoctrination! "I have to see if there is a fire."

Having experienced fires at a high school where I taught, at an apartment building where I lived, at a house that I cared for, and several warehouse fires at my father's business, this type of calamity was not unusual. When I first approached the building, I laughed. This has happened to me before. Tomorrow, we'll scrub down the walls and clean the soot off of the desks. But as I watched the evening news, the smoking building was a flaming inferno. By the next day, the fire had consumed the floors and walls. We had no classes that week. It continued to burn for several days. The shock of that disaster superseded the shock of the trial.

"Cathy, there's a very serious matter. Redding's lawyer has accused you of tampering with the jury. You must come back." I laughed. *How could I tamper with the jury when I had no contact with them!* "Joel, what's the evidence?" "His sister saw you talking with the foreperson." "His sister saw me talking to the security guard and not the foreperson. There was a security guard in the courtroom when the foreperson returned to retrieve an item from the jury room. Joel, I do want Redding convicted, but I did not tamper with the jurors. I didn't even try. I am not returning. There is no evidence against me." "Well, the judge will hear the defense attorney's argument tomorrow, and I'll be in touch." "Joel, could I get Haily's address? Since the cases are separate now, I'd like to meet her." "Yes, I think that's OK." Joel called the following day to inform me that the judge had dismissed the defense attorney's charges against me due to lack of evidence.

September 1991: News—Trial postponed, Again. Court of appeals to decide validity of third indictment. Stop. Other victim's trial was 8/12/91. Jury deliberated for a week. Hung jury—> Mistrial. Stop. Result of TV and press coverage = investigation of 3 other unsolved rape cases. Suspect: Redding the rapist. Stop. College of Arts and Sciences, including my department, burned down on 8/26/91. Stop. And that's the whole truth. Stop. Good News = bought old blue car. Stop.

January 2, 1992: After the August TV interview, the DA informed me that they had decided—surprise, surprise!—to go ahead with the case with the other VISA testifying. At the trial, most people felt that since my testimony was out, I could go alone. Luckily a few really good friends found a day or two to help me through it and understood my trauma. The TV reporter and I simultaneously came up with this brilliant plan. She could interview me daily from the VISA's perspective. VISAs' Rights, Yes!! On the first day of the trial, the judge gagged me. This was not a dilemma for the reporter because she had approval for a camera in the courtroom. Instead the TV people took pictures of me during the trial proceedings, repeated my comments from the earlier interview, and then stated that the judge had gagged me.

The trial was awful. On the one hand, my reactions were to remain muted during the trial, and on the other hand, everyone worried about my reactions. As a result, emotional turmoil reigned. The defense attorney brought in a geneticist who makes money ($3–4,000 per case for 15 past cases/year = $45–60,000/year) by testifying for rapists and raising doubts about the DNA. He challenged the band shifting and the statistics. The laboratory expert's statistics were 1/100,000 and the statistics of the defense attorney's geneticist were 1/250. Suspicious!

To be honest, Joel did a brilliant job on the scientific part of the trial. He knew that jargon. But by burying himself in the scientific argument and in beating the geneticist, he forgot about the jury's need to understand the labyrinth of complicated points. The trial ended with a hung jury. The jury foreperson (he's about 65 years old) stated in the newspaper: "This has been the most gruesome thing I've ever been through because of the bickering, the arguing, and the stubbornness of some people." The DA's interviews with the other jury members showed that they had figured out who I was. First, the DA had inadvertently stated my name during the case, and the lab had rerouted the second VISA's results. They figured out why the rerouting had occurred. One woman juror felt that this was a white scam by the DA. She refused to believe any of the evidence. Every time there was a dispute, the jury went back into the courtroom and listened to the testimony. After a week, she stated that there was no rape. The other jurors pointed out to her that the defense attorney stated explicitly at the beginning of the trial that there was a rape but the defendant was not the culprit. When she took that position, the situation was hopeless. Despite the 100 percent conviction rate with DNA in 30 other states, this was a mistrial.

The next move by Joel was to send the three other cases to the lab, but Bill Sr. stated that they couldn't do this because there was no blood from the rapist. Therefore, those cases were over. I stated that the defendant's blood was in preponderant supply: They had three samples. Then he stated there was no money. I told him I could raise the money. Then, the laboratory sent back the wrong blood; they sent the defendant/rapist's 1988 blood and not the 1990 blood. The 1988 blood is illegal because the first search warrant was illegal. They therefore have to send the 1990 blood. But we all know that the 1990 blood and 1988 blood are the same and a match. If the argument between whether to use the 1988 or the 1990 blood is logical, please point it out to me. At this point in time, Joel has sent the 1990 blood off to another laboratory because of his dislike of the first lab and their error. He cannot use the state crime lab's DNA equipment because they will not do DNA tests on cases prior to December 1990. Every prisoner wants the test.

A few weeks later, I went to find Haily (figure 10.1). She had a nice low-income place but with defects like no window screens or air conditioning. I met her mother and three kids. The latter were like monkeys playing all over me: loveable and funny. "Hey, kids. That's enough. Go outside and play for a while." "Haily, I'm glad you testified in August. The evidence in Redding's attack against me is still in legal limbo." "Hey, did the jury convict him?" "Didn't Joel call you?" "No. I don't have a phone. They picked me up to testify that one day, and that's it." "The jury deliberated for a week but were hung. The judge called a mistrial. Now we'll have to see what will happen. Haily, I'm not giving up, and I wanted to know your position." "Hey, this is not the first time for me. About ten years ago, two guys raped me. I knew them. They waited in jail five months for the trial. Jury found them guilty, and the judge gave them time served. After that trial, they walked out of the courthouse with me. But they'll rape again, and they'll be in jail longer next time. My conviction will bust them later." Her statement revealed that she understood the women's movement: Every time we speak up, we help someone else. "Cathy, I can testify again. I want to stop that son of a bitch."

Six months later, they found the other VISAs and sent off their blood. The DNA testing would take another three to four months. Since the DA was not in a hurry for the results, the lab could delay. Joel regularly remarked about the difficulty of the court of appeals and that maybe we wouldn't need it. "Joel, if Redding did not rape the other women, then the court of appeals is our last chance. We have to try it. Yes, I want you to pursue it." This conversation occurred many times. The meaning of his words demonstrated Bill Sr.'s desire to drop the case. Persuading me to drop the court of appeals' process and depend on the new VISAs' evidence was their goal. From my perspective, they could not discard any option.

Stalling Games

And I could do nothing. How can I get media support when Bill Sr. could demonstrate that they had ordered more DNA tests for three other cases?

Figure 10.1   Haily Betten

Who wouldn't believe that this rapist had attacked other women? Aren't rapists serial? Doesn't this rapist have a 1980 indictment against him? Maybe, just maybe, he did rape those other women. I could believe that, I wanted to believe that, and I did not want to be the person who testifies. The latter is a hellish job that I would gladly pass over.

Joel said to me, "Cathy, sadly the DNA from those other victims doesn't match. But you know what? For two of those victims, the DNA matches, and the same guy raped them. Can you believe it?" This patriarch again exposes his ideology of lies. Why is this a surprise to Joel that the DNA matches for two of the VISAs? He told me previously that he would bet his job that the same man raped all three of these VISAs, and that man was Redding. If the cases were so similar, why aren't there three DNA matches? Joel's reaction revealed the plot by him and Bill Sr. Use those other VISAs to hush me. In silencing me, they falsely raised those VISAs' and my hopes for conviction. They spent the county's sparse money to find the women and to do the expensive DNA tests. The purpose of their actions was not to seek justice but an effort to gag me. In September 1992, "Cathy, the court of appeals' decision is in, and they agree that the third indictment does not jeopardize the rights of the

225

defendant." "When is the trial?" "There are still some other issues. As you probably know, Bill Sr. gave up the DA position, and Tim is the new DA. He makes that decision. If he did go ahead with this case, then we still have the issue of the lab error." "But I thought you told me that the lab could explain the error." "Yes, but the judge has to accept it as valid and accept that there is no alteration of the evidence." "Thanks, I guess." "Also, Redding fired Marble for poor representation." "He's kept Redding from conviction for four years!" "Well, anyway, a public defender, Statel, who is the best, wants the case. She goes for high-profile cases."

Another year of wait-and-see. The case was on the back burner of my life. I focused instead on my work and life. In the meantime, activity in Bill Sr.'s life was at an all-time high. While the supercop position fell through, he had another agenda: to run for representative to the U.S. Congress. That year Bill Sr. needed to quiet me because he was in the public light. His goal was to hush all negative publicity. He succeeded. I could think of no effective way to expose him. Bill Sr. borrowed $50,000 as a personal loan and ran against a woman for the position. Ironically, the woman won the primary beating Bill Sr., but she lost the election. Bill Sr. gave up his DA's position and was on the job market.

The lab did admit the error, but, because of the contractual arrangements, kept all the money. The DA, or our taxes, paid for this $11,000 error by the "best laboratory in the world." The lab did send the following apology to the DA: "We regret any inconvenience this may have caused." The lab did not apologize to the VISAs, nor did the lab have to provide monetary compensation to them.

Although the stalling continued, I put together a package on the case: legal explanation and past strategies employed along with my article on the rape attack. I sent it to several investigative magazine shows. Exposure was not my intent. Rather, these shows call and check on the cases. Whatever happened with those packages, I don't know. But I do remember Tim's reaction when he met me in October. We had a late brunch on a Sunday morning. I chose a calm time of the day and week, a time when Tim would feel relaxed and comfortable. He was nervous. "Tim, I'm Cathy Winkler." "Yes, I've seen you in the office." His voice nervously echoed his negative feelings. Everyone in the office knew me! "Tim, what are your plans for the case? The court of appeals has approved the third indictment, and the lab says they can explain the error."

"Cathy, this isn't the best case." "Tim, is there such an entity as the best case? This guy rapes women. Don't we have to try?" He looked down and away from me. Clearly, he had to say yes to my questions, but these were questions that he did not want to answer. "Yes, we'll try. We'll see what happens at the pretrial." "Tim, if the judge turns down the case, will you proceed with the case that involves Haily?" "I can't make that decision right now." Avoidance meant no: He didn't want to proceed with that case either unless I brought more media pressure on him, and he didn't want media pressure. Later in November, Joel called: "Cathy, as you probably know [in other words, Joel knew about the meeting with me and Tim], Tim gave the go ahead for the pretrial on your case." "Joel, it's not *my* case; it's Redding's case." "Cathy, I just say that to distinguish you and Haily." "Fine, then please say Redding's case that involves Cathy and Redding's case that involves Haily. I'm not the rapist. I don't like it when you use those words." "Whatever." He never changed. "In January and February, I have two big cases coming up, and I talked with Judge Foible, and March is a good time for the pretrial. We haven't set a date yet."

January 2, 1992: Dear Coalition of Freedom Fighters: This is a quaint place with few movies and restaurants, but close to a large city. The common social activity is dinner parties where people fix fabulous dishes and then sit around and talk for hours. Quite humane! Jogging continues with its regional variations. I began in August in the 110-degree heat. Well, maybe I didn't jog, but I did walk. We won't discuss the pace, just note that I covered the distance. The route takes me by cows and deer, both of whom glance at my dog Logan and myself and then continue on with their grass cutting projects. If these animals don't play tag like squirrels, Logan has no interest. At the end of September, some friends invited me to the beach. Surprisingly, I saw fish swimming in one to two feet of water. My original thought, before I learned that this is the cleanest beach in the U.S., was that an oil spill forced the fish into these shallow waters. Sounds reasonable, doesn't it?

The fire was more a shock to my system than I realized. Since I didn't lose any personal items, I thought I was "sitting pretty." The difficulty was that I was without a place to sit. A month seemed reasonable to get new offices. While some of the departments in the social sciences got offices within a month, our situation took longer. The issue was the reconstruction of three other buildings that began before the fire. Space is a premium. By November, we had places, but negotiations were necessary for revamping those places into offices. To date, we do not have locks on the doors. An additional problem is that a second fire occurred: the science building located by the airport burnt to the ground. Since this is the fifth building in the town to burn—a local high school, grade school, and a church, some people are suspicious that there is an arsonist around. When the work people were ready to start on our offices, the second fire occurred. The debate became which fire disaster took precedence. Oh well! On teaching, the students rated me high on all points except office hours. Students are rough these days!

I haven't written an update for a while and realized that these are more for my own benefit: The letters eliminate repetition. One letter allows me to give the same explanation to every single person, and my life is more pleasant. My delay in writing was a result of emotional exhaustion: for some crazy reason, it happened! The shenanigans don't end. This past month, Joel called to inform me that the parole board will release the rapist. What else was there to do anyway? Another batch of calls. My overworked friends get the most calls! They are smart though; they use answering machines. It saves us both a lot of time. The parole board had failed to advise me because they had sent the notice to a three-year-old address despite my up-to-date notices of each move, including this last one. The notice of release was also an error: the parole board stated that it did not know of the current indictment. Joel stated that they had sent it. Since both sides make errors, and since overwork and understaffing define the conditions of both, the cause was irrelevant, but the result was crucial! The rapist will stay in prison a bit longer. At the next parole hearing, the board will notify me and other VISAs to testify against the rapist. The parole board did state that I was *not* the only person protesting his release. I wonder who else is! The people on the parole board are wonderful because they stated that I can complain and call all I want.

If you would like to take action, please write a note to the address below, informing them that you protest the release of this dangerous guy and to notify you of future decisions regarding his release: Re: Kenneth Redding, EF-220577, State Board of Pardons and Paroles. One way that students could get five extra points in my class was to send a letter of protest: good class assignment! For fairness, a protest letter to anyone on any issue could also earn five points.

The conclusion is that this is a horrible and disgusting wart in my life. In part, I'm glad to do it even though it is hell at times. Learning about other people like me makes me realize that this is a common, not an isolated, case. I finished another article on my research on rape trauma and plan to finish my book next semester because I'm teaching it: the

228

course reading *is* my book. By the way, the daffodils will be blooming here no later than February 15. Yes!

For the next pretrial hearing, the box with the unopened and untested tubes of blood was necessary. The question was: Where was this box? Joel called with the news: "The police can't find your tubes of blood from 1988. They're in the warehouse, but they can't locate them." "I'll find them. I'm persistent." "Well, we can't do that. Detective Roth is sure they're there. We'll find them." A month later, "Joel, how are you and your big cases for next year?" "Everything's good." "Does that also mean that they found the missing blood?" "Cathy, they did look again, but no, they haven't found them yet." So I called Roth: "Are you still good looking?" He laughed: "I try. I try." "Roth, Joel said they can't find the 1988 tubes of my blood in the warehouse. What's going on?" "That's right. The box is probably behind other evidence." "Roth, could I go over there and look?" "Cathy, I know what the box looks like. Let me try first." "You know that I'm persistent. If you don't find it, I'll get myself in the warehouse to find it." He laughed again: "I'll find it and call you." He did both.

With a March date, the reorganization of my life occurred again. But Joel told me, "The date is moved to April 19." "Why?" "One of the scientists has a conference he wants to attend." "That's the reason?" "Yes. His is a favor to testify for us. The judge has to change his schedule to fit the scientists!" Shouldn't testifying be a duty? A conference takes precedence over the conviction of a rapist! What could I do but rearrange my schedule—again! Anger kept my energy renewed: I contacted the newspaper and was assigned a reporter. To hear about an article a month ahead of time was a thrill for Beverly Sheperd. I sent her the materials to review and answered her questions.

At the pretrial, the lab experts explained the error. Slides illustrated the calamity. Dr. Gemal the lab technician inadvertently picked up the wrong tube: "537" instead of "531." The numbers "7" and "1", written in an almost identical shape, were the cause of the error. When questioned by the defense attorney on whose blood was "531," she did not know. *The lab didn't know!* The judge ruled that the lab explained the error, and the evidence was legally acceptable. He protected the integrity of the lab and admitted the 1988 DNA semen evidence. The judge wanted another pretrial on the already approved-by-the-state-supreme-court evidence of that same 1988 DNA analysis on the semen. Since scientists had agreed on the validity of this evidence, this was another, albeit unnecessary, hurdle. After that, a trial would happen.

Media Pressure

Beverly Shepard's article caught the attention of a news magazine show that wanted to cover the case. *48 Hours* planned not a fifteen-minute segment but an hour on me, my research, the case, and my students. What option did I have but to say yes? There were no guarantees with the DA. Media pressure was my only means of support. I did not have a lawyer. Another dream surfaced in my waking memory. We were in the courtroom awaiting the judge's decision on the next pretrial issue. Redding tried to escape. The guard shot him dead. The judge lackadaisically commented: "Thank goodness that's over." No doubt about the meaning of that dream existed. I told the media people about it: a good sign for them and the show. The end was near. The next pretrial issue would go well, and the law, not a bullet, would stop Redding.

"Cathy, I'm worried about the next pretrial. I just got a letter from Dr. Pompousie and he does not accept the 1988 semen evidence despite the explainable error." "Does he think there is something wrong?" "Let me read it to you." And he did. Pompousie's points were pointless. He made up unsubstantiated criticisms. He implied irrelevant points. Pompousie's argument for discarding valid evidence against a rapist is that today there are better methods. With his argument, every criminal would go free because every few years there are better methods. The question should be: Are the quality and validity of the methods still accurate today? Yes.

"Joel, you know that none of those points are valid. Why is he doing this?" Silence. Another attacker in my life, and this one uses academic force. "Joel, this is the opposite of what he said two years ago, isn't it?" "Yes." "Can anything be done? Can you exclude him from testifying?" "Well, I'll not call him, but the new defense attorney Clare Statel gets a copy of his report. She will call him. I called Michael Glue who used to work for us in forensics. He now runs a private lab. He agrees that Pompousie is wrong on every single point. But, since Pompousie raises eight points, the jury will think that one of those points is accurate even if the others are wrong. More importantly, Michael told me about a new method called PCR Amplification." "It's not a new method. It's at least six years old." "Yes, that's true. But this last year it reached acceptable legal usage, and he thinks we can get Redding with it. He's really hopeful.

If there's a problem with the pretrial, then we have this option." On the one hand, Joel—for the first time—had offered me hope beyond the next defeat. This was the impact of the media. On the other hand, the roller coaster ride was not ending, but only starting over AGAIN.

On April 19–20, 1993, at the pretrial motion on DNA, Joel asked: "Would you call this analysis seriously flawed, Dr. Pompousie?" "I would say that it does not meet the standards of scientific rigor which are called for in cases of this kind." "What would be the preferred way, if you were a scientist and received this, what would you like to do to be for sure?" "I would, of course, want to run it over." One cannot retest or duplicate forensic evidence: There isn't enough. On the next witness, Prey started: "Dr. Musher, does the DNA analysis in this case meet the [today's] accepted scientific standards?" "No, it does not." "Is this work done by the lab scientifically reliable, in your opinion?" "Well, that is a slightly different question. The experiments that were performed are reliable. What is an issue here is how interpretable the results are. The lab did not commit any mistakes in terms of how they actually ran the test." Even Dr. Bland, the defense attorney's expert, had a favorable comment: "I think they [lab experts] did a good job."

In the file, I found letters from both scientists written to Joel saying that the evidence was a match: Pompousie stated that "I agree with the analysis of the lab that these samples match"; and Musher stated "I know they match"! The semen collected from me and the blood collected from Redding matched. Despite their agreement on the validity of the evidence, they testified against it.

It was unusual for Judge Foible—except in this case—to postpone his decision. A wait with Judge Foible meant problems. Scientifically and legally, the evidence was valid. It was the last day of school. The media was on campus to film my class on "Victimization and Violence." Arriving at my office, I saw the message light on the answering machine blinking. With my student Katrina nearby, I pushed the replay button: "Judge Foible denied the motion. Here are the reasons," and Joel stated them. Katrina left for class. Disillusionment gripped me, but strength still seemed to glue me together until I walked down the stairs. No one was around. On the stairs, my knees buckled and I crumbled down the steps. My arms reached out for the banister to hold my body from falling and tumbling to the bottom. The trauma of another illogical and unfair step in this legal process crippled me momentarily. My throat choked. I could not call out for help. If the media and my students had not been waiting for me and if I could have gone into hiding, tears would have swollen my body. *But you can't cry,* I told myself. *You're a professional. You must act objectively.* Breathing deeply and focusing on the task in front of me, I forced myself to put aside my emotions, my distress, and my pain, and to teach the class. Festering inside me was the trauma.

As I walked into the classroom, the cameraperson followed me. Initially I was calm. When I began to speak, tears of despair rushed forth. My body contracted in pain. Professionalism flew out the window. My hands covered the water flow. Here was a professor who had maintained distance on this subject in front of her students for six years. Now my face printed the pain. The tension and surprise of my students wrapped the room into togetherness. Breathing deeply for control, I got out a few words: "Katrina, please tell them." Hearing the words, the students demonstrated anger with their own tears also, choking back rage. What option did we have? A classroom of fifteen people sobbing was not what we wanted on film.

The hour and the semester ended in hopelessness. The judge eliminated the evidence, and future alternatives were unclear. I called Joel. "I got the message." "Well, we did expect it." "No, I didn't expect it. Joel, Pompousie was wrong on every single point. Foible is smart enough to know it. Pompousie's argument is not scientifically valid." "Well, his decision is final. I do feel hopeful about this PCR Amplification. I've checked with the lab, and they have slides with the sperm cells collected at the hospital after the attack. The lab expert checked the slides, and there still is a sperm cell to do the PCR Amplification for both cases. It looks good, Cathy." "Let's try it. Do you need my blood?" "No, that's not necessary." "How long does the test take?" "About three to four weeks." "Joel, the DNA Fingerprinting test takes eight to nine weeks, but due to the backup in the lab the real length of time is fourteen to fifteen weeks. How backed up is this lab?" "Cathy, with this media coverage, the case will get top priority. We'll know in a month."

I called Joel. "Did you notice that a month has passed?" "Yes, I called the lab, and they want to run some other tests to be sure. The results are positive as we expected but the lab wanted to have all the aces in their hand." Another month and a half passed, and the media arrived at my house for the phone call. Without event, they departed. One week later, bright and early, they knocked on my door again. The phone call would come today, they thought, because Judge Foible was to leave on vacation and would clear his desk before departure. The morning was uneventful except that my cracked phone got a lot of attention from the camera person. Lori, a friend, stopped by with her five-month-old baby and broke the tension. This child was fantastic: He laughed and smiled and thoroughly enjoyed himself in my arms. The child made me feel like a star.

Joel called at 1:30 p.m.: "As we expected, it's a match. The lab ran other tests just to make triply sure. Now, we have to do the tests over again with yours and Haily's blood. This is to ensure that there is no problem in chain of custody this time. Can you make it to town next week?" "Oh Joel, I'll make it any time and any place." Why repeat the tests? Why didn't they draw mine and Haily's blood initially? What problem is there with the chain of custody? Is Joel continuing not to think clearly, is he overworked, or does he feel the pressure of the media? The following week the cameras followed me to the clinic, meticulously noting and recording the chain of custody. Who could doubt this? Certainly not the lab, as they did last time. My anger at the process continued. Having my blood drawn again was not the issue. Rather, the repetition of the PCR test with our blood was the origin of the most recent rage. This second set of PCR tests would mean at least another month or two of waiting before the scheduling of another set of pretrial motions. Why the delays?

By September, Joel reported. "We've got the results back, and the scientific experts for our side are examining them. Then Clare gets to have her experts review the results." "How long until pretrial?" "Oh, not long." In October, Joel said, "Our experts just finished up and Clare still needs to examine the results." "How many experts do you have?" "We want to be on the safe side. There's Pompousie and Musher." "Not them again?" "Oh, it's all right this time." "Isn't that what we thought last time? They are not trustworthy." "This is a different situation. Anyway, then Dr. Glue. They each need a few days to find time to look over the tests." "Joel, does a few days frequently mean two weeks plus postal time?" "That's about it." With Clare's three expert witnesses and Joel's, the total examining period could take up to three or more months. Stalling continued. Prior to Thanksgiving, I asked, "Any information on the pretrial date?" "Not yet." "Is it possible the judge would schedule a pretrial in December?" "Oh, quite likely." I had to cancel my plans to return to Mexico—again. Seven years had passed, and I couldn't leave the country. With my absence, the legal people would permanently end the case.

Around December 15, Joel called me. "Cathy, Judge Foible squeezed us in on December 30. He's even making his clerk come back that day. Do you plan on attending?" "Sure, why not?" December 30 was an odd date to call the pretrial. He had had over a month and half to schedule this pretrial, why did he pick that day? That call from Joel ensured that trauma would define my holiday season, another season without pleasure.

On the morning of December 30, I called the television stations to notify them of this new scientific evidence. The media decides each morning which stories to cover: "Is the media interested in covering a six-and-half-year-old rape case that introduces new evidence, never before used in this state?" I asked when I called. At 9 A.M., I peeked into the courtroom. Surprise. In the unused jury box, since this was a pretrial situation, were five cameras. There were more camerapeople than people in the courtroom. This is a judge who is antipublicity, anti-media, anti-interference in *his* court. This would not please the judge. Afterward, the pretrial left me completely exhausted. I felt I couldn't go on. No energy. On December 31, I spent four hours on the phone calling all the people who would tell me: "You can't give up." "You've got the national media now." "Success has to be possible." Or "How can you possibly consider quitting?" Without energy, my will knew that the choice to quit was not an option.

The first three weeks of January were nerve wracking as I awaited the judge's decision. The phone didn't ring. I called and questioned Joel, "Joel, has the judge made a decision?" "No, not yet." "Do you have any idea when?" "No." "Do you know why he is taking so long?" "It is long, but I don't have any idea." Something else was on their agenda, and I didn't know what it was. Ironically, those two months were peaceful and productive. I wrote a grant proposal and paper for publication. In addition, my sinuses cleared up, and for that period my breathing was calm and restful. My stress lowered. At the end of February, Mary, the media producer called: "I wanted you to know that the judge wrote his decision and will review it tomorrow, Friday. If there are no changes, according to the secretary, then he releases it today, and if there are changes, he will release it on Monday or Tuesday." "Great." Friday came and passed. Then Monday, Tuesday, Wednesday, Thursday. My patience had reached its limit. "Mary, what's going on?" "Beats me. I keep calling. The secretary doesn't know. The judge refuses to release the decision. I'll contact you as soon as I hear."

At the end of March, the judge scheduled another pretrial for DNA Band Shifting in the case involving Haily. Clare had put a motion in front of the judge to squelch this evidence. Logically, no pretrial hearing was necessary. First, the judge had already had a pretrial hearing on this evidence and accepted it. Second, the state supreme court had ruled on the admissibility of this same type of evidence. Judge Foible insisted on a hearing anyway. The wait continued. No decision. By April, the judge had refused to release either pretrial decision: on PCR Amplification for both cases, the wait was more than four months, and for the one on DNA involving Haily, that wait was more than a month. Anger turned up my energy level.

I called: "Cheryl, it's been five months and Foible has not released any of the pretrial decisions. Can you check with your friend on the inside to find out what's going on? I know crime has increased almost fivefold. Does Foible have a problem scheduling and keeping up with the work? Why doesn't he release the pretrial decisions? They're completed and sitting on his desk. What is the problem?" Politics had reared its head again. "It is not a problem with court overload or anything like that. Foible is running for reelection and does not want anyone to run against him. Ergo, he does not want any publicity. A low profile is a successful profile. You're involved in a high-profile case. As soon as he releases the decisions, the media will broadcast the results. I don't think he'll do that until after the filing date."

"That is his reason for stalling? And Joel is part of it. Joel stalled initially by not sending my blood along with the first PCR tests. Then he stalled by using the scientists as an excuse. Then the judge stalled by separating the pretrial dates. The first pretrial date he selected on a day when the media would not want to give much attention to a case of violence and would prefer holiday coverage. Then the useless pretrial on the DNA Band Shifting. Now the refusal to release already-written pretrial decisions to ensure his reelection. He has caused me a year of pain to safeguard his throne. Last July should have ended my terror. All of them tried to control my life. What do they have—a system? First a rapist bludgeons me, then the lawyers argue irrelevant issues, next the lab fouls up, the scientists disqualify internationally accepted evidence, and now the judge places his position over the importance of convicting a rapist. If I didn't know better, I'd think they sat down to plan this like a conspiracy. They safeguard their status positions by stepping on VISAs. And stepping on VISAs is what they define as protecting the rights of the defendant. They are full of _____ and that's the gospel truth."

"Mary, this waiting for the judge's decision is preposterously long," I said. "I know. I get up and call the judge's secretary every day. I could do a biography on her life. Does this ever end?" "Perhaps we think alike. Let's end the television show. It's not that I've lost interest or I'm displeased with working with you. Quite the contrary. All of you are great. But, this judge always makes instantaneous decisions. That's his history. And a long wait for him is three weeks. He believes in speedy justice. He jerks you around just like he jerked me around for years. Besides, to end without knowing if there is a trial is a trauma. Let people experience the reality of the victimization." "Yes, we do think the same. We'll come down on Friday and do the closing interview with you."

That weekend I left to spend time with my friends Daisy and Darrell and their adopted kids Emiko and Pedro. On Monday, May 9, 1994, the second day of my vacation and two days before the show was to air, the judge released the pretrial motions. Mary, who always knew my where-abouts, informed me: "Foible ruled in favor of the prosecution each time and admits all evidence: DNA Band Shifting in the case with Haily and PCR Amplification for both cases. The trial is on May 23. We'll announce that at the end of the show." "Joel hasn't called." "He hasn't?" On May 9, 1994, Judge Foible ruled:

> Although Dr. Pompousie has changed his opinion concerning the relia-bility of these tests and now questions the appropriateness of correcting for band shifting, the court finds that the evidence, taken as a whole, still shows that these tests have reached a scientific stage of verifiable certainty. Therefore, this court will not change its *earlier* ruling admit-ting this evidence [emphasis added].

Due to national media coverage, Judge Foible, this time, did not agree with Dr. Pompousie.

The next day, Daisy and I headed out for the stores, and I informed her immediately that this was not a good day. Trauma enveloped me. To hear the confirmation of the trial date, the absolute certainty now of a trial, stunned me. Joel's failure to inform me confirmed his attitude toward VISAs. I learned later that no one notified Haily: Not only did Joel not notify her about the trial, but since she had moved, she did not know about the airing of the show. The trial date also meant the abbreviation of my vacation.

While we shopped, I confided to Daisy. "This is a terrific second-hand store with these great forties-looking dresses—a favorite period of mine in fashion design, but I'm too exhausted to try them on. We have to go home. I'm wasted. You know, Daisy, if I could stay a few more days, then we could come back and shop here." "No problem, Cathy. Just tell that to the DA. Postpone the trial. You need a few more days of shop-ping." We laughed. "Hell, why not? The scientists postpone trials and pretrials because they want to travel and visit their buddies. Don't they call those vacations 'conferences'? Judges postpone trials for reelection. DAs cancel trials to ensure their political status." "Yeah, you're the VISA. You tell them when you want the trial." "That will be the day."

PUBLICIZING THE PAIN

Naming

"Cathy, this is Roth. Your trial, as the first DNA case, will be on television. Isn't that great! They don't use victims' names." During the meeting with Bill Sr. and Stan, I was told, "Cathy, we will have news coverage on the DNA and trial. Don't worry. The media will not mention your name." Although many friends called and energetically announced: "The case is in the newspaper," the nameless victim didn't matter. My friends knew who the victim was. Every time I read the word "victim," my mind read my name. The publication of that first news article without any notice instigated a reaction, mild but emotionally uncomfortable, because the details of the article and my friends' calls highlighted the rape. Surprise was the advantage of the rapist, and the lack of media warning left me unprepared again. The anonymity of the VISA is for protection—is that always necessary? My friends did not need a name to read my pain in those articles. The issue is that publicizing the pain was not my choice or my decision. Neither the media nor the rapist asked me what I wanted.

Without a name, the media still centered their articles on me. One account read: "The victim was assaulted in her dimly lighted bedroom and she could give only a general description of her *attacker*" (Green, June 4, 1988, emphasis added). The subject of the sentence was not the attacker but the victim. Passive voice hides the criminal and highlights the VISA, nameless or not.

Simple, unobtrusive words described the rape, but my mind read a different meaning: The shading of the night slowly revealed a man, a rapist, who stood over me and who at the first moment generated such a hate that without touching me, he had traumatized me with his threat of rape. The reporter's unobtrusive words obtrusively invaded my existence. Although the media coverage was important to educate people about rape, rapists, and DNA, a notice of up-and-coming news could have prepared me to better deal with the unwanted resurfacing and reliving of the trauma. With Stan's aid, the publication date of the next article reached me in time for me to prepare myself for the trauma and for my friends' comments—favorable and unfavorable. I appreciated his gesture.

On the first day after the attack, I had told the detectives to use my name publicly; I likewise gave that same information to Bill Sr. and Stan. All disagreed with me by making decisions for me and without discussion. As well, the media, in its protective mold, did not use my name or ask me if I cared about the use of my name. They did not think to ask me. Historically we have assumed the need for protection of VISAs. Assumption of the VISA's wishes and decisions is a pattern of the legal system, the media, and the assaulter alike: We know what VISAs want. As the rapist left my home, he promised: "You can remain in the neighborhood. I'll protect you." Protection is exclusionary if it denies a person his or her right to decide: He, they, wanted to protect me. On the other hand, the rape survivor advocate supported me to stand up and stop the rapist: She worked with me to protect myself. The decision to go public or not is the right of the VISA. Could the media people advise people to stand up to the rapist's horror for their own strength, to speak up in order to stop the rapist's attacks against other people, to educate people about the crime in our communities, and to speak to provide pressure for justice?

The first news articles emphasized DNA—the crux of the articles—as the critical evidence to find the rapist:

> [The victim] could give only a general description of the rapist. [The police] identified a suspect on information from the victim and *other pieces of evidence* (Green, June 4, 1988a, emphases added).

> [t]he victim . . . could give only a general description of her attacker, such as height, weight, race, and approximate age. "She cannot identify him at all. We have *other circumstantial evidence*" Stan Rest said (Green, July 1, 1988a, emphases added).

Eighty percent of my details matched the rapist. The media people repeated the position of Bill Sr. and Stan, doubting my data against the rapist. Excluding me left the DA in a position to glorify himself—"we have other evidence"—and to protect the view of an undependable victim. What was the "other" evidence that the DA used to write a search warrant? The questionability of DNA as valid was the crux of these first articles: "Judge Foible will have to determine the admissibility. The judge will want to know whether it's generally accepted in the scientific community, the prosecutor said" (Green, July 1, 1988b). The focus of the article on the evidence as "on trial" deleted the focus from the defendant: "It is the DNA test itself that has been on trial" (Green, July 1, 1988b). But why? For the previous decade and a half, DNA Fingerprinting was a subject of study in high schools across the nation. Many scientists had published on its validity. Argentina had even used this evidence to reunite grandchildren with their grandparents after a regime of horror in which upper-level military and wealthy people stole children from their murdered biological parents. Why didn't the media mention that the use of this unquestioned evidence throughout our country, our educational system, and internationally? The reporter did note that five other states accepted this evidence, and that with admissibility in this state, the state crime lab would buy the equipment to conduct these tests.

Although the first articles highlighted the words only of Bill Sr., the first full-length article (Renaud, October 11, 1988) on DNA included the words also of the defense attorney, the judge, and scientists. The media people highlighted not only these people's names and words, but the photos of two of the white males—Bill Sr. and the judge. Status meant quotability, but not the quality of the quote. The defense attorney commented:

> At that stage, where although the theoretical aspects [of DNA] may appear to be valid, there have not been sufficient quantities of applications in the field to determine its validity. Our trial court cannot judicially note the acceptance of the DNA typing test since the test has never previously been introduced in a court in this state.

There has to be a first time! For Stan Rest, "[He] is confident the [DNA] test meets the state's standards: 'Every expert I've spoken to in the field,' he says, 'has told me that the test has reached a verifiable stage of scientific certainty.'" Stan spoke to three scientists! For the media's objectivity, there was one scientific expert for each side. "The techniques involved, we have been using for over fifteen years. But the application to forensics is new." The opposition's objective scientist was a psychologist/assistant professor: "[T]he procedure does not yet meet a test of 'verifiable certainty.'" The media people also included the perspective of Judge Foible: "Foible has indicated to attorneys for both sides he will issue a certificate of review [on DNA admissibility] with his rule." The media people reinforced and honored the organizational structure of the members of the court.

Just as critical to the discussion of DNA is its impact as evidence for people raped. For VISAs, DNA eliminates the need for the VISA to identify the defendant as the rapist and a grueling cross-examination by the defense attorney. If I could not remember, the police, lawyers, and judges could not badger me, intimidate me, doubt me, or denigrate me. DNA is a protection, a favorable protection, for VISAs. Without our voices, the media failed to mention that point. The media muted the VISA, like the rapist and the legal people.

Since no lawyer or legal protection exist for VISAs, VISAs have no voice. The media is then of great value. Without a voice, status, position, or protection, I needed another institution to counter the misdeeds of the legal people. With the help of Quinn, who edited my press releases, I contacted all members of the media from television to radio stations to newspapers: Columnists, editors, reporters, and producers received a package that included one of my papers and a press release about the case.

Three points made me a favorable subject in the eyes of the media: First, once the media commit to a story, then additional media coverage is possible. Second, Bill Sr. as the candidate for supercop was a hot issue in the news. The media people connected Redding's case to Bill Sr.'s supercop bid, increasing the possibility of coverage. Third, my education campaign about rape was important. Media people who read my article "Rape as Social Murder" liked its conciseness and detail. Copies of that article also left their offices for elsewhere. Education gave me a privileged—if unpaid—position of status with the media. I was Dr. Winkler.

Pain in Print

The columnist who had the power, position, and status to pressure the DA was Jane Hansen. After reading my material and interviewing me for hours by telephone, she called with the publication date of my interview. Nothing appeared. I called and asked, "What happened, Jane?" "The editors argue that it is too sexually specific." "You read the article to me. There wasn't anything about sex or even graphic about the rape. What could they possibly object to?" "It's the quote from your article: 'His sweat drenched down from his face and fell over my forehead and cheeks, drops of which I could not turn away from.' " "They think the word 'sweat' is too sexually specific? What are you going to do?" "This is not your problem. I will publish the article as is. I'll take a stand on this." "The article is criminally, not sexually, specific. Why are you taking a stand for me?" "Cathy, it is the issue and my reputation that are crucial." Two days later, the column was in print.

Her article (June 8, 1991) began: "Hers was a particularly brutal rape, a story not for the squeamish. But then the details of rape rarely are." Pointing out the hierarchy of pain—this rape is "a particularly brutal rape"—is common. Hadn't many people said to me: "Your rape is worse than mine"? But all rapes are brutal. Did a person have to suffer "a particularly brutal rape" to be media worthy? Or was "the particularly brutal rape" a result not of my suffering but of my ability to write the details of that brutality? I could defend myself articulately both verbally and in print; others did not have that ability.

In her article, Jane raised the issue of publicizing the victim's name and noted that this is the choice of the victim. Further she noted that "[o]nly by then [going public] can the dehumanization of what happened to her [Cathy Winkler] be turned into *healing* [emphasis added]." I went public for several reasons explicitly stated: to stop the rapist, to protect other women, and to alter the rapist-favoring methods of Bill Sr., Joel, and the judge. My actions were not healing. Rather, due to the media, I had to have self-therapy on the days prior to the interviews to preserve myself through those ordeals, and I had to continue therapy after the interview to cope with reliving the rape attack and the negative responses of people. Going public was not therapeutic, nor desirable. It was for justice.

The Limits of Media Justice

Hansen, like many media people, covers issues briefly. "Cathy said he was the wrong man." My statement is incomplete. Missing is my identification of the defendant's body shape as that of the rapist, the artist composite that, to all people but myself, is photographically perfect, and the body scar. It was written that, "Bill Sr. argues that the case was never dead. 'Unfortunately,' he says, 'Cathy got caught on the cusp of DNA evidence.' He now says the reindictment of Redding is imminent." The support of the DNA evidence remained unexplained in the media's simplistic retelling. The point that Bill Sr. dismissed the case is likewise ignored. The minimalist approach preserved Bill Sr.'s status. Despite my criticisms of it, this one article was critical in Bill Sr.'s actions: "the reindictment of Redding is imminent."

With the reindictment came more news coverage: "Man Indicted

Third Time in Two Rape Cases" (Foskett, July 4, 1991). This reporter noted that the errors in the case were "investigative foul-ups," blaming the detectives whose words were not in print. Mute was the detective's position in the media. Moreover, phrasing has an impact: "Lab mix-up called into question the match in Redding's blood and the DNA found in semen taken from one of the victims." Scrutinize this quote. At first reading, a person comes to the conclusion that the DNA of the defendant probably does not match the DNA of the rapist. Reread the sentence with a focus on the words "called into question." The reporter did not say that those two DNAs did not match. Rather, the issue was that a mix-up in my blood sample raised doubts on the ability to use the DNA from the semen. There were three years of DNA matches between defendant's blood and rapist's semen. The media did not mention this. The media also did not name the offending lab. Is this protection of people with power and status again?

On details, media coverage is often inaccurate. Some examples from an article by Barbara Walters (July 3, 1991) on the left demonstrate this. On the right is the correct information.

1) Arrested on the basis of the police drawing.	1) Redding's arrest was a result of DNA evidence.
2) He beat her with her bedside lamp.	2) He beat me with his fist. His swing hit the lamp.
3) After the DNA test in Feb 1989, Winkler could see that Redding was the face she saw the night she was raped.	3) In March 1991, after my confrontation with Bill Sr., I saw a resemblance between the drawing and Redding. A match with the rapist's face never occurred.
4) Winkler's knowledge of the unusual scar . . . was also considered a strong point for the case.	4) My sight of one, not two scars, was always a problem in the case for the detectives, Bill Sr., and Stan.
5) DNA experts asked that Redding's brother . . . also be tested.	5) I asked that Redding's brother be tested.
6) Police officers accused her of being "obsessive."	6) Friends, not the detectives, accused me of being obsessive.
7) Through a lab error, another woman's blood sample was switched with Winkler's.	7) The only information from the lab was a switch of blood samples, but not the sex of the person.

| 8) The dismissal was modified to allow for an indictment within six months. | 8) The type of dismissal always allowed for reindictment within six months. No modification occurred. |

The focus of the articles is more important than errors in minor details. In that regard, Walters focused on crucial points: DNA education, activism of people criminalized, ability to survive brutality of rapist, recognition of the brutality of the rapist, ability to survive the brutality of the DAs, ability to confront DAs to act justly, and more. Like Jane Hansen, she published my words; she discussed in her column my actions from writing to teaching to newsletters to legal confrontation to my publications. Her photograph of me, at my request, was not one of a sad, depressed, long-suffering victim with her head turned downward but of a person secure, content, and unafraid to hold her head up. She did not hierarchialize the rape: "the rape of Cathy Winkler was no different than any other rape." Highlighting the contradictions of Joel was important: his words—"a very, very nasty crime" versus his actions—"dismissal of the case." The unjust acts of Bill Sr. and Joel received recognition: "Surviving this [legal] battle was one Winkler found as tough and as important as surviving the physical battle with the rapist." A subtle but important point was the publication date of July 3: the day before Independence Day. July 4 has quietly become a symbol of the lack of independence for many people within this country. Barbara Walters' demonstration of respect for me, in so many ways, helped my recuperation from the pain of the printed word.

In August 1990, I called a television reporter interested in interviewing me. After Bill Sr. had postponed the case again and again, the need for justice via public exposure was at hand. In this media experience, I learned that the order in which the media people organize the interviews favors those in status and those in status know how to organize the timing of the interview to favor themselves. In the interview, I stated that the DNA evidence scientifically and legally is valid. The reporter omitted that vital information. With two hours of interviewing, the reporter selected only one or two of my sentences that fit her angle on the story. The media people aired on August 3, 1991 Bill Sr.'s point that the problem with the case centered on my inability to ID the rapist, completely avoiding the issue of DNA identification. Afterward, when I told the media person that my identification was irrelevant with DNA as evidence, she responded: "Juries like it when the victim points to the defendant as the rapist." She'd never seen a DNA case and had no idea how the jury would react. "There has been a 100 percent conviction rate in hundreds of DNA cases across the nation, and juries from most regions in this country believe the evidence. The scientists, not the victim, point to the defendant as the rapist," I told her. Nevertheless, the critical importance on the airing of the interview is that Bill Sr. agreed to try Redding with Haily testifying.

The announcement of the dismissal of the case in which I would have testified was news: "Suspect Charged Three Times in Rape Wins a Reprieve" (Foskett, August 7, 1991), with my picture next to the headline. The reporter asked my view of his article. "My photograph is next to the word 'suspect' and the emphasis on the defendant 'winning a reprieve,' as if he is innocent, leaves me with a double blow of embarrassment and anger. I am not the suspect, and the word 'win' should not be used in association with a defendant who has DNA evidence against him. Do you doubt his guilt?" "Let me know if anything happens in the case." He did not agree, and his response indicated his belief that the case was over. That reporter duplicated the legal word games:

> A defendant cannot be prosecuted if two previous indictments returned by a grand jury on the same offense have been squashed. Judge Foible wrote in his ruling that no other case has directly answered the question of whether a motion by the prosecution *to dismiss* an indictment was the same as to *squash* the indictment under the law (emphases added).

Another word game was also in the discussion of the DNA: "The case also has been complicated by the reliance on DNA evidence." The reporter leads one to believe that there are doubts in the validity of the evidence instead of its highly successful use worldwide. Further, the questioning of DNA plants the idea that identification was problematic. How many smoking guns were necessary in a case? Other wording—"a mix-up in the genetics testing lab raised doubt"—had a twofold impact in favoring and protecting the scientists' status: not naming the lab and the use of the words that it "raised a doubt." "Raise a doubt" of the identity of the rapist? I think not. Those words are less explicit than "failed to test the VISA's blood." Like so many reporters thereafter, Redding's case received the title "the Winkler case." Vocalizing the need for justice placed me on trial.

The trial with Haily Betten testifying began August 19, 1991, and the news media covered it. With the gag order given by the judge, the media had to avoid me. That was fine. On the sixth day of deliberation, the newspaper reported Joel's interpretation of the lengthy discussions: "[I]n such a complicated trial . . . there was a lot of technical testimony" (Lewis,

August 30, 1991). The supposed difficulty in explaining science was the excuse for a delayed jury decision. Difficult issues are explainable and understandable. As my friend Faye commented, they're just words, and one can comprehend words. The media did not point out that Joel or Sefaborb raced through their explanations and used words that are not part of the jury's everyday vocabulary. The judge's gag order muted my interpretation of the proceedings and protected his colleague's—the DA's—status.

"Mistrial Declared in DNA Rape Case" (Lewis, August 30, 1991) proclaimed the result of the jury deliberations. Joel had his explanation:

> "We were in essence asking the jury to make a scientific decision. That is maybe not the fairest way to deal with jurors." ADA Joel Prey knew the case would be tough because of the lack of industry wide standards on DNA Testing. Marble, Redding's attorney, said: "I would conclude that the expert testimony in this case was confusing."

Since I was not at the courthouse, I could not correct their misstatements. Likewise, the absence of the scientists—money defines their presence—left their opinions unregistered. Without them, reporters depended on the words of the lawyers—justified or not.

Getting It Right

With Bill Sr. pursuing his political career and wanting my silence, Joel focused on locating the three women in the Mumford area and sending off their blood samples for DNA testing. This approach took one and a half years. Due to local gossip, a news reporter, Judy Sheppard, contacted me. She did a three-part series that paralleled my three-part approach in this book. "Society's Shame—Victims Suffer Lasting, Crippling Affects" (August 16, 1992) focused on the physical assault. That title left the impression that the rapist had permanently destroyed me emotionally. A reader might wonder if I could even hold down a job. This first article involved two stories and an additional side article "One Woman's Nightmare Journey." My name and photo were foremost: The photo, with much accentuated dark background, covered the length of half the page and the width of two columns. Yet, the editor's note, next to my photo, stated that "At their request, the last names of the women interviewed will not be used." The layout implied that my name was a pseudonym: it was not.

Judy wrote many comprehensive points about physical rape: "[Cathy Winkler] was determined to survive . . . [b]ut . . . she also was frozen with fear and dread." She showed my strength and my vulnerability. Of importance were her comments on the brutality of the rapist: "It was a three and a half hour tour of hell guided by a brutal stranger who wanted, inexplicably, to hurt and humiliate. . . . Strangely, he lapsed occasionally into kindness." Also Judy noted my activism and education of students.

Trauma leaves deep thrusts of pain, and the emotional scarring is critical to understand. Although Judy made a good attempt at her explanations, some of the words disturbed me. On my inability to identify the defendant as the rapist on street surveillance, "It was as if . . . she had deep down decided she could not come face to face with the attacker." Such words leave the impression that I made a conscious decision not to recognize the rapist, and the phrase "decided she could not" also implies my lack of strength. Such subtle word choices imprint upon all of us the image of a poor decision maker and an ineffectual VISA, when, in actuality, neither of those is true. It is the rapist's traumatization that scorches people. The reporter further reinforced her position by adding, "It was a disastrous lapse in her otherwise clear, comprehensive account." In other words, "such a brilliant person can act so inappropriately and illogically." Trauma is not illogical and neither is the person raped.

Part II had the title "Victim's Worst Trauma Comes Later in a 'Bomb of Emotions'" (August 17, 1992). Comments like "Winkler still talks and writes with anger and dismay" and "Winkler says angrily" stress that VISAs are out of control. Interestingly, these denigrating comments juxtaposed comments of praise. The first sentence followed a note on my book and its title. The second followed an insightful presentation on the face-to-face confrontation with the attacker. The position of such phrases is a cunning way of saying to the readers that Cathy Winkler is great but still out of control. And out-of-control people are not honorable or trustworthy.

Part III led with the title "Victim's Fight for Justice Reveals Tenacious Stance" (August 18, 1991). While Judy used "survivor-activist" in the contents of the three articles, none of the titles held that wording. This article began with my phrases: "I am not a fanatic. I am not crazy . . . People say I'm obsessed." Reading such words at the beginning of an article gives the reader the impression that those negative qualities are those of the speaker herself. The words that describe my actions further raise the readers' suspicions of my credibility. Instead of using examples as Judy did in Part II, this article presents judgment calls:

she says . . . [Bill Sr.] has *lied to her, ignored her, mocked and insulted her.* Had she not *organized pickets and public stunts*—including taking her story to the media *wherever she lives*—she believes this case would have long ago been left to molder in the place where unresolved, unpunished crimes go to rot (emphases added).

My supposed description of Bill Sr.'s and Joel's action in print was a surprise. Those were not my words nor were the points about "pickets" and "stunts." Such inappropriate descriptive statements gave a view of an intemperate VISA. The rapist wanted me to be out of touch with reality, and so, it appears, did this article.

For a rebuttal to the points I made in my interview, the reporter interviewed the lawyers. Prey said, "We have handled this case . . . professionally. . . . Dr. Winkler is a difficult person to deal with sometimes. She will tell you that. . . . We have done everything we humanly could."

My title was used rarely. When Joel wanted to denigrate me, he used my title "Dr." Marble commented: "It is true there has been a horrible miscarriage of justice. She was attacked. . . . I'm sort of getting upset about people writing articles about my client from only one point of view."

The reporter summarizes the lawyers' positions:

In some ways, imply both sets of attorneys, Winkler herself is to blame for the failure to reach a conviction. After all, she was for months unable to identify Redding, though she gave police a detailed description.

Once again, the reporter never mentioned DNA. Reading the lawyers' statements left me with a feeling that questioned my right to ask for justice. Denigration is disabling. Public humiliation insults one's identity. The rapist used such words, and this reporter parroted the lawyers and used comparable words.

Wording continued to favor the people with status. When the lawyers made a comment, the words "said" or "says" were without descriptive adverbs. Yet in my quotes, the reporter used the adverbs like "angrily" or "forcefully." There was one exception in the case of Joel: " 'And there's no way she's going to get full satisfaction from this case or be returned to her pre-rape self,' he says quietly. 'I'm not sure if she consciously wants that.' " The use of the word "quietly" leaves Prey as not culpable.

The pictures varied. In Part I, the photograph was of a complacent person looking up. In Part II, the photo was of a serious, maybe angry person, staring up (the sun was in my eyes and I kept asking them to retake the picture). In Part III, the photograph was a happy, carefree, attention-getting shot. Along with that photo, the reporter discussed my desire for media "wherever she lives." The photo paralleled that theme.

Judy Sheppard worked long hours on this three-part series. I called to thank her for her efforts and many of her points: "I'm sorry, Cathy." "Are you sorry for some of the discrepancies in the article? Please don't be. That happens. There are so many good points." "Cathy, the editor changed the article in many areas and denigrated my theme and thus you. Those are articles I worked on so hard. I really worked on the words and sentences. He chopped it up and edited them in a way that severely altered the ideas. I'm so angry. That editor ruins all my good work." I suspect that my points of contention with Judy may stem from words inserted by the editor: He marked both me and Judy.

With another pretrial in April 1993, more than one year after the discovery of the lab's error, I sent my materials to the reporter. "Thanks for the notice. I usually have little or no time to spend on an article," said Beverly Sheperd. Her article generated further media interest. While one could castigate her for initiating the article with the phrase "Cathy Winkler's case," that would be the end of my negative criticisms. Her title was "Rape Case Finally Hears Trial [this gives hope]—Botched Procedures" (April 6, 1993). She began, "An anthropologist has used her own personal nightmare to develop a college course on rape and victimization." Her approach was complimentary, action-oriented. The photo she used was of my students taking notes and studying the court procedures. Beverly asked the photographer for that shot. Great. The focus is on someone else. Quotes from students were in the article:

> The students skipped breakfast and sacrificed other classes to take the 140-mile drive [to arrive] on time for the 9 A.M. hearing. "I wanted to see first hand how the justice system would handle it," said Shawn Conwell, and Glenn Testamark . . . said that he "has been inspired to help rape victims in his hoped-for political career."

Beverly used Joel's words to describe the problems in the case: "glitches" and "bugaboos." Those were the only words quoted from Joel. Another insightful approach by Beverly was naming all participants in the case: Sherry Sutton, county commissioner, and Rev. L. W. Hope, eighty-one-year-old former neighbor. Her inclusiveness in detail was the reason that *48 Hours* contacted me.

Beverly did the follow-up article on the judge's decision that stated:

"The DNA evidence in this case is not sufficiently reliable to be used as evidence" (May 5, 1993).

She wrote this about me:

> While praising both Joel and the judge, Dr. Winkler said the decision sends a negative message. "If a criminal waits a year or two before a trial, he might never come to trial," said Dr. Winkler, an anthropology professor. "The legal and scientific experts have made it impossible for a rapist to get convicted."

Sheperd's respect for me, education on the legal labyrinth, presentation of my support, and disagreement with Bill Sr. and Joel were points that pleased me.

In *Anthropology Today* (1993), an international journal for my profession, the editor chose to publish one of my papers and to follow up on the results of anthropology in action:

> [Due to her paper], two columnists pursued the case personally, and a local television station decided to publicize it. . . . [T]he article has also been found useful by women's groups to help victims of rape confront their experiences and in teaching courses.

Bill Sr. received a copy of the complete excerpt. Anthropology—once a bastion of study of countries distant from the researchers' residence and with a focus on mostly themes of passivity—needs to include more studies in the countries of the researchers and action-oriented research including the area of violence. The publication of details of my research demonstrated that some people in power agree with the perspective.

Spreading the Word

In February 1991, a man attempted to attack my friend in her car at 5 P.M. at her apartment complex in front of ten men playing basketball. Her screams brought others who pulled the man out of the car. Despite a stranglehold, he initially escaped, but the police quickly apprehended him. My friend called me immediately. She had read my material, wanted justice, and asked my advice: "Go to the media." I found a humane local reporter, Penny Pool, and then advised my friend on interview techniques: what to say and what not to say. A week later, when my friend returned to her classes and to church, both groups stood up and applauded her. Three months later, the jury convicted her attacker.

Penny contacted me. She wanted me as an expert. While the title of the article was "Land of the Free?" (September 19, 1993), to my surprise her full-page article was on me. Because I lived in a community where people never discuss violence, crises, or problems publicly, no one harassed me, or even made a reference to the article. She began, "Violence in America is a fact of life. . . . Questions abound about violence in America but answers are rare. Dr. Cathy Winkler, an anthropology professor, has struggled to find some of those answers." Penny had remarkable insight, and I noted that in a letter to the editor. Amazingly, the editors published the entire letter.

> I would like to applaud your coverage. . . . The publication of such horrors can be a horror in and of itself. The uniqueness [of one of your quotes] is in the respect for my efforts and respect for me. . . . [B]y employing those terms of respect ["Dr" and "Professor"], you were educating people that rape does occur to people of status, and not just people with low economic lives. (October 8, 1993)

The editors titled my letter: "Thanks for sensitive approach."

While *48 Hours* began their almost monthly visits in April 1993, a local newspaper began research on an expose on rape in the courtroom. The reporter, Sandra McIntosh, spent five months on her research. My first press release with my article was in April, and the reporter published her article in October. "Getting Away With Rape?" (McIntosh, October 10, 1993) started with the statistics "for 44 of every 45 victims, filing a crime report is as close as they will get to seeing their attacker convicted." In the article, one of the women ADAs commented, "If you're a rapist, you want to rape here . . . because you won't do any time." Sandra pointed out reasons for high rape crime rate: "Because sex offenders are considered likely to repeat their crime, the inefficient law enforcement may well be contributing to the city's high rape rate." Other statistics, although not startling if compared across the nation, are still sad:

1) three out of four defendants accused of rape were found innocent;
2) plea bargains result in much more lenient sentences, and 54 percent who pleaded to reduced charges . . . walked out of court free men;
3) the median sentence for guilty pleas was five years in prison; and
4) the conviction rate for rape trials in which female judges presided was 60 percent, compared to 9 percent for trials with male judges.

When Judge Foible scheduled the pretrial on the validity of PCR Amplification, a method that duplicates the DNA and provides a pattern of recognition of genes, I contacted the television stations. All stations had cameras present, and I thought I was ready for them. In the interview, I offered my prepared sound bite: "With one cell from saliva, blood, or semen, PCR amplification can identify the attacker. Scientific evidence exists to stop rapists." Many times I repeated the gist of these sentences. The reporters pressured me to respond emotionally, and unfortunately, I did: "Emotionally, this experience is draining and taxes one's ability to exist." On the news that night, no television station mentioned PCR and all focused on my one statement of emotional upheaval. People remained unaware and uneducated about this legal asset.

For five months (January–May 1994), Judge Foible refused to release the pretrial decisions in order to stop media coverage. Even though Foible postponed news coverage on the case that involved me, an important news coverage did occur on January 6, 1994. The governor signed into law get-tough sentencing: No parole for two-time offenders of violent crimes. Rape is violent. The law now existed if Redding went to trial.

Foible's attempt to stop publicity ended with the publication of an article on his court behavior on April 11, 1994. Foible ordered John Kappers, a nurse who contacted AIDS and later a rare form of untreatable tuberculosis, confined to his home despite his noncontagious state. In the courtroom, Foible also ordered all people to wear masks. He did not provide masks for the family and friends prevented from entering the courthouse. Foible, without deliberation, ruled immediately on house imprisonment. Kappers, author of an article on fraudulent practices by the health board, believed his article was the board's impetus to banish him. Foible complied. The local newspapers complied. But one local magazine didn't.

National Television

On May 14, 1994, *48 Hours* went public with their show "Shreds of Evidence." While they had specifically requested my permission to use photos of me after the attack, the highlighting of these photos in the promos sent me to the phone to warn my mother. She had never seen these and knew little about the bruising. Pictures highlight the patterns of pain. The theme of the show was on rape trauma and the benefits of DNA evidence to traumatized VISAs. Without considering trauma, Joel had his comments: "Cathy Winkler gave an incredibly detailed, much more detailed description than we usually get. How can you rationalize incredible detail and not ID him?" Roth noted that "Kenneth Redding fit the description and was the first person to come to my mind." Both men recognized the photographically identical drawing as Redding, and yet they could not comprehend the impact of trauma on my ability to visualize the rapist.

People interviewed had their ideas about me. Joel noted that "This [case] is just my nightmare. Overall, we are prosecuting the right person. Cathy is as frustrating and frustrated a victim as I have ever met." And Joel added that "[Cathy Winkler] is very adamant about her position in the case." Haily said that "If I thought about it constantly day in and day out, I'd be in a mental institute. I worry about how [Cathy Winkler] is handling it. Every time I've met her, I worry about her." Haily and I had had contact twice in seven years. Redding's sister said that "Cathy Winkler is nuts. Bringing attention to herself." The mother of Redding pointed out that "Cathy Winkler is just confused." Statel, Redding's lawyer, said:

Cathy Winkler has convinced herself of Redding's guilt. The DA ought to be very careful given the weak ID, nonevidence that they have the right guy. If we don't have the right guy, it doesn't matter what she is suffering from, we shouldn't lock him up for life. Miss Winkler is part of the reason we are still at trial.

Susan Estrich, a lawyer and VISA who published *Real Rape*, said: "They ought to be very careful, in regard to the weak evidence, nonevidence. If we don't have the right guy, it doesn't make any difference what she is suffering. We shouldn't lock him up for life." The ideas and phrasing of the words by Statel and Estrich are almost identical! One wonders if Estrich is aware of the DNA evidence from two rapes.

A local columnist, Phil Kloer, generally harsh in his criticisms, reviewed the *48 Hours* show (May 11, 1994).

The trial of Kenneth Redding, accused of raping a former professor (who has gone very public), is set for May 23. . . . Although waiting for a resolution would have been preferable, CBS does have a point—there seems to be no end to the story of Redding and Cathy Winkler, a case full of bizarre legal somersaults. . . . Winkler . . . is an articulate spokeswoman for her own cause and has hounded officials to keep after Redding. . . . Although the local media have been sympathetic to Winkler, whose courage is undeniable, *48 Hours* correspondent Richard Schlesinger plays it very fair. . . . [*48 Hours*] followed the case for more than a year. That's to the good—some stories just aren't wrapped up in 48 hours.

The approach and compliments are great. On the approach, "trial of Redding" and "no end to story" point out who is the criminal and the need to take action. Intermixed within those insightful words are negative patterns that affirm the DA's position. "A case full of bizarre legal somersaults" stresses the supposedly unpredictable calamities happening in one case. There is another interpretation: Those bizarre legal somersaults are a regularity in our legally criminalized system. The only uniqueness of so many somersaults in this case is a result of my ability along with supporters and the media to keep the case open and expose the negative patterning of abuse by the DAs, scientists, and judge. Word choices such as "hounded officials" raise the issue of our right to speak up for justice.

Mark Silk was the courthouse reporter, and after the *48 Hours* show he asked, "How did people react to you as a result of *48 Hours*?" It was a sensible question. The reactions of people were few in part because I was not available and not out in public. Some friends and students left supportive messages on my answering machine. Days before the show, an editor of a soon-to-be published book with an article of mine had a dispute with me over the rapist's name in print. According to the editor, conviction and sentencing were not sufficient evidence of the rapist's guilt because the rapist could appeal and the conviction could be overturned. What more proof does a person need of the rapist's acts and guilt? He sent me the following fax.

> The point is that he is not yet the convicted rapist. None of what you include in your letter—Judge Foible's pretrial statement, the scientific standards of DNA matching, or your willingness to assume legal responsibility—address that issue. While my editor at the press had recommended a pseudonym, there is another way to deal with this issue. In my view the way *TV Guide* refers to him as a "suspect" is unsatisfactory—for the same reasons as you have stated. I'm unwilling to say "suspected rapist Redding" or "alleged rapist Redding." What I have decided as volume editor is simply to delete the name so that the text reads "the rapist's words to me."

I did not receive the fax for several weeks due to my relocation for the trial. That night after the show, he telephoned me: "Cathy, please excuse my fax." "I haven't seen it. Did you send it to the university?" "Yes, but I just saw the show and now I understand." For years, I would not read my own article in print because I did not want to see the space where the editor deleted the rapist's name. Finally, I did, and I read the name:

Kenneth Redding. It took *48 Hours* with its visualization of the seven years of my struggle for the editor to comprehend the meaning of my printed words.

"Rape Victim to Make Her Case" (Silk, May 23, 1994a) initiated the trial coverage. It was not "her case"! Contentious words continued in old and new forms. Reporters still described me as "hounding" for justice. "It is a case that Winkler has refused to let die . . . turning to the news media when prosecutors seemed to be moving too slowly." Is seven years slow? Informatively, the reporter presented the chronology of the Redding case. Haily, who had remained nameless to this point, including in her *48 Hours* coverage, remained anonymous here as well. Anonymity impacted word choice: "Redding is indicted in the Winkler rape and indicted in the rape of the other victim." "Her case" is now "the Winkler rape." "Victim has made a study of rape" was the subtitle for the third section of the article. Favorably, the reporter highlighted my current and Mexican research, but other errors continued: "The PCR tests show evidence of 'band shifting.' " No, the DNA shows band shifting. PCR is a method where there is no possibility of band shifting because it depends on visualization of dots in color and tone. He did use my interpretation, albeit I did not receive credit for it, of the scientists: forensic v. ivory tower perspectives.

A few days later, the placement of photographs angered me: a photo of me was next to Redding as if I was looking at him. The positioning of myself, even photographically, near the rapist abhorred me. "Never associate me with the rapist, not even photographically." The reporter's contradictory treatment of me continued: "Like a fury [a woman out of control] she used her experience as the basis for a new life of scholarship into the place of rape in U.S. society" (Silk, May 25, 1994b).

Media Rape

I have described the cultural patterning against the VISA in the media as a form of rape. Despite this experience of the raping culturing patterns against me, I argue that the media people did not rape me. How can I argue this? Let us examine anthropologist Peggy Sanday's analysis from her book *Fraternity Gang Rape*. She states that initiates agree to a period of terror and horror that attacks their self-esteem, denigrates them in every form, victimizes them through harassments and insults, and bodily violates them. According to Sanday, the victimization of pledges is part of a process designed to bring about a transformation of consciousness so that group identity [target self-esteem] and attitudes [control] become personalized. . . . Reinforced by a vow of secrecy [silence and isolation], the covenant promises masculinity [position] and superior power [hierarchical control] (1990: 135).

The following is a list of a few practices against the initiates: made to wear diapers, exposed genitals and ridiculed, self-applied makeup and perfume, pelted with eggs, washed in shower with buckets of feces, forced to vomit and clean it up, drank milk with hydrogen peroxide, gagged and hands tied, dripped hot wax down back, lie in closed caskets lowered into ground with sand shoveled on top, and subjected to a noose around the neck with a blindfold and platform release.

The initiates agree to such humiliation and violence because survival of that period provides them with lifelong status in a group. At the beginning of that period of terror, the initiates—and this is a group, not individuals—know that endurance and patience lead to the gift of power, control, hierarchy, and status—for life. Since the initiates know their future horrors, the beforehand knowledge minimizes the trauma. And in my experience with the media, the same happened. While the reporting felt like a continuation of the patterns of rape, the media aided in the prosecution of the case.

In 1990, Quinn, a public relations expert, gave me advice: All news—agreeable or not—is favorable. After Jane Hansen's article that detailed the crime and grabbed the attention of her readers, the DA reindicted Redding. When the DA postponed the trial in August 1990, the television interview resulted in Redding's trial with Haily testifying. In the sixth year after six pretrials, five courts of appeals, a state supreme court decision, three DNA tests, two search warrants, and three indictments, Beverly Sheperd used her African American perspective and caught the attention of a national investigative show. Due to *48 Hours*, the DA tried Redding.

On a personal note, I want to thank all of the media individuals with whom I worked. Although I am sometimes critical of their word selections and use of phrases and titles, these are often the result of editors' decisions, not these reporters whose names are on the articles. Many media people either had shouting matches with editors over those news items or called me to apologize for the results. The anonymous editors— the people with high status in news organizations—are more likely the ones who promote those raping patterns. Moreover, the number of articles per day that most reporters need to produce to earn a salary limits their time to research and write. I want to thank the media for aiding in the conviction of the rapist, and I hope my points will generate a recognition among editors of the need for humane treatment of both VISAs and journalists who report on them.

JUDGING CRIMINAL JUSTICE

The media exposure forced the issue of a trial. What evidence would the jury believe? Originally the DNA statistics demonstrated 1 out of 49,000,000 probability that Redding was the rapist. "DNA saved my ass in this case," Joel commented in an interview prior to the trial. PCR had a probability of 1 out of 1,200. Could the jury understand DNA Band Shifting? What would the scientists testify to this time? So often, they changed their position on objective scientific evidence and testified against themselves.

And how would the jury react to Haily and me? We couldn't identify the rapist, but our artist composites were similar, quite similar. "I told the police there was probably no way I'd ever be able to identify him. I just saw him *ten* seconds. I mainly focused on the knife," said Haily, and I had said that, "I don't see any similarity between the artist composite and Redding; they don't look alike at all."

The data from this chapter are a combination of trial transcripts, media coverage, my memory, and notes. The only evidence recorded in a trial are words. Hence, there is no transcript or videotaping of emotions. Juries may judge witnesses based on presentation of self, but without video recordings, no record exists.

Pretrial Preparation

On the Thursday, May 19, 1994, before the trial, I waited in Joel's office. Unfortunately, he had spent part of the morning in the emergency room—a small calamity. The visit at the hospital constricted his time. His information was minimal. "You and Haily will be the first witnesses. I want to present the horror of the crime first." Joel wanted me to be graphic. Without reliance on blood or knife wounds, he wanted my words about the attack to wound the jury. He wanted my trauma to become theirs. "The jury will remember that and keep those memories alive when listening to the scientific evidence, which at times is boring."

My worry from the previous trial surfaced: Joel had unintentionally acted in a racist manner. This turned off the jurors. He can't repeat that behavior again. I raised the issue diplomatically. "Joel, do you remember how the jury reacted in the last trial?" "No, I never look at the jury." *Isn't the jury critical?* Lawyers hire specialists to interpret the facial responses and gestures of members of a jury.

My strategy with Joel was to reveal his past faux pas by exposing my own. "Joel, since I've been teaching black students, I've learned a lot. There are two cultures, and when they mix, racism might define those traits. When a white person gets excited about an idea, s/he might speak quickly, raise their voice, and use elegant words to enhance their argument. The fast-paced, loud voice and long-winded words appear to Blacks to be a ploy to hide the truth. Sometimes, that is true. Therefore, any time a white person uses this approach, Blacks suspect racism.

"Many African Americans believe that whites who are not racists speak slowly, understandably, and with everyday words. While you did not intend it, Joel, I think your involvement in the scientific argument revealed those characteristics. I remember that woman juror initially listening intently and then getting disgusted when those traits appeared. You were proud of yourself and you should have been, but that approach doesn't work with Blacks." Joel listened carefully as he digested my ideas. My media visibility gave me status with Joel.

"Can I testify when Redding spoke the words of the rapist to me after the arraignment? He was getting on the elevator." "Was it a threat?" "Well, yes, but for me it was proof that he was the rapist." "Did you tell Stan at that time?" "No, why should I? Redding was in chains. What could Stan do?" "It's too late. It's not evidence."

Loneliness defined my weekend before the trial. Some of the time I prepared for my testimony. I wrote multiple outlines, trying to present the details in a fashion that would prevent my emotions from overtaking me. Each practice session ended in disaster: to overcome those barriers of pain was impossible. *Would the pain prevent me from testifying effectively or at all?*

Forming a Jury

Joel asked me to be at the courthouse at noon on Monday. No one was sure how long jury selection would take. As I walked up to the courthouse, a reporter with a cameraperson ran up to me, surrounded me, and pushed a microphone in my face. In the mode to testify, their actions exposed my feelings of horror from the attack. "The DA does not want me to speak to the media until after the trial. I'm sorry. I can't help you in your job." Their disappointment was apparent. Their anxiousness made me angry. What were the media people thinking? Would they do any story even if it meant destroying a positive verdict? If the release of Redding occurred, my life was in danger, not theirs. And speaking to the media could result in a mistrial. I wouldn't risk it.

During a break, Joel notified me that "We won't finish jury selection today." "Joel, I am nervous about testifying." "Cathy, if you weren't nervous, I would worry. That's a good sign." "I realize it's a good sign, but it feels like a bad sign. What if I forget what happened? There's so much to remember." "I'll help you." At 9 that night, Joel called. "Cathy, do you want to go over the testimony tonight?" "Isn't it better if I appear unprepared?" "Cathy, you've taken a lot of major exams." "This is a bigger exam." "That's true, but if you're worried, you can use cards tomorrow." "Doesn't that look bad to the jury?" "It does come across better if you speak from memory." "Maybe the petrification will work to our advantage." "That's true. I have to show you some pictures, taken after the beating. I'm going to have to ask you some questions that might annoy you like, 'did you have these bruises before the attack?' Just answer them. You never know what a juror will think, and we have to answer all of their questions. I can show those to you tomorrow before you testify." "Joel, don't do that. Those pictures might set off my trauma, and I would rather that the jury see that. Can you wait?" "Sure, no problem." "Joel, I don't think I can talk about the ass-licking or penile-anal incident in front of the jury. With everything else he did, do those matter?" "I'll be there, Cathy. I'll help you with questions."

"Joel, could I be addressed as Dr. Winkler? I earned that status and I don't want to be looked at as just a VISA." "Cathy, I don't think that's a good idea. Jurors would have more sympathy for you if I don't use that address." "All right. I've gone this far. I don't want to lose now. Joel, did you know that for my research in Mexico I did pen-and-ink sketches of people's faces? People in the community recognized the faces. Joel, I'm aware of people's features." With the bulk of details on Joel's mind, I had to remind him of points that I thought were important. Joel did store that information away and use it in court.

"Cathy, there is one more point I wanted you to know. Clare axed almost every woman from the jury. I argued with the judge that there was a pattern of discrimination because nine out of ten strikes were against women. She had an argument for each one. One woman was head of a Women's Studies department, and Clare argued that's prejudicial. The judge overruled me." I said, "That figures. Anyway, I've heard that women don't believe women raped. Maybe this is Clare's favor to us." The illogic of the law: If a woman supports women's issues, then she is biased! If a man supports men's issues, is he biased? If the defendant-rapist is a man, are all men biased? Eight months earlier, the DA, Tim, had addressed that issue in a letter to the editor: "In Sunday's Perspective you failed to recognize the most significant problem. Only in this state can the defense in a criminal prosecution of rape effectively remove all the female prospective jurors" (Morgan, August 17, 1993).

"I'm also worried about the racial makeup of the jury. There are eight Blacks, and almost all men." "That's great. Blacks don't want violence in their community any more than any other ethnicity wants it." "Also, it's a young jury. Many are in their twenties, thirties, and just a few are older." "That could work in our favor. Younger people have a better education about violence than some older people. They are also more open about issues of rape than sixty- and seventy-year-old people." Joel said, "Well, I hope that's true. See you tomorrow." Not only did I believe those points, but I felt that Joel began to believe them also.

Statel made several motions prior to the trial:

> Miss Winkler is a very vocal person. In just these hearings, she has been talking about the case, talking to the TV cameras, talking it up. And my concern is that the jury not be exposed to any of this. She always has an entourage with her. They are always out in the courtroom, as I say, talking about the case.

One camera was an entourage! Statel also made this request: "I would ask the court to at some point admonish people—the spectators in the courtroom to conduct themselves appropriately, his family, and his friends." Recorded was the adjective "his." What was Statel worried about?

The Trial Begins

That morning I waited outside the courtroom with Haily to testify. A well-dressed twenty-year-old woman, young not only in age but also actions, introduced herself as the rape advocate. She had had this job, she informed us, for nine months. Shock hit me. She was to provide any support that we needed. Despite her presence on the job for months, she never informed us of her existence. The pretrial period is hell, *and yet she did not contact us!* Now she offered us "support." "What kind of support can you offer?" "Whatever you need." "Well, could you be specific? What support have you offered other VISAs in the past?" "Whatever a victim needs." I asked her, "Could you list those types of support?" "Whatever the victims ask for." Her answers matched her support for us.

VISAs are not allowed to hear opening statements. Although not evidence, unless the defense attorney pays for the court reporter, they are not part of the trial transcripts. Television provided that information. Joel ended with the words: "The bottom line, ladies and gentlemen, is that every single piece of scientific evidence on which there was enough to test and to declare a match, it matches Kenneth Redding." Clare dwelled on the defendant's innocence:

> We are here today because through Kenneth's pleas of "not guilty," he maintains that he is innocent of all of these charges, and that the state has the wrong man. Ladies and gentlemen, it is horrific to convict an innocent man.

Outside the courtroom, Haily, who had testified twice before in rape trials, advised me: "Breathe deeply. Just focus on the issues. Don't worry. Look at Joel throughout. He'll help you. Don't look at Redding or people in the courtroom. Just keep focusing on getting through it. You know you will." "What are your feelings, Haily?" "I'll never feel safe again," she said. Haily left to testify. Even though I have only included excerpts, Haily's testimony was a narrative of the rape.

> Around seven o'clock, it was just starting to get daylight. I felt something touch the left side of my face, not sure what it was. When I turned over, I saw a black man with a knife in his hand over me—about *ten* seconds. He told me to close my eyes and keep them closed. During the course of sexual intercourse, my little girl had gotten up. She was used to getting up and getting in bed with me sometime in the morning. He told me to tell her to go back to bed or he would hurt her. I told her to go back to bed. She didn't want to, but she did.

Joel interjected: "Were you through with intercourse, or still having intercourse?" It was good that I was not in the courtroom because my eyes

would have popped out of my head when Joel said the word "intercourse."
It's RAPE, RAPE, RAPE. Seven years and you still don't get it.

> Still having intercourse. I knew that there was a knife there and I
> thought that he would hurt her. I took him at his word when he said
> that he would hurt her. So I had her go back to bed. During the time
> of the intercourse, he kept telling me to close my eyes. At one point, he
> told me, he said, "I need money. I need $500." I told him I had no
> money in the house.
>
> While he was actually having intercourse with you, um, uh, while he
> was raping you?
> Yes sir.
> How long was the knife he held against you?
> Four inches, sir.
> To the best of your recollection, did he have an erection during the
> time that he forced you to commit oral sodomy on him?
> To the best of my recollection, I would say maybe partial but not a
> full one. When he put his penis in my vagina, the kids were there. I
> value their lives more than I do my own. He had a lot of pubic hair, and
> he did have hair on his chest. I felt it. I was examined at the hospital.
> They told me that during the rape that he had turned my uterus.
> Objection, your honor.

Judge Foible ruled: "I'll grant the motion. Do not state what anybody told
you."
In her cross examination, Statel had a few points:

> Your assailant was not wearing a hat. Is that correct?
> If he had a hat, I wouldn't remember if I saw it or not.
> You were still—kind of in that sleep daze.
> When I turned over and saw the knife, I immediately woke up,
> fully—fully awake.
> Because I know that you testified that you only really looked at the
> man for about *four* seconds, and because of that, is why you have only
> been able to get a general description of a Black man with a thin mus-
> tache, average height, on the skinny side. Is that correct?
> Yes, ma'am.
> In regard to the knife, since you couldn't really see it either, could it
> have been maybe 2 or 2½ inches?

The law is specific about the length of the knife and the seriousness of the
crime: 4 inches or more equals a felony.

No, I know it was 4 inches long.
But 3, 4 inches is hard to measure and tell a difference in that length during such a traumatic situation?
It was 4 inches. I know it was.

The next day Haily's anger at Clare was strong: "How could she question me on the length of that knife? Why didn't she believe me?" "Haily, you know that it is a felony if the knife is 4 inches and not a felony if the knife is 3 inches—even though both knives could do a hell of a lot of damage." "Cathy, I know it was 4 inches." "I know, Haily. There are certain points that are unquestionable for us." "No, Cathy, I know because the knife was mine. Redding grabbed my own knife after he broke in." "You, devil, you. Everyone assumed that the knife that Redding carried was his. No one asked that question." Haily had a huge smile on her face. The hatred against Clare's questions dissolved as Haily realized her power in testifying: She had outwitted those lawyers who described her as an uneducated Appalachian woman.

While waiting for Haily to finish testifying, the advocate sat next to me. Any conversation seemed better than silence. "How's your life these days?" She began to ramble about her new house, her wonderful husband, her marvelous honeymoon, and her fantastic life. While bombs of horror exploded throughout my body, she described her idyllic life. During her soliloquy, she failed to note my silence. She made only one point of substance: "Victims should have their own room to wait in." Later I saw her private office where I could have waited comfortably. But that was *her* office, and she did not allow VISAs to wait in her office. The scientists waited upstairs in comfort in Joel's office.

On the Stand

The bailiff called a name. I didn't move. He had mispronounced my name. Seconds later, I gasped in understanding—I was the only person in the hallway waiting to testify. I got up, but my legs shook. *Keep those jello-like legs moving until you reach the stand.* My concentration was so strong that, even though I veered around Redding (see figure 12.1), I did not notice him. *Just make it to the chair. Try not to fumble when you climb into it.* Deliberate movements were crucial. Sitting did not stop the shaking. Part of me wanted to scream, but my counseling voice calmed me. Joel began with obvious questions: "What is your name?" "Cathy Winkler." "What is your job?" "I teach at a local university."

Figure 12.1   Redding at Trial

And then he asked: "Where do you live?" I remember hesitating and glancing around. He wanted me to answer *that* question. *That* question meant the rapist would know my whereabouts. The media people always hid that information and were even discrete on pictures of the house by editing out street signs. Redding sat in the courtroom, and I imagined him leaning forward in his chair to hear the details. *What should I answer? Why was Joel asking this question? Does this mean Joel knows he's going to win and I'll be safe?* Then I recalled that even if we lost, Redding had several more years in prison. But, he had told me he had friends. To give the city was the same as giving my address: To track me down was easy. For seven years, I'd worked to make myself stand up to Redding's terror, to face him and the fear he buried inside of me. Now was not the time to back down: "Springfield, State."

With the first tissue in hand, I started the hours of blotting away tears.

I woke up and there was a man with his arms open standing in my room. I jumped out of bed and backed up towards the wall. I thought I was dreaming at first and I said to him: "What are you doing here?" And he said: "You know what I'm doing here." Then I said something like "do you want my money?" or "are you here just for robbery?" He said, "You know what I want."

The media's summary: "The attacker forced Winkler to take off her clothes. He then pushed her to her knees and ordered her to perform oral sex on him."

I said, "Then, I wouldn't move." Joel interjected: "You're still kneeling beside him." "Yes, then he took his right hand off of my wrist and moved it up and put it behind my head and forced my head down on his groin. And that's when he put my eyes over his left groin." My voice changed from one of a nervous and scared victim to strong, accurate, and self-assured, the voice of a VISA. The next information revealed my confidence. "And I saw a scar. The scar I saw was about a nickel or dime in shape, and it had two concentric circles. The inner circle was smooth skin, and the outer concentric circle was wavy skin." "Excuse me, your honor." Defense attorneys never excuse themselves to VISAs. "Judge, I object to this narrative account. The prosecution should use the court method of question and answer." She did not object to Haily's narration or with the scientists later. Judge Foible let me testify.

> When I saw that scar, I thought, maybe I could identify him, and if I told the police about the scar, they would believe me that he had broken in. I decided to fight back. I raised my right hand and hit him in the groin. I was ready to run, but he . . .

and I stated this with a halting, surprised voice, "he got up really quick. And, he swung and hit me."

> Where did he hit you?
> He hit me on the left side of the face. Because it was a bit dark and he had swung wide enough that he hit the lamp at the same time, he didn't give full force. I decided to keep fighting. I wanted to get out of there. I grabbed his penis and pulled it as hard as I could. He just kept hitting me and grabbed both of my arms to position me so he could hold me in place while he kept swinging at me. Then I just said "OK, I'll do it"; he can stop. I let him know that I wouldn't fight any more. I was afraid he would kill me. The blows were . . . [pause]. I knew he could have hurt me worse.

The defense attorney stood: "Your honor, I'm going to object. This is just pure speculation at this point." "Your honor. This is not speculation. This is what is going through the victim's mind at that particular time to explain her actions." "Overruled." I restated the point that she objected to and made it clear that the rapist's violence led me to my interpretation.

During the narrative, my eyes avoided everyone. I looked at the ceiling or down at my hands. To exchange eye contact was to share that pain and trauma. I didn't want anyone closer to that emotional chaos than my words. My concentration now was entirely on the attack. The next interruption therefore came without notice. Joel stood up: "Judge . . ." Before Joel could continue, the judge hit the hammer and asked the jurors to please excuse themselves to the jury room. The lawyers approached the bench and had a discussion, which I, sitting but three to four feet away, could not hear. Once the lawyers had resumed their seats, Foible spoke:

> When a victim testifies, there will be no intrusion. The law states that people may not enter or leave during the testifying, and the doors to the courtroom will be locked. Therefore, if there is anyone who is not going to stay for the whole testimony of this witness, please leave now. No one may enter after the bailiff locks the door.

Judge Foible paused and glanced around. "Bailiff, will you please lock the doors? During this testimony, no one will make noises or any type of intrusive movements. Bailiff, please ask the jury members to return to the courtroom."

Afterward, my friends explained the disruption. Redding's sister had come in late. This happens. She was noisy when she sat down. This happens to all of us, too. But as she sat down and glared at me, she made noises of disgust at my testimony and did not stop her interruptions. I hoped that the jury members noticed but the drama of my testimony probably usurped their attention also.

> He kept doing it. And I didn't count because he kept getting on his back, and kept getting on top of me. He just went on and on. I did try to look at his face sometimes when he was on top of me. He would put his hand on my face and then tell me to look away. And then he finished or I thought he was finished. Then he said: "Where's your money? I need $500."

The media's summary: "Winkler testifies that the rapist led her around the house, looking for valuables. Finding nothing more than a few dollars, he took her back upstairs."

I continued testifying: "He probably said you gotta have money again. I said I don't; I haven't been paid. Then he said I might as well get everything I came for." Tears took over my existence. "Then he took off his clothes again." The tears deluged and forced me to hide my face behind the mike. With my hands over my face, I turned my head away from the jury and down into my chest as I curled my body into itself. I didn't want people to feel that pain. "And it started all over." Prey knew I needed help and interjected: "On the scar, did you ever attempt to look into his abdominal groin area again?" "No, I didn't even—I didn't even want to look at—look at those genitals at all. I was too afraid." Several times in the retelling, the horror seized my being and left me speechless. Joel was there to help me through. "When he said 'suck it,' did you, in fact, put his penis in your mouth when he ordered you to?" "Yes, it happened in terms of him getting on top of me and getting inside of me. And it would go limp, and then he would have me do it again. I don't know how many times." Unconsciously, I had deleted the two most horrifying parts of the attack. Joel reminded me: "Did he ever involve himself with you, did he ever force himself on you in any other type of oral sodomy?" "Yes." And I described the anal ordeal. Yet on dissociation, when I stepped out of my body, that part I deleted from the police statement and the chapter that I had given Stan six years ago. To legal people, this is not a reproducible fact and is legally incomprehensible. I could not tell them what I knew they would not believe.

On surveillance with Det. Doil, can you tell the ladies and gentlemen of the jury if you were able to meet anyone while you were out with Det. Doil?

When Kenneth Redding walked toward the car, I—I noticed a change in my body. And I couldn't recognize his face. Well, I—I all of a sudden got really scared.

And the court reporter spoke up: "Repeat that, please?"

I got really scared. And I started feeling inside of myself exactly like I felt during the—the rape attack. And I didn't know what was going on, because I couldn't recognize Redding's face as the rapist, but something was going on. And I was afraid to move because—I wanted to run from the car, because I wanted to get away from there, or I wanted to grab onto Det. Doil, but I—I—I, you know, I thought he wouldn't believe that I—that I was a good victim. For some reason or another, the fear of the attack was coming back, but I couldn't understand why. And then Kenneth Redding walked away from the car, and then, I—I didn't feel any—I didn't—I didn't feel that fear. And I said to Det. Doil, but, you know, remember that body. That's the exact shape. And I remember stating the head shape was exactly the same and the body shape.

Before Statel started with her questions, my digestive system tied itself into knots. The rapidly increasing pain and the tightening of the guts pulled my body toward itself. My body leaned over to ease the burning inside of me. The media narrator interprets: "The defense attorney gently questions Winkler." My perspective: Redding's attorney enraged me. *How dare you rigorously defend a man who would gladly rape you! How dare you arduously work to free a man who you know is guilty!*

On the same day of the attack you did, in fact, give a description—or a statement as to what happened, and that would have been at 12:25 P.M., is that correct?

That's when we started. I gave a description of what he looked liked and what he did. It took us three or more hours. She typed a five page— five pages of what I said. She then had me read it over. I made changes. She put in the changes, but I never read over the changes.

And then you did, in fact, sign the statement, is that correct?

Yes.

Miss Winkler, isn't it true that there is no mention of the fact that your assailant testified—or, excuse me—that your assailant told you that he had a knife?

I—I might not have said it, because the police told me that there were only two things that they wanted. And that was things that would describe him and things of the crime. And since he didn't have a knife, there was no reason, I thought, to put all of that in the statement.

You didn't think that was important to mention.

There was no knife.

And isn't it true also in the statement that was given, Miss Winkler, there is nothing in the statement indicating that the assailant forced you to lick his anus?

I didn't know if that was a crime.

And I believe you've testified here on direct that you did not notice any other scars on this individual?

I—didn't—notice—because—I—didn't—look.

The media narrator interpreted: "She [defense attorney] focuses on Winkler's description of only one scar. 'I believe you testified here on direct that you did not notice any other scars on this individual.'" The defense attorney repeated her point. *Be patient*, I told myself. *Don't become angry. Answer the questions simply and directly. The interrogation will end soon. You have held on for seven years. You can hold on for a few more hours.* I answered again, "I never looked at any other part of his chest or his groin. So—I— didn't—look." "You didn't notice any other scars on your assailant?"

Joel had told me that lawyers ask the same question three times for emphasis, but Statel's questions were destructive. My body further tightened up, and my insides coiled. Her questions were intolerable. *"I—didn't—notice,"* and I looked at her directly and with the explicit meaning to stop her attack or she would feel my anger. Emphatically and slowly, I said: "Because—*I—didn't—look.*" "Did you notice the huge scar that runs from the stomach to the upper chest?" "I did not notice what I did not look at." She dropped that line of questioning.

In your statement to the police, you did not state the act of licking? Why not?

The police asked me to put in my statement anything that might describe the rapist from physical appearance to mannerisms to words stated, and to include the crimes he committed. I did not know what crime that was.

The truth is that exclusion was due to its horror. A trait of the testimony of people raped is to delete or minimize discussion of the worst parts of the attack. In my statement to the police and to the jury, my mind protected me from those horrifying acts. To explain to someone the abhorrence of rape is to share the pain. Words can make us feel the disgust. Legally, that rapist's act was not a crime: It is not against the rape laws in that state to force a person to lick his ass. That's not rape; that's not forced oral sex; and that's not the beatings or aggravated assault. Most state laws do not encompass, cover, or understand rape. Simplistically, we say that rape is the unwanted and forced insertion of a penis into a vagina. That definition fails to recognize that men rape men and in rare incidents women rape men, and women rape women. Moreover, it does not include the plethora of acts of horror in the rapist's bag of tricks.

The defense attorney then conferred with Joel. Redding and I looked at each other: a unique moment. Here we were, the two of us, the only two who were at the attack, the only people who had experienced those three and a half hours. His look showed amazement at the precision and accuracy of the details. He couldn't believe how much I remembered. Our eyes looked through each other: we both knew the truth. While my description of the rape attack took about an hour and a half—and even at that I deleted several of his acts—the cross-examination lasted about fifteen minutes. My boiling anger abbreviated Clare's questions. She did not want to look like the villain to the jury. If she aggravated the VISA, the one who had gained everyone's sympathy, her defense was over.

Joel had begun the discussion of the attack with a question that allowed for a narrative answer: "Tell us what happened on the night of September 29, 1987." Even before beginning my description of the rape, tears seeped out of my eyes. Joel grabbed a box of tissues, a glass, and a pitcher of water to help me. After all those years, an emotional description of the attack was at hand. That was hard. The training of professionals is one of dispassion. To be a professor is to be a person without tears. The profession taught me to bury and hide my emotions, my pain. And, I was ugly when I cried. My face got puffy and full of huge, distorted blotches. My voice heaved and halted constantly, and my face and neck became an inflamed red. It would last for hours. After the attack, I carried makeup in case salty drops seeped out. Following tears, I would get out my mirror, foundation, powder, mascara, eyebrow pencil, and eye shadow. Crying always left my eyes swollen, and eye shadow partially hid those bulbous lids. Three strategies in testifying were a result of the seven-year wait.

First, cry. For years, I did not want to do this and still don't. My real reason to hide the tears was my fear that with the tears would come the explosion of pain. The volcanic eruptions of pain when I was alone were a part of my life. No one else should ever see those. Any emotional expression, I feared, might reawaken that pain. The years of tears and writing about the anger and emotional explosions gave me insight that my inner self protects me by appropriately letting out those pained feelings. For the jurors, I could now release those tears and let the enormity of the pain show in my voice. In our society, pain is most real when it is visible.

Second, describe the attack in detail. A vocabulary to describe a rape attack enables people from friends to family to police to lawyers to judges to jurors to understand the depth of pain that we suffer. With more education about the tortures of rapists, the less VISAs will need to elaborate on every single excruciating moment. The media people told me that my VISA's testimony impacted them greater than anyone else's. My anthropological education gave me the ability to verbally explain people's behavior and to translate ideas from one culture to another: the culture of VISAs to the culture of non-VISAs.

Third, correct mistakes and defeat the defense attorneys. On mistakes, explain to the jury why one made the mistake. I couldn't remember the house number of where the rape occurred. I said that I think it is, . . . but it is a number that I wanted to forget. The jury found this explanation plausible. To outwit defense attorneys ask them to repeat their questions and explain the meaning of the queries. Clare had read my statement, learned of my involvement in keeping the case alive, and noted my effectiveness on television: Joel thought she feared questioning me. All defense attorneys need to fear VISAs in pain. The interrogation of people raped is their job, their worst nightmare. Moreover, an excellent method against the defense attorney is expression of our emotional pain. She wanted to avoid getting me upset: the jury would then consider her and her client guilty. The defense attorney felt my anger. She knew that a few more questions would result in my verbal debasement of her. That would be her downfall. Also, she did not want to aggravate me into further crying. That's another VISA method of defense: cry in shock at their questions. The questions make us want to scream and cry at their cruelty, a cruelty that judges allow.

After testifying, the judge said some words, unregistered by me. I sat there for what seemed like a few minutes but was probably a few seconds before I realized: IT WAS OVER. I picked up a half-dozen used tissues and left the chair. As I walked across the courtroom, my legs shook. As I put each foot in place to get out of the room, my abdomen contracted and ached. While I had a right to listen to the witnesses after me, the testifying had sapped my strength.

My friends rushed out of the courtroom and hugged me. The witless rape advocate suddenly appeared, in front of the cameras and media people, and asked me if I needed a ride. Her act angered me. She had not asked me if I needed a ride to the courtroom to testify. And, she did not offer Haily, who had also testified and who had also endured the seven-year wait, a ride home. Haily needed a ride. She had no car nor friends to comfort her nor was she staying within blocks of the courthouse like I was. The witless one perceived me as a sufferer and Haily—who had not cried—as a person without pain. In front of the media people, I ordered her: "Help Haily now."

The Other Witnesses

The trial continued without me. Prey questioned Det. Carson: "At what time did you take an initial report from Miss Winkler at the hospital?" "I don't remember the exact time." "And what time was it that she returned to her residence?" "That, I can't give you an exact time." "Were there other persons with Miss Winkler at the hospital?" "I do not remember." "Did you have an opportunity to be with Miss Winkler to show her a group of photographs in an attempt to see if she could identify anybody?" "I had taken an entire file drawer of photographs and let her go through every one of them that was there." She gave me twenty photos. "Does

Kenneth Redding appear to you the same today as he did then?" "His facial features do. His hair does. I think he has gained some weight and perhaps been lifting weights, or something. He looks more muscular."

Statel cross-examined: "Nowhere in her statement does she mention that her attacker told her that he was carrying a knife, is that correct and is that important?" "No, there is no mention of that, and yes, it is important." "And also, nowhere in her statement—is there any mention in her statement about how the assailant forced her to lick his anus? Would that be an important circumstance of a crime?" "She stated he had . . . let me look here a moment. It doesn't mention anything about being forced. Yes, this is important." "During the giving of this statement with these very specific details, did she appear to be rational and coherent?" "I think that she varied at times. She would be calm, and sometimes she was very upset emotionally. It lasted a couple of hours because we would take a break so that she could get her composure and get her something to drink." My emotional variation was crucial to understand: Calmness demonstrated accuracy in the details of the crime, and my rattled moments held the details of the horrors.

The three-minute exchange between Redding, Doil, and myself was a focal point. In court, Det. Doil testified:

> I asked him to come over to the car. He came over, said a couple of words, stooped down far enough so that Cathy would really get a good look at his face. And I could also make eye contact with him. After he left, I asked Cathy if that was the guy. She said no that was not the guy who raped me. I asked her if she was sure. She said "yes, I'm sure it's not him."

Statel emphasized that point: "You asked her a second time, and she answered positively, unequivocally that this was not the man who raped her. Is that correct?" "Correct." Det. Doil didn't remember the rest of my words—"But remember that body and head. This is exactly the same shape and size as the rapist." The media narrator noted: "Police investigator Kenneth Doil is asked about the *infamous* ride around six years before when Cathy Winkler encountered Kenneth Redding" [emphasis added].

The scar I never looked for and never saw continued to be an issue for Statel when she questioned Det. Roth: "The scar that runs down the stomach of Kenneth Redding, was that a raised scar back in 1988?" "I believe it was." "So, if someone had their eyes closed and ran their hand over the chest, it is possibly something that you would feel." "If you ran your hand across the scar, yes." The words "ran their hand over the chest" indicates a gesture of desire. And the judge allowed those words. "She did not mention any other scar that her assailant had, did she?" "No, she didn't." "She did not mention at all that her assailant had this very large scar down the center of the stomach." "Yes, ma'am."

In her media interviews, Statel pressed the point of the scar: "The fact that she missed the scar down the middle of the torso is a very important piece of information. That's why we have a photograph. Looking at the scar, you cannot say that someone who noticed a small, half-inch scar on the hip, would have missed one larger scar." The defense attorney's strategy was not to protect the defendant legally but to attack the VISA. Luckily, Joel, in his media interview, remembered my position:

> She saw the scar very briefly. She tried to fight him at that point. He literally beat her black and blue. The pictures that we have of her injuries from that night are truly frightening. She saw an identifying mark. She decided at that point I don't want to look in this area anymore; he will realize I've seen his round scar, and he will kill me.

The photograph of Redding's scar after the attack did not exactly match the more recent photograph due to his significant increase in weight: his weight had moved the scar that was two inches below the hip line up several inches. No lawyer bothered to ask—Did his weight change affect the placement of the scar?

After testifying, Haily decided to attend the trial with me. The next day, two of my students showed up too. The students were there in the courtroom before I arrived, observing the expert on hair analysis. CoSandra noted the defendant's actions immediately: "He's guilty." "CoSandra, I know you're on my side, but how can you say that?" "He blinks almost constantly." I had never noticed this trait despite the fact that I had taught her in class to pick up on behavioral cues. "My mother told me that a blinker is a liar. That guy is a liar. He's guilty, guilty, guilty." Throughout the rest of the trial, Redding blinked—incessantly. Did he blink that constantly during my testifying? We'll never know. He didn't blink during the rape attack. Later in the trial, there was only one time when he did not blink frequently.

Mr. Dependable's hair analysis focused on details. Off the record, he had told us that he knew positively that the hair of the rapist matched the hair of the defendant. The hair strands for the defendant, he said, were unique. On the 100,000 hair identities he had identified in his career, there were only three he couldn't match confidently. Hair demonstrates what people have or have not eaten in the last months. Redding's hair showed signs of malnutrition that correlated with his drug periods. In court, he described the hairs found and the reasons for the match with Redding and then said, "And there was one dyed red hair unaccounted for." That was why Roth had questioned me so many times! *Whose hair was it? How did it get in my home? Did Redding meet someone earlier with that hair color?* Statel questioned the reliability of his hair analysis: "Hair analysis is not like a fingerprint. Is that correct?" "That is correct." She presented no rebuttal witness to his testimony. The media noted that, "Two crime lab analysts gave uncontested testimony that hairs recovered from both incidents [that is, both rapes] were consistent with hairs taken from Redding."

As we waited to go to lunch, the DA Tim passed me in the hall. He did not speak, look, or even recognize my existence. Throughout the trial, he continued this treatment. *Was I his nightmare?* Tim invited Laurie, the media person from a local television station who had first interviewed me and kept the case alive, to lunch. Their discussion remained a mystery until after the trial. Haily came to lunch with my students and me but did not order. After multiple queries, she admitted that she had used her last coins for the bus to get to the trial. I paid for her lunch. She wrapped up half of the food for her kids. We gave her a ride home that night and thereafter. The advocate offered no help. During lunch, my students told me about their exchanges with Redding's family. "Dr. Winkler is our teacher, and we're here to support her." The Reddings had an answer: "You belong to the Black mafia." CoSandra ignored them and walked away. Libretta chose to answer them: "Kenneth is guilty."

When I initially walked into the restaurant, the eyes of three of the women jurors caught my attention. There was only one section of the restaurant with a free table, and that was in the section with the jurors. Since the family of Redding had previously accused me of jury tampering, caution was a necessity. One juror focused on me with a positive and supportive look. I only surmised, as others had at my table, that we had her vote. I diverted my eyes. How does one communicate to a juror without talking to them? It's great we have your vote, but don't, please don't give this away. Throughout the trial, her glances continued. After that, I noticed each day another juror or two glancing at me. By the second to last day, almost every juror had looked at me. A look is never a guarantee in the voting process, but it was a clue.

When we returned to the courtroom, I noticed another pattern among the jurors. They never sat in the same row, same seat, or next to the same person. This also occurred at lunch. I couldn't predict which jurors would eat together. During discussions at the bench among Foible, Joel, and Statel, jurors talked to each other. Their pattern of interaction was flexible. At other times, they passed notes that were obviously congenial and enjoyable. These observations raised my hopes: These jury members are open-minded, they get along with many types of people, and they don't have exclusionary ideas. There was no evidence of distrust among them. Friends who came to watch also noticed this pattern of multiple associations. Nevertheless, there was still a juror or two whose feelings on the case were a mystery.

DNA Evidence Verifies the Rapist

After the hair analysis, the boring part of the trial began: DNA Fingerprinting. The experts first explained the method and then what is unique in this case—Band Shifting. Only one lab in the United States uses a method to correct for the shift. The argument was between two sets of scientists: forensic versus ivory tower. If there is evidence of environmental contamination, the university scientists throw the sample away and use a new sample until the test results are perfect. These scientists are aware that environmental contamination exists, and they have actually introduced intrusive elements into the testing to show that band shifting occurs. Other than that, these scientists never study the process of environmental contamination. All their lab tests are with perfect DNA material.

On the other hand, forensic scientists seldom come in contact with perfect material. Contamination due to transportation or contact with the real world occurs with most evidence. For that reason, the FBI uses a 5 percent margin of error as their standard. There is a DNA match if the two examples are identical within 5 percent variance. Dr. Sefaborb was less pompous than the last time. Joel must have approached him. He still had a smile of a rich fat white guy who owned the world. The media ignored him in their coverage.

Laura Gemal, the other DNA specialist, surpassed her usual superb performance. Joel gave her the floor—literally. He sat down with the few observers in the courtroom and listened. She stepped down from the chair and explained the details of DNA and Band Shifting to the jurors. Her explanation was clear, understandable, and presented with complete respect for the jurors. Her voice was cordial and amiable. Her ideas were in words that a person off the street could understand. She looked directly at the jurors. She did a great job.

When Clare began the questioning, Gemal's approach changed. She turned her body away from the jurors, arched her back as she sat forward, and kept eye contact only with Clare. The media did not note these subtle but explicit behavioral changes. There was even a slight difference in intonation. She replaced her calm work-with-you approach with a reserved voice of authority and control. Laura also altered her word choices from a comprehensible to a scientific vocabulary. As she answered Clare's questions, I wondered how well the jury understood her answers. Many times, I—a university professor—couldn't comprehend her high-minded words. While her company prepared her for court, I felt that Laura showed anger at the defense attorney. A case that had lingered too long and hurt Dr. Gemal's reputation.

That night I began a practice that continued every evening thereafter. Very late at night I called Joel's answering machine at work. My purpose was twofold: first, to applaud and encourage him, and second, to correct his errors through words of support. "Joel, this is Cathy. I wanted you to know what a great job you did. You impressed everyone with your performance. You were calm and secure, and demonstrated control of those scientific terms. You used understandable words. My students felt you exuded confidence and belief in your side. They told me that I'm lucky to have such a great lawyer." This last point was important because a mostly Black jury worried Joel.

Thursday had more scientists droning on. The number of media people present declined significantly, and the jurors showed signs of boredom. The Redding family contingent decreased to two who showed up late, took long lunch breaks, and left early. In the courtroom, they noisily turned the pages of magazines. At one point, they began a conversation among themselves. Once, I noted that everyone watched them, especially the annoyed jurors whose focus was to understand the complexities of DNA. This time the judge and lawyers said nothing.

Support from my friends dropped off too. Friend A was on vacation. Friend B had just delivered her baby and needed to recuperate. Friend C had a new position and could only take off one day of work. Friend D came when she could but she was fighting off economic hardships. Friends E's previous efforts in supporting me had worn them out. Friend F had had foot surgery. Friends G never contacted me after their divorce. Friend H—who had originally wanted to attend the trial the first year— told me that the emotional roller coaster ride was too much. Rev. Hope was seriously ill and died a month later, knowing that he had worked for justice in this case. My sisters came for the last two days. On the other hand, Joyce, a woman I didn't know, attended for two days. Twenty years ago, a gang of bikers kidnapped and raped her for three months. She came just to support me.

The publicity of the case two weeks earlier on *48 Hours* and the comprehensive media coverage in the newspapers, on the radio stations, and on television made this case well known. In spite of the publicity, no group, no organization, nor individual from the city stepped forward to support me. There were hours when I sat there by myself.

Friday had its own character. One of my students said her mother would show up. I approached a woman seated alone. She was kind to me but informed me that she was the sister of the mother of Redding. During the trial, she resolutely refused to look at or interact with Kenneth. He tried to greet her. She rebuffed him.

This was the third day of scientists testifying. Musher, one of the many scientists who I feared, took the stand. He was slightly nervous. During his initial testimony, he made a reference to the fact that he had testified for both sides in this case. "But, in this particular instance, I am in agreement with the DA." He was testifying on the validity of DNA Band Shifting. Anticipating his testimony, I had contacted a friend of his wife. I explained that she was in a vulnerable situation. Redding might not have forgotten that Musher previously testified against him. If he gets free, the wife of Musher is a possible target.

This time Musher supported the prosecution and testified, against his boss's position and for the reliability of Band Shifting evidence. Here was a witness who received $1,000 for testifying and another $1,000 for preparation, and yet his work was a grade-school quality foldout, a chart hand drawn on two pieces of graph paper taped together. I cringed. The chart displayed two parallel lines to represent the DNA of the defendant and the DNA of the rapist. He explained that these lines were parallel at every point and the separation between these lines was minuscule. Therefore, he declared the DNA of Redding as a match to the DNA of the rapist. Then Dr. Glue testified on PCR Amplification that duplicates a cell and demonstrates the DNA match. According to my scientist friends, this method was very common in DNA research. The media had another view: "Polymerase chain reaction is cutting-edge science."

Joel rested his case. Clare had three witnesses. The first was a woman scientist. Her last performance was poor. With the cameras on her, maybe she would behave professionally. As she walked into the courtroom, her appearance was a significant step above the sweatsuit she had worn previously. Her answers were concise and well stated. She explained the issues and her disagreements with the evidence. At the beginning of her testimony, the juror who favored me gave me this look of concern, as if she was saying to me: Oh no, this woman sounds credible. On my face, I tried to respond: Don't worry, Joel has yet to question her.

Joel began his questioning, and his elegant subtlety showed his control of the situation. His first questions were direct and inquisitory, establishing a base of knowledge. He presented questions as a naive person, letting her answer as the professional. She looked good under the first part of his inquiry. Then, "How do you know that the DNA of Redding does not match the DNA of the rapist?" "If one looks, they do not see a match." "Did you do any measurements to verify your position?" "No, I didn't think that was necessary." Five months ago, she did no measurements to verify her position either. Twice the court paid her to testify, and twice she testified unprepared. The juror looked at me with satisfaction, and I gave her that look: I knew it would be all right.

The next witness was Dr. Soo. I hoped that he would repeat his arrogant performance of last time. He leaned back in the chair, legs open, arms protruding out, and constantly swung the chair back and forth like a pendulum. Joel exposed Soo's ivory tower approach. The case was still solid. The defense attorney requested to continue the following week because her last witness had a conflict and couldn't appear. What could we do? The whole courtroom—judge, two lawyers, fourteen jurors, two bailiffs, one defendant and family, and two victims with friends—would just have to wait until the scientist could fit us into his schedule. His obligations were more important than the law.

Now that the weekend was upon us and the trial trauma had overtaken my life, I needed the break. My emotional exhaustion demanded time to relax and to recover from the days of tension. The scientists' testimonies tired the jurors. The weekend would allow them to relax from the tedium and give them time to think over the evidence. Time helps us to learn. Joel will replay the details on Tuesday, and further increase their understanding.

Saturday and Sunday were my days. I tried to revive my self: hot tub baths, soothing music, a drink, an herbal smoke, a good book, a funny movie, and times for nothingness with my body in a relaxed horizontal position. No intrusions. My sister Mary Carol arrived Sunday morning. She took the red-eye special, and likewise needed a day of relaxation. On

Monday, a holiday, my other sister Anne arrived with her five-month-old child, Nathan.

Tuesday morning, we showed up bright and early. I was as usual the first person the jurors saw when they arrived and the last person they saw when they left. My face would constantly remind them of the reason they were there. As jurors, they held women's lives in their hands. Nathan occupied our attention as we waited. Another baby showed up. The Reddings had brought one of their young relatives. Kenneth's sisters caressed and smiled at the gorgeous child. At one point, the two children noticed each other. We made comments among ourselves: Wouldn't it be wonderful if the two children could play together? But could people overlook the present crisis and work for future nonviolence and peace? In Olinalá, Mexico, it is a social crime to impose the sins of the parents upon the children. All adults must safeguard and keep secret from children the mistakes and crimes of parents.

Dr. Pompousie was the last witness of the trial and an end to the boring scientists. He acted in an authoritarian manner. He tried to justify his position. "I realize that other scientists have a different position, but I take the more cautious position. We must be absolutely certain." Joel had the right questions. "Didn't you testify previously that you accepted this evidence?" "Yes, but now we have looked more closely at the evidence, and I feel it does not reach our standard of certitude." Four years ago he wanted to absolutely, positively convict the rapist, and today he wanted to free him.

Verdict

Then came the summary statements. Clare began with the idea of justice: "As horrific as the assaults that occurred on Miss Betten and on Miss Winkler were, I submit to you, ladies and gentlemen, it is equally as horrific to convict an innocent man of that crime." After twenty minutes, she began to speak about the evidence. Each of her points surprised me.

- The artist composite does not look like the defendant.

- We know there were men across the street in both attacks. Both victims told us they heard voices and saw men there later. One of those men could be the rapist.

- The hair analysis is not an absolute certainty.

279

- Cathy Winkler had some bruises, but let's be realistic, she was not battered.

- DNA Band Shifting throws the evidence in serious doubt.

- PCR Amplification is only an approximation: 1 out of 1,200.

- Cathy Winkler did not see a scar on the stomach. How could she miss it?

Joel's summation reflected what I had told him before the trial: "Joel, you've got the evidence. Let the jury decide." He gave the jurors their rights.

- *You* decide whether or not this artist composite looks like Redding.

Joel grabbed the composite, took it over to Redding, and held it next to his face.

- Let's look at the scars on Redding's body. Now look at this small scar and remember Cathy Winkler's words. Don't those words match this scar? Did Cathy Winkler fail to see the other scar? Let's remember the situation that she was in.

- Was Cathy Winkler battered? Here's the pictures. Look at them. What do you think?

He then placed each of the six pictures on the rail in front of the jury box. The placement of the pictures initiated a response from a juror that surprised me: the stoic, hard-faced Black woman cried. She believed me.

- Clare says the hair analysis is in doubt. Well, if there was any expert witness that agreed with her, she would have had him in here on the stand. Note that no one testified against the hair analyst.

- Clare thinks that one of those guys across the street is the rapist. Believe me, if she had evidence that could link those men to the rape, she would have had them in court testifying. She didn't bring them in, ladies and gentlemen.

- Ladies and gentlemen, every single piece of evidence points to Redding.

And Joel pointed at him. "This man is the rapist. This man raped Cathy Winkler, and he raped Haily Betten." He jumped up and down to emphasize his point.

- Every single piece of scientific evidence in this case that can be attributed to the man who robbed and raped and sodomized those two women matches somebody. Who in the world does the evidence match? Who in the world matches hair to hair, DNA strand to DNA strand, pubic hair to pubic hair, facial hair to facial hair, DNA Band Shift strand to DNA Band Shift strand? Who else? What are the probabilities, what are the odds on the face of this earth that more than one person matches every piece of evidence, matches item to item, and line to line?

Unnoticed by me but noticed by a media person, Clare's eyes became red and moist. Joel's summary—at least from her perspective—was not a damnation of the rapist, but a personal attack against her. Her desire to win had become personal. Due to the extensive workload, long hours, sleepless nights of study, and media pressure, she identified with the case, with the defendant, with the criminal. Was winning more important than justice?

The judge then read the counts and dismissed the jury to deliberate. After lunch, the media took turns interviewing me for four hours. My sisters loved it, but for me it was not a pleasurable task. The questions were standard: "What does this feel like?" "What do you think the decision will be?" "What will you do afterward?"

At 5:30, we rushed back to the courtroom only to hear that the judge had dismissed the jury for the night. The judge noted a typographical error on the formal sheet that they have to sign. One count against Redding was missing. The jury was to return the next day and resume deliberation. Early the next day, I was once again in front of the elevators. The jury saw my face before they walked into the courtroom. Previously the jury members had come in casual clothes. Today the door opened and I saw one of the jurors dressed up, her face with makeup on it. Several other jurors got off the next elevator, likewise dressed up and hair arranged. Then, I spotted the bailiffs talking into the mikes on their shoulders and giving orders for others to assemble: "It's time." I gathered my sisters and rushed in for seats. Within minutes, Haily was beside me. A bailiff downstairs had notified her, but the Redding family had not arrived. The advocate—missing daily for the past week—suddenly showed up to sit next to us in front of the cameras. "We don't need you. Get out of here." Flustered, she searched for a reason: "Uh, I wanted to see if Haily needed a ride." "You've never offered her one before." Red-faced, she left as the media and bailiffs stared at her.

For the verdict, the judge allowed other camerapeople into the room: The media wanted to capture the reactions of both VISAs. The judge read the first count, and the foreperson read the verdict. I watched Redding's face: His eyes never blinked. "Guilty." That was the word of the day: Guilty, Guilty, Guilty, Guilty, Guilty, Guilty, Guilty, Guilty, Guilty, Guilty, Guilty, Guilty, Guilty, and Not Guilty. On count 14, stating the carrying of a gun, they voted not guilty. No one explained to them that a lethal weapon such as a knife could suffice. The thirteen guilty verdicts were not sufficient responses for Statel. She wanted each juror to say that they agreed with the verdict. Twelve more times, the jury repeated the word "guilty" and emphatically. They were relaxed and confident in their decision.

What evidence influenced the jurors?

> I don't think there was any juror who went strictly on DNA evidence. I may be one that was the closest to doing it because of the way I looked at it. But I looked at everything together. I just didn't examine DNA itself.

> I voted guilty because of DNA information that was presented, because of the composite sketch, because of the testimonies of the expert witnesses, and also because of the testimony of Cathy Winkler.

Even though I could never identify the rapist, my evidence in terms of the artist composite and details such as the scar did convince the jurors. My answers explained how the trauma had impacted my details. They believed me.

As we left the courtroom, I went up to Joel in front of the cameras and stretched out my hand. He awkwardly switched his box of legal papers from one hand to the other: "Joel, I want to thank you for your work and for winning the case. I would also like to say good-bye." Stunned and speechless, he smiled embarrassingly. He became a star in legal circles for this win. To him, my testimony and energy were only minor ingredients. He never thanked me. As I walked outside, I ran into the highly supportive media person Shirley. She and I looked at each other, only briefly, and quickly hugged. "Thanks for not making this racist." "It never was, Shirley." "I know, but you know how some people are." The rest of the media people waited in front of the courthouse. Haily and I walked out together. This is how I addressed the media. "First," and then my emotions skyrocketed to the surface in bolts of tears and sobs,

> I hope that all past victims of Redding hear this guilty verdict. He is stopped. You do not have to fear this man. You can release the trauma of past fear. Today we experienced a miracle: the conviction of a rapist.

After the media exchanges, I asked for the nearest pay phone and called Cheryl first, but of course she was on the phone and would have to wait for the announcement in person. Then I called my mother. My emotionless mother let out tears of joy. Her friends said she really cried happy tears. How unlike her! I called other friends to invite them to the conviction party: their response—"Unbelievable." We returned to Cheryl's house to tell her the good news. As we walked in, she had a worried look. Immediately I pronounced the word: "Guilty." Shock framed her face. As she questioned me "Really?" I reached out to hug her. Grabbing each other, we swung around as we gyrated up and down. Our feet pounded with the strength of two joyous giants, and the floor absorbed the waves of happiness. She stated those famous words that people kept repeating to me thereafter: "I can't believe it." Then she explained the real reason she didn't attend the trial: "Tim had told me the first day that they expected to lose. He worried about the $20,000 cost of this case." The lawyers had no belief in themselves! "Cheryl, did Tim tell Laurie this, and did she tell the others in the media they expected to fail?" "Yes." I estimated that I spent $25,000 to keep the case alive, and their worries were over less money. My lost funds were out of my pocket, and theirs was from a budget.

Why did people not believe in the possibility of conviction? The evidence was explicit and clear. How could people doubt DNA? Didn't the picture-perfect artist composite raise issues of high probability? How could I know that Redding had a scar? How could people doubt that I would work so hard for an issue that did not have substance? How could people doubt my ability to succeed? Hadn't I succeeded in most issues around this case: keeping it alive, getting media support, maintaining a job despite academic opposition to the research? What were their reasons? The parole board told me they believed in me. Yet most had doubts.

Mrs. Redding, Kenneth's mother, was on the news that night and stated that she hoped that Cathy Winkler could live with herself for putting the wrong man in prison. It was a racist verdict, she declared. Both comments were painful. I never testified that her son was the rapist. I could not identify him as the rapist. Mrs. Redding and her family had not listened to the DNA evidence. Supporting the sexism in our society, her family attacked the woman VISA, not the male DA, male scientists, male detectives, and male hair analysis expert who identified Redding as the rapist. Some of these men were African American. The skin tone of the rapist was never an issue. The detectives, the private investigators, many of the people in the neighborhood, and my students were Black. I worked with, lived with, and taught African American people who believed in me and supported me. The issue was sexual violence against women, not race.

The party that night, entitled "People with Conviction," was an odd experience. Although people showed up singularly and slowly, many did not make it. Tim showed up without an invitation. "Sorry about the cost of the trial." "It was $40,000, but that is not important, Cathy. We won. Money is not a problem." *Only a win legitimates spending money to stop a rapist?* Redding had probably raped at least 100 women in his life: the county spent $400 per woman. Stan Rest, also without an invitation, showed up with a gift—a picture of the courthouse, my home-away-from-home. He always did have a sense of humor.

The next day, still accustomed to the pattern of waking early to prepare for whatever was in store, I retrieved the morning newspaper. The editor had asked me for my reaction; my unstated feelings were that this was a job for justice, and I wanted to walk away from all of it. The newspaper had a picture and article of me on the front page, had another picture—can you believe it?—and article on the editorial page surrounded with words of praise, and a third article—no picture this time—in the local news section. Although I was flattered, I wondered if the extra coverage took away from other relevant issues. Still and all, Jane Hansen, the editor, with whom I had dealt when she was a columnist, knew how rare such a success was. Perhaps she wanted others to know that my efforts deserved praise. The editorial "Justice the hard way" pointed out the magnitude of work a VISA must exert for justice:

> She had the education. She had the self-confidence to consistently push prosecutors. She knew how to write letters and make phone calls to poli-

ticians and the media. No victim should have to fight so hard for justice. (June 2, 1994)

Letters to the editor appeared:

[Cathy Winkler] won a victory for all women. (Ann Latham Agreda, June 12, 1994)

If it hadn't been for Cathy Winkler's persistence, her attacker would never have been tried. It's about time that our courts begin paying as much attention to the rights of the victim as they do to the rights of criminals. (Pat Jorgensen, June 8, 1994)

I take issue with the recent headline "Victim applauds rape conviction." Cathy Winkler may have been victimized, but she will never be a victim. . . . Women everywhere have been psychologically empowered. No, that is not the work of a victim. (Kenyada, June 5, 1994)

The next day my sisters and I recuperated at a museum with calliopes. After scampering up to the dollar change machine, I put my money in the first calliope: the biggest and loudest. A smile covered my face before the music had a chance to begin, and quickly I turned to watch my sisters' looks as the music churned out. A soothing peace seeped into our faces. The music returned the joy of life and the memories of feeling carefree.

Sentencing was Friday. On the one hand, there was reason to worry: the 1993 U.S. Senate Judiciary Report stated that almost half of all convicted rapists can expect to serve one year or less behind bars. On the other hand, the reputation of Judge Foible was well known around the courthouse: His nickname was "Forever Foible." Those convicted could expect to live in prison forever. At the sentencing, Haily brought her daughter. We had decided not to speak at the sentencing. We had given our testimonies. This time with the cameras running, I trusted the judge to give a fair sentence. The Redding's family was present. Scott Redding was in a state: Rage molded his face. His eyes bulged in anger, an anger that screamed to get out. It was directed at me. For five minutes or more, he stared directly and unstoppably at me. I wondered if he would act on it—not here—but later.

Mrs. Redding took the stand. She asked for the mercy of the court. And I think that she was, unnecessarily, asking for the forgiveness of others: My son was good when he was home with me. Ironically, she never stated that her son was innocent. Too many of us blame parents for the fall of their children. Sometimes the parents could be better, sometimes the parents need to work hard, and there are other pressures that minimize their contact with children. Nor is there a correlation between the quality of the parents and the quality of the child: considerate, loving parents can produce an out-of-control child, and irresponsible, loveless parents can produce a caring, intuitive child.

> I would like the court to consider that he is still a human being and have mercy on him. I ask the judge to consider that Kenneth has some good in him. The worst of us has some good in us, and the best of us has bad in us. I hope and pray that God will set the record straight.

Scott took the stand and said little: "This is racist. My brother didn't do it." At that point, the rage almost exploded out of him. He ran out of the courtroom. Statel's arguments in defense were contradictory: "Mr. Kenneth Redding is an innocent man who has been unlawfully convicted. The defense recommends a sentence of twenty years." The judge read the expected verdict: five life terms plus forty years, and added:

> Certainly Mr. Redding needs to be punished for these brutal acts. Based on your history, if you are released from prison, the question is not if you will commit another crime but when and where. I don't think you should ever be released from prison.

As we left the room, the bailiffs surrounded us and asked us to wait. The rage of the Redding family was apparent. For several minutes, we stood together, cornered by the security officers. "As soon as we have an elevator for you, we'll escort you out." Several minutes later as I walked out past the Redding family, likewise protected by security officers, Mrs. Redding spoke out: "Cathy Winkler." Everyone became tense. I walked onto the elevator. Silence. Even from the media people. Joel took us to his office to explain the sentencing, or so he said. For forty-five minutes, he reviewed the issues. The length of time revealed to me their worry about the Reddings' rage in the hallway below.

Joel ended with words that were on his mind for the previous forty-eight hours since I'd congratulated him: "Cathy, I hope with the knowledge of this sentencing, you won't feel inhibited about speaking up or feel like a wallflower." His line was humorous, and for that reason, I repeated it to a number of people. But his words reminded me of the parts of me that had felt inhibited and the parts that I had wallpapered out of existence for years. For the first time in seven years, Haily's daughter slept, slept without nightmares, slept a sleep of peace.

RAPED THREE TIMES

Argument Summary

The first rape was physical. 1) The rapist isolated and silenced me, embodying me in a state of horror and torture. 2) He denigrated my self—"you like it." 3) His contradictions from "you're my girl-friend" to "I raped you" created a chaotic and insane-like existence. 4) The rapist controlled me internally and externally with feelings of horror. 5) The rapist cycled the hateful pain after the attack through trauma with bodily scars, mental stigmas, and emotional gashes.

Silence is the choice of most victims. Why do people raped choose not to tell others or to file a police report? Silence is a method of protection, protection from more rapes.

The second rape was social. 1) Isolation was the result of my friends' avoidance of me. 2) Those who spoke dictated my feelings—"you are obsessive for stopping a rapist" or "*your* rape is destroying the department." 3) Contradictions existed: success at my job and denigration for that success. 4) Hierarchical control defined me as a "victim," a nonentity. 5) The pain cycled through and through my life from unmoderated counselors' advice to administrators' denial of my rights to my job.

The third rape was legal. 1) DAs and the judge silenced, even gagged, my rights to justice: No legal advice or protection existed for me. 2) Their verbal attacks of me in the media left my self-esteem battered. 3) Contradictions existed: scientists, DAs, and the judge spoke about justice, and yet acted unjustly. 4) Their hierarchical control in decision making became a seven-year plague. 5) The highway of legal briefs and pretrials on word games continued the cycling of rape pain.

People's Reactions

A letter arrived from Bill Sr.:

> I was delighted by the verdict and sentence. Redding is a dangerous individual, and I am pleased to know he will remain behind bars. Given

287

the significant problems encountered in the Redding case, you are to be commended for "staying the course" and for seeing the matter through to its successful conclusion. I believe some degree of justice has been achieved, but of course it in no way eradicates the unjustifiable pain inflicted upon you.

Bill Sr. showed up in the courthouse for the case, and that was his first sighting in the halls of justice since his departure two years earlier.

My research revealed interesting information. Bill Sr.'s staff and lawyers informed me that he described himself as a dictator, and the DA's office was his dictatorship. Joel Prey suggested to me that his preferred pseudonym for my book should be Buck Rogers who wears a white hat. When I shared that information with people in his office, an uproarious laughter reverberated against the walls. In reviewing the files, I found a stick-man sketch of him by a security guard, drawn during the 1991 trial and labeled: "Super Ego."

I met a man who went to high school with Redding. "We both played football." "What was he like?" "After he ran over me [beat me up] several times, I learned to avoid him. I think that's the only strategy that would work with him." "What position did he play in football?" "He was a linesman." "But he's not very big." "No, he didn't need size. He was so full of hate and madness that no one could stop him. He was good at that. After high school, we parted ways." "What happened?" "I went into the marine corps." "That must have been hard." "After Redding, no."

I heard from many other people as well. I share these comments and letters with the many people who over decades have worked to change people's negative culturing patterns. Your efforts aided me in this case. It began with a delivery man: "You don't know how many people you have helped." Humor was present: "Cathy, how long did it take the lawyers to convict the rapist?" "Tony, seven years." "Wow, wasn't World War II shorter?"

Comments arrived in the mail. "Congratulations! You are definitely a relative!" (Cousin, Missouri). On a postcard from a friend in Mongolia,

> This yak (actually, a yak hybrid) doesn't give a darn about your court victory, but I do, Yeah! Yeah! Yeah! Congrats! There is justice in the universe, and individual persistence is its conduit. (Friend, Mongolia)

Other words of support came from strangers:

> [The trial you suffered] makes my problems seem so minor, and yet at the same time, watching you on television gave me hope and strength. (Stranger, New York)

The women whom your perseverance has saved from being raped will never be able to thank you, but I know that you must take heart from knowing that others will not have to go through what you did. (Stranger, California)

I read about your story printed on the Op-Ed page and clipped it and saved it. I put it in my "inspiration" file which is fuel for my personal statement for the law school applications. (Stranger, Georgia)

From a couple dozen participants, strangers at a national women's conference on peace and freedom,

What an extraordinary survival! Your courage and strength of character to persist is remarkable in light of the ongoing "emotional" battering you received. You've empowered all who learn of this ordeal and your determination. Thanks.

And my sister Mary Carol gave me a T-shirt with the slogan: "This is no ordinary person you're dealing with." Margery, daughter of Haily Betten, sent me a card: "Thanks $510,000.49! That's 'thanks a million' *after* taxes."

More letters arrived at both my house and office:

I wrote to you earlier in the year about your case but back then I was under the impression that you're Black. But after seeing you on *48 Hours*, I was surprised to learn that you're in fact White—not that it makes any difference because you were still brutally attacked the night of the rape. In watching the case unfold and listening to you, I was able to put one issue to rest: the racial issue. I was deeply moved by your openness and honesty, but more than that, I am in awe of your courage and drive in pursuing the case and seeking justice after all these years and heartaches. (Stranger, Georgia)

I saw the episode of *48 Hours*. I cried throughout the whole show. I felt as if I was in class again listening to you tell us what happened. (Student, Alabama)

I want you to know how much I admire your willingness to allow your vulnerability to be on television. You do not stand alone. (Stranger, Georgia)

Many victims of rape declare that it's "A Walking Death," but Cathy, to understand that as long as you keep sharing your story, you can only be called "A Walking Testimony." It warms my heart to know there is someone who's in the ring with me, and we're not fighting each other. (Stranger, California)

If telling the truth makes the police/DAs look bad . . . then tough! They need to be made accountable. It's our taxpayers' dollars, and we want to know where and how those dollars are/are not spent. (Friend, Massachusetts)

Please forgive me for not having been more supportive over the years. I just finished watching and crying through *48 Hours*, and I understand so many things much better now. Now I understand, in a small way, all those letters you've been sending out, and what you were going through. I had no idea that there were so many of us (letter recipients, that is) with whom you kept in touch. No wonder you hardly had time for more than a little line now and then in your own handwriting. (Friend, Indiana)

To thank people personally, I sent out 225 framed pictures of the symbol of three rapes and of the successes in dealing with them (see figure E.1). Joel placed his frame on his book shelves behind his chair: when facing Joel, one faces the frame of three levels of injustice. The following message was on the back:

This gift is a thank you for the years ('87–'94) of endurance, patience, stamina, and caring in an ordeal of violence and threats. The ribbon points out that a rape attack is also a threat of AIDS. The shoestring reminds us that rape crisis centers and VISAs live on shoestring budgets. The laurel represents the success with your help that resulted in a guilty verdict on 6/1/94 with a sentencing of five consecutive life terms. Thanks for your greatness.

Aftermath

Afterward, anger defined my emotions. How could the defense attorney attack me on my narrative testimony, on failure to overcome the ID trauma, or on not seeing another scar? How could the scientists question the validity of methods that they use every day? How could Joel debase me in the media? Why did the DAs make me remember the details of that rape attack for seven years? Why did the judge viciously manipulate

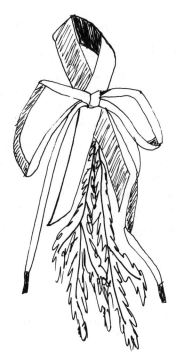

Figure E.1   Gift to Supporters: AIDS Ribbon, Shoestring, and Laurel Symbol

the trial date—to add a year to my torture? Why didn't women's groups come out and support the cause?

I wanted solitude. In the back of the rental home, the abandoned garden became my land to turn into a paradise. Azaleas grew twelve feet long, covering the back stairs and hiding dozens of bulbs. Vines entangled and choked the bushes and trees, and privet and weeds tried to extinguish all other growth. This garden reflected my life. The entangled mess covered a hidden beauty that I would slowly uncover. One day as I whacked through the brush, I found several bushes, ripe with juicy blueberries. Some days I swung from the vines as I used my strength to pull them down: On those days I was Tawana the wonder VISA. Trimming back a circle of azaleas were two contented turtles, one on top of the other. Stopping my work, I gave them their space and time: They did not change position for four hours! Each day I worked a few hours in the garden to take away the choking debris that represented the hate in my world: a hate that has deep roots historically and grows feverishly. Working daily to completely rid those out-of-control, malignant growths from the garden

291

was impossible. More importantly, the work gave me an opportunity to rediscover feelings of solace and contentment about life.

Conviction stopped the rapist, but it did not stop the ongoing pain buried inside of me: "It is such a secret place, the land of tears," wrote Saint-Exupery (1993: 31). I wanted that hate and anger—planted by the DAs and the judge and the scientists and the defense attorneys—out of me. Each day I wrote about the details of the trial, my feelings, and my remembrances. The writing recorded the pain but was not therapeutic. In the garden, my therapy began: at first it was only for five minutes once a week. In those five minutes, peace defined my inner self. I felt how unimportant people's accusations about my efforts and actions were. My past did not define me. Nevertheless, suffering daily depression for two months, I called my therapist friend Linda: "When is it going to stop?" "Call me in two years."

Crises Continue

Crises do not take a holiday. Two months after the trial, I received a letter in the mail from Haily:

> Cathy, please come here and pick up my religious pictures. The mayor has condemned this house and is kicking me out. I am going to go homeless and put my children in foster care. They know they have to give up everything. I trust you to take care of my special pictures.

The next day I drove there. Margery gave me her teddy bear to keep safe. Otis and Zacchary each had a special toy that they wanted safeguarded. "Haily, why is this happening? Isn't there something you can do?" "I cleaned up the house, but there's a whole list of problems on why they condemned the house. Here it is. I talked to the mayor but she's an ornery person." "Most of these we can take care of. The structural issues we could get help. What do you think of my talking with her?" "Well, you can try, but it's never worked for me."

"Mayor Spitun, how nice to meet you. I'm Dr. Winkler, a friend of Haily. Haily and I met through the trial that was recently on *48 Hours*. As a professional, I'm always pleased to meet other women who have succeeded, and as mayor, that is fantastic." We discussed the problems. "Dr. Winkler, we put in for a grant to redo the house, but due to a technicality, Haily doesn't qualify." "Well, Mayor Spitun, Haily has testified three times in her life against rapists. The juries convicted the rapists. This is a person who protects the community. Shouldn't we help to protect her from economic doom? She's a good mother. The media wants to report her story. Is there a way we could keep it out of the media? If we can begin fixing the small problems and if you'll give us a little more time to take care of the larger ones, could we have the condemnation order lifted?" The media was a threat to the mayor: it would make her look like a dispassionate person. "The media! Oh, we are concerned about Haily. And I am so glad there is someone to help her. If you make changes, we might be able to work something out."

Each week I gave Haily a list of chores on the house, and my group of supporters raised $2,000 to buy supplies and pay the back taxes. A church group donated a roof. One of Haily's personal priorities was a pair of teeth so she could eat a chocolate bar again: We bought her the teeth—and the chocolate. The mayor lifted the condemnation order a month later. I took Haily to buy a plant for the Mayor. "I'm not going to do that. She's a mean old witch and was going to kick me and my kids out of our house." "You're right. But, we don't want her to forget you. And this plant on her desk will force her to remember your heroic acts and to think twice before she takes action against you." "Well, in that case, I'll give the witch the plant." Every Saturday for a year, I worked with Haily on the house. We replaced the broken windows; both inside and outside we painted; removed the trash; cut the weeds; planted flowers; fixed gas pipes; checked the electrical work; and a few zillion more projects. The first year after the trial centered on saving Haily and her kids from homelessness. Haily had worked for the safety of the community, and the community wanted her to live unsafely—homeless with her children in foster care.

The second year after the verdict began with another crisis. My mother had not attended the trial due to two years of abdominal bloating. The doctor's diagnosis: "You're old. You retain fluids. You're tense. Get a massage." Then, "Cathy, I have ovarian cancer that has metastasized. When the time comes, I want you to help me do it." Suffering like my brother did in those last weeks of his life was against my mother's wishes. After Jack had died, we had discussed the issue of euthanasia. His life ended in an unimaginable hell of pain, a pain so severe that he slept all of the time. The medical people had the technology to keep Jack alive, only to suffer.

With death looming, my mother told me about the rapes in the late 1960s. My father, the year before his heart attack, demanded marital sex rights. Stress and overwork had seized him, leaving him challenged and physically altered. My father came home from work—late as always—

and, after dinner, raped my mother. "Mom, what did you do?" "I drugged his coffee to stop it. And I don't feel guilty." In the 1960s, the idea of marital rape did not exist. My mother hated what he did to her, but she had no name for it. She told no one. If she had gone to the police then I believe that my dad would have pleaded guilty and gone to jail.

This did happen to one friend of mine. She went to the police to stop her husband. He pleaded guilty and served a one-year sentence. He apologized, accepted responsibility, and worked on his problems that drove him to be a terrorist. Today they are together and happy. This case is rare. Rapists almost never apologize, never say they're wrong, never take responsibility, and never seek help. My experience with rape educated my mother on the tortures she had suffered. Death gave her the courage to speak the truth. On my mother's deathbed, she told me to tell the truth about my father raping her. For my father, he was an honest, hardworking person, and he too believed in the truth.

The executor of my mother's will told us her last oral requests: "Mary Catherine wanted Cathy to be paid extra out of the estate for each of the four areas: her four-month salary, which she gave up to take care of Mary, her time spent cleaning the inside and outside of the house and preparing it for sale, her full-time, 24-hour nursing care, and her legal responsibility to help Mary die." Everyone agreed. Two months later, I received a check for one month replacement salary for my job. For my mother's care, it was less than the executors had paid the painters: they received $80 per hour and I received $6 per hour. Women's sacrifice to care for others has little value, even when money is available, in this society.

The following year, the administration at my university denied me tenure. My honors included the Teacher and Advisor of the Year Awards, publications with Cambridge and California University Presses among others, committee work from security to human rights research to accreditation, and highly favorable national and international publicity for the university. Sarah had heard the administrators' views:

Cathy had embarrassed the school and embarrassed "manhood" by saying what had happened to her. Universities are closed societies, and especially for anyone who wants to get ahead, s/he must keep his or her mouth shut. I seriously believe that the compulsion to suppress truth at most universities is so strong that, if a female faculty member was raped, she might have also suffered repercussions for "airing dirty laundry," unless she were granted tenure to remain silent. The punishment was quadrupled, however, because Cathy was young and successful and raped and in a state nearby.

Without a job, I wrote this book living off of my savings. I applied for academic jobs for two years. At one university where a friend worked: "Cathy, I would love to have you as a colleague but the competition is stiff." "Competition is stiff" means "your publications are too few." Since I had been in academics ten years, my half-dozen articles and two book contracts (not yet in print) were insufficient for a professional position. Not listed on my resume was the time spent on a seven-year legal case.

The legal case, my book, or myself will not change the horrors. Weeds will always fight to grow in our gardens, trying to choke the beauty out of life, and we must work daily to confront the weeds and unearth the beauty. Sometimes our efforts can actually result in a conviction of a rapist. At the same moment of triumph, we watch the DAs and judges and scientists reinstitute practices that continue to negate VISAs. We help someone die with respect and dignity while those who never cared-to-care refuse her last wishes. I relocated, worked some, wrote another book—this time focusing on love rather than hatred—and still search for employment. Despite the negative impact, I was lucky. I had the chance to try. I do not regret my decision to stop a rapist even though it has led to a professionally unfavorable outcome.

Is the legal case over? No. For the rest of my life, I will have to be in touch with the Parole Board.

BIBLIOGRAPHY

Agreda, A. 1994. Sisters in Spirit. *Atlanta Journal Constitution*, June 12.
Anthropology Today. 1993. Editorial Comment. Vol. 9(4):20.
Barry, K. 1979. *Female Sexual Slavery*. New York: New York University Press.
Bierwert, C. 1990. "Somatic Transformations." Paper presented at the American
 Ethnological Society Meetings, Atlanta, Georgia.
Boston Women's Health Book Collective. 1984. *The New Our Bodies, Ourselves*.
 New York: Simon & Schuster.
Brownmiller, S. 1975. *Against Our Will*. New York: Simon and Schuster.
Buchwald, E. et al. 1993. *Transforming a Rape Culture*. Minneapolis, Minn.:
 Milkweed Editions Press.
Burgess, A. and L. Holmstrom. 1974a. Rape Trauma Syndrome. *American Jour-
 nal of Psychiatry*, Vol. 131:981–6.
 1974b. *Rape: Victims of Crisis*. Bowie, MD.: Prentice-Hall.
Burt, M. 1980. Cultural Myths and Support for Rape. *Journal of Personality &
 Social Psychology*, Vol. 38:217–30.
Cash, C. 1994. Kappers Put Under Home Quarantine. *Southern Voice*, April 21.
Chau, M. et al. 1993. Introduction. In *The Subject of Rape*, 8–12. New York:
 Whitney Museum of American Art.
Colao, F. and M. Hunt. 1983. Therapists Coping with Sexual Assault. In *Women
 Changing Therapy*, eds. L. Robbins and R. Siegel, 205–14. New York: Har-
 rington Park Press.
Du Bois, W.E.B. 1967. *The Philadelphia Negro*. New York: Schocken Books.
Ellis, E. 1983. A Review of Empirical Rape Research. *Clinical Psychology Review*
 Vol. 3:473–90.
Estrich, S. 1987. *Real Rape*. Cambridge, Mass.: Harvard University Press.
Federal Bureau of Investigation, U.S. Dept. of Justice. 1992. *Crime in the U.S.
 1991*.
Index of Crimes, United States, 1972–1991.
Feldman, H. 1993. More than Confessional Testimonial and the Subject of
 Rape. In *The Subject of Rape*, eds. M. Chau et al., 13–42. New York: Whit-
 ney Museum of American Art.
Finkelhor, D. 1979. *Sexually Victimized Children*. New York: Free Press.

Foskett, K. 1991. Suspect Charged Three Times. *Atlanta Journal-Constitution,* August 7.

Freire, P. 1970. *Pedagogy of the Oppressed.* New York: Seabury Press.

Green, C. 1988a. Genetic Evidence Facing Trial. *Atlanta Journal-Constitution,* June 4.

———. 1988b. Man's Indictment on Rape Charge. *Atlanta Journal-Constitution,* July 1.

Hansen, J. 1991. Victim of Rape. *Atlanta Journal-Constitution,* June 8.

———. 1994. Justice the Hard Way, *Atlanta Journal-Constitution,* June 2.

Harlow, C. 1991. *Female Victims of Violent Crimes.* Washington, DC: U.S. Dept. of Justice, Bureau of Justice Statistics.

Herriot, J. 1992. *All Creatures Great and Small.* New York: St. Martin's Press.

Janoff-Bulman, R. and I. Freize. 1983. A Theoretical Perspective for Understanding Reactions to Victimization. *Journal of Social Issues,* Vol. 39:1–17.

Jorgensen, P. 1994. Justice System is Lax. *Atlanta Journal-Constitution,* June 8.

Katz, J. 1984. *No Fairy Godmothers.* Saratoga, Calif.: R & E P.

Kenyada, R. 1994. Empowerment. *Atlanta Journal-Constitution,* June 5.

Kloer, P. 1994. Local Rape Case. *Atlanta Journal-Constitution,* May 11.

Koss, M. and M. Harvey. 1991. *The Rape Victim.* Newbury Park, Calif.: Sage.

Lewis, D. 1991. Mistrial declared in DNA Rape Case. *Atlanta Journal-Constitution,* August 30.

Long, K. 1991. Man Indicted Third Time. *Atlanta Journal-Constitution,* August 8.

MacKinnon, C. 1982. Feminism, Marxism, Method and the State. *Signs,* Vol. 7(3):515–44.

McIntosh, S. 1993. Getting Away with Rape? *Atlanta Journal-Constitution,* October 10.

Metzger, D. 1976. It is Always the Woman Who is Raped. *American Journal of Psychiatry,* Vol. 133(4):405–8.

Millett, K. 1971. *The Prostitution Papers.* New York: Basic.

Morgan, J. 1993. A Bias in Court. *Atlanta Journal-Constitution,* August 17.

National Crime Victimization Survey Report. 1992. *Criminal Victimization in the U.S., 1991.* In *Female Victims of Violent Crime,* Caroline Harlow, 1–3, 7. Washington, D.C.: U.S. Department of Justice, Bureau of Justice Statistics.

National Victim Center and the Crime Victims Research & Treatment Center. 1992. *Rape in America.* A Report to the Nation, April 23, 1992, pp. 1–16.

Panourgia, N. 1995. *Fragments of Death.* Madison: University of Wisconsin Press.

Poole, P. 1993. Land of the Free? *Opelika-Auburn News,* September 19.

Raine, N. 1998. *After Silence.* New York: Crown Press.

Renaud, T. 1988. DNA: Criminal Code? *The Fulton County Daily Report,* October 11.

Russell, D. 1984. *Sexual Exploitation.* Beverly Hills, Calif.: Sage.

Saint-Exupery, A. 1993 *The Little Prince*. San Diego: Harcourt Brace Jovanovich.

Sanday, P. 1990. *Fraternity Gang Rape*. New York: New York University Press.

Sanders, W. 1980. *Rape and Woman's Identity*. Beverly Hills, Calif.: Sage.

Sheffield, C. 1987. Sexual Terrorism. In *Analyzing Gender*, eds. B. Hess and M. Ferree. Newbury Park, Calif.: Sage.

Sheperd, B. 1993a. Rape Case Finally Hears Trial. *Atlanta Journal-Constitution*, April 6.

1993b. Rape Case's DNA Tests botched. *Atlanta Journal-Constitution*, May 5.

Sheppard, J. 1992a. Society's Shame. *Columbus Ledger-Enquirer*, August 16.

1992b. Victim's Worst Trauma. *Columbus Ledger-Enquirer*, August 17.

1992c. Victim's Fight for Justice. *Columbus Ledger-Enquirer*, August 18.

Silk, M. 1994a. Rape Victim to make Her Case. *Atlanta Journal-Constitution*, May 23.

1994b. Rape Victim Describes Attack. *Atlanta Journal-Constitution*. May 25.

1994c. Man is Guilty of Two Rapes. *Atlanta Journal-Constitution*, June 1.

1994d. Victim Applauds Rape Conviction. *Atlanta Journal-Constitution*, June 1.

1994e. Man, 39, Convicted. *Atlanta Journal-Constitution*, June 2.

Tomaselli, S. and R. Porter. 1986. *Rape*. New York: Basil Blackwell Press.

Veronen, L. and D. Kilpatrick. 1983. Stress Management for Rape Victims. In *Stress Reduction and Prevention*, eds. D. Meichenbaum and M. Jaremko. New York: Plenum Press.

Walters, B. 1991. Justice Delayed. *Kalamazoo Gazette*, July 3.

Weis, K. and S. Borges 1973. Victimology and Rape. *Issues in Criminology*, Vol. 8:71–115.

Williams, J. and K. Holmes. 1981. *The Second Assault*. Westport, Conn.: Greenwood.

Winkler, C . 1996. Review Essay of "A Woman Scorned by P. Sanday." *Violence Again Women*, Vol. 2(2):215–24.

1995. Rape Attack; Ethnography of the Ethnographer. In *Fieldwork Under Fire*, eds. C. Nordstrom and T. Robbins. Berkeley: University of California Press.

1994a. Rape Trauma: Context of Meaning. In *Embodiment and Experience*, ed. T. Csordas. Cambridge: Cambridge University Press.

1994b. The Contexts of Meanings Behind Rape Trauma. In *Many Mirrors*, ed. N. Sault. New Brunswick, N.J.: Rutgers.

1993. Thanks for Sensitive Approach in Story. *Opelika-Auburn News*, October 8.

1991. Rape As Social Murder. *Anthropology Today*, Vol. 7(3):12–14.

1987. "Changing Power and Authority in Gender Roles." Ph.D. Diss. Bloomington, Ind., University of Indiana, University of Michigan Microfilms Films.

DEDICATION AND ACKNOWLEDGMENTS

Dedication

Part of the profits from this book are for the Rape Crisis Center called CPASA (pronounced 'k-pasa'; in Spanish this means "What is happening?"), Community Program Against Sexual Assault, located in Roxbury, a section of Boston, Massachusetts. This center works for the prevention of rape by educating communities of people, and as a truly multicultural center, it aids survivors of rape by helping them to stand up to rapists and to integrate their therapy into their daily lives. I would like to especially thank Barbara Bullette (pronounced "bul-léh"), who has worked for over twenty years in this center, and Dr. D. E. Dale, whose work also includes support for persons with AIDS. They treated me not like a victim but like a human being who had suffered a tragedy, and, even though I was a victim and an activist, they were not afraid to be my friend, to accept me as an active member of a rape crisis organization, and to be part of my foundational support. Thank you.

This book is also for the Heroic People who have spoken and organized against rapists and rape, and to all the anonymous Heroic People who have survived rape(s) and rapist(s), and most importantly, who become activists by working against the barriers of rape in our society from institutional denigration to the misunderstandings promulgated by rape-prone statements. Those Heroic People stood up against the misconceptions and harassments of rape and rapists, and provided the foundation of support for my success in surviving and activating my work against sex discrimination at the university due to the rape, in my plight to find the rapist, and in confrontations with the district attorney and scientists' crowd. These Heroic People altered erroneous ideas and provided a new arena for fairness in which comprehension of VISAs' plight is possible. I thank you and want you to know that I felt your efforts throughout the process. Your work, although anonymous in name, is writ large in the words and actions of this book. For every Heroic Person who spoke up, even though s/he spoke only to one other person, I thank you.

Also, I dedicate this book to my brother Jack: Together we supported each other against the negators in our society in the areas of AIDS and rape. While he worked to try and save his physical life and I strived to save my identity, simultaneously we stood strong against discrimination. Moreover, for reasons explained in the book, I also dedicate this book to my mother Mary Catherine Mooney Winkler.

Acknowledgments

I would like to thank the following people for their support. They helped me over and over again, and acted in a compassionate and understanding manner. If only all people in our society could have the insight into disaster and sensitivity toward VISAs as these people have shown me! To stop rapists is not something that a person can do alone but lots of people are needed to help. I thank:

M Allen, D Arello, J Ullian, P Bart, D Bathrick, S Barr, D Cook, J Bauer, M Wade, S Bery, H Bennett, C Bierwert, A Bingham, B Detweiler-Blakely, B Blakely, K Bonner, J Borden, C Bostik, L Boyd, D Braaten, M Bradley, J Brashler, J Brewer, R Brinker, J Norton, F Brown, C Browner, E Brusco, B Bullette, V Burt, A Burson-Tolpin, S Butler, L Ronald, Det. Carpenter, A Carter, S Claire, M Chrisholm, J Cole, S Cole, J Collier, J Branscamb-Collier, S Collier, N Constable-Alters, V Commons, R Conwell, F Coolie, B Corless, J Cowan, D Culp, Dr. D. E. Dale, R David-Floyd, K Dawson, K Dettwyler, M Dickson, J Dobson, B Donnelly, P Dressle, P Dorn-Sezgin, M Dorsey, J Ebbott, E Ebosele, Bishop & Mrs. J Embry, E Endicott, K Endicott, K Endicott, E Eule, N Evans, F Farmer, M Foley, D Foley, K Foskett, D Fry, K Fry, M Fields, V Fennell, L Ferguson, C Gailey, J Galvin, G Galvin, M K Gamel, B Garland, B Garland, M Geewax, D Gillette, D Goerger, J Goerger, P Goerger, O Goerger, H Golder, W Grant, K Griffon, G Groover, J Hanson, D Halpern, C Harris, F Harrison, C Ghoirsi Hart, G Hart, H Hecker, L Heisner, A Helweg, U Helweg, M Herzfeld, J Hill, R Hodges, G Hodges, L A Hoff, Rev. L Hope, M L Hope, Rev. J Hope, Q Hudson, B Hull, S Hull, J Hunt, S Imara-Bello, L Israel, E Israel, B Jack, E Jackson, R Jackson, R Jackson, P Jemian, W Jemian, P Johnson, A Jones, R Kandel, D Kaufman, P Kaurouma, B Keely, M Keely, R Keely, B Kelly, L Kellogg, R Kennedy, D King, N Koertge, J Kulstand, G Landberg, J Laude, M Lawson, R Lane, J Lewis, D Leonard, Laura X, T Leonard,

B Rosen, R Litmon Jr, E Loeffler-Friedl, Rev. F Lloyd, K Long, M Loring, H-S Lu, G Lyles, A Makurat, S Makurat, K Manthey, J Malcolm, P Malmquist-Sigman, V Sigman, W Marbaugh, S Simonton, R Marbaugh, C Marbaugh, M Manning, W Mayfield, E McKindley, R McMullen, S E Mears, S Mikula, F Mikula, E Mooney, C Mooney, J Mooney, L Mooney, K Moore, O Morgan, M F Mueller, M Murphy, M Neal, P Landsberg, S Neiderbach, R Nolan, B Oaks, S O'Farrell, E Otake, A M Petrokubi, J Pettis, D Picchi, M Pike, S Porter, D Powell, L Powell, M Richards, S Roberts, C-S Roche, D Rosaldo, D Rosenberg, P Rosenberg, C Ross, D Ross, W Rosser, A Peterson Royce, R Royce, P Sanday, B Santos, H Sargeant, M Satterwhite, R Jemian, N Sault, P Reynolds, M P Schildmeyer, A Seeger, H Serrie, K Seibold, A Singer, R Beckman, N Singer-Beckman, M Singer, Macki Sissoko, M Sissoko, T Sissoko, H Sissoko, B Schwartz, M Smith, P Smith, S Smith, S Smith, GA Pardons & Paroles, K Steinberg, L Stephens, S Stephens, J Stulp, S Suman, S Sutton, B Torvert, B Torbert, J Tatum, B Nobel, G Testamark, A Totenberg, A Tsuru, C Van Voorhies, J Van Voorhies, B Van, B Vernado, B Walters, R Washington, J Wheeler, J Williams, C Williams, K Williams, J Wilson, L Wilson, P Wilson, D Williams, K Wininger, M C Winkler, A E Winkler, J Winkler, B Yarbrough, S Chen Yeng, B Zabawa, and A Zabawa.

I am sure that names are missing because first, some are anonymous to me, second, my errors, and third, the large number of great people who helped me succeed. Students who aided me are:
1987–1991 Unfortunately, the names of the students during these years who magnanimously supported me were not available through the schools. Nevertheless, I want to thank these students for their understanding, insight, caring, intelligence, and great humor. You, and the following students, supported this success in the conviction of the rapist.
1991–1992 I Abraham, C Alexander, L Alexander, L Anderson, N Arnold, M Artis, C Ashley, C Askew, S Austin, K Banks, L Baskerville, B Bateman, E Beavers, E Belin, M Bell, K Bonner, J Borden, L Boyd, P Branker, S Brown, T Brownridge, M Buford, T Burton, C Clark, T Cliett, L Cole, Y Coleman, C Collington, S Conwell, C Cox, M Davis, W Davis, A Duboise, D Ellington, D Ellis, L Ellison, N Farrell, M Fisher, R Fluker, H Ford, R Franklin, D Frazier, G Gager, R Gentry, M Gilbert, S Gordon, R Grant, B Gray, P Gray, P Hale, K Hardy, C Harris, M Harris, Q Harrison, L Heard, G Hicks, R Hiligh, K Holifield, J Howard, G Hunt, C Hunter, J Hyde, W Ivey, D Jackson, K Jackson, M James, C Johnson, S Johnson, O Jones, R Jones, A M Jordan, Ar Jordan, Av

Jordan, K Jordan, D Kenney, C A King, C J King, P Knight, M Lamar, D Ligon, R Macon, J Malcolm, E Malveaux, S Mann, T Marshall, C McLemore, S McLoyd, K Miller, T Moffit, C Moore, G Moore, E Motley, W Nelson, C Nicols, A Oden, N O'Neill, M Outland, S Owens, A Parks, J Peebles, T Pelham, A Perkins, B Pettway, R Phillips, M Pointer, B Pollard, S Porter, U Pritchett, A Pryce, K Radcliffe, R Randell, K Ranson, R Raymond, I Regis, K Riley, T Robbins, D Robinson, C-S Roche, M Ross, S Sanford, A Scott, J Shanks, M Shon, J Smith, L Smith, W Smith, A Spears, W Stephens, C Stevens, C Strong, G Sumlin, J Sumner, V Taplin, L Taylor, C Terry, E Terry, G Testamark, A Toney, V Ugh, B Varnada, K Ward, A Washington, J Washington, A B Watkins, A Y Watkins, G Wells, D Wesley, J West, K White, V White, J Wilkins, K Williams, T Williams, A Wilson, A Wimberly, M Wright, M Zellner, M Zenburg

1992–1993 R Adams, R Alexander, R Antoine, M Ashley, L Ates, C Atkins, K Bailey, T Bailey, S Barnes, R Barzey, N Bell, W Bell, A Bentley, T Billingslea, D Billingslea, T Bluford, J Boyd, G Broadnax, C Brown, D Brown, L Brown, L S Brown, S Brown, D Buch, R Buddock, J Burks, V Burnett, A Butler, N Calvin, A Carter, Q Carter, C Chance, K Chappelle, J Cherry, J Clark, J Coleman, Y Coleman, S Conwell, C Cooper, J Coprich, T Covington, J Cox, D Cross, T Crowell, T Crum, C Culver, C Davis, L Desadier, A Dodd, S Donald, M Dorsey, E Drew, M Dula, M Faison, H Fambrough, T Farmer, C Farthing, R Favors, M Foley, C Foster, D Francis, M Franklin, M Fuller, B Garner, S Garvin, B Gary, H Gatson, A Gess, D Gipson, D Goodman, A Graham, J Graham, H Grant, E Green, D Greene, D Greenway, A Grenshaw, K Griffon, J Hall, L Hall, L Halloway, P Hamilton, L Harrigan, C. Harris, L Harris, N Henderson, P Hogan, F Hogue, B Holliday, A Hopewell, C Hubbard, S Huffman, D Hunter, F Huntley, J Jackson, S Jackson, S Jamison, E Jarmon, A Jarvis, G Johnson, N Johnson, E Knighton, A Lamar, N Lanier, K Leaner, K Lewis, J Liner, A Mace, B Martin, J Matthews, N McDonald, D McGlothen, A McKenzie, T McKenzie, S McLeod, I McMillian, A McNulty, M Miller, C Minga, P Missick, C Mitchell, V Mitchell, N Moody, C Moore, L Moore, T Moore, S Moshette, A Mullings, B Murray, T Murray, L Nathan, J Ngola, E Oates, J Obleton, S Oliver, K Ottison, N Outlaw, T Owens, S Patterson, R Perry, S Pinkney, M Pinkston, C Pinnock, P Pointer, G Pope, V Porter, B Portier, A Powell, D Prewitt, M Pswarayi, B Purnell, I Quinn, C Raines, J Raudenbush, K Ransom, W Reed, K Riley, T Riley, V Robinson, K Rocker, F Rouse, D Rue, A Russell, N Russell, I Ryan, T Salter, K Scales, Ka Scott,

Ke Scott, L Scott, R Sewill, R Shann, R Singleton, L Slusher, E Smalls, R Smith, S Smith, T Soles, V Springer, K Stevenson, D Steward, L Strong, A Sturgis, D Swain, D Sydnor, A Tate, B Taylor, G Testamark, A Thomas, C Thomas, T Thomas, A Thompson, C Thompson, A Toles, R Turner, U Ugokue, D Upchurch, T Upchurch, J Vandee, J Vital, S Walker, M Wallace, M Webster, E Wesley, D Wheeler, S Wideman, A Willians, K Williams, Et Williams, Ea Williams, N Williams, C Wilson, E Wilson, N Wilson, N Wims, J Woodard, K Wright, W Wright

1993–1994 J Abubakai, C Adams, M Arrington, L Atkins, D Bailey, S Baker, J Ball, Y Ball, K Barron, Y Benjamin, S Benn, S Blaise, N Boggs, W Bowers, M Brown, R Bryan, C Bullock, M Burnette, E Burton, A Butler, T Byrd, A Calloway, N Calvin, S Carr, M Carter, Z Carter, D Chapman, A Cheatham, W Chevalier, C Christian, J Clark, V Clay, D Coffie, R Coleman, B Coston, B Coulon, T Crawford, N Curry, E David, A Davis, R Deavers, K Dias, H Dixon, M Dixon, A Durrah, M Eaton, T Fanning, J Farrakhan, S Foster, T Francis, S Gardner, K Gilliam, M Glover, N Gomez, R Grayson, E Guilford, G Guiy-Brown, S Hambry, J Hamilton, L Harbison, P Harmon, H Harriel, F Harris, L Harris, O Harris, Y Higgins, K Higgs, L Holloway, C Hubbard, D Hunter, S Hutchins, C Inglis, A Jackson, J Jackson, K Jones, Y Jones, K Kendric, T Key, D King, V King, J Khan, S Lane, A Lankford, K A Leaner, R Lee, K Lewis, T Lewis, E Lightsey, T Lomax, A Lucas, J Mack, L Mack, T Marshall, C Martin, H Massaquoi, K Mayo, D Mays, P McCauley, A McClaney, B McFadden, T McKinnies, M McNeil, A McNulty, S Mohamed, K Moore, I Moses, K Moss, T Mourning, J Murdock, J Murray, M Nunnally, S Oliver, E Pearson, R Phelps, R Phillips, D Radford, L Raines, J Rawdenbush, M Richardson, T Rickey, N Roberts, T Robinson, S Rodrigues, J Rouse, C Towe, L Samuel, F Sanders, T Sanders, T Scarbough, T Sealey, R Shabazz, I Shaw, C Simmons, S Simmons, L Slusher, J Small, J Smalls, V Springer, M Stallings, B Stargel, V Stewart, D Sydnor, Q Sylvester, J Taylor, N Taylor, C Thomas, H Thomas, N Thomas, T Thomas, W Thomas, D Tidwell, C Tucker, N Wade, F Walker, O Walker, K Washington, S Watts, A White, H White, R White, C Wiggins, K Woodard, B Woods

1998—Victimization and Violence Class: J Barrow, E Baruch, K Bullock, Q Frasier, T Gibbs, T Lawson, R Outland, T Solomon, S Turner, Z Washington, E Wilson

Thank you. You were always terrific: laughing and listening.

ABOUT THE AUTHOR

Dr. Cathy Winkler is an anthropologist who researched women's acquisition and expression of authority in a rural artisan Mexican town. Although she taught anthropology in the 1980s and 1990s at various universities and colleges, her current employment is as a high school math teacher. She relaxes by gardening, planting easy-to-grow varieties. She continues to write and speak publicly about the crime of rape.